KNIGHT-CAPRON LIBRARY
LYNCHBURG COLLEGE
LYNCHBURG, VIRGINIA 24501

TOWARDS A HISTORY OF PHONETICS

PAPERS CONTRIBUTED IN HONOUR OF

DAVID ABERCROMBIE

J.R. FIRTH, DAVID ABERCROMBIE, DANIEL JONES
St Peter's Hall, Oxford 1955

TOWARDS A HISTORY OF
PHONETICS

edited by R.E. Asher
and Eugénie J.A. Henderson

AT THE UNIVERSITY PRESS
EDINBURGH

1981

KNIGHT-CAPRON LIBRARY
LYNCHBURG COLLEGE
LYNCHBURG, VIRGINIA 24501

P
221
.T68

© Edinburgh University Press 1981
22 George Square, Edinburgh
ISBN 0 85224 374 X
Printed in Great Britain by
Redwood Burn Limited
Trowbridge & Esher

NEH

Contents

Introduction

The idea of this book was conceived some three years ago through a wish to honour David Abercrombie on the occasion of his seventieth birthday and consequent retirement from the Chair of Phonetics in the University of Edinburgh. After discussing the project with Mr Archie Turnbull, Secretary to the Edinburgh University Press, the present editors and the late Dr W.E. Jones agreed to put together a book that would not be a festschrift of the more traditional type but rather a collection of papers on a unified theme. Dr Jones' sudden death early in the planning stages not only deprived the editorial committee of his valuable advice and collaboration but also took from their midst a good friend and a particularly close and long-time colleague of David Abercrombie during his years at the University of Edinburgh.

Though the decision to seek contributions in one restricted area in the field of phonetics has clear advantages in being likely to produce something that will hang together better as a book than would a collection of essays on miscellaneous topics, it was not taken without some feeling of regret, for it inevitably meant denying an opportunity of participating in the venture to a large proportion of those colleagues, friends, and past and present students of David Abercrombie who would have been happy to contribute a paper in his honour and indeed were most anxious to do so. It is, furthermore, with sadness that we record that death deprived us not only of a chapter that was promised by Dr Jones but also one by Professor A.E. Sharp of the University College of North Wales.

The choice of theme for this book was determined mainly by two factors: firstly, a growing interest in the history of our discipline and the lack of a comprehensive work on the history of phonetics and, secondly, the fact that this subject has been one of the major interests for many years of the recipient of the volume. To symbolise the importance of his work in the historiography of his subject, it was decided to take the perhaps rather unconventional step of including a revised version of one of David Abercrombie's own papers, first published in 1963 in *The Monotype Recorder*.

Readers will not expect the volume to be a complete and fully integrated history of phonetics. Rather it presents groups of papers on some of the important topics that such a history would have to be concerned with. Thus the sections on the history of ideas in phonetics (our Parts 1 and 2) could and should be vastly expanded, bearing in mind what J.R. Firth termed the 'clear continuity of studies in all the main topics of interest to phonetics from the Restoration to the time of Sir William Jones'. A comprehensive section on national contributions (our Part 4) would need to say something about phonetics in ancient India and in the Arab world; an account of phonetics in Europe would not pass over in silence the work of the twelfth-century Icelander, author of the 'First Grammatical Treatise', a discussion of which might properly lead to an account of the many other proposals for the reform of the spelling of European languages that were to be made in the following eight centuries. There would also be more on the description of the sounds of non-European languages by European scholars, starting perhaps with the various *Alphabeta* published by the Sacra Congregatio de Propaganda Fide in Rome from the eighteenth century onwards; more on the development of instrumental techniques of investigation; more on the individual contributions of those who have in their time been dominant in the field.

In the middle years of the present century there has been no more important figure than David Abercrombie, who on his retirement in September of this year had completed fifty years in phonetics. This half-century began in 1930 when, at the age of twenty, he joined the Department of Phonetics at University College London as a postgraduate student. The earlier part of his education was at Leeds Grammar School and Leeds University, where he took a B.A. in English in 1930. David Abercrombie's close links with University College continued until 1937, with a two-year break in Paris from 1931 to 1933. He thus had the inestimable good fortune for a phonetician of being trained in a department headed by Daniel Jones, for a festschrift in whose honour he was appropriately to be one of the editors many years later. We can assume that it was above all from Daniel Jones that he derived his interest in the practical side of phonetics and his appreciation of the value to a phonetician of an ability, obtained only through a very rigorous training, to produce accurately utterances in a variety of different languages.

It is only recently that Linguistics has been linked with Phonetics in the name of the Department at University College. It should not however be thought that the Department was concerned half a century ago only with phonetics taken in a very narrow sense. There were, for instance, courses on the teaching of English to foreign learners, which doubtless contributed to David Abercrombie's qualifications for posts he was to take up subsequently. From this later practical experience were to result papers setting out his thoughts on the problems and principles involved in the study and learning of languages, some of which papers were collected and republished in one volume in 1956. There were classes, too, on speech therapy by Ida Ward, who later became Professor of African Languages at the School of Oriental Studies, and one thinks in this connection of David Abercrombie's unobtrusive but nevertheless invaluable work in the fostering of the study of speech therapy in Edinburgh and elsewhere in Britain.

Jonesian theoretical discussion had two focal points, namely the notion of cardinal vowels and the idea of the phoneme as a family of sounds, and although it is difficult to imagine any course on linguistic phonetics at the time that paid no attention to the issues raised, the work of Jones himself and of his closest associates always remained relatively unalloyed by the work of their contemporaries elsewhere. Yet this did not inhibit the development of other theoretical approaches in Jones' own department, of which J.R. Firth was a member. Already in the early 1930s Firth was beginning to feel dissatisfaction with the phoneme concept and began to express his doubts in a number of publications. In the laboratory there was Stephen Jones to provide training in instrumental phonetics. One can thus see the Department as a remarkably stimulating environment for a young phonetician.

Training in phonetics for David Abercrombie did not, however, end there. It was held at that time, notably in the University College Department of Phonetics, that a proper requirement for a phonetician was that he should be able to speak at least one foreign language fluently and well, and French was considered to represent a good choice. Accordingly, David Abercrombie spent the years 1931 to 1933 in Paris as an English Assistant at the Lycée Louis-le-Grand. Simultaneously with this appointment he followed courses at the Institut de Phonétique, of which Pierre Fouché was Director. While in France he was awarded the International Phonetic Association Certificate on the basis of an examination conducted, in French, by Paul Passy.

Some time after his return to London, David Abercrombie was appointed to an Assistant Lectureship in English at the London School of Economics, a post he held from 1934 to 1938. His main work was the teaching of English to foreign students working for degrees in Commerce and in Economics and he took part also in the teaching of French. One of his colleagues there was one of the regrettably few scholars working in a British university to make a really solid contribution in both linguistcs and anthropology, Bronislaw Malinowski, who exerted a great, if indirect influence on him. A further influence at this time was that of C.K. Ogden, co-author with I.A. Richards of *The Meaning of Meaning*, a book to which Malinowski contributed an influential supplement. A tangible outcome of David Abercrombie's association with Ogden is the phonetic transcription he devised for use in Ogden's *General Basic Dictionary* published in 1940. In later years he was to give much thought to the subject of phonetic transcription, its varieties and complexities, and to the need for a precise classification of the different types and their relative appropriateness for different purposes. This interest in notation and writing systems which plays such an important role in the history of phonetics is reflected in Part 6 of the present volume.

David Abercrombie's four years at the London School of Economics were followed by two years (1938-40) in British Council posts in Athens, Cyprus and Egypt. He was in Athens at the outbreak of the Second World War and became Ministry of Information representative in Greece and the person in charge of the Ministry's office in the British Legation. After moving to Cairo in 1940 he took up an appointment as Lecturer in English at Cairo University, a post he held until the end of the war. During these five years he was also an announcer in Egyptian State Broadcasting, and Assistant Censor in the Control Headquarters of Anglo-Egyptian Censorship. There was also, in 1942, a brief spell in the army. From the end of the war until December 1947 he was back at the London School of Economics as Lecturer in English. During his last two terms there he was simultaneously Lecturer in Phonetics at the University of Leeds and he was thus at last able to devote his energies fully to the subject that had formed the centre of his interests since his days as a full-time student.

In 1948 he moved from Leeds to Edinburgh to found a Phonetics Department there. After promotion to a Senior Lectureship in 1950 and a Readership in 1957, he was appointed to the Chair of Phonetics in 1964. During his first year the sole representative of his subject to Edinburgh, he was to see his Department grow to one of ten members by 1967, when it amalgamated with the Department of General Linguistics to form the Department of Phonetics and Linguistics. A further amalgamation three years later – with the Department of Applied Linguistics – led to the present Department of Linguistics.

These successive amalgamations have in no way lessened Edinburgh's commitment to teaching and research in phonetics. Indeed, over the last decade there has been a steady increase in undergraduate courses in phonetics, in particular for third- and fourth-year students. That such an increase has been found both possible and desirable is the result of David Abercrombie's work during his earlier years in Edinburgh. From the time of his first involvement in phonetics it had been one of his main ambitions to see the full acceptance of phonetics as a subject for undergraduate study in its own right, and not merely as an ancillary subject for courses in modern languages. His first year in Edinburgh saw the setting up of an Introductory Course for undergraduates as well as a Postgraduate Diploma Course. But it was with the establishment of the 'First Ordinary Course' in Phonetics in 1950 and its subsequent success that his ambition was to be fully realised. Out of this course arose his *Elements of General Phonetics* (1967), than which there is surely no better introduction to the subject and which one may regard as his most important single publication. Now the passage of time has necessitated his retirement from the Chair that he has filled with such distinction. Happily, this does not represent the end of his teaching life, for when this volume appears he will be in the middle of a year as Lecturer in the Department of Linguistics and Phonetics at the University of Glasgow.

David Abercrombie has during the last fifty years taught and written on a wide range of topics in the general area of the study of language, and his speaking and writing share a number of estimable characteristics, among them elegance, clarity and humanity. High in the list of his special interests are rhythm in speech and the history of phonetics. In the latter area one of his most valuable publications is his paper on 'Forgotten Phoneticians' (1949). Such is his stature and the nature of his lasting contribution to his subject that we can be sure that this is not a category which will ever include David Abercrombie.

*

The editors are indebted to Mrs Mary Abercrombie, who kindly loaned a copy of the photograph of J.R. Firth, David Abercrombie and Daniel Jones that forms what it is hoped will seem a particularly appropriate frontispiece to this book, and to the staff of Edinburgh University Press who guided the work through the press and gave much valued help and advice.

Edinburgh and London, October 1980

PART ONE

HISTORY OF IDEAS IN PHONETICS :
BASIC CONCEPTS

Early Views of
Distinctive Features

Partly thanks to David Abercrombie, few people still hold the 'unfortunate opinion ... that before about 1830 there was no such thing as phonetics' (Abercrombie 1965, p.5). But it is still commonly believed that the notion of distinctive features burst upon the scene in the second half of this century. However, a little humbling history will show us that our present-day feature theory is largely foreshadowed by traditional work. Even the arguments that are to be found in current literature are often only sharpened forms of the questions that were being asked centuries ago. Thus we are now concerned with whether there are two kinds of differences between speech sounds, those that are phonemic and can change the meaning of a word or phrase in a language, and those that are merely phonetic, and serve only to distinguish the sounds of one language from those of another. In distinctive feature terms we ask 'whether the set of features required for describing systematic phonetic contrasts is greater than or equal to the set required for classifying the lexical contrasts in all the languages of the world' (Ladefoged 1971); and we then conclude there is 'no clear evidence showing that the set of features required for specifying phonetic contrasts is the same as that required for specifying the natural classes of sounds required in phonological rules' (ibid). We begin this paper by showing that this question and answer is almost parallel to the seventeenth-century search for a universal phonetic alphabet that could be distinguished from the separate alphabets required for particular languages.

We could, of course, have gone back much further, to the writings of Aristotle, Dionysius Thrax, Cicero, Quintilian, and many others; or to the English spelling reformers of the sixteenth century, such as Thomas Smith (1568) and John Hart (Danielssen 1955) who, driven by their practical aims, gave phonetic descriptions of, for example, syllabic consonants and the voiced/voiceless distinction. But it is the seventeenth-century writers like William Holder, John Wallis, and Francis Lodwick who provide the more interesting parallels to our modern arguments.

Holder's concern for the education of the deaf led him to describe the components of the speech organs in considerable detail. His *Elements of Speech* (Holder 1669) provides an unusually complete set of what we would now call features, based on an analysis and classification of sounds according to the place and manner of their articulation. He was, moreover, concerned

3

with features which were distinctive. Abercrombie (1965) has shown that Holder's contemporary, John Bulwer, noted in 1648 that 'Letters, the true elements of speech [are] made of Motions, and [are] nothing else but locall motions of the part of the Mouth'. Holder goes a step further in noting that a letter (which we would now call a phoneme) is composed of distinctive motions (or features). He writes:

> the Learning of a Language is (or at least needs be) nothing else, but the informing our selves, and remembering what Composures of Letters are, by consent and Institution, to signifie such certain Notions of things, with their Modalities and Accidents: I say, the *Motions* of the *Mouth* (speaking largely) by which the voice is discriminated, and the Sound thereof in distinct formes received by the Ear, according to the number of their variety, are the *Natural Elements* of *Speech*; and the Application of them in their several compositions, or Words made of them, to signifie things or the Modalities of things, and to serve for communication of Notions. (Holder 1669 [1967], emphasis in the original)

Holder often emphasises the ability of sounds to distinguish meaning, their distinctive aspects. In so doing, he points out that a finite number of signals or symbols can produce a large number of meanings. Thus he notes that four bells can produce twenty-four signals (p.3), but that the human voice is far more variable and can produce a very large number of sounds, which combine into syllables, which combine into words. The phonetic properties that he uses for his classification thus serve, like the finite set of distinctive features, to specify all possible sounds and classes of sounds.

It is interesting to consider Holder's distinction between consonants and vowels in the light of modern discussions on this topic. These two major classes of sounds were of course distinguished by all linguists and phoneticians attempting to discuss speech sounds, including the early Greeks, Romans, and Hindus. But Holder states:

> That I may be the easier understood, I do comply with the Antients, in distinguishing Letters into *Vowels* and *Consonants*; yet not wholly upon their reason, *viz.* That a *Vowel* may be sounded alone, a *Consonant* not without a *Vowel*; which if examined will not be found all true, for many of the Consonants may be sounded alone, and some joyned together, without a Vowel, as *Bl*, *St*; and as we pronounce the later Syllable of People, Rifle, &c, though it be true of some Consonants, as the Mutes, P.T.K. that they can make no sound alone. (p.28)

Holder instead distinguishes these classes by the feature that one might today call obstruction saying 'That in all *Vowels* the passage of the mouth is open and free, without an appulse of an Organ of Speech to another: But in all Consonants, there is an Appulse of the Organs...' (p.29).

Holder also clearly recognises the distinctive nature of the feature 'voicing' or [± Voice] when he writes: 'The Distinction of *Articulation of Breath* and the *Articulation of Voice* must be well heeded, because in it consists the only difference of many letters' (p.31). He even gives us the following chart (p.43):

p	t	k	f	th	s	sh
b	d	g	v	dh	z	zh

That Holder is concerned with a universal set of features is also clear since he suggests that in describing the differences between consonants, he will take 'the number of Consonants, not from the *Grammatical Alphabets* of any language, but from the *diversity of Sounds* framed by single Articulations with Appulse, which I find in any usage' (pp.36–7). In his definition of the class of possible consonants he even considered the question discussed at the beginning of this paper: 'It will give much light to what hath hitherto been spoken concerning *Consonants*, to take view of what has already been hinted, and to lay this Hypothesis; *viz.* That the number of Letters in Nature, is equal to the number of Articulations, severally applyed to every distinct matter of Sound.' Can anyone doubt that Holder was interested in developing a theory which would make explicit 'the phonetic capabilities of man' (Chomsky and Halle 1968)? The same might be said of Holder's contemporary, John Wallis. Wallis showed great insights into phonetic theory in his *Treatise of Speech (de loquela)* in which he

> philosophically considered the Formation of all Sounds used in Articulate Speech (as well of our own, as of any other Language that I know); By what Organs, and in what Position each sound was formed; with the nice distinctions of each (which in some letters of the same Organ, is very subtil:) so that, by such Organs, in such Position, the Breath issuing from the Lungs, will form such Sounds, whether the Person do or do not hear himself speak. (Kemp 1972, pp.18–19)

Wallis considered his phonetic framework to be a universal theory in which the classificatory devices or features had a substantive, phonetic, basis, rather than being the product of an ad hoc, arbitrary, classification.

Similar points can be made with reference to the work of Francis Lodwick, one of the 'forgotten phoneticians' now remembered owing to Abercrombie (1965) and to the subsequent reprinting of Lodwick's writings published together with the excellent study by Salmon (1972). Lodwick wished to devise a schema which could 'the more regularly ... sort (all the necessary sounds) into Classes, and to express the derivation of Letters of the same Organe, the one from the other' (Lodwick 1686, p.132, as reprinted in Salmon 1972, p.241).

Abercrombie (1965) discusses Lodwick's Universal alphabet in great detail. He shows that the classification scheme used by Lodwick was not radically different from those to be used three hundred years later, especially in specifying consonants. (Lodwick's vowels and diphthongs were largely unanalysable properties of syllables.) Lodwick's schema permits generalisations not possible with indissoluble segments, because the files and ranks by which he organised consonants produce at least a subset of the natural classes required by phonological rules. Files 1 to 6 distinguish the classes of bilabials, dentals, palatals, velars, labiodentals, and alveolars. His ranks for the most part correspond to classes of voiced stops, voiceless stops, nasals, voiced fricatives, voiceless fricatives. Using this schema, one could develop a formalism to permit feature counting as proposed by Chomsky and Halle (1968). Thus, for example, a class of segments could be designated by numbers, with the file number (place of articulation feature) stated first, followed by the rank number (the manner feature). The class of bilabials would then be simply represented as $(1:0)$, the class of voiced stops as $(0:1)$, the class of voiced and voiceless oral stops as $(0:1, 2)$. One can see that Lodwick's schema has some of the same problems as are found in the first eight chapters of *The Sound Pattern of English* (Chomsky and Halle 1968) in that by this system we do not always get the simplest classes designated by the fewest numbers. The single sound [t] can be specified by only two numbers $(2:2)$, whereas the more general class including all voiced and voiceless consonants would require 9 numbers, $(1, 2, 3, 4, 5, 6, 7:1, 2)$. We could amuse ourselves with 'translating' Lodwick into current feature notation if we like. Not surprisingly Lodwick would be found poorer in comparison to more modern theories. His classificatory scheme is not as appropriate in some respects as that of his contemporary, Holder. As we have noted, Holder has a clear chart illustrating the difference between voiced and voiceless sounds, whereas Lodwick has no way of designating all voiced (or all voiceless) consonants as members of a single class.

Lodwick's *An Essay Towards An Universal Alphabet* was first published as a pamphlet in 1685, and then reprinted in the Philosophical Transactions in 1686. According to Salmon (1972), however, it was the culmination of twenty years' work, since Robert Hooke noted in 1673 that he had borrowed Lodwick's 'new Universal alphabet'. Lodwick's 'organic' classification of speech sounds came a century after a notation on similar principles by Honorat Rambaud of Marseilles in his *La Declaration des Abus que lon commet en escriuant*, published in Lyons in 1578, as pointed out by Abercrombie (1965).

It is interesting to note that Lodwick's earliest concern, like that of so many of his contemporaries, was to develop a 'universal character' and a 'universal language'. At first he did not consider a universal phonetic framework to be necessary for this enterprise, because he intended to form an alphabet of symbols that would represent objects or ideas directly, such that the speakers of any language could 'read' them in the sounds of their own language (Knowlson 1975). It may have been his eventual recognition of the difficulties and shortcomings of this approach that led him to seek, instead, a universal alphabet 'Which should contain an Enumeration of all such Single Sounds or Letters as are used in any Language', proposing the alphabet and classification scheme discussed above.

The insights of the seventeenth century were not more clearly developed until the nineteenth and early twentieth centuries. It took the genius of Sweet and his contemporaries to provide the additional insights that provide the foundation for our current theories. Sweet explicitly states his notion of the difference between a broad and a narrow transcription in a way that is compatible with both seventeenth-century universalist views, and with present-day discussions on differences between languages. He writes:

> A broad notation is one which makes only the practically necessary distinctions of sound in each language and makes them in the simplest manner possible, omitting all that is superflous. But in comparing the sounds of a variety of languages or dialects of a language, and still more in dealing with sounds in general, we require a 'narrow', that is, a minutely accurate notation covering the whole field of possible sounds. (Sweet 1908)

Although Sweet talks in terms of notation and transcription, the principles behind 'broad' and 'narrow' notations are the same principles as those that are found in the Prague school view of distinctive features. Sweet is suggesting a theory of phonetic features that meets the two criteria of modern phonetic theory, a framework for describing all the phonological oppositions in a single language ('broad' transcriptions) and for describing all the systematic differences between one language and another ('narrow' transcriptions).

Another basic notion in distinctive feature theory – that the segment is not the most basic element of speech – is also explicitly recognised by Sweet. After years of attempting to develop a Romic alphabet for phonetic notation, he finally decided that 'what is wanted, for scientific purposes especially, is a notation independent of the Roman alphabet, built up systematically – an alphabet in which there is a definite relation between sound and symbol' (Henderson 1971, pp.239–40). Sweet reached this conclusion in the course of his detailed examination and criticism of Bell's *Visible Speech* (1867). Bell, we may recall, presented a systematic description of the capabilities of each speech organ as well as the speech sounds that resulted from their simultaneous actions. Clearly, Bell and Sweet were interested in 'the phonetic capabilities of man' (Chomsky and Halle 1968) long before distinctive feature theory came to be an integral part of phonological theory. Bell's and Sweet's organic alphabets – the set of iconic symbols representing 'the elementary actions by which all sounds are formed' (1880–1, Henderson 1971, p.240) – are phonetic features which can be combined to represent all the possible speech sounds. In distinctive feature terminology, each symbol was viewed as a composite 'bundle' or cell in a phonetic matrix. These organic alphabets are clearly related to both their seventeenth-century predecessors (on which they are obvious improvements), and to current universal phonetic theories (from which they do not differ very much).

Neither Sweet, nor his predecessors and contemporaries, gave these properties of the speech organs, or the properties of the sounds that were related to them, independent theoretical status. As we have shown, there were indications that the distinctive nature of the features was recognised. But the theoretical importance of these semi-independent phonetic properties was not clearly delineated until the advent of the Prague school. The main contribution of distinctive feature phonology is this change of emphasis. Modern generative phonology borrowed heavily not only from Jakobson and the Prague school of phonologists, but also from all the linguists and phoneticians who from the earliest times used features to define the intersecting sets of speech sounds that are used in the sound systems of languages. We are where we are because, in the words of Newton, we stand on the backs of giants.

References

ABERCROMBIE, D. (1965) *Studies in Phonetics and Linguistics*, London (Oxford University Press).

BELL, A.M. (1867) *Visible Speech: the Science of Universal Alphabetics*, 3rd ed., Washington (Volta Bureau) 1907.

CHOMSKY, N. and HALLE, M. (1968) *The Sound Pattern of English*, New York (Harper and Row).

DANIELSSEN, B. ed. (1955) *John Hart's Works*, Stockholm (Stockholm Studies in English).

HENDERSON, E.J.A. (1971) *The Indispensable Foundation*, London (Oxford University Press).

HOLDER, W. (1669) *The Elements of Speech*, London; facsimile reprint, Scolar Press, London, 1967.

KEMP, J.A. (1972) *John Wallis's Grammar of the English Language*, London (Longman).

KNOWLSON, J. (1975) *Universal Language Schemes in England and France 1600–1800*, Toronto (University of Toronto Press).

LADEFOGED, P. (1971) *Preliminaries to Linguistic Phonetics*, Chicago (University of Chicago Press).

RAMBAUD, HONORAT (1578) *La declaration des abus que lon commet en escriuant et le moyen de les euiter, & representer nayuement les paroles, ce que iamais homme n'a facit*, Lyon (I. de Tournes).

SALMON, V. (1972) *The Works of Francis Lodwick*, London (Longman).

SMITH, T. (1568) *De recta et emendata linguae Anglicanae scriptione dialogus*, [ed. O. Deibel, 1913] Paris (Halle); facsimile reprint, Scolar Press, London, 1968.

SWEET, H. (1908) *The Sounds of English*, 2nd ed., Oxford (Clarendon Press) 1929.

The Kazan' School and
the London School

The last ten years or so has seen a great interest and a great industry, relatively speaking, in bringing many of the original works of the Kazan' School, particularly those of Baudouin de Courtenay, in translation, to the attention of the English-speaking world. In addition to these translations, we have also had the influence of Kruszewski on Baudouin de Courtenay (Jakobson 1971b, pp.429–50) (we had already had that a good many years earlier, as I shall be pointing out later); the possible influence of each on Saussure (Koerner 1973, pp.133–65); and, going back somewhat further, the influence, particularly and specifically, of Baudouin's and Kruszewski's ideas on the development of the lowest ranked unit of phonology, in its phonemic aspect, in Russia, Western Europe, America and Japan (Jones 1957; Jakobson 1971a, pp.394–428).

As I consider those translations of the original works that I have been able to consult, I find myself asking about their influence on another personality, and on a quite different approach to phonology, indeed on another approach to linguistic analysis in general – namely, on J.R. Firth and certain British attitudes; and thus I suggest on the recipient of this volume. And I find that their influence may well be profound, especially that of Mikołaj Habdank Kruszewski, as I hope to show.

When people consider the emergence and growth of the phonetics / phonology distinction in the Slav world, it seems to be generally agreed that it was Kruszewski who really lay at the heart of it. We have been told this comparatively recently by Jakobson (1971), by Koerner (1973) and by Stankiewicz (1972). But in what fashion, exactly, does he so lie? To judge by much ostensibly written in his praise, in a rather weak way.

I take it that Roman Jakobson is a fair representative of the panegyric mode in this connection. He has written the two reasonably long articles already referred to, one about Baudouin de Courtenay and Kruszewski (op. cit., 394–428) and one about Kruszewski alone (op. cit., 429–50). In the first, we find the following statement (407):

> Alternations of the latter type are called by Baudouin 'purely phonetic divergences', and he cites Russian examples of such 'combinatory variants', as he later labelled them ...: in the forms *èta | èti, cel | cel'nyj* a close *e* before a soft palatalized [sic] consonant alternates with an open *ε* in other positions; in the endings of the words *baly | koroli* a

back *y* after hard (non-palatalized) consonants alternates with a front *i* in other positions.

Again, a few pages further on we find (410):

Thus Baudouin's magnificent discovery (even today [original Polish version, 1960] not understood by all linguists) – the merger of the Russian and Polish combinatory variants *y* and *i* into one phoneme, called *i mutabile* – was made, as we have seen, by comparing two forms of one and the same morpheme, e.g. the nominal plural endings that occur after hard and soft final stem consonants.

This is essentially the same example, though see below concerning 'one and the same morpheme'.

In the article on Kruszewski (I translate from the Russian of the 1971 version) we again find (442):

The question of unilateral or bilateral predictability was clearly stated by Kruszewski and lay at the bottom of the remarks of Baudouin on 'purely phonetic divergence', as e.g. the Russian alternation of close *e* before 'soft' (mjagkie) consonants and open in other positions ([ét'i]−[ɛtu]) or of back *y* after 'hard' consonants and front *i* in other positions ([darý]−[car'i]).

– again the same or comparable examples.

In passing it seems to me extraordinary that in what Jakobson writes about these two, for their time, highly original Polish linguists, he should stress and restress little more in the general area of 'phonology' than these rather mundane and simple examples of realisations of some postulated phonological unit, referred to by Baudouin and Kruszewski merely as the anthropophonic alternations; and that he should desire nothing deeper to handle these alternations than what I will call a structuralist-type phoneme (otherwise dubbed, from about this same time, taxonomic). For there was surely more to what they were saying than that. True, Jakobson refers in the second quotation to Baudouin's establishing his *i mutabile* 'by comparing two forms of one and the same morpheme', and, in the article on Kruszewski, to the interest of the latter in the other ('traditional') alternations, but no particular interest is seen to attach to the first point, and the second occurs under the head of morphology. One might be excused for believing that phonology was not involved at all here. But the fact is that even at that early date Kruszewski's *fonema* was at the very least trying to be a systematic one, to put it in generative terms; or, to put it in terms of prosodic phonology, a phonematic one. Though the deeper aspects of the Kazan' phoneme are referred to in passing, they cannot be said to be stressed.

The person to see the deeper aspects most clearly, indeed perhaps the only person to see them at all, and that many years before the other writers to whom I have referred, was Firth (1957, pp.1–2; original publication, 1934a). This is what he says there at the end of his discussion of Kruszewski:

Kruszewski, however, extended the term 'phoneme' to include sound alternances associated with changes of morphological categories. In English, for instance, -s, -z, -iz would be one morphological phoneme, represented naturally enough in orthography by one sign, s.

Firth adds:

He also extended it to include interlingual correspondences between sounds in related words in parallel morphological categories. And here he came near to the concept of what Professor Jones calls the diaphone.

This is surely better and, I take it, nearer the mark. For it seems that Kruszewski was interested in deeper relationships than are assumed or handled in setting up the later European and American 'phonemes'. And this was also true I believe of Baudouin, even if, as suggested by Stankiewicz (1972, p.25) 'he [Baudouin], no doubt, also tried to assert his claim to the authorship of the theory vis-à-vis Kruszewski' (through 'An attempt at a theory of phonetic alternations' that is to say). One has only to consider some of the examples in this work, to see something of what Firth was referring to in the case of Kruszewski, exemplified in de Courtenay. Such pairs as Polish *mróz* [mrus] / *mrozu*, *ród* [rut] / *rodu*, German *gab* [-p] / *geben* instanced there are evidence of interest in this deeper relationship; and when we come to such examples as *Frost* / *frieren*, *Verlust* / *verloren*, *Last* / *laden*, if we take into consideration the C-elements only (and one could adduce many such examples from a variety of languages), we can see that we are a very long way beyond even the first set of examples, and correspondingly far from the later phoneme with its allophones.

There is little doubt that it was Firth who put his finger on the real point concerning Kruszewski and his 'master'. The above are of course all examples of what Kazan' referred to as 'traditional alternations'. Only Firth seems to have been interested in this aspect of the Kazan' linguists' phonology, and what he said seems to have been ignored rather than noted; though it is heartening to be able to record at this point that Koerner (1973), who does refer to Firth's above-quoted short article, describes it as 'a beautiful statement of the principal ideas of Kruszewski's theory [of ablaut]' (p.161n.11). It is refreshing for once to see Firth referred to in this context, and to see the point he was making in 1934 recognised in 1973. True, Firth did not discuss the matter at any great length, but he did at least notice it, and that under 'phonology' it should be pointed out, where it surely belongs.

One may ask then, in view of this awareness on the part of J.R. Firth, how far Baudouin and Kruszewski may not be found to be 'responsible' for Firth, in addition to those mentioned already, and for others in Britain, in respect of some of their views on phonology. In some cases we do not realise the extent of the debt to our Polish forerunners. It is clear that Firth knew of Kruszewski and his theory – after all, he wrote about him, as we have seen. He was also, surely, the first to suggest in English that it was Kruszewski who was responsible for Baudouin in this connection. It is securely established of course that these linguists were, jointly, ultimately responsible for what I will call the more surface view of phonology, which reached this country through the person of Daniel Jones. I am not unmindful of this. Daniel Jones himself tells us that, having seen how Ščerba, one of Baudouin's later Petersburg students, had used the 'unextended' phoneme concept in his description of the Petersburg pronunciation of Russian, he (Daniel Jones) realised its importance for the sort of systematic representation of pronunciation that he was interested in. Tytus Benni also explained and filled in the details through personal contact (Jones 1957). Through Jones, the concept in this form passed as we know to Jones's own students (among them David Abercrombie) and, in most cases, to their students again.

But, if I may be allowed a personal note, it did not, significantly enough, so pass from Firth and others at the School of Oriental and African Studies at the beginning of the 1950s to me; and I recall being slightly amused later, when I joined the Department of Phonetics at the University of Edinburgh, at the thought that I had to check up on certain aspects of this, to most people, basic concept, before lecturing on the (Jonesian) phoneme.

If we now return to consider the other, deeper aspect, however, what of Firth and those associated with him? Is it the case, first of all, that his own work shows, from early on, this understanding of and interest in the so-called traditional alternances? The answer is yes. Firth's early papers, dating from just after the one cited above in which he discusses Kruszewski, papers such as 'The use and distribution of certain English sounds' (Firth 1935) and 'Linguistics and the functional point of view' (Firth 1934b), deal with sound function and relationships from precisely the sort of viewpoint that interested the Kazan' linguists. What Firth called 'major function' corresponds essentially to their traditional alternation, though in some respects it went further. Elsewhere in his writings too, Firth, unlike most of his British contemporaries, constantly stresses wider linguistic considerations of the function of sounds and sound attributes (as both he and Daniel Jones called prosodic features at that time) as carriers of distinctions at other formal levels. This was presumably why Trubetskoy identified him, in a letter to Roman Jakobson from London in May 1934, as the only person he had met who was to him a linguist in the sense that would be understood in Prague (Jakobson et al. 1975).

Such formulations by Firth as 'the phonetico-grammatical study of the language' – used in reference to the development of a notation at what we would now call the phonological level – 'will show how the sounds and sound attributes are used'; 'phonetic or phonological grammar' (a contradictory phrase if taken literally, but one which has to be understood in the spirit in which it was meant); 'phonetics is purely descriptive and non-linguistic, since it ignores phonological structure and function', if rightly understood, take precisely the same view of phonology, and hence of phonological units, as that taken by our diachronic colleagues in Kazan'. It is the same sort of view, whether admitted or not, as that of our synchronic colleagues of the generative school, at any rate in this respect; or rather *they* are now taking the same sort of view as Firth and the Kazan' school. Notice by the way that Firth always stressed the importance in grammatical function of intonation, stress and other traditionally 'prosodic' features, as had Henry Sweet before him. Here, however, he perhaps went further than Kruszewski and Baudouin de Courtenay.

But to return to the subjects of our discussion. I do not go so far as to suggest that the embryo of the 'articulatory' prosody, as I may call it, was already there in the work of the Kazan' school. This would perhaps be too much to expect along with the other advances – but other ideas that became important to Firth, were in phonology, and, it would seem, in other areas too, even if they were not explicitly worked out in a consistent theory.

For example, what Firth and his followers were later to present as polysystemicness can be recognised in the work of Kazan'. (This is also to be found in embryo in Twaddell (1935), though not in the particular form that I have in mind.) In Baudouin's 'An attempt at a theory of phonetic alternations' (see Stankiewicz 1972), following the discussion of anthropophonic and traditional alternations, chapter VI is devoted to 'Foreign alternations, i.e. alternations which are due to the influence of another language'. Here we find such examples as:

1. Both members of the alternation being of foreign origin –
   '*h*//*z* [in *błahy*/*błazen* ...]', borrowed from Czech.
2. One member is native, the other foreign – 'French *š*//*k*
   [*chose*/*cause, champs*/*camp* ...]'

There is a *z* in Polish, (e.g. in *za, Zakopane*), but not normally at this place in structure in such forms, and thus not alternating with *h*. Similarly, there is such a thing as *k* in French, but not commonly one must suppose before *o* where this is written ⟨au⟩. Admittedly this involves reference to the written medium, and is thus invalidated in terms of spoken French in the case of the first example from that language, but could probably be upheld in the case of the second, even at the present day. In any case, the principle is clear – the units concerned in these alternations are being proposed for treatment separately from others in the language, that is to say, to use the term of the London School, polysystemically.

These examples represent only one of the ways in which the prosodic-polysystemic approach later developed this concept (for this application, cf. e.g. Henderson (1951) 'The phonology of loan-words in some South-east Asian languages'). If we now look back at the previous quotations from Jakobson, however, there is at least a hint there, at the end of the second, at polysystemicness having another origin. To quote again: 'Baudouin's magnificent discovery ... was made, as we have seen, by comparing two forms of one and the same morpheme' – where the morpheme concerned is a purely grammatical one, as evidenced by the examples quoted. There is probably no evidence that either Baudouin or Kruszewski seriously set up the *i mutabile* here as a term in a separate system from that in say *byt / bit* (using Jakobson's notation, as I have throughout) – certainly not from Jakobson; but it is interesting, surely, that they should have chosen such elements of structure to set some phonemes up, and the existence of the evidence concerning loan-words means that it would have required only a step to treat the two *i*'s ('grammatical' and 'lexical') separately. And if one goes to set up, compara-bly, a 'phoneme' or phonemes in the case of the English *dogs / docks* (the example instanced by Firth), it is well known, or if it is not it should be (I suspect that generally it is not), that one does not arrive at a traditional (lexical) phoneme. But after all why should one? This Firth already took for granted in the place referred to. One arrives, on the contrary, and that without benefit of morphophoneme, at a phonematic unit, in Firthian terms, as a term in a system expounding grammatical elements of structure. Perhaps it was felt that the place concerned in Russian and Polish was different, even then. Things are not necessarily what they seem, in linguistics or in meta-linguistics. The *i mutabile* of that time as exponent of the nominative plural in Russian or Polish may look like any other *i*, but was it? Or, to put it more pointedly, should it be so?

So I find, with Firth, though it must be confessed too, to a large extent through Firth, that these linguists dealt in 'deep' phonology in a way that did not obtain elsewhere, I believe, until Firth and his colleagues of the London School worked in terms of prosodies and polysystems, and still does not apply in any real sense outside this theory.

To take a further example, it was not only in relation to grammatical morphemes that there was, as we have seen, at least a hint at a deeper phoneme, though both Firth and Jakobson refer mainly to this type of exam-ple. If we return to such pairs as German *Verlust / verloren*, *Last / laden*, cited above; and one could add, for Slavonic, Russian *dast / dadut*, or, more strik-ingly perhaps, Polish *idzie / idą / iść*; also Russian *jest / jedjat*; we have the possibility of deep phonological units as part exponents of lexical roots as well. The *s / d* alternation, in German and in Slavonic, would seem best re-garded as some sort of apical stop, basically 'voiced', and the *s / r* one an 'alveolar fricative', basically 'voiceless', each having the exponents appro-priate to particular environments, which can be characterised. In my opinion a prosodic treatment, in the London sense of that term, in a polysystemic framework, is the only way to achieve such an analysis; indeed, if rightly understood, the above formulation already says this. Naturally enough perhaps, Baudouin and Kruszewski were not going to reach the point of making the statement in the above terms – after all, and to adapt Jakobson's phrase, this too is 'not understood by all linguists even to this day' – the *d*'s referred to are not the *d*'s of *Dach* or *dat*', nor perhaps is the *s* referred to the *s* of *lesen*. In some sense they must have intended this.

There is yet another way in which Kazan' is reflected in the London

School more than in others, and that is in the matter of the clear separation of levels. This idea is made most clear by some who have followed Firth, through their further elaboration of the theory of the scale of exponence, so that it is quite clear that a morpheme, word or whatever, is *expounded* at the phonological level by phonological categories; it does not *consist of* phonological units, of whatever sort. I believe this was equally clear with Baudouin and Kruszewski. If I may be allowed to quote Jakobson again, he would not, it seems, have us believe in this separation of levels in the Kazan' School (Jakobson 1971a (1960) 409); though it seems at first as though he would. (The quotations from Baudouin are said to be from Programma II, 1877–8.)

He [Baudouin] took into account 'the twofold division of human speech'. The sound matter gets dismembered from an 'anthropophonic' point of view: 'The whole of *audible* speech is divided into anthropophonic sentences; sentences, into anthropophonic words; words, into anthropophonic syllables; syllables, into sounds'. On the other hand 'from the phonetic-morphological point of view the whole of connected speech is divided into sentences, or meaningful syntactic wholes; sentences, into meaningful words; words, into *morphological* syllables or *morphemes*' (units indivisible from the morphological point of view), the term 'morpheme' being Baudouin's neologism on the model of phoneme. If, Baudouin argued further, 'a morpheme can be divided into its component parts, then these components must be homogeneous with it'; Baudouin rightly considered the division of such semiotic units as morphemes into bare physical sounds to be 'an unjustified and illogical jump in the process of division';

– all fine so far. But the quotation ends:

morphemes are divisible, not into sounds, *but into minimal semiotic elements, i.e. phonemes* [my italics].

But suppose that Baudouin was acuter even than we are generally told. In the first section of this quotation (which, be it noted, is ostensibly from a fairly early source – see above), Baudouin is apparently dealing with phonetics/phonology. It is just perhaps that he lacks terms such as foot, stress group, and tone group, and thus uses 'anthropophonic sentence' etc. instead. Jakobson does not suggest at this point that the occurrence of the terms sentence and word mean that we are dealing with grammar. Then let us suppose, contrariwise as Tweedledee has it, that in the second section he is, equally, completely involved with grammar, despite the hint at phonology in one formulation used. This is unclear, admittedly, but there is no actual reference to anything 'phonetic' (phonological) in the passage as quoted. What, then, might 'an unjustified and illogical jump in the process of division' mean, other than what Jakobson states? For notice it is Jakobson who states that morphemes divide into phonemes, not into sounds. He does not show that Baudouin himself said this, although he may have. But since Baudouin has already said that *syllables* divide into sounds (like Firth, perhaps he felt that sounds would 'do less harm'; but no, he did not really have the word phoneme then, nor the concept of a separate phonological level – this is 1877–8); he must surely mean that morphemes are indivisible. And in fact Baudouin says as much elsewhere, in the introduction to 'An attempt at a theory of phonetic alternations', to which we are also referred by Jakobson, (original Polish version 1894) – 'the *morpheme* ... is ... not further divisible'. I suspect therefore that here we have a misinterpretation, in terms of what we want to understand or see in an exposition, rather than in terms of what is actually there. Of course morphemes do not divide into phonemes. This is one point about which the British tradition has arrived at a sensible conclusion. As Halliday once said to me apropos the formulation 'The phonetics of the sentence': 'The sentence *has* no phonetics' (thus agreeing so far with Jakobson); he could have added 'and no phonology either'. Sentence, word and morpheme are at the grammatical level, and if once we start to talk of dividing morphemes into phonemes, why should we not talk of dividing them into sounds? The one, I suggest, is not really any better than the other. And I believe that both Baudouin and Kruszewski were aware of this.

But we have neglected Kruszewski in all this. I should like to return to him now to show again his connection with Firthian linguistics, even though this goes outside the scope of this volume.

I have noted above a remarkable similarity between Kruszewski's and Firth's phonological theories. I wish to refer briefly now to Kruszewski's views relative to some other linguistic matters. First, he distinguished clearly in linguistics in general between the two formal 'dimensions' of structure and system, so important for Firth later. It does not perhaps appear that Kruszewski extended the concept to the phonological level, but it would have required only a small step to do so. Kruszewski referred to these two sets of relationships as *Ähnlichkeitsassociationen* and *Angrenzungsassociationen*. It is true that he probably regarded them primarily as relationships obtaining in the mind; nevertheless they are clearly comparable to the other concepts. In referring to them, Kruszewski related the discussion to the word, largely in a lexical sense, though also in a grammatical one, too. Thus we have reference to related forms of the same item, but also to semantically related sets of items (these exemplify relations of similarity of course; they are on the paradigmatic axis). And then, a word or words, Kruszewski says, will call up other words with which it / they are commonly associated, as for example the item *wear out* is associated with such items as *clothes, dress, trousers* (Koerner's example); but not presumably *head, house* or even *cups* or *plates*. We get used to employing a particular item more often with one item than another. I found the realisation of this particularly interesting. For here is 'the company words keep', to use Firth's phrase. In other words here is Firth's lexical concept of collocation. I find this similarity between Kazan' and London remarkable.

Now I am aware of two possible reactions to the foregoing. One is that if so many of Firth's views and ideas are to be found already in the writings of the Kazan' school, and particularly in the work of Kruszewski, then perhaps much, or worse still most, of what we regard as typically Firthian is called in question. As I have already said, it is clear that Firth knew Kruszewski, even if only through *Über die Lautabwechslung*. I do not think, however, that the fact that Firth may have been inspired by Kruszewski, detracts from what he himself achieved. He may, in any case, have come on some of the ideas that seem to be comparable, quite independently. I think he was likely, for example, to have favoured deeper phonology quite independently. In either case, he made the ideas his own and developed them beyond the point that Kruszewski had reached, or was able to reach, in the short time allowed to him. And Firth's approval of Kruszewski, though only briefly evinced by what he wrote, is none the less clear from his reference in 'The word "phoneme"'' (1934a).

This leads on to the second point, however. I have suggested earlier that Jakobson, in laying such stress on the importance of Kazan' in giving us the simpler view of the phoneme, was seeing what he wanted to see and no more, and so overlooking the more important aspect, which Firth saw (and by the same token overlooking Firth): overlooking, that is to say, something that was there, but that did not agree with his own objectives. Am I not also seeing what I wish to see? Well, possibly. Why allow all the best tunes to one faction? But if not, and in this instance I believe not, it is high time that the striking similarity was pointed out, for the sake of British linguistics, and equally for the sake of Kruszewski, whose 'contribution', as Koerner has said (1973,148) 'to linguistic thought has been even more ignored by western linguists and historians than Baudouin's work'. As Palmer says with reference to Firthian phonology, in the introduction to *Prosodic Analysis* (Palmer 1970, xv): 'Ironically, today when prosodic analysis is no longer being championed with the fervour that it was in the late 1950s, many of the points that were made are now quite widely accepted'. Some of these points, as I have tried to suggest, were in fact there in the Kazan' School, right at the beginnings of phonology as we know it. Firth, I believe, saw the significance of what this school had in mind, and particularly of what Kruszewski had in mind. It seems to me that when we praise him and Baudouin de Courtenay, we should do so as fully as we can, and more fully than has usually been the case, in terms of what they really stood for. And when we hear Kruszewski say 'Ax, kak bystro prošel ja čerez scenu', 'Oh, how quickly I have crossed the stage', I cannot help wondering how much nearer, at the beginning of this century, we might have been to phonology in a more linguistic sense, if Kruszewski had lived.

References

FIRTH, J.R. (1934a) 'The Word "Phoneme"', *M Phon*, no. 46, 44–6. Also in Firth (1957).

— (1934b) 'Linguistics and the functional point of view', *English Studies* XVI, no. 1, 18–24.

— (1934c) 'The principles of phonetic notation in descriptive grammar', *Congrès international des sciences anthropologiques et ethnologiques*, London, 325–8. Also in Firth (1957).

— (1935) 'The use and distribution of certain English sounds', *English Studies* XVII, no. 1, 8–18. Also in Firth (1957).

— (1957) *Papers in Linguistics, 1934–1951*, London (Oxford University Press).

HENDERSON, E.J.A. (1951) 'The phonology of loanwords in some South-East Asian languages', *T Ph S*, 131–58. Also in Palmer (1970).

JAKOBSON, ROMAN (1971a) 'The Kazan' school of Polish linguistics', in *Selected Writings II*, 394–428, The Hague (Mouton).

— (1971b) 'Značenie Kruševskogo v razvitii nauki o jazyke', in *Selected Writings II*, 429–50, The Hague (Mouton).

— et al. (1975) *N.S. Trubetzkoy's letters and notes*, no. CXXX, p.299, The Hague (Mouton).

JONES, D. (1957) '*The history and meaning of the term "phoneme"*', supplement to *Le Maître Phonétique*.

KOERNER, E.F.K. (1973) *Ferdinand de Saussure: the Origin and Development of his Linguistic Thought in Western Studies of Language. A Contribution to the History and Theory of Linguistics*, Braunschweig (Vieweg).

KRUSZEWSKI, MIKOŁAJ (1881) *Über die Lautabwechslung*, Kazan' (University Press).

PALMER, F.R. ed. (1970) *Prosodic Analysis*, London (Oxford University Press).

STANKIEWICZ, EDWARD (1972) *A Baudouin de Courtenay Anthology*, Ontario (Fitzhenry and Whiteside, Ltd.).

TWADDELL, W. FREEMAN (1935) *On Defining the Phoneme*, Language Monograph no. 16, Linguistic Society of America, Baltimore.

Observations on the Recent History
of Vowel Classification

It is generally acknowledged that the 'traditional' classification of vowels in terms of 'horizontal' and 'vertical' tongue-position was invented by Melville Bell (1867) and further developed and popularised by Henry Sweet (1877). It is this 'Bell–Sweet' model of vowel production and system of classification that underlies most modern description of vowels; including the system of Cardinal Vowels developed by Daniel Jones and used by the International Phonetic Association.

The Bell–Sweet model of vowel production has long been criticised: among the best-known of the critics are Meyer (1910), Viëtor (1914) and Russell (1928, 1936). Their criticism was that instrumental methods of investigation – notably radiography and Meyer's 'plastography' – failed to confirm, indeed at times totally contradicted, the tongue-configurations postulated by the Bell–Sweet model.

With the advent of refined methods of acoustic analysis of speech a new element entered into the criticism of Bell–Sweet. Joos (1948, pp.53–6) pointed out that when vowels were plotted in terms of their first and second formants on the type of formant chart that he introduced 'the classical or IPA tongue-position quadrilateral rather more closely resembles the acoustic vowel quadrilateral than it resembles the Carmody X-ray tongue-position quadrilateral'.

The sound-spectrograph then became a powerful tool in supporting the view already proposed by Russell (1928) that 'phoneticians are thinking in terms of acoustic fact and using physiological phantasy to express the idea'. Ladefoged (1967, p.68) put the same point of view very clearly.

> With the later work of Bell [i.e. Bell's *Visible Speech*, 1867] we enter an era when phoneticians had the avowed intention of doing one thing but actually succeeded in doing another. They set out to describe the positions of the vocal organs during the production of different sounds; but their success in this enterprise was partial. They did, however, succeed in providing categories with which to describe their auditory impressions.

Ladefoged has also criticised the tongue-position model on the basis of its non-correspondence with X-ray data, for example, in Ladefoged (1976), and a good deal of evidence apparently supporting this type of criticism has been presented by Sidney Wood in his publications of 1975 and 1977.

A confusing side-issue in the controversy about the validity of the Bell–Sweet model is the frequent reference by users of this model to the location of the *highest point of the tongue*. It has been pointed out by several people (including myself in Catford 1977, pp.182–7) that the location of this 'highest point' is not the most relevant determinant of vowel quality: that the location of the narrowest constriction is much more relevant. Stevens (1972) and especially Wood (1977) make the point not only that constriction-location is important, but also introduce the idea of *discrete*, quantal, articulatory types for vowels (hard-palate, soft-palate, upper-pharynx, lower-pharynx) as against the *continua* (front-to-back, high-to-low) of Bell–Sweet, and Wood evidently considers this as another defect of the traditional system.

I have not carried out the historical research that would be necessary to determine who first introduced 'the highest point of the tongue' into discussions of vowel production. So far as I know neither Bell nor Sweet did so, but Jespersen (1889, p.18) treats this expression as current, and makes the very point that has been raised by recent critics. He refers to measuring 'not from the highest part of the tongue, absolutely speaking, but from *that part of the tongue which is nearest to the palate*. In consequence of the arched shape of the palate, these two parts do not always coincide' (Italics Jespersen's).

In view of the mobility and extreme polymorphism of the tongue it is obviously difficult to specify precisely what is meant by the labels for different 'tongue positions' – 'high-front', 'mid-mixed' etc. – and it was not unreasonable to seek some kind of reference-point for the purpose of comparing tongue-positions. The summit of the tongue-hump may not have been a bad choice for this purpose. The danger in using it, however, was that one might come to believe that the tongue-summit was itself some kind of functionally important locus in vowel production, instead of being merely a reference point.

The main points that I want to discuss in the present paper are:
i) Were Bell and Sweet deluding themselves: talking of tongue-positions but unaware that they were *really* talking about auditory sensations?
ii) A matter of recent history – the problem of reconciling the cardinal vowel diagram with acoustic formant charts.
iii) The Russell-type criticism of the mismatch between the tongue-position model and radiographic data is partly grossly exaggerated, and partly based on a particular fallacy in the interpretation of phonetic data.

Bell and Sweet

With respect to my first point, it seems to me that there is ample internal evidence in the works of both Bell and Sweet to show that they (and no doubt many of their contemporaries and successors) were *not* deluding themselves. They really were taking note primarily of *perceived tongue-positions* and not of auditory sensations. Bell's description in his *Visible Speech* pp.15–16 of how he discovered that 'labial modification' was an independent variable that could be added to, or subtracted from, any vowel articulation strongly suggests articulatory experimentation rather than mere auditory introspection. On the next page there is explicit reference to the articulatory experimentation underlying the system:

> experiments proved that the missing sounds could all be produced by organic arrangements corresponding with the theoretical classification. In fact, any desired sound, known or unknown, could be produced at pleasure by first adjusting the organs tentatively for its neighbour-sounds and then allowing these to coalesce, as it were, into an intermediate.

This is an articulatory, proprioceptive, (and only very marginally auditory) procedure which must be familiar to anyone who has made extensive motor experimentation in his own mouth.

Further down page 17 he says:

> The Consonants were much more easily classified, as their organic formation was more obvious; and former results had left comparatively little to be done in order to form a correspondingly complete scale. An important discovery was, however, made in tabulating these elements: their relation to the various parts of the Vowel Scale was ascertained; the true cause of consonantal, as distinct from vowel effect, was made manifest, and a New Class of Elements, intermediate to vowels and consonants, was recognised. These 'glides', or true semi-vowels, completed the scheme of Linguistic Sounds, joining the vowels and consonants into one harmonious scale.

Throughout all this there is a clear implication of motor experimentation: one can hardly associate *auditory* impressions of vowels with the *articulatory* locations of consonants. But Bell makes it clear here, and even more on p.75 where he discusses the relationship between various vowels and pharyngal, velar, and palatal consonants, that he is equating tongue-positions, not auditory sensations. Incidentally, although they used a different terminology for vowels (high-low, front-back), both Bell and Sweet were well aware of the relationship between vowel locations, and consonantal locations: their use of the special vowel terminology did not conceal from them the fact that vowels were indeed articulated in the palatal, velar and pharyngal zones referred to by Wood (1977).

In the 1877 *Handbook of Phonetics*, as also in his later *Primer*, Sweet was even more explicit than Bell on the question of the *articulatory* basis of vowel classification. This is particularly clear in his paragraph on the Practical Mastery of Vowels, pp.17–18, where he says:

> Whispering the vowels will be found a great help in analysing their formation. After a time the student will be able to recognise each vowel solely by the muscular sensations associated with its formation:

21

he will be able to say to himself, 'Now my tongue is in the position for (i),' 'Now I have changed (i) into (ih),' &c., while not uttering the slightest sound, confident that if voiced or whispered breath is allowed to pass through the mouth the required sound will be produced.

In subsequent paragraphs dealing with lengthening and shortening vowels (p.18), with comparing unrounded and rounded vowels, high and low and front and back vowels (p.19) it is equally clear that Sweet is talking all the time about experiments on articulatory postures and movements. Again, his instructions (pp.19–20) for the acquisition of unfamiliar vowels clearly refer to actual articulatory activities in the mouth.

> The student ... has only to follow the analogies of the changes he has already made, to produce without difficulty many sounds that he perhaps never heard before in his life. ... If from a comparison of (ɐ) [IPA ɤ] and (o) he has learnt the medium degree of rounding that belongs to a mid vowel, he has only to apply it to (e) and he will have (ə) [IPA ø] ... Mixed vowels are best learnt by arresting the transition between the nearest back and front vowels. Thus if the student wishes to acquire the Swedish (uh) [IPA ʉ], he only has to pass from (u) to (y) backwards and forwards several times without intermission, and then to arrest his tongue half-way.

Finally, on page 20, in the section headed Acoustic Qualities of Vowels, Sweet says:

> We have hitherto entirely ignored the acoustic effects of the vowels. This has been done designedly. The first and indispensable qualification of the phonetician is a thorough practical knowledge of the formation of the vowels. Those who try to learn new sounds by ear alone, without any systematic training in the use of their vocal organs generally succeed only partially .... There can be no question that flexible organs well trained together with only an average ear, can yield better results than even an exceptionally good ear without organic training.

It seems clear that Bell and Sweet relied primarily on their perceptions of tongue-positions – that is, on tactile and proprioceptive sensations – in describing and classifying vowels. The Bell–Sweet model was thus a system genuinely based on the organic perceptions of highly competent phoneticians, and not a delusive misinterpretation of auditory sensations by phonetic illiterates.

Quite apart from the evidence quoted above, one can verify the feasibility of the Bell–Sweet proprioceptive approach in much the same way as some archaeologists have verified the feasibility of manufacturing flint implements – by actually doing it. When, as a boy, I studied Sweet's *Primer of Phonetics*, without a live teacher, I naturally followed Sweet's instructions meticulously. Hours spent in producing silent vowels, correlating the proprioceptive sensations with direct observations in a mirror, checking, by

22

voicing, the acoustic-auditory result of this or that posture, and so on, demonstrated conclusively that the Bell–Sweet vowel production model was articulatorily, not auditorily, based. After having learnt Jones' cardinal vowels, I always used that system in a basically proprioceptive way – estimating the relationship of heard vowels to the cardinal vowels by imitation and silent comparison of proprioceptive sensations. I grew up assuming that this was how all phoneticians did it – but now I wonder if this is so!

Another verification of the basically proprioceptive nature of the Bell–Sweet model is derived from teaching. In teaching the cardinal vowels (as in all teaching of phonetics) *silent* experimentation, and intensive *silent* practice is very effective in helping students to acquire a practical control of the system. Incidentally, in a relevant, though rather tentative, experiment (Catford and Pisoni 1970) it was found that *silent*, purely articulatory instruction in the production of a few 'exotic' vowels and consonants was significantly more effective than purely *auditory* instruction with no articulatory guidance.

It is important, I think, to emphasise the point that I have repeatedly mentioned above – namely that the Bell–Sweet model is not based on objective (radiographic) records of tongue-position, but on *proprioceptive and tactile* sensations. Obviously there is a close correlation between the objective and proprioceptive data, but one should not expect them to be identical. Moreover, Bell and Sweet were estimating relative tongue-positions from such data as degree of contraction of the *genioglossus* muscle determining 'tongue-height' (perhaps with some help from *styloglossus* for high back vowels), contraction of *pharyngeal constrictors* for the less high back vowels, and so on. Consequently, what they arrived at and described were primarily general estimates of total tongue-position rather than estimates of the location of the 'highest point', or of the narrowest constriction: the actual proprioceptive data that they relied upon were derived from muscles often widely separated in space from these particular points. As mentioned earlier, however, they were both well aware of the location of the narrowest constriction – as is shown by their explicit correlation of certain vowels with consonantal articulations. But this correlation was a thing apart from the basic proprioceptive classification of general tongue configurations.

Cardinal Vowels and Formant Charts

The second point I want to discuss is the problem of correlating the cardinal vowel diagram, ultimately based on a Bell–Sweet type model, with acoustic data and acoustic formant charts. Figure 1 shows the primary and secondary cardinal vowels plotted on the original type of formant chart devised by Joos (1948). It is clear that the relative positions of the points representing the primary cardinal vowels, joined by unbroken lines, show, as Joos pointed out, a rough resemblance to their positions on a cardinal vowel diagram. But the fit is not very good, and various authors have tried to devise methods of

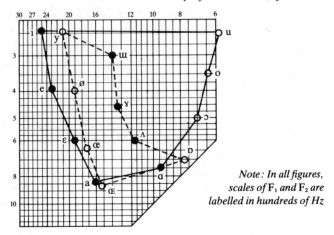

FIGURE 1. Primary and secondary cardinal vowels on a Joos-type formant chart. Open circles represent rounded vowels.

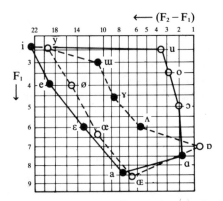

FIGURE 2. Primary and secondary cardinal vowels on a Ladefoged-type formant chart.

improving the fit between the traditional vowel diagram and a two-formant chart: one such method was to use the mel scale of units of *pitch* devised from psycho-acoustic, perceptual, experiments, but this was not particularly effective.

Another expedient was to use the normal physical frequency scales, calibrated in Hz, but in place of F2 to use, as the horizontal axis of the formant chart, a scale representing the *difference* between F2 and F1. This scale is used, for example, in Ladefoged (1976) and in several other publications of Ladefoged and his associates. Our figure 2 shows the cardinal vowels plotted on a formant chart of this type.

Obviously this type of chart provides a better fit. The slopes of the lines representing the front and back series of cardinal vowels more nearly match the slopes they have in the traditional cardinal vowel diagram. But the match is not perfect, and with respect to the secondary cardinal vowels, particularly the unrounded vowels [ɯ ɤ ʌ], it is still wildly off. Incidentally, the extreme separation of pairs of back vowels like [ɯ] and [u] or [ɤ] and [o] on the formant chart (and hence, by implication, in terms of auditory sensations) is additional evidence against the hypothesis that the Bell–Sweet tongue-position model was in reality an auditory model. Both Bell and Sweet un-hesitatingly equated pairs of rounded and unrounded back vowels. It is perfectly obvious from figures 1 and 2 that this kind of equation would be utterly impossible in an auditorily-based system.

Incidentally, figure 2 provides some evidence for the proprioceptive basis of the cardinal vowel system. The cardinal vowels are supposed to be a scale of *equidistant* vowel sounds. It is clear from figure 2 that, acoustically speaking, this is not the case: the acoustic distance (particularly as repre-sented by F1) between successive vowels increases as they become more open. But a deviation from acoustic equidistance in precisely this direction is what one must expect if a speaker attempts to produce a series of vowels that are articulatorily or proprioceptively equidistant. Owing to the shape of the roof of the mouth, which widens as one moves downwards, equal increments of tongue-lowering result in increasing increments of cross-sectional area (and of volume) and this, of course, is reflected in increasing increments of formant frequency.

The types of formant chart presented in figures 1 and 2 may be described (even though this may not have been the primary intention of their authors) as attempts to reconcile the cardinal vowel diagram with a formant chart primarily by *distorting the cardinal vowel diagram*. As we have seen, they are only partly successful. It has for some time seemed to me to be worth while approaching this problem from the other end; that is, by *distorting the formant chart* to fit the cardinal vowel diagram. Taking values for cardinal vowels derived, by averaging, from a number of recordings of my own cardinal vowels together with those of Daniel Jones, I proceeded, by trial and error, to fit scales of F1 and F2 to a cardinal vowel diagram. It is, of course, obvious that we must have two distinct vowel diagrams: one for unrounded vowels and a second for rounded vowels. As a matter of fact, ideally one should have a whole series of intermediate vowel diagrams for intermediate degrees of rounding. As a compromise I have found it useful sometimes to use a cardinal vowel+formant (CVF) diagram with intermediate values between those for unrounded and rounded vowels. Finally, of course, one can combine the formant scales for rounded and unrounded vowels in a single CVF diagram and hence plot both types of vowels on the same chart.

Figure 3 illustrates the original CVF diagrams, for unrounded and rounded vowels, with plots of the average formant values for the cardinal vowels of eleven phoneticians, as reported by Ladefoged (1967, pp.88,89). It was necessary to convert Ladefoged's data from the mel scale in which they

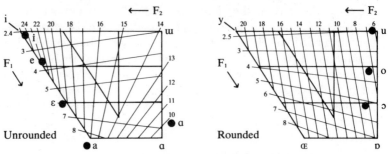

FIGURE 3. Cardinal vowel plus formant (CVF) diagrams. Average values of cardinal vowels for 11 phoneticians.

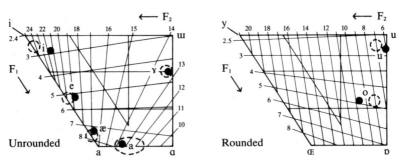

FIGURE 4. Vowels of Svan. Dots represent spectrographic data. Broken-lined circles and elipse represent auditory-proprioceptive data.

were presented to Hertz, and in doing this some slight degree of approximation is introduced. It is interesting to see that the positions of the points representing these average values correspond rather well with the locations of the cardinal vowels on the CVF diagrams. This is an encouraging indication of the usefulness of the CVF diagram, and a little surprising since the specific formant values of particular individuals depend upon the dimensions of their individual vocal tracts. There is no doubt that in some cases special CVF diagrams would have to be devised to fit individuals whose vocal tracts were unusually small or large.

However, I have found that these CVF diagrams work rather well in practice, and they are being used in work in progress on Caucasian languages. The value of this method of displaying vowel formants is emphasised by superimposing upon the spectrographically obtained vowel plots an indication of the placing of vowels on a cardinal vowel chart 'by ear' – which, of course really means by imitation and proprioceptive comparison with cardinal vowels. Figure 4 shows average formant values of vowels in the Kartvelian language Svan, and figure 5 the short stressed vowels of the Nakh Language, Chechen, with 'auditory-proprioceptive' plots (carried out in the

26

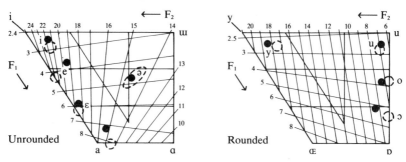

FIGURE 5. Stressed short vowels of Chechen. Spectrographic and auditory-proprioceptive data as in figure 4.

field before spectrographic data were available) indicated by larger broken-lined circles or ellipses. These figures tend to show the validity of the cardinal vowel diagram as indicating a proprioceptive scale of 'tongue-positions' as well as an acoustic scale.

Tongue Position and Radiographic Data

I come now to my final point, and here CVF diagrams will be of some use, which is indeed why they had to be introduced earlier. The point I want to examine here is the claim, made by such scholars as Russell, Ladefoged and Wood, that X-ray photographs of tongue-positions invalidate the tongue-positions model of vowel classification.

One must first point out that the critics of the Bell–Sweet model have tended to exaggerate: as Lindau (1978) points out 'when additional radiographic data are analysed, it becomes apparent that Ladefoged has overstated his case: the traditional highest point of the tongue is virtually as good a measure of height and backness as the formant chart is'. Not only Ladefoged, of course, but Russell (1928, 1936) Wood (1975, 1977) and other critics of the Bell–Sweet model have tended to exaggerate. Ladefoged (1976) does, however, provide a clear example of 'overstatement'. Commenting on relative positions of the highest point of the tongue in X-rays of his own pronunciation of vowels he comments that 'We can only pretend, for example, that the vowel in "food" is higher than the vowel in "hid" by considerably warping the line separating high vowels from non-high vowels'. In fact, his X-rays indicate rather good agreement of radiographic data with the tongue-positions postulated by Bell–Sweet and the cardinal vowel system. There is nothing in the traditional tongue-position model that says that all high vowels must be at the same absolute height (above what?) and, indeed, the earliest version of the cardinal vowel diagram, as used in Jones (1922) actually represents 'close back' [u] as being at almost as low a level in the diagram as 'half-close front' [e]. In the same article Ladefoged implies that the Daniel Jones cardinal vowels deviate extremely from their postulated

27

tongue-positions. But this implication is derived from critical examination of a set of X-ray pictures of cardinal vowels pronounced by Daniel Jones' colleague (but no relation) Stephen Jones. These pictures, published in 1929, are rather badly reproduced on a small scale. They are thus not too easy to interpret. Moreover, they are all produced with one chain lying along the surface of the tongue (to provide an X-ray opaque indicator of tongue-configuration) and another chain through the nose and hanging down behind the uvula (to show the position of the soft-palate). Although S. Jones claims in the accompanying article that the chains did not interfere with his pronunciation, one cannot be certain that they did not do so. In general, these X-ray pictures of S. Jones are not very convincing evidence against the validity of the tongue-position model. Other X-ray pictures of some of the cardinal vowels, for example those reproduced in Daniel Jones (1950) show, as far as they go, tongue-positions of the appropriate kind. The fact is that when one examines a wide range of published (and unpublished) X-ray pictures of vowels one finds a great deal of general agreement between the traditional tongue-positions and the configurations actually recorded by X-rays.

The other defect in some of the criticism of the Bell–Sweet model is perhaps more subtle, more easily overlooked, than simple exaggeration. It is what I referred to above as 'a fallacy in the interpretation of phonetic data' – perhaps it would be more accurate to say a fallacy in interpretation of transcriptions. What I mean can be illustrated by Russell's paper (1935) published in the Proceedings of the Second International Congress of Phonetic Sciences. Here Russell presents four X-ray negatives, of pronunciation of what he claims are 'the same vowel' namely [ɑ] in the words *pop tot* and *cock* embedded in sentences and a 'prolonged vowel **ɑ** where the subject is told to "open your mouth and prolong the **ɑ** in *cock* until I tell you to stop"'. Now in spite of the fact that Russell represents all four of these vowels by the symbol **ɑ**, it is practically certain that they do not all represent an identical articulation, nor an identical sound. It is practically certain that a competent phonetician, using the auditory-proprioceptive technique of vowel identification, would have postulated quite different tongue-positions for them and plotted them differently on a cardinal vowel diagram.

Unfortunately we have no means of verifying the claim made in the last paragraph, but I recently came across an example which is very instructive in this connection. In an article on the vowels of the literary Avar language of Dagestan, the Georgian phonetician Džaparidze (1967) presents a number of tracings from X-ray pictures of vowel articulation. Among these are examples of Avar **a** and **o**. These turn out, as is clearly shown in one figure where their tongue-profiles are superimposed, to have almost identical tongue positions. Now, this is precisely the kind of example that would have been seized on by a critic of the Russell type as conclusively demonstrating the falsity of the traditional tongue-position model of vowel production.

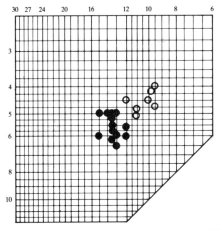

FIGURE 6. Spectrographic data for Avar **a** (filled circles) and **o** (open circles) on a Joos-type formant chart.

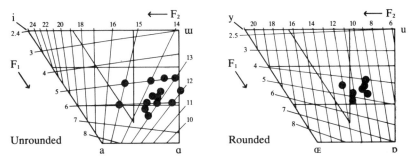

FIGURE 7. The same data for Avar **a** and **o** on CVF diagrams.

'Everyone knows,' he might say 'that **a** is traditionally classified as an *open* vowel and **o** as a *mid* or half-close vowel. The X-ray shows them to have the *same* tongue-position. Therefore the traditional classification is wrong'. However what would be *wrong* in this case would be the phonetic interpretation of the *letters* **a** and **o**, as we shall see.

Even before seeing Džaparidze's article I had noticed in field work with three speakers of Avar that their **a** and **o** vowels were neither of them necessarily *back* vowels (being usually rather strongly centralised) and that both were about half open. I tentatively transcribed them as something like [ɔ̈] and [ɜ] or [ä]. I later made spectrograms of these vowels in a short text by one of my informants, and plotted his vowels on a regular formant chart (figure 6). In this figure the filled circles represent examples of **a**, the open circles examples of **o**. In figure 7 we see the same vowels plotted on a CVF diagram for unrounded and rounded vowels. Finally, figure 8 shows the area occupied by these examples of **a** and **o** on a composite CVF diagram. It is

29

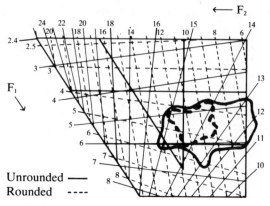

FIGURE 8. The areas covered by Avar **a** (full line) and
o (broken line).

clear from figures 7 and 8 that Avar **a** and **o** are acoustically (and so, presumably, auditorily) quite similar, and secondly, from figure 8, that some occurrences of **o** may be presumed to have the same tongue-position as some occurrences of **a**.

Wood (1975, p.75) presents four 'anomalous' examples of X-ray data showing American and German 'lax ɪ' with a lower tongue-height than 'tense ē'. I am not competent to discuss the German examples, but the American examples are not at all convincing indictments of the Bell–Sweet model! In the first place, American ɪ and ē are very commonly diphthongs of the types [ɪə] and [eɪ], and there is no indication here of the particular point in the diphthongal glide captured by the X-ray photographs. But apart from that, it is not uncommon for American ɪ-vowels to be quite low – of a type which would be plotted by the auditory-proprioceptive technique on a cardinal vowel diagram below the half-close line. It is not surprising, therefore, that some examples of American ɪ turn out to have lower tongue-positions than ē – precisely as predicted by the traditional Bell–Sweet model of vowel formation when properly applied.

To conclude, then, it seems to me that there is convincing evidence to show that the great nineteenth-century phoneticians Bell and Sweet were not self-deluded incompetents. Their classification of vowels was primarily based upon their highly trained perception of proprioceptive and tactile sensations, not upon the misinterpretation of auditory sensations. It was thus in some sense genuinely based upon tongue-configurations – that is, perceptions of the general positioning of the tongue as a whole, not of the highest point of the tongue. The 'tongue-summit' as a reference point was introduced by others, and has led to some misconceptions. Bell and Sweet, concentrating on perceptual information from the muscles which positioned the tongue as a whole were not much concerned with 'the highest point'. Moreover, they were perfectly well aware of the relationship between vowel articulation and consonant articulation in the palatal, velar, uvular, and pharyngeal areas – but they defined vowels differently from consonants, just because their vowel classification relied more heavily on *proprioceptive* information than the *tactile* information that played a greater role in consonant classification.

Critics of the Bell–Sweet model using radiographic and other instrumental techniques have overstated their case. They have sometimes exaggerated the discrepancies between traditional auditory-proprioceptive evaluation of tongue-configuration and their instrumental data, and they have sometimes interpreted the graphic (often phonemic) representation of the sounds they were studying in an arbitrary and incorrect way which has introduced spurious discrepancies between their data and the appropriate Bell–Sweet type description of the sounds.

The traditional proprioceptive system of vowel classification, which we have inherited from Bell, Sweet and Daniel Jones, appears to exhibit some marginal inadequacies. It does not, for instance, have built into it the ability to cope with such features as 'tongue-root advancement', 'pharyngalisation', 'rhotacised' and so on, though, in fact, a careful perusal of Bell's *Visible Speech* shows that he did allow for more modifications than we realise. Nevertheless, it still works remarkably well in practice, and, as I have shown above by means of the cardinal vowel + formant diagram, it can be brought into harmony with modern methods of acoustic analysis. Bell's 'break-through' in vowel classification of 1867 was indeed a key event in the history of phonetics the results of which are still far from being superseded by new approaches and techniques.

References
BELL, A.M. (1867) *Visible Speech: the Science of Universal Alphabetics*, London (Simpkin, Marshall & Co.).
CATFORD, J.C. (1977) *Fundamental Problems in Phonetics*, Edinburgh (Edinburgh University Press).
CATFORD, J.C. and PISONI, D.B. (1970) 'Auditory vs. Articulatory Training in Exotic Sounds', *Mod. Lang. J.* LIV, 7, 447–81.
DŽAPARIDZE, Z.N. (1967) 'Salit'erat'uro xundzuri enis xmovnebi' ('The vowels of literary Avar' – in Georgian with Russian summary). *Met'qvelebis analizis, sinteza da st'at'ist'ik'is sak'itxebi* (Questions of analysis, synthesis and statistics of speech) II, Tbilisi, 112–21.
JESPERSEN, OTTO (1889) *The Articulations of Speech Sounds represented by means of Analphabetic Symbols*, Marburg (N.G. Elwert).
JONES, DANIEL (1922) *An Outline of English Phonetics*, 2nd ed., Leipzig (Teubner).
— (1950) *The Pronunciation of English*, Cambridge (Cambridge University Press).
JOOS, MARTIN (1948) *Acoustic Phonetics*, Language Monograph no.23, Linguisitic Society of America, Baltimore.
LADEFOGED, PETER (1967) *Three Areas of Experimental Phonetics*, London (Oxford University Press).
— (1976) 'The Phonetic Specification of the Languages of the World', *UCLA Working Papers in Phonetics No. 31*, March, Los Angeles 3–21.

LINDAU, MONA (1978) 'Vowel Features', *Language* 54.3 Sept. 541–63.

MEYER, E. (1910) 'Untersuchungen über Lautbildung', *Festschrift Wilhem Viëtor* (Special issue of *Die neueren Sprachen*) 166–248.

RUSSELL, GEORGE OSCAR (1928) *The Vowel: Some X-ray and Photo Laringoperiskopik Evidence*, Columbus (Ohio State University Press).

— (1936) 'Synchronised X-ray, oscillograph, sound and movie experiments showing the fallacy of vowel triangle and open-closed theories', in D. Jones and D.B. Fry (eds.) *Proc. 2nd Int. Congr. of Phonetic Sciences*, London 1935, Cambridge (Cambridge University Press) 198–205.

STEVENS, K.N. (1972) 'The Quantal Nature of Speech, evidence from articulatory-acoustic data', in E.E. David and P.B. Denes (eds.) *Human Communication, a unified view*, New York (McGraw-Hill) 51–6.

SWEET, H. (1877) *A Handbook of Phonetics*, Oxford (Clarendon Press).

VIËTOR, W. (1914) 'Zur Systematik der Vokalartikulation', *Miscellania Phonetica* IPA, 1–5.

WOOD, SIDNEY (1975) 'The weakness of the tongue-arching model of vowel articulation', *Working Papers No. 11*; Phonetics Laboratory, Lund University, Lund, 55–107.

— (1977) 'A radiographic analysis of constriction locations for vowels', *Working Papers No. 15*; Phonetics Laboratory, Lund University, Lund, 101–31.

PART TWO

HISTORY OF IDEAS IN PHONETICS :
PROCESSES

Early Descriptions
of Nasality

In traditional phonetic terms 'nasal sounds' are sounds in the production of which the nasal cavity crucially participates. The velum is lowered, thus linking the nasal cavity with the vocal tract below it. An airstream from the lungs may then pass through the 'nasal port' into the nasal cavity. Simultaneously the airstream may enter the oral cavity; modifications of the flow by action of the tongue, teeth or lips gives rise to different varieties of nasal sounds. The auditory character of these sounds, at least if there is simultaneous voicing, derives from the configuration of the cavities involved, and the associated resonances. In recent years the acoustic characteristics of nasal sounds have been given detailed descriptions; see, for example, Lindqvist and Sundberg (1976), Delattre (1969a, 1969b), Hecker (1962), Fujimura (1961, 1962), Fant (1960). Research over some fifty years has demonstrated that the equations, 'nasal' = 'with velic opening', and 'oral' = 'with velic closure' are in fact an oversimplification of the true state of affairs. It has been clearly established that a sound may be produced with some degree of velic opening and yet not be perceived as nasal in quality. Conversely, utterances perceived as having a nasal quality may be produced without any velic opening. Cagliari (1977, p.105) cites Eijkman (1926, pp.212 and 277–8) as perhaps the first to contest the belief that the nasal cavities necessarily participate in the production of sounds that are perceived as having a nasal quality. (On nasality as a feature of voice quality see Laver 1980, pp.68–92.)

However, it is not the purpose of this article to examine recent research into nasality but to give some account of the way in which nasal sounds are described in some of the early works in the western tradition of phonetic description, with very brief references to the ancient Indian and Arabic traditions.

The western tradition starts with the Greeks. In ancient Greek there were two nasal consonant phonemes – / m / and / n /; the velar nasal [ŋ] occurred in certain limited environments (see Allen 1968, pp.33ff.). These nasal consonants were not treated in any of the Greek descriptions as a class on their own. In the grammar of Dionysius Thrax (ed. Uhlig, p.11) they are grouped with /l/, /r/, /s/ and the double consonants – /ps/, /ks/ and /dz/ (or /zd/) under the heading *hēmiphōna*. The group is characterised as being less 'euphonious' than the vowels; that is, they possess *phōnē* to a lesser degree. It is difficult to find a suitable translation for this word, comprising as

35

it does auditory characteristics of both voiced and voiceless continuants (to use modern terminology). 'Sonority' might do, although we usually associate this with voiced sounds. The group is, on the other hand, different from the oral stops, which do not possess *phōnē* at all. The *hēmiphōna* are described as audible without any accompanying vowel, unlike the oral stops (Aristotle, *Poetics*, xx, 1456b). However, they do not function in Greek as the nucleus of a syllable. (See also Allen's discussion of these terms in his paper in this volume, pp.115–22.)

The nasal consonants in Greek are also part of a smaller class, excluding /s/ and the double consonants, which are called *hugra* (Dionysius Thrax, p.14). The literal translation of this is 'moist' or 'fluid'. Explanations of the term in ancient sources vary; the commonest relates it to the effect of this group of sounds, /m, n, l, r/, on metrical quantity. When forming the second element of a sequence of two consonants, the first being an oral stop, they did not, in Attic Greek, necessarily result in the preceding syllable becoming metrically 'heavy'. In this they differed from the other consonants. So 'fluid' could be taken as signifying 'holding up the flow of the rhythm less'. The term *hugra* was translated into Latin as *liquidus*, but referred now only to /l/ and /r/, not the nasals. This is normally the sense it has in later tradition.

The Greek descriptions of speech are more auditory than articulatory. Although references are made to the action of articulators they are sporadic and unsystematic. This contrasts markedly with the approach of the ancient Indian phoneticians (see below). One example of this is the fact that the Greeks do not link together the nasal consonants with the oral stops. This link, where it is made, is an articulatory one. For the Greeks the oral stops, we have seen, were separated from the nasal consonants by an auditory criterion. However, they were aware of the crucial part played in the formation of nasal sounds by the airflow into the nose. Dionysius of Halicarnassus (1st century B.C.) describes /m/ as formed with a closure of the lips 'while the breath is divided and passes through the nostrils'; /n/ is said to be formed by 'the tongue intercepting the current of the breath, and diverting the sound towards the nostrils' (*De compositione verborum* xiv; tr. by Rhys Roberts); see also below pp.44,45.

The ancient Indian phoneticians (*c*.500 B.C.) based their descriptions of the sounds of speech on the articulations involved in their production, classifying according to criteria that correspond closely with the modern 'place of articulation' and 'degree of articulatory stricture'. They regard nasality as a process (*prayatna*), parallel with the processes responsible for voicing and aspiration. The combination of these three processes with the stricture of complete oral closure gives a symmetrical set of *sparśa* letters, comprising four groups of oral stops, and the one group of nasals, each group represented at five different places of articulation (see Allen 1953, pp.46–7). This separation of nasality as a component that may be combined with other speech processes and places of articulation is satisfying in its economy of statement, and one wonders what sort of difference it might have made if this Indian tradition had reached Europe a few hundred years earlier than it did. The nasals are described as having 'an opening of the nasal cavity', but the mechanism by which this was controlled is not specified. Nasalisation of vowels is described – they are referred to in some treatises as 'coloured' (*rakta*) in contrast with the 'pure' (*śuddha*) non-nasalised vowels (Allen 1953, pp.39–40). Certain details of the Indian description are obscure and are discussed by Allen at some length, but these relate not so much to the basic segmental classification of nasals as to junctural features involving nasality.

Sibawayhi (8th century A.D.) is one of the pioneers of the description of the sounds of Arabic. He divided consonants into 'tense' – *hurūf-el-shidda* (the stops), and 'slack' – *hurūf-el-rakhāwa* (the fricatives). The nasals, /m/ and /n/, are associated with the first of these categories, because of their oral closure, in spite of the simultaneous sound flowing out of the nose. A later tradition introduced an intermediate category comprising /m, n, r, l, w, j, ʕ/; this may well be the result of influence from the Graeco-Roman tradition.

The Greek classification formed the basis of the one adopted by the Latin grammarians; corresponding to *hēmiphōna* is the group of *semivocales*, /l, m, n, r, s, z, f/. The criterion for classification is still an auditory one, and there is no hint of an articulatory link with the oral stops. Subsequent descriptions in the western tradition tend to retain the terminology of the classical writers, no less than they did in grammar generally. During the Middle Ages grammarians paid comparatively little attention to phonetics. However, the First Grammarian (see Haugen 1972), in his attempt to provide a new orthography for Icelandic, suggests an analysis of the vowels which separates out nasality as a distinctive feature, and gives as many nasalised as there are oral vowels. Vowel nasalisation is also recognised in some early French grammars, for example Palsgrave (1530). In England at the same period the movement for spelling reform led to notable phonetic works by Sir Thomas Smith (1568) and John Hart (1569). In their classification they follow very much the classical grouping, although Hart remarks on the capacity of certain sounds, including nasals, to form 'half-syllables' without a vowel. As it became acceptable in scholarly circles to devote attention to the grammar of languages other than Greek and Latin we begin to find attempts not just to describe the sounds of European vernaculars but also to provide a framework of description that could be applied to any language. Another very practical reason which led to an improvement of phonetic observation was the start of deaf teaching. Before we look at some early descriptions of this kind it will be useful to consider the extent to which the anatomy of the vocal organs in relation to the production of nasals was understood.

The uvula was known to writers in classical antiquity, and was given a variety of names – Greek *kiōn* or *kionis* (lit. 'pillar'), *staphulē*, *staphulis* (lit. 'bunch of grapes') *gargareōn*, Latin *uva* ('grape'), *columella* ('pillar'), *gurgulio* (also used meaning 'gullet' or 'windpipe'). However, its function in speech was not understood. Classical writers noted its condition when affected by disease, and the term *staphulē* was applied in particular to the swollen uvula (Aristotle, *Historia animalium*, I, 493a). There was no suggestion that any part of the palate (*ouranos*) played a part in regulating airflow through the nose, although the passage from mouth to nose is mentioned in classical authors (*Historia animalium*, I, 495a; pseudo-Arist., *Problems*, XXXIII, 14). The uvula was thought by some to be involved in the voicing mechanism, acting as a plectrum (Galen, *De usu partium,* VII, 5, ed. Kühn).

Anatomists of the fifteenth and sixteenth centuries give drawings and descriptions of the uvula (e.g. Leonardo da Vinci, Mondino, Fallopius, Vesalius, Fabricius ab Aquapendente, Casserius). Leonardo's remarkable anatomical drawings include one of the soft palate and uvula, but give no indication of the way they function in speech. Nor did Vesalius (1514–64), in his pioneer work on anatomy, give any account of this. His pupil, Fallopius (1523–62), does discuss the function of the uvula, in terms which typify the state of knowledge at the time:

> In the throat (*faucibus*) hangs the uvula .... If it becomes moist it hangs down and moistens the throat; this causes hoarseness of the voice .... (p.792,22)

Compare p.477, 51ff:

> Also in the throat we have not mentioned that the palate which is visible is not completely bony, but approximately the rearmost half of it, terminating in the throat, consists from one side to the other of taut, glandulous flesh, which is quite thick, though on its lower surface it is covered by the membrane of the palate and on its upper surface by the membrane of the nose (*narium tunica*). From about the middle of this glandulous part of the palate hangs another glandulous but not fleshy body, which the Greeks call *gargareōn* and we call '*gurgulio*', covered in a loose and very soft skin. Hanging over the epiglottis and that middle part of the larynx it drips onto them some very transparent substance, and moistens them. For that is the function of this pendulous. body, and not the functions they suggest, namely to temper the air, or to moderate the voice. (trans. J.A.K.)

Fallopius goes on to say that infection of the uvula in the 'French disease' on its own does not affect the voice, but only if the French ulcers have eaten away 'an extensive part of that glandulous body, which forms the end of the palate (*extremum palatum*)'. However, he does mention that the uvula may play a part in the production of speech sounds in another passage (pp.507, 1ff.), where he says that voice is formed as the air strikes the *aspera arteria* (i.e. the trachea) and the sound is articulated by the tongue and teeth (*a lingua dentibusque coarticulatus*), and so makes speech

> with some help from that small part (*concurrente etiam aliquantulum illa particula*) which can be seen hanging on the back of the palate in

front of the opening into the larynx, called '*uva*' or '*gurgulio*', although they say that it has been formed by nature rather more so that air is drawn by it and held up for a short time, and has a preparation in the mouth to prevent it from being so cold, on entering the lungs, as to cause them injury.

This last view is one that is to be found widely in descriptions of the period.

Somewhat later Fabricius ab Aquapendente (1601), in discussing the formation of vowels (chapter 8) criticises the view that they are formed in the throat (*in faucibus*) on the grounds that they would then be transmitted through the nose 'since the region of the throat is shared also by the nose', but, he says, this clearly does not happen. He tries to explain why the nose does not affect vowel sounds by the fact that the 'hollow and smooth palate' transmits the sound effectively whereas 'as the nasal cavity is twisting, curved, long and angular ... the sound ceases to be a proper vowel sound' (trans. J.A.K.) Fabricius also gives a diagram of the vocal organs, showing the passage into the nose.

Uncertainty about the nasal cavity and nasality in general is apparent also in what is one of the earliest attempts in the western tradition at providing an articulatory description of speech, namely Jacob Madsen's *De Literis*, published in Basle in 1586. Madsen, who came from Aarhus in Denmark, takes as his objective the description of 'the doctrine of letters common to all languages' and not just the sounds of a specific language. He says that he has used such earlier sources as were available and also has applied himself 'to the observation of nature itself', comparing his observations with the written sources – an admirable way of proceeding, although he often seems to give rather too much weight to his written sources and too little to his observations. On p.11 he states that the nose is important for speech

> for the letters and speech also resound in the nose. For which reason those whose noses are more open than is normal, seem as though they are speaking through the nose. And those whose noses are filled and obstructed by the phlegm which flows down from the head have voices that are duller and more obscure. (trans. J.A.K.) Cp. Amman's remarks on this (p.44 below).

On p.33 he describes the diversion of air though the nose when the passage through the mouth is blocked by the articulators, but he makes no mention of the uvula or soft palate. This diversion is necessary, he says, for [m], [n] and [ŋ] but he also believes it to be important in the production of [t] and [d] (p.45). They are formed, according to his description 'by the application of the tongue tip to the upper teeth, the tongue being long,' for which reason the nose is also used'. Similarly, in describing the labial stops [p] and [b] (p.88) he says that there is resonance in the nose. It sounds as though he believed that any oral closure would cause air to be forced into the nose, although he does not mention this participation of the nose in the velar stops [k] and [g]. He suggests testing the degree to which the passage of the air through the nose occurs for different consonants by holding the nose closed. To denote the auditory effect of nasality he uses the verb *tinnio* 'to ring, jingle' – following the example of Quintilian (*Institutiones oratoriae*, XII, 10, 31), whom he frequently quotes. There is no mention of the nose being involved in the production of consonants without oral closure or of vowels, unless one can read some significance into his remark at the beginning of his description of the consonants 'and here the nose plays a greater part than it does with the vowels' (*atque hic narium maior est usus quam in vocali*).

In 1635 Petrus Montanus (1595–1638), a Dutchman, published *De Spreeckonst* (The Art of Speech). (This account of Montanus is much indebted to Vos 1962). It describes the formation of speech sounds in considerable detail, and in a highly systematic way, proceeding by a series of dichotomies to a close sub-classification. Montanus does not mention Madsen, although Møller (see Madsen 1586) suggests that Montanus was greatly influenced by him. His description of nasality, however, is a considerable improvement on Madsen's. He calls the nasal cavity the 'nose-vessel', and divides it for descriptive purposes into a posterior part (from the uvula to the beginning of the nostrils) called the 'nose-pipe', and an anterior part (divided by the septum) – the nostrils. He observes correctly that it is possible to widen or narrow the nostrils – something that is not thought worthy of mention in most descriptions. At the posterior end the 'nose-door', which is connected with the uvula, operates to close off the nose-pipe or to open it up. Montanus emphasises the importance of this action of the nose-door in speech in bringing about differences in the voice. He correctly describes the open position of the door for [m] and [n] and the closed position for the oral stops, and observes that it is only when producing an oral stop followed by a homorganic nasal (e.g. [dn]) that one becomes conscious of the movement of the nose-door. Montanus is rather vague about the position of the nose-door for segments without an oral closure, although he indicates that it may be open for the vowel [i], and in talking of [l] he says that some sound leaves via the nose. In addition to [m] and [n] he recognises palatal, velar and uvular nasals, and envisages the possibility of voiceless nasals. The nasal consonants are included in the wider term *semivocales*, which is divided into two sub-groups – *firmae* (Montanus's so-called 'steady' vowels) and *liquidae* (nasals and l, r, j, w); *liquidae* in turn are divided into *obtusae* 'blunt, dull' – the nasals, and *acutae* 'sharp' – [l, r, w, j] (cp. pp.46–7 below). Speech sounds are ranked on a sonority scale, namely (from maximum to minimum) vowels, trills, [j, w, l,], nasals, fricatives, stops. This bears a close resemblance to the ordering suggested in the nineteenth century by phoneticians such as Sievers, Viëtor and Jespersen. Regrettably Montanus's work remained relatively unknown, for it offers many new insights.

In Britain in the seventeenth century a number of significant works dealing with phonetics were published, notably Robinson (1617), Wallis (1st ed. 1653), Wilkins (1668), Holder (1669) and Cooper (1685). Robinson is notable for his introduction of the term 'semi-mutes' for the nasals, which he thus associates closely with his 'mutes', the oral stops, by reason of their complete stoppage in the mouth, 'so in their own proper places of restraint they give no sound at all, but by a contrary course, having a restricted passage through the nostrils, they thereby admit of a sound'. He gives no account of the mechanism involved in the production of nasals, nor does he mention nasality in segments without oral closure, or voiceless nasals.

Wallis, like Robinson, associates the nasals with the oral stops, labelling them both 'closed' consonants. He chooses, however, to call them *semivocales*, using this traditional term in a sense of his own. As in the traditional classification, *vocales* (vowels) are at one end of the scale, and *mutae* at the other, but for Wallis *mutae* refers only to what we would label 'voiceless oral stops'. The voiced oral stops (in our terms) are given the label *semimutae* by Wallis. This seems straightforward, but Wallis's criterion for his division was somewhat different from ours. It arose from his belief that what we now distinguish as 'voiced' consonants are not, or should not be, distinguished crucially from the corresponding 'voiceless' ones by what happens in the larynx. Wallis believed that the larynx was responsible for the difference between 'full voice' (*aperta loquela*) and whisper, but that it was possible to distinguish the *semimutae* from the *mutae* even when both were whispered. He therefore looked for another explanation for the difference between them, and the answer he arrived at was that the nose is responsible. Whereas for the *semivocales* (i.e. nasals) all the air passes through the nose, striking the air in the oral cavity only in passing, for the *semimutae*, he says, the air is divided equally between nose and mouth. He supports this explanation by saying that the *semimutae* produce a small sound in the nose, which can be heard on its own without the addition of the sound of any other letters (Wallis, ed. Kemp, p.159). The *mutae* have no such sound, because no air passes through the nose. It appears that Wallis was not enough of an experimentalist to try closing his nostrils while producing the *semimutae* and *semivocales*; or did he perhaps think it unnecessary for air actually to pass out of the nostrils for the *semimutae*, as long as it passed in? He allows for 'open' *semivocales*, that is, what corresponds to our 'nasalised fricatives', but not as speech sounds – if labial they are equivalent to 'mooing' and if palatal or guttural to 'groaning'. He does not mention the possibility of nasalised vowels, although he refers to the French vowel *e* before *n* in *entendement* (see below p.46). Nor does he include voiceless nasals; they would presumably have to have an air-stream entirely through the nose and be distinguished from the *semivocales* simply as whispered forms.

Wallis attributes control over the direction of the airstream to different positions of the uvula, but does not mention any participation of the posterior part of the palate in this (Wallis, ed. Kemp, p.155).

In the chapter he devotes to word-formation he comments on the association of the sequence *sn* with the nose – snout, sneeze, snort, etc. (6th ed.

p.146), and later (p.166) on the common insertion of a stop after a nasal in the course of language change for example, *humilis* > humble, *camera* > chamber. He does not define the phonological environment associated with the change, but quotes examples from several languages.

John Wilkins (1668), in his remarkable attempt to provide a new universal language, devotes chapters x–xiv of part iii to a description of the formation of sounds. His account of the nasals says nothing about the mechanism involved, simply identifying them as having air passing through the nose. They are grouped with the open consonants, not the stops. However, Wilkins records the existence of 'mute' forms of the nasals (i.e. voiceless), which he notates as *hm, hn, hng*; the first two, he maintains, occur in Welsh and Irish, and the third, according to some, is Hebrew **ע**. He says nothing of nasalised open consonants or vowels.

William Holder's *Elements of Speech* (1669) has more elements of modernity in its approach than any other seventeenth-century description of speech. In some respects it reminds one of the Indian phoneticians, in particular their view of voicing and nasality as processes. Holder, like Wallis, was concerned among other things with the teaching of deaf people to speak, and his approach is obviously influenced by the special needs of those without auditory feedback. He describes speech as composed of a material part and a formal part. The former involves participation of the lungs, trachea, larynx, uvula, nose, and the arch of the palate; the latter involves the tongue, palate, gums, jaw, teeth and lips. The material of speech is determined in particular by the breath from the lungs and the modification of it, if any, by the larynx and the nose. The following passages are relevant to our topic:

> The *Uvula*, as a Valve, opens and shuts the passage of Breath or Voice through the nose. The *Nose*, sometimes giving passage to Breath or Voice, in speaking alters their sound, and gives a Material discrimination, by which the general sound of Breath or Voice may be distinguished into *Oral* or *Nasall*, or (to speak more accurately) *Ore-Nasal*. (pp.23–4)
>
> ... the same Articulation, if of *Breath*, makes one letter; if of *Breath vocalized*, or voice, another; If of *voice Nasall* (i.e. when the *Uvula* is opened, and the voice passeth into the Mouth and is there Articulated, and at the same time hath a free passage through the Nose) then it makes another; and lastly, if of *Breath Nasal*, then another. (pp.33–4)
>
> M. is an articulation of voice, by close Appulse of the Lips; so far perfectly the same with B: but there is this difference added, that at the same time, passage is opened for the Voice through the Nose. And the like is N. in the Goums [sic], and Nĝ in the Palat. Thus in *respect* of *Appulse of Organ* P.B.M. are the same. (p.39)
>
> ... it were easie to add a *Nasal* letter to each of the other pair of *Lisping* and *Sibilant* letters, but they are not found to be so gracefully

42

pronounced nor sufficiently discriminated in *Pervious* Appulses [i.e. strictures other than complete closure], where the Breath hath passage through the Mouth and Nose both at once; but onely in the Appulses, which are *Occluse*; where the voice is stopt, and onely murmures within the Mouth, and passeth freely by the Nose. (p.45)

... the number of Letters in Nature, is equal to the number of Articulations, severally applied to every distinct matter of Sound. (p.54)

Thus there will be one *Primary* [i.e. the articulation] joyn'd severally with Four *Secondary* differences, four times Nine Consonants, *viz.* 9. Spiral [i.e. voiceless], 9. Vocal, 9. Naso-Spiral, and 9. Naso-Vocal; in all 36. (p.56)

Having thus envisaged the theoretical possibility of voiceless oral, voiced oral, voiceless nasal and voiced nasal at each place of articulation Holder rejects the six voiced nasals having no 'Occluse Appulse' (i.e. those with no stop closure) as 'not easie or graceful to pronounce'; he also rejects the corresponding six voiceless nasals without stop closure. He goes on

And for the other 3. [i.e. the voiceless nasal stops] though some Nations possibly may take the pains to pronounce them, (especially the last of them, formed in the palate, Nĝ. which may perhaps be the Genuin sound of the *Hebrew* ע), yet being found harsh and troublesome, they are more generally disused, whilst most Nations rather study to sweeten and soften their Pronunciation. (p.57)

As concerns the vowels he says

... the same Vowels ... if there were any use of it, ... may be pronounced *Nasal*, both *Spiral* and *Vocal*; but in Vocal Speech they are all *Ore-vocals*, as to common and ready use .... (pp.81–2)

Holder also refers to nasality as characteristic of certain languages

... where some Nations may be found to have a peculiar *Guttural* or *Nasal* smatch in their language, it will be found also, that they labour to retain in their pronunciation ... some of those Letters, whose use is more generally rejected. (pp.59–60)

Although modern descriptions would probably avoid such terms as 'harsh and troublesome', in most respects Holder's analysis is accurate, and lucidly expressed, and enables him to accommodate sounds that are potentially speech sounds, even if he does regard them as peripheral. His reference to voiceless and nasalised vowels is particularly noteworthy.

Cooper (1685) puts the voiced nasals under the heading *semivocales* like the classical grammarians and Wallis, but his usage of the term is different again. By *semivocales* he understands all consonants with some compression or interruption of the air-stream, but without a total stoppage, and always accompanied by voice (*vocis sonorae*) in normal (as opposed to whispered) speech. The class thus includes the voiced nasals, /l/, /r/, and the voiced fricatives, but excludes the voiceless nasals and voiceless fricatives, which he classifies as *aspiratae*. Nasals are characterised as having an airflow through the nose, and both Welsh and Irish are said to possess all three voiceless nasals – [m̥ n̥] and [ŋ̊] (cp. Wilkins's [m̥] and [n̥] only). Like Wilkins he makes no mention of nasalised consonants other than stops, or of nasalised vowels.

At the turn of the century the Swiss doctor, Conrad Amman, another celebrated teacher of the deaf, published his *Dissertatio de Loquela* (1700). He, like Holder, gives an accurate description of the valve-like action of the uvula, and associates with it a movement of the soft palate also. As one would expect from a doctor there are some comments on possible malfunctions of the speech apparatus,

> If the valve is missing or if the entry into the nose is too large for it to close off properly, the letters p.t.k. are pronounced through the nose, in a most unbecoming way. (p.38)
> The nasal passage is sometimes too wide, so that the voice and breath escape mostly through the nose; hence, in addition to a general speech defect and a marked distortion of the voice, arises a particular fault – none of the letters which should be exploded through the mouth only, like k, t, p etc., can be pronounced. The only really effective way of helping in this situation is by blocking up the gap with a thin plate ...
> If the defect is only slight the letters k, t, p etc. should be pronounced with the nostrils compressed or blocked up, or the back part of the tongue must be trained to close up the gap. (p.109)
> Sometimes the nasal passage is not wide enough, or is completely blocked; if this is so m, n, ng can only be pronounced with difficulty, or not at all ... Those who suffer from serious catarrh, and whose nose is blocked by the very viscid phlegm, have difficulty in pronouncing those letters and are commonly said to speak through the nose, but wrongly; for they do not speak through the nose enough. (p.110, trans. J.A.K.)

This was by no means the first discussion of speech defects such as cleft palate. Attempts to repair the cleft had been mentioned by Renner, Lusitanus and Paré from the sixteenth century onwards (see Panconcelli-Calzia 1961, pp.84–5).

Amman classifies the nasals as *semivocales*, a group that includes [m n ŋ l r] – more or less the classical grouping, but he does not include *semivocales* within his class *consonantes*; this comprises the stops and fricatives only. He notes that any letter may be 'breathed' (i.e. voiceless), or 'voiced', but does not specifically mention voiceless nasals. Nor does he seem to allow for nasalised vowels or non-stop consonants.

Amman's concern with the deaf followed in the same line as Bonet (1620), Wallis and Holder. In classical antiquity there were only sporadic references to the problems of the deaf, such as that in pseudo-Aristotle, *Problems*, XXXIII.14. 962b–963a. The author asks 'Why do the deaf usually talk out of their noses?' His attempted explanation attributes it to a malfunction of the lungs leading to the breath being 'forced out through the nostrils'. This passage is interesting as being one of the few references in classical literature to the anatomy of the nose. The passage goes on

> As it (sc. the air) is forced out of the nostrils, friction produces the noise. For talking through the nose occurs when the upper part of the nose, towards the palate, where there is a passageway through, becomes roomier (*koilon*); for it resounds like a bell, the lower part being narrow. (trans. J.A.K.)

This passage may lead us to consider the common auditory associations of nasal resonance. We have already come across the use of the Latin word *tinnio* 'to ring, jingle, tinkle' by Quintilian and others. Allen (1953, p.40) quotes from the Sarvasaṃmata-Sikṣā the passage 'The nasal colour should arise from the heart, with a sound like that of bells' (trans. A.O. Franke). Dionysius of Halicarnassus (*De compositione verborum* XIV) in describing the *hēmiphōna* or 'half–resonants' says (trans. Rhys Roberts)

> They cannot all affect the sense of hearing in the same way. *l* falls pleasurably upon it, and is the sweetest … while *r* has a rough quality, and is the noblest of its class. The ear is affected in a sort of intermediate way by *m* and *n*, which are pronounced with nasal resonance, and produce sounds similar to those of a horn.

The comparison with bells is, of course, implicit in many of the expressions used to refer to the sound of bells, which include nasal sounds – ding-dong, bim-bam, and so on. There is an interesting passage in Ved Mehta's *Face to Face* (pp.73–4), where the author relates how he was given a demonstration in his childhood in India by a guru of the phenomenon of *ghungrus* – the imitation without any instrumental aids of the jingling sound of the small bells worn by Indian dancers round their ankles. He describes the final stages as follows:

> Then I would hear a sound like blowing a noiseless whistle, and if I had not known what was to follow I might have thought he was out of breath. Then this blowing sound would assume a more regular character. Finally he would break into the bell-like notes. Slowly but surely the sound would grow more and more like the low jingling of real bells.

As mentioned at the beginning of this article the auditory effect of nasality can be produced without air entering the nasal cavity. Cagliari (1977) discusses this question and reviews earlier literature (p.105ff.). The mouth normally acts like a side-chamber in the production of the nasal consonants, and resembles 'a topped organ pipe' (Eijkman 1926, p.218, cited by Cagliari). This produces only odd partials so that 'a great many tones sound hollow and even twangy' (Eijkman, p.214). Cagliari goes on to refer to experiments by Paget (1924), Russell (1931), West, et al. (1937) and others, which suggested that constrictions in the area of the pharynx or larynx could of themselves produce a nasal resonance, without participation of the nasal cavity. Several early descriptions (Wallis, Wilkins, Cooper) suggest that

Hebrew *Ayin*, which it seems at one stage represented a pharyngeal consonant, was the only symbol used in languages to represent the velar nasal, either voiced or voiceless. And this pronunciation of it is attested in other sources also. Matisoff (1975) quotes a number of examples from languages of rhinoglottophilia – an affinity between the feature of nasality and the articulatory involvement of the glottis. He instances nasalisation of vowels in the environment of [h] and [ʔ], and cites Hetzron (1969) for a similar report concerning pharyngeal consonants in Semitic languages. Ohala (1975, pp.300f.) points out that this phenomenon can be related to two factors: 1) A velic opening is not inconsistent with a sufficient build-up of air pressure behind the strictures for glottal and pharyngeal obstruents, and 2) Oral-nasal coupling would have very little acoustic effect on the voiceless glottal and pharyngeal obstruents. This assumes that there is lowering of the velum. He also mentions (p.303) an effect of [s] and glottal and pharyngeal consonants on vowels that 'mocks' that of nasalisation.

Apart from the connection with bells, a common association, especially in the case of the bilabial nasal, is with 'mooing', and in general with an 'enclosed' sort of noise. Plato (*Cratylus*, 427c) talks of [n] as having an 'inner' sound, and relates this to its use in words meaning 'inside'. Terentianus (*De litteris*, 235) says that it 'gives a kind of moo inside the closed mouth' (*clauso quasi mugit intus ore*). In the sixteenth century Petrus Ramus uses *mugio* of *m* and *tinnio* of *n* (*Grammatica*, 1559). He goes on to make additional distinctions, describing *m* as having a 'fuller' sound (*plenius*) initially, an 'obscurer' one finally (*obscurius*), and an intermediate one when medial. He describes *n*, however, as sounding 'sharper' (*acutius*) initially and finally and 'flatter' or 'duller' medially (*obtusius*) (Cp. Priscian, *Institutiones grammaticae* I. 7, 38–9 for similar comments).

Auditory descriptions of this kind are notoriously unsatisfactory as a basis for description, although they can often be put into relationship with more rigorously defined and established terms. Fónagy (1963, p.13) points out that nasalised vowels are characteristically described as 'obscure', 'dark' or 'dull' as compared with oral vowels, and refers to Wallis's comparison of the English vowel 'thin a' (a *exile*), as in the word *bat*, with the French vowel represented by *en*, as in *entendement* (Wallis, ed. Kemp, p.237). Wallis says that they are pronounced in approximately the same way, but the English vowel is a little sharper and clearer (*acutius et clarius*). He does not mention any nasality in the French vowel, and, as we have seen, few authors describe nasalised vowels, even as a possibility. It may be that those who were familiar with languages containing nasalised vowels, such as French, did not associate the auditory quality of these vowels with that of the nasalised consonants. It has been clearly demonstrated that nasalised vowels are acoustically characterised very differently from nasal consonants (Delattre 1969a), and that a nasalised vowel, at least in French, sounds qualitatively opener than the corresponding oral vowel. Sylvius (1531), cited by Thurot (1881), uses Latin *exilis* ('thin', 'slight') to describe the quality of vowels in French when preceding *m* or *n* in the same syllable (cp. Wallis, above).

Nasality as a semi-permanent feature of an individual's voice quality does not seem to have evoked any comment in the writers we have considered, except where it was clearly severe, as when Amman describes it as a 'defect' (*vitium*) and a 'distortion of the voice' (*vocis depravationem*). One often comes across unfavourable reactions to a nasal voice quality, especially as perceived in other people's accents; the term 'nasal twang' tends to be used in a pejorative sense.

We have seen that different writers take different views about whether nasal consonants are to be associated more closely with oral stops (Indian grammarians, Sibawayhi, Robinson, Wallis, Holder), with continuant consonants (Greek and Latin grammarians, later Arabic tradition), or with neither. Arguments about which is the 'best' grouping can really only be substantiated in relation to particular languages, or groups of languages. For some the articulatory relationship may be more crucial, and for others the auditory associations.

The absence in most descriptions of any reference to nasal segments other than those with a stop closure, or even other than [m] and [n], reflects the influence of orthography, and probably also the relative 'normality' of these sounds in languages with which the writers were familiar (see Ferguson 1975). The same applies, though more so, to the voiceless nasals. They are rare in languages of the world, and often derive from fricative-nasal clusters (Ohala 1975, pp.295–6). Acoustically they are very different from voiced nasals. Holder mentions them, only to dismiss them as 'harsh and troublesome' and so to be avoided. Wilkins and Cooper both provide symbols for them by prefixing the letter *h* to the voiced nasals; in addition to attributing them to Welsh and Irish, Cooper interprets the initial consonant sequence *kn* in English as standing for the voiceless alveolar nasal (1685, p.67).

None of the writers we have mentioned comments on the common use of nasal consonants in expressions for assent, negation and hesitation.

We have seen that by the end of the seventeenth century the mechanism of nasality had been correctly described. Later writers progressively refined the description. Von Kempelen, in the late eighteenth century, gives a clear account of nasal vowels and consonants. By the early part of the nineteenth century acoustic investigations of speech were being undertaken, and the advent of scientific techniques opened the way for a more delicate and detailed examination of the various aspects of nasality: anatomical, physiological, aerodynamic, acoustic and perceptual. An account of these later developments would go beyond what is possible within the scope of this paper. Cagliari (1977) provides a useful survey of work done in investigating nasality in more recent times, and the collection of papers entitled *Nasálfest* (1975) is an indication of some of the research currently being pursued.

References

ALLEN, W.S. (1953) *Phonetics in Ancient India*, London (Oxford University Press).
— (1968) *Vox Graeca; a guide to the pronunciation of classical Greek*, London (Cambridge University Press).
AMMAN, J.C. (1700) *Dissertatio de Loquela*, Amsterdam (J. Wolters).
ARISTOTLE, *Historia animalium*, ed. D'Arcy Wentworth Thompson, Oxford (Clarendon Press) 1910.
— *Aristotle's Theory of Poetry and Fine Art* with a critical text and translation of the Poetics by S.H. Butcher, 4th ed., London (Constable) 1951.
pseudo-ARISTOTLE, *Problems*, tr. W.S. Hett, Loeb Classical Library, London (Heinemann) 1956.
BONET, J.P. (1620) *Reduction de las letras*, Madrid (F. Abarco de Angulo).
CAGLIARI, L.C. (1977) *An Experimental Study of Nasality with particular reference to Brazilian Portuguese*. Ph.D. Thesis, University of Edinburgh.
COOPER, C. (1685) *Grammatica linguae Anglicanae*, London; facsimile reprint, Scolar Press, London, 1968.
DELATTRE, P. (1969a) 'Two types of nasality: vocalic and consonantal', in *The General Phonetic Characteristics of Languages*, U.S. Department of Health, Education and Welfare, Office of Education Institute of International Studies, 81–100.
— (1969b) 'Explaining the chronology of nasal vowels by acoustic and radiographic analysis', in *The General Phonetic Characteristics of Languages*, U.S. Department of Health, Education and Welfare, Office of Education Institute of International Studies, 101–19.
DIONYSIUS OF HALICARNASSUS, *On Literary Composition*, being the Greek text of the *De compositione verborum*, edited with introduction, translation etc. by W. Rhys Roberts, London (Macmillan) 1910.
DIONYSIUS THRAX, *Ars grammatica*, ed. Gustav Uhlig, Lipsiae (Teubner) 1883.
EIJKMAN, L.P.H. (1926) 'The soft palate and nasality', *Neophilologus* 11, 207–18 and 277–8.
FABRICIUS, H., ab Aquapendente (1601) *De locutione et eius instrumentis*, Venice.
FALLOPIUS, G. (1584) *Opera quae adhuc extant omnia*, Frankfurt (A. Wechelus).
FANT, G. (1960) *Acoustic Theory of Speech Production*, The Hague (Mouton).
FERGUSON, C.A. (1975) 'Universal tendencies and 'normal' nasality', in *Nasálfest*, 175–96.
FÓNAGY, I. (1963) *Die Metaphern in der Phonetik*, The Hague (Mouton).
FUJIMURA, O. (1961) 'Analysis of nasal consonants', *Quarterly Progress Report*, Research Lab. of Electronics MIT, 60, 184–8.
— (1962) 'Analysis of nasal consonants', *J. Acoust. Soc. Am.* 34, 1865–75.
GALEN, *Complete Works*, ed. C.G. Kühn (in the series Medicorum Graecorum Opera quae supersunt), Lipsiae, (Car. Cnoblochius) 1821–30.
HART, J. (1569) *An Orthographie*, London (W. Serres).
HAUGEN, EINAR I. ed. (1972) *First Grammatical Treatise; the earliest Germanic phonology*: an edition, translation and commentary, 2nd rev. ed. London (Longman).
HECKER, M.H.L. (1962) 'Studies of nasal consonants with an articulatory speech synthesizer', *J. Acoust. Soc. Am.* 34, 179–88.
HETZRON, R. (1969) 'Two notes on Semitic laryngeals in East Gurage', *Phonetica* 19, 69–81.
HOLDER, W. (1669) *Elements of Speech: an Essay of Inquiry into the Natural Production of Letters*, London (J. Martyn); facsimile reprint, Scolar Press, London, 1967.

LAVER, J.D.M.H. (1980) *The Phonetic Description of Voice Quality*, Cambridge Studies in Linguistics 31, London (Cambridge University Press).

LINDQUIST, J. and SUNDBERG, J. (1976) 'Acoustic properties of the nasal tract', *Phonetica* 33, 161–8.

MADSEN, J. (1586) *De Literis*, Basle (C. Waldkirch); ed. C. Møller and P. Skautrup, *Acta Jutlandica*, II.3 (1930) and III.1. (1931).

MATISOFF, J.A. (1975) 'Rhinoglottophilia; the mysterious connection between nasality and glottality', in *Nasálfest*, 265–88.

MEHTA, VED. P. (1967) *Face to Face: an autobiography*, 2nd ed., London (Collins).

MONTANUS, P. (1635) *De Spreeckonst*, Delft (P. Waalpot), see also VOS (1962).

NASÁLFEST (1975) Papers from a symposium on nasals and nasalization, Stanford (Language Universals Project, Department of Linguistics, Stanford University).

OHALA, J. (1975) 'Phonetic explanations for nasal sound patterns', in *Nasálfest*, 289–316.

PAGET, R. (1924) 'The nature and artificial production of consonant sounds', *Proc. R. Soc.* A 106, 1, 150.

PALSGRAVE, J. (1530) *L'esclarcissement de la langue Francoyse*, London (R. Pynson).

PANCONCELLI-CALZIA, G. (1961) *3000 Jahre Stimmforschung*, Marburg (N.G. Elwert Verlag).

PLATO *Cratylus*, tr. H. N. Fowler, Loeb Classical Library, London (Heinemann) 1956.

PRISCIAN *Institutiones grammaticae*, ed. M. Hertz (Keil, H. *Grammatici Latini*, vols. 2–3) Lipsiae (Teubner) 1855–80.

QUINTILIAN *Institutiones oratoriae*, ed. M. Winterbottom, London (Oxford University Press) 1970.

RAMUS, PETRUS (Pierre de la Ramée) (1572) *Grammatica*, Paris (A. Wechelus).

ROBINSON, R. (1617) *The Art of Pronuntiation*, London (N. Okes).

RUSSELL, G.O. (1931) *Speech and Voice*, New York (MacMillan).

SIBAWAYHI, 'Amr Ibn 'Uthman, *Sibawaihi's Buch über die Grammatik*, introduction and translation by Gustav Jahn, Hildesheim (G. Olms) 1969.

SMITH, T. (1568) *De recta et emendata linguae Anglicae scriptione dialogus*, Paris (R. Stephanus).

SYLVIUS, J. (1531) *In linguam gallicam Isagoge*, Paris (R. Stephanus).

TERENTIANUS MAURUS *De litteris, de syllabis, de metris* (Keil, H. *Grammatici Latini*, vol. 6) Lipsiae (Teubner) 1855–80.

THUROT, C. (1881–3) *De la prononciation française depuis le commencement du XVIe siècle*, Paris (Imprimerie nationale).

VON KEMPELEN, W. (1791) *Le Méchanisme de la parole, suivi de la description d'une machine parlante*, Vienna (J.V. Degen).

VOS, A.L. (1962) *Tradition and Innovation in Petrus Montanus, The Art of Speech, 1635*. Ph.D. Thesis, University of Edinburgh.

WALLIS, J. (1653) *Grammatica linguae Anglicanae*, Oxford (Leon Lichfield); ed. J.A. Kemp, London (Longman) 1972.

WEST, R., KENNEDY, L. and CARR, A. (1937) *The Rehabilitation of Speech*, New York (Harper and Brothers).

WILKINS, J. (1668) *An Essay towards a Real Character and a Philosophical Language*, London (S. Gellibrand).

Experimental Studies in
Lingual Coarticulation

The general principle that speech sounds are influenced by neighbouring sounds has long been recognised by linguists and is, in fact, implicit in traditional treatments of familiar concepts such as assimilation, elision, metathesis etc. One way in which this mutual influence is said to be manifested is for two adjacent sounds to become more 'similar' to or 'adapt' to each other. An example would be a typical pronunciation of the word 'coo' where the initial plosive /k/ is influenced in at least two ways by the nature of the following vowel. It is articulated in a post-velar region and it is labialised. Both these features of tongue retraction and lip-rounding are typical characteristics of the vowel articulation, so it can be said in a sequence such as this the /k/ 'assimilates' to or 'adapts' to the following vowel. The process exemplified in 'coo' has been given a variety of names. Daniel Jones (1932) called it 'similitude' and reserved the word 'assimilation' for phonological changes such as final /z/ in 'is' becoming /ʒ/ under the influence of a following /ʃ/ in the sequence 'is she'. The terminology in this area becomes particularly confusing as assimilation is also used in the context of historical sound changes to descibe, for example, a process such as Latin 'octo' becoming Italian 'otto'.

Nowadays, with the current interest in problems of the motor control and serial ordering of speech, most experimental phoneticians prefer to use the term coarticulation rather than assimilation so as to focus attention more specifically on the physiological mechanisms underlying the articulation of a speech sequence (see e.g. Daniloff and Moll 1968, MacNeilage and De Clerk 1969, Daniloff and Hammarberg 1973, Kent and Minifie 1977). The physiological concept implicit in the notion of coarticulation is the well-attested observation of varying degrees of 'overlapping' or simultaneous movement of the different organs involved in the production of a speech sequence.

The term 'coarticulation' itself has an interesting history. It appears to have originated with P. Menzerath in the first half of the twentieth century (Menzerath and De Lacerda 1933, Menzerath 1935, 1938) as 'Koartikulation', a concept which Menzerath (1935) exemplifies as follows 'Bei *pu* ist es deutlich so; die *Artikulation der beiden Laute erfolgt in weitem Masse gleichzeitig.* Die Lippenbewegung für *u*, wie auch die Zungenbewegung dafür, setzen genau im selben Moment ein wo die Bewegung für *p* beginnt. ... Ich bezeichne das also 'Koartikulation' oder 'Synkinese' und stelle damit ein neues Artikulationsprinzip auf, das so lautet: *jeder Laut beginnt artikulatorisch sobald er beginnen kann'* (p.65). Menzerath claims this is a new concept ('ein neues Artikulationsprinzip'). In actual fact, however, the principle of simultaneous articulatory activity was already well known to the early experimental phoneticians at the end of the nineteenth and early twentieth centuries, although their formulation of the concept was perhaps not as precise as Menzerath's. During that period the first systematic investigations of speech production using quantitative scientific methods were begun by scholars such as Rousselot (1897–1901, 1901–8), Scripture (1902), Grützner (1879), Viëtor (1894, 1898) Lenz (1888) and others in England, France, Germany and the U.S.A. Detailed analysis of speech records convinced these early investigators that the stream of speech could not readily be segmented into discrete elements like 'sounds' or 'letters' (as some of their predecessors believed) but was a continuously changing process with articulatory movements 'overlapping' in time and sounds 'fusing' into each other. Many insightful observations on the dynamics of articulatory organs were made during this period in spite of the relatively crude instrumentation available.

In this paper I shall discuss some of the results of these early investigations and assess their relevance for modern experimental phonetic research. In order to restrict the scope of the paper, I shall be concerned mainly with studies of lingual function, the various techniques that have been developed over the last hundred years and how the results from these techniques have influenced theoretical viewpoints.

Experimental phonetics as a discipline in its own right probably began with Rousselot who was basically a philologist but with a keen interest in studying details of speech production using scientific methods of analysis. During Rousselot's most active years at the end of the nineteenth century phonetic research was dominated by two main groups of workers. There were those such as Henry Sweet, A.J. Ellis, Paul Passy and A.M. Bell, who were interested primarily in the description and classification of sounds and in the development of a suitable notation system for recording speech in written form. The efforts of such phoneticians culminated in the inauguration of the International Phonetic Association in France in 1886. Another group of phoneticians from a wide variety of different disciplines including physics, psychology, philology, was concerned primarily with the quantitative analysis of the physiological and acoustic aspects of speech and in developing instrumentation suitable for this purpose. Rousselot belonged to this latter group and he was among the first to adopt for the purposes of speech analysis the so-called graphic recording methods at that time in widespread use in physiology, astronomy, physics, and meteorology (see Panconcelli-Calzia 1957). The basic graphic recording technique involved the use of a movement detector or tambour (most commonly a Marey tambour, named after its developer M. Marey of Paris) made of some elastic membrane, a stylus, and a recording medium such as smoked paper on a con-

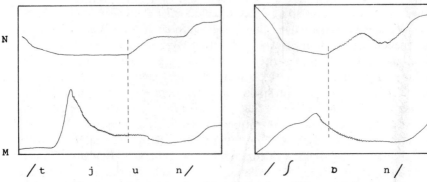

FIGURE 1. Kymograph tracings showing nasalisation of the vowels in two English words 'tune' and 'shone'. The top trace (N) shows nasal air-flow (nasal olive) and the bottom trace (M) shows air-flow from the mouth (adapted from Rousselot 1924, pp.551–552).

tinuously revolving drum (kymograph). By using a rubber mask placed before the mouth or a nasal olive in the nose, gross changes in air-flow could be registered and individual vocal fold vibrations could be detected as fine fluctuations in this air-flow curve (see figure 1). These basic recording techniques were quite accurate but had, of course, relatively slow response times due mainly to the inherent characteristics of the materials used. However, one could study many aspects of the dynamics of speech using these techniques, such as the timing of voice onset associated with plosives, the degree and timing of nasalisation, the manner of articulation (e.g. stop versus fricative), relative duration and extent of voicing etc. Specialised instruments using the Marey tambours were soon developed for a variety of purposes. For investigation of tongue activity, devices such as exploratory bulbs and tongue tambours (Rousselot 1924, pp.86ff., Scripture 1902, p.333) were widely used. These were basically flat hollow rubber bulbs inserted into the mouth to record by air transmission the pressure of tongue contact at different points. Another development was the geniohyoid tambour (Rousselot 1924, p.95, Scripture 1902, p.335) designed to register by means of a lever system the elevation of the floor of the mouth and so by inference the height of the tongue during speech (see figure 2).

The development of many of these techniques was motivated partly by a revival of interest in new methods of teaching foreign languages with increasing emphasis on the spoken word. Proponents of the new methods, particularly the influential W. Viëtor, enthusiastically welcomed any attempts to provide more accurate descriptions of the sounds of foreign languages, and a large number of comparative studies were made using much of the available instrumentation including the exploratory bulbs, geniohyoid tambours and another technique, palatography (see below). During this time the sounds of most European languages particularly English, German, French and Italian were exhaustively described by Rousselot and his experimentally-minded

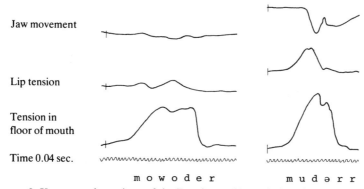

Jaw movement

Lip tension

Tension in
floor of mouth

Time 0.04 sec.

m o w o d e r   m u ə r r

FIGURE 2. Kymograph tracings of the Dutch word 'moeder' spoken
in the Deventer (left) and North Holland (right) dialects. The third
trace from the top (labelled 'tension in floor of mouth') is obtained
with a geniohyoid tambour (adapted from Scripture 1902, p.371).

contemporaries such as Grandgent (1890, 1892), Lenz (1888), Scripture
(1902), Viëtor (1898) and many others. There was a keen interest also in the
physiological mechanisms underlying the articulation of sounds in more
'exotic' languages as well and investigators such as Scripture (1902) included
in his major work references to experimental work done on languages such as
Hungarian, Finnish and Russian.

Detailed analysis of records from these early graphic techniques showed
the difficulty of segmenting the speech signal into discrete, readily identifiable
units. As Scripture (1906, p.59) says: 'Speech elements have no absolutely
definite limits. One sound shades off more or less gradually into the next one;
even the passage from a vowel to an occlusive is not sudden'. In the air-flow
trace of a sequence such as [ap] some arbitrary segmentation decisions could
be made but with other types of sounds problems remain. Thus: 'If we
determine to place the end of [a] at the first indication of the implosion, and
the beginning of [p] at the cessation of the vowel vibrations and to call the
sonant implosion a glide, we get out of the difficulty in this case fairly well.
But in many other cases, particularly combinations of vowels and liquids, no
such solution is possible; one sound changes gradually into another'
(Scripture 1906, p.59). The merging of one sound into another, reflected in
the difficulty in segmenting the speech signal, was frequently related specifically to the articulatory movements taking place during the sequence.
Physiological descriptions of such articulatory processes were commonplace
at the time. E. Sievers, for example, in the influential *Grundzüge der
Lautphysiologie* (1876), relying on subjective observations rather than scientific quantification gives a detailed description of some of the articulatory
manoeuvres during the sequence [mi]: 'Hierbei drängen sich also in den einen
Uebergangsmoment drei oder vier Articulationsbewegungen zusammen. Um
dies zu vermeiden, kann man aber die Zunge bereits während der Dauer des

m gleichzeitig mit dessen Einsatz, zur *i* – Stellung erheben und auch die Lippen können sich neben dem Verschlusse auch spaltformig erweitern, ohne dass dem *m* seine Eigenschaft als labialer Nasal genommen wird, dann bleiben für den Uebergangsmoment nur zwei Articulationsbewegungen übrig' (p.103).

The concept of simultaneous articulatory activities where speech movements 'overlap' and produce 'sound fusion' as it was sometimes called became a recurring theme in much of the work done during this period. Scripture saw this notion as a breakthrough in the study of speech dynamics and vigorously attacked traditional viewpoints which regarded speech as a sequence of static isolated sounds linked by glides. He showed clearly by means of the graphic recording techniques available at the time that speech is a dynamic process where articulatory organs are continuously in a state of flux with 'contiguous articulations ... modified to produce easy passage from one to another' (Scripture 1902, p.455). The rather vague notion of 'ease of articulation' or 'economy of effort' became the most frequently expounded principle to account for this transitional felicity.

As a psychologist, Scripture clearly saw the implications of the concept of simultaneous articulatory activity for the neural encoding of speech. Some thirty years after *Elements of Experimental Phonetics* he was to claim: 'Overlapping is an inner, or psychic matter that happens before the impulses are expressed in speech. The impulses must occur more or less simultaneously. Inner activity, or mind, must therefore possess a dimension of simultaneity in addition to those of time and intensity. This means simply that several things can occur in the mind at the same time' (Scripture 1936, p.219). Scripture obviously recognised the implications of this basic principle of physiological activity for all sorts of sound phenomena. He states, for example, (Scripture 1935, p.759) that overlapping 'may well prove fertile in explaining the phenomena of sound change'. Presumably he was thinking here primarily of historical assimilations.

Experiments with exploratory bulbs and the smoked-drum kymograph produced some interesting results concerning the influence that contiguous sounds can exert on each other. Scripture (1902, p.372) quotes some research by Laclotte which showed that in CV syllables the tongue position during the consonant element depends on the nature of the following vowel. When the pairs *ba*, *bi* and *za*, *zi* were compared it was found that the tongue position during the consonant was lower in the first member of each pair. According to Scripture, Laclotte claimed that the records showed 'that the tongue takes for the beginning of the work of articulation for the syllable the position necessary for the vowel and maintains it throughout the consonant and its explosion' (Scripture 1902, p.372). This is, in essence, the idea of simultaneous activity expressed by Menzerath in his notion of 'Koartikulation'. Recently the principle has been formulated by Kozhevnikov and Chistovich (1965) as the theoretical basis for their model of speech production. Kozhevnikov and Chistovich posit as the basic neural encoding unit in speech an 'articulatory syllable' which is basically a CV type unit where 'all the movements of a vowel which are not contradictory to the articulation of the consonant begin with the beginning of the syllable' (p.122). Coarticulatory effects are said to be maximal within such an articulatory syllable and minimal between successive syllables. Some details of the model remain controversial, for example the concept of 'contradictory' articulatory movements (see MacNeilage 1972), but it has nevertheless prompted a great deal of research in the area of speech production during the last few years which has contributed greatly to our knowledge of coarticulatory processes (see discussions in Kent 1976, Gay 1977). In addition to his studies using CV type syllables Laclotte also examined coarticulatory effects in VCV utterances (see Scripture 1902, p.372). Using the exploratory bulb technique once more, he showed that a vowel may influence not only an immediately preceding consonant as in the CV syllables but also the vowel before this consonant. Thus in sequences such as *ela* and *eli* the records showed that the articulations differed for *e*, the tongue being higher and nearer to the *i* position in *eli* than in *ela*. Similar results were found for *eba* and *ebi* (see figure 3). Thus coarticulatory effects were found to extend beyond the CV syllable. Recent spectrographic research by Öhman (1966) on Swedish and American English has demonstrated that in VCV type syllables formant transition characteristics of the first vowel depend not only on the consonant but also on the nature of the second vowel. Öhman interpreted his results in terms of a model of speech production appropriate for VCV type utterances, the basic tenets of which are that such a sequence consists of a relatively slow moving diphthongal V-V gesture involving mainly the extrinsic muscle system of the tongue and a relatively independent fast moving consonantal gesture involving primarily intrinsic tongue muscles, which is superimposed on this basic diphthongal gesture. Although the data were restricted to Swedish and

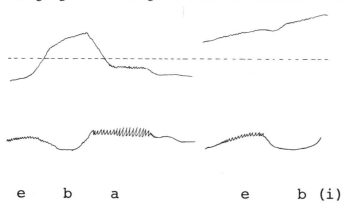

e   b   a   e   b (i)

FIGURE 3. Kymograph tracings of two utterances 'eba' and 'ebi' showing tongue activity from an exploratory bulb (top trace) and air-flow from the mouth (bottom trace) (from Rousselot 1924, p.984 after Laclotte 1899).

American English there are some claims for generality in the theory. It would be interesting to test this model on a number of different languages using articulatory techniques more accurate than Laclotte's exploratory bulbs, such as, for example, electropalatography (e.g. Hardcastle 1972).

Other results of early investigations using exploratory bulbs, geniohyoid tambours and air-flow registration techniques mentioned in Scripture (1902) of interest to today's experimental phoneticians are as follows:

1) Voiceless stops involve more pressure of contact than their voiced counterparts.

2) The degree of nasalisation of a nasal vowel in French varies with the nature of the preceding sound, being complete for the initial position and after /s/, /ʃ/ and probably all continuants, but lacking in the first portions after /p, b, t, d, k, g/.

3) Final voiced consonants often become voiceless before they end.

4) In groups of consonants between vowels in French there is frequently an assimilation of the first consonant to the second in respect of voicing, very rarely of the second to the first.

5) In Italian the nasalisation required for a 'nasal' regularly extends to the neighbouring sounds and sometimes to the entire word.

Although valuable because they focused attention on the dynamics of speech the various graphic recording devices were limited in that they provided indirect and relatively gross information on the activities of the different speech organs. There was a need to obtain more detailed direct information on the function of the tongue particularly its positions and configurations during the production of speech sounds. Abercrombie (1957) mentions a number of early attempts to record the position and shape of the tongue, including Erasmus Darwin's (1803) technique where cylinders of tin-foil are inserted into the mouth and deformed during the production of various vowels. Rousselot (1897–1901) describes an interesting method which involved the use of a strip of softened vulcanised rubber fastened anteriorly to the front incisors which upon production of various sounds showed the curvature of the tongue and its relation to the front teeth. A plaster model of the palate and teeth was then cut in half to give a sagittal section and the strip of the now hardened rubber material attached to this section. Diagrams could then be drawn from this model. The technique was said to have been devised by Atkinson who also developed the ingenious Atkinson's Mouth Measurer (Atkinson 1899) to obtain the position of points of the tongue in relation to the upper front incisors and palate. The method is described in full in Scripture (1902) and various diagrams of tongue contours during the production of sustained vowel sounds are presented (p.332). But there were obvious disadvantages with these relatively primitive techniques. Grandgent (1890) recognises the difficulties involved in investigating tongue activity when he says of the various devices: 'Here the greatest drawback is the unwillingness of the organs to perform their natural functions when in contact with any foreign substance. Only by long and patient practice can the rebellious tongue and palate be entirely subjected to their owner's will' (p.154).

Another limitation of these techniques was that they gave information primarily on tongue proximity to the palate so could be used only in the analysis of sustained vowel sounds. They were not of course suitable for investigating consonants which involved the formation of a narrow constriction in the oral cavity. Thus attempts were made to develop methods of obtaining accurate and detailed information on consonant characteristics, particularly the place of articulation of consonants. One of these new methods was that described by Grützner (1879). He first dried the tongue and coated it with either carmine water-colour or Chinese ink. Then he articulated the required sound. The places where the painted tongue touched the palate could be seen by means of a small lamp and suitably positioned mirror and the outline of the contact area could be sketched by hand onto a plaster model of the subject's upper palate and teeth. Grützer mentions in a footnote the work of another investigator Oakley Coles (1872) whose work had just been brought to his attention. Oakley Coles, generally regarded as being the originator of the technique which became known as 'direct' palatography (Abercrombie 1957), had coated the palate and teeth rather than the tongue with his adhering mixture. He then observed the wipe-off of material directly from the palate and teeth. This basic technique is still used today with various refinements such as facility for directly photographing the wipe-off area, and remains one of the most convenient ways to obtain accurate data on the place of articulation for speech sounds (Ladefoged 1957).

A modification of the Oakley Coles technique (see Kingsley 1879) involving the use of a thin artificial palate normally made of vulcanite or similar material was favoured by most researchers in the late nineteenth and early twentieth century. This modification was thought to give a clearer outline of tongue-palate contact and the contact area could be sketched at leisure after removing the artificial palate. (For details of manufacture of the artificial palates and methods of measurement see Moses 1940, and Keller 1971.) Using this technique researchers carried out detailed investigations on the place of articulation of the sounds of many different languages, including English, French, Italian, German, Spanish, Hungarian, (see bibliography in Keller 1971).

One of the problems facing the early researchers using the palatographic technique was how to represent what is essentially a three-dimensional structure in a two-dimensional diagram. It was clearly recognised early that individual palates varied considerably in shape (Kaiser 1936) and that the tongue palate contact diagrams should somehow be able to represent this variation in palate shape particularly the variations in the depth of the palate. One technique was that described by Russell (1928). Using a base metal model of the hard palate he made pin-holes in the entire surface at centimetre intervals beginning at the median line. A paper was then placed on top of the

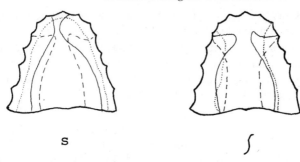

s   ∫

FIGURE 4. Schematic diagrams made from palatograms showing outlines of tongue contact for [s] *and* [∫] in English (---), German (——) and French (····) (adapted from Viëtor 1898).

palate and a light shining through the pin-holes allowed the dots to be traced onto the paper. The result showed a two dimensional plan of the palate where the proximity of the dots illustrated the degree of slope of the palate. The outline of the tongue contact area could then be traced if desired onto this plan. Other, more recent techniques for representing the contours of the palate are described in Ladefoged (1957).

In accordance with their desire to quantify aspects of articulatory behaviour, the early investigators tried various methods of determining the area of contact from the two-dimensional palatograms. Some of these methods are described in detail in Moses (1940) and included the use of squared paper and the planimeter. (For a more recent attempt to quantify area of contact using the planimeter see Wictorin and Agnello 1970.)

Much of the early work done with palatography was comparative in nature to show differences in the articulation of various speech sounds in a wide variety of languages. Thus Viëtor (1898) illustrates his phonetic textbook on the sounds of English, German and French with palatograms of these three languages made by himself and his contemporaries Kingsley and Rousselot. It is interesting to note that palatograms of the grooved fricatives [s] and [∫] show consistent differences for French on the one hand, and German and English on the other (see figure 4). In French both the [s] and [∫] have more forward contact than in English or German and the [s] in French has much less contact along the sides of the palate than in the other languages. Scripture in his *Elements of Experimental Phonetics* (1902) includes palatograms made by his contemporaries of American English, Irish, Hungarian, German, French and Italian.

Although traditional palatography allows the accurate study of single isolated sounds only and is hardly suited to the study of the dynamics of articulation, nevertheless many of the early researchers were able to demonstrate coarticulatory effects using the technique (see Scripture 1902, p.302). The palatalisation of velars before front vowels could be illustrated easily by the somewhat artificial exercise of articulating isolated plosives or fricatives with imagined vowels following such as [i], or [e]. Another strategy was to obtain a 'reference' pattern for a given sound in isolation and to compare this reference pattern with that obtained from the articulation of a sequence. Clearly, the early investigators were fully aware of the difficulties in studying sound sequences using palatography. As Scripture says 'to obtain records for a sound in the interior of a word, such words should be selected to give no other records or no records which can be confused with the one desired' (1902, p.301). The practice of using single isolated sounds was of course less than satisfactory, as isolated sounds often bear little resemblance to the sounds in connected speech. But for sequences such as /ki/, where the palatogram shows a composite pattern for the /k/ and /i/ contacts, it was extremely difficult to obtain unambiguous evidence of /k/ fronting from the single palatogram. It was not until much later (e.g. in Ladefoged 1957) with the technique of cineradiography that one was able to show conclusively that the *closure* for /k/ was in fact made much further forward in the mouth than in 'coo'.

In spite of these difficulties, however, the early investigators found some interesting contextual effects using palatography. Rousselot (1901–8), for example, claims that for Irish, /e/ and /i/ palatalise the preceding consonant more consistently than appeared to be the case in other languages. In French, for instance, Rousselot found that one of his subjects palatalised /k/ and /g/ before front vowels not consistently but only in moments of 'negligence'. It is possible that the constraints on contextual effects are more complex in French than in Irish. E. Haden (1938), for example, on the basis of a palatographic study of French consonants claimed there was greater 'accord' between the consonant and the following vowel than between the consonant and the preceding vowel. It is possible this is a language-specific constraint and as such certainly would seem to warrant further investigation.

Apart from the immediate sound environment there were other factors found to affect the contact pattern for particular sounds. Scripture (1902), for example, suggests differences in contact patterns for /t/ depending on rate and degree of aspiration. 'The contact for *t* shows complete alveolar contact of the tongue. If this contact was marginal, the release was probably quick with a sharp explosion; if predorsal, slower with a slight following aspiration' (p.302). The effect of rate of utterance on contact pattern was to be explored more thoroughly later by Stetson, Hudgins and Moses (1940, p.56). They found that the contact areas for alveolar stops change in at least two ways with increasing rate of utterance. Not only is the area of anterior contact reduced in size with the more rapid speech but the main contact area is shifted backward from the front teeth and covers only the posterior part of the alveolar ridge and a narrow strip of the front palatal arch.

The optional nature of many of these coarticulatory effects was clearly recognised by phoneticians writing at the turn of the century. Henry Sweet (1877) lists a number of assimilations occurring in rapid speech such as /ŋ/ in 'going' changing to /n/ when followed by /t, d, n/ and the /t/ being 'dropped' in 'I can't go' with the alveolar nasal becoming velar under the influence of the following /g/. Many of these coarticulatory effects were regarded as belonging strictly to fluent conversational speech and were to be avoided in formal styles. Thus Viëtor (1909), writing about German, lists three effects that are 'tolerated in fluent conversational German not however in public speaking, in reading etc.' (p.99). These are: /pf/ becoming /f/ (thus /kamf/ instead of /kampf/); /t/ omitted in /nt/ followed by a third consonant (especially /s/) (thus /gans/ instead of /gants/); /ən/ becoming, 'in rather slovenly speech' /m/ after labials, /n/ after dentals, and /ŋ/ after gutturals. A more prescriptive view of these processes was taken by Dumville (1909) and Soames (1913). Dumville (1909) states: 'It is obvious that assimilation is a laboursaving process. It arises from carelessness – often unconscious – in rapid speech' (p.115), there being 'insufficient time and insufficient energy for the speaker to perform all the movements which would be made in slow and careful speech' (p.118). Soames (1913) regards many of these coarticulatory processes as being undesirable, claiming that assimilations such as /s/ becoming /ʃ/ before /j/, and /t/ becoming /tʃ/ before /j/ are 'to be avoided' as 'slipshod habits' although she does admit the process /z/ becoming /ʃ/ before /ʃ/ (as in 'is she') seems to be 'unavoidable in rapid speech' (p.119). It is interesting to note in this regard that the early phoneticians, grammarians and orthoepists writing between 1500 and 1900 such as Hart, Bulloker, Herries, Wallis, Robinson, Gill, Holder, Kenrick etc. rarely mention variations in the production of sounds owing to phonetic context, although there is the occasional reference to the elision of alveolar stops and variant pronunciations of sounds owing to their position in the word. Thus Herries (1773) in a chapter on impediments of speech allows the possibility of omitted /t, d/ when followed by another alveolar. Thus of the passage 'of man's first disobedience, and the fruit – And sing th' infusive force of spring on man –' he says 'As the *t* in "firs*t*", and the *d* in "*d*isobedience", and the *v* in "infusi*v*e", and the *f* in "*f*orce" are formed in the same place, it is necessary to make a pause between these words, else there is only ONE of the single sounds pronounced. But in just speaking, no pause ought to be made between the substantive and the adjective: therefore in the one line, either the *t* and *d* is lost; and in the other, either the *v* or *f*'. Also William Kenrick (1784) discusses positional variation thus: 'The consonants also change their nature frequently by position: thus *l, m, n, r, f* and *s* are called half vowels, and are said to have a kind of obscure sound, while *b, c, d, g, k, p, g, t* are said to have no sound at all. But let us place *m* at the beginning of a syllable, and it is nearly as mute as *b*. You cannot open your lips to pronounce either without making it serve to articulate some following vowel. Again, the sound of *c* and *g* at the beginning of words is equally vocal with that of *s*. Again *b, d, p, t* at the end of words are considerably more vocal than even *l, m, n, r,* at the beginning of them'. Descriptions of positional variants such as these seemed to have been rare up until the latter half of the nineteenth century, in fact until the writings of phoneticians such as Ellis, Sweet and Jones. For these phoneticians the task was to provide not only a descriptive framework for single isolated sounds but to describe what happens to these sounds in spontaneous connected speech.

It is somewhat difficult often to determine what the early researchers regarded as being the main constraints on coarticulatory processes. Factors influencing the degree and type of coarticulation obviously included rate of utterance and certain stylistic variables but there was some suggestion also amongst the early investigators that certain coarticulation effects were language specific. Apart from Rousselot (see above) other phoneticians often indicated the language-specific nature of some coarticulatory phenomena. Thus a non-experimentalist, Kruisinga (1935), makes the (somewhat doubtful) claim: 'as a general rule there is no assimilation of place between neighbouring sounds in English but in Dutch it is common' (p.51). Speculations on the constraints on coarticulatory processes continued well into the twentieth century. In the course of what was perhaps the most far-reaching and detailed palatographic investigation ever undertaken L. Kaiser (1942) specifically investigated the phenomenon of assimilation of place in Dutch pairs such as 'moed' versus 'maat' where the tongue contact for the final alveolar stop would normally be affected by the preceding vowel – the contact area typically being more retracted for 'moed' than for 'maat'. She found the degree of influence depended largely on four main factors: the speech 'tradition' of the subjects, their sex, their dialect and their rate of utterance.

A detailed experimental analysis of the constraints on coarticulatory processes has still to be carried out although recent researchers have widened the field considerably by examining constraints such as the prosodic and syntactic environment (e.g. McClean 1973). Some of the early investigators did in fact mention many of these constraints (e.g. Rousselot 1897–1908) but in most cases lacked the theoretical framework for a systematic study.

Towards the middle of the twentieth century more sophisticated instrumental techniques were developed offering greater possibilities of research on lingual dynamics. Radiography had become a fairly standard part of the experimental phoneticians' research tools, although there were severe restrictions on its widespread use. Most of the early work using X-ray techniques was aimed at establishing tongue contours for continuously spoken or sung vowels (see e.g. Jones 1929, Russell 1928, Parmenter and Treviño 1932) and as such were rather limited (Moll 1960). Menzerath (1938) in his paper at the Fourth International Congress of Linguists in 1936 was among the first to demonstrate new techniques of cineradiography in the study of lingual dynamics. Today new developments in X-ray technology (see e.g. Fujimura et al. 1973, Bladon and Nolan 1977) have made it possible to obtain detailed information on the co-ordination between articulatory organs relatively safely and research is already underway into coarticulatory phenomena (e.g.

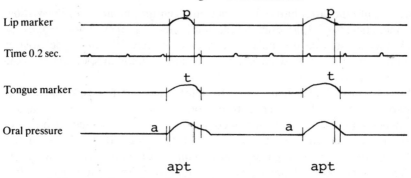

FIGURE 5. Kymograph tracings showing the temporal relationships of bilabial and lingual contacts during two occurrences of the word 'apt' (after Stetson 1951, p.86).

Kiritani 1977, Fujimura et al. 1977, Giles and Moll 1975).

Another investigator about the middle of this century who considerably refined the instrumentation used by Rousselot and his contemporaries was the psychologist Stetson (1951). He is mainly remembered today for his influential work on respiratory activity during speech and his formulation of a 'chest-pulse' theory of syllable production (see recent modification of his theory in Ladefoged 1967). In addition, however, he carried out some detailed experiments on consonant combinations of the type /pt/ in, for example, the word 'apt' to determine the degree of overlapping articulatory movement. To register tongue contact he used a 'tongue marker' which was essentially a modification of Rousselot's exploratory bulb but with a faster response time. Basically the tongue markers were made of taut rubber either fastened to a wire frame shaped to a plaster impression of the subject's palate, or stretched over two small 'windows' (one in the alveolar region and one in the velar) cut into an artificial palate. Lip closure was registered by a lip marker using a similar principle.

Kymograph tracings of sequences such as 'apt' showed the lip closure for the /p/ occurring almost simultaneously with the tongue contact for /t/ with the /p/ normally slightly earlier. It is interesting to note in the illustration of one of these consonant sequences (see figure 5) that the closure for /t/ actually occurs slightly earlier than for /p/ in the same sequence. A recent experiment using new techniques for registering tongue and lip dynamics (see Hardcastle and Roach 1977) showed instances where the closure for the 'two' stops in a two-stop combination occurred simultaneously, and in an informal experiment the closure for the 'second' stop has been found actually to precede the closure for the 'first' stop. In this experiment the technique of electropalatography (e.g. Hardcastle 1972) which provides spatial and temporal details of tongue-palate contacts during continuous speech was synchronised with a cine-camera to enable frame-by-frame analysis of lip movements. It was possible using this experimental set-up to examine temporal details of articulatory closure in sequences such as /pt/, /pk/, /tk/, /kt/, etc. Interestingly it was in the /kt/ sequences (in words such as 'acting') that one of the subjects made the /t/ closure slightly *before* the /k/ closure, although this seemed to be rather atypical. The general pattern was for the velar contact to precede the alveolar contact and then for the two contacts to overlap in time for a period of around 30 per cent of the total duration for the stops before the /k/ contact was released. It may well be that Stetson's results and the results of this experiment both involving alveolar articulation may be interpreted in terms of intrinsic mechano-muscular features of tongue activity. Further research is necessary in this area.

The theme of lingual dynamics and the overlapping nature of speech was explored thoroughly by Menzerath (Menzerath and De Lacerda 1933). He showed convincingly as did Scripture before him that at no time during speech were the articulatory organs fixed in position, thus discrediting the traditional view of speech as a set of isolated static postures of the articulatory organs linked together by glides. Menzerath attacked the ideas of the older phoneticians such as Sievers whose theory of speech production stated that each sound was characterised by three articulatory phases: two dynamic phases ('Anglitt' and 'Abglitt') with one static phase or 'Stellungsphase'. By means of air-flow measurements, labiograms and later cine-X-ray techniques, Menzerath demonstrated convincingly that articulatory organs during speech production were continually in a state of flux even during the so-called closure phase of a plosive. He gives an example: 'Ich bitte Sie nun, ganz verurteilsfrei mit mir einmal zu beobachten, was vor sich geht, wenn man *apa* oder noch einfacher *ap* sagt ... Man macht den Mund stumm (!) auf und schliesst ihn, und *während dieser Schliessbewegung* wird das *a* lautbar, bis es in *p* übergeht. Hier ist also kein lautbarer Anglitt vorhanden, keine Stellung, kein Abglitt des *a* ebensowenig ein Anglitt des *p*. Das *a* wird von der *a*-Grenze aus in das *p* hineingesprochen, oder in einer anderer Konsonanten, der ihm folgt. Diesen Vorgang habe ich also "Steuerung" bezeichnet' (Menzerath 1935, p.61). He draws a distinction between this situation and that exemplified by the overlapping movements in a case such as a sequence /pu/ which he calls 'Koartikulation' (see above). He claims this phenomenon is different from that described traditionally by linguists, as 'assimilation' but does not explain how. Presumably the main difference lies in the fact that 'Koartikulation' describes the physiological processes themselves involved in speech production rather than the acoustic effect these processes can produce (assimilation).

Phoneticians continued to refine the notion of coarticulation throughout this century, introducing new experimental techniques and new knowledge particularly from the field of physiology. Shohara (1939) in a discussion on overlapping movements in speech distinguishes three forms of such movements (1) those involving different portions of the same organ (e.g. 'act, ask' etc.) (2) those involving different organs adjacent to each other (e.g. /pt/ in 'baptize',) and (3) those involving different organs remote from each other (e.g. /pm/ in 'equipment'). She presents experimental evidence to show that many of the muscular activities involved in these three types of movements must occur simultaneously and she urges that this extensive overlapping be taken into account in areas such as speech training. She also notes that much of this overlapping 'affords only partial auditory and visual check' thus challenging 'further investigation of the neuromuscular mechanism involved' (p.27).

In the last decade interest in coarticulation has increased greatly. We now have at our disposal techniques available for examining not only the activities of individual articulatory organs directly (e.g. various radiographic techniques, cine photography, electropalatography etc.) but also the electrical potentials in the muscles contributing to these articulatory activities (by electromyography). One should not forget however our considerable debt to the older phoneticians who influenced many of our theoretical viewpoints and gave us much valuable data in this important area of phonetic research.

References

ABERCROMBIE, D. (1957) 'Direct Palatography', *Zeitschrift für Phonetik und allgemeine Sprachwissenschaft* 10 (1), 21–5.

ATKINSON, H.W. (1899) 'Methods of mouth-mapping', *Die Neueren Sprachen* 6, 494–503.

BLADON, R.A.W. and NOLAN, F.J. (1977) 'A video-fluorographic investigation of tip and blade alveolars in English', *J. Phonetics* 5, 185–93.

COLES, J. OAKLEY (1872) 'A plan for ascertaining more accurately the physiology of speech', *Trans. Odontological Soc. Great Britain* 4, 110–23.

DANILOFF, R.G. and HAMMARBERG, R.E. (1973) 'On defining coarticulation', *J. Phonetics* 1, 239–48.

DANILOFF, R. and MOLL, K. (1968) 'Coarticulation of lip-rounding', *J. Speech Hearing Res.* 11, 707–21.

DARWIN, ERASMUS (1803) *The Temple of Nature or The Origin of Society*: A poem with philosophical notes, London (J. Johnson, St Paul's Churchyard); facsimile reprint, Scolar Press, London, 1973.

DUMVILLE, B. (1909) *The Science of Speech: an Elementary Manual of English Phonetics for Teachers*, London (W.B. Clive).

FUJIMURA, O., KIRITANI, S. and ISHIDA, H. (1973) 'Computer controlled radiography for observation of movements of articulatory and other human organs', *Computers in Medicine and Biology* 3, 371–84.

FUJIMURA, O., MILLER, J.E. and KIRITANI, S. (1977) 'A computer controlled x-ray microbeam study of articulatory characteristics of nasal consonants in English and Japanese', Paper presented at 9th Int. Congr. Acoustics, Madrid Spain, July 4–9.

GAY, T. (1977) 'Cinefluorographic and electromyographic studies of articulatory organization', in M. Sawashima and F.S. Cooper (eds.) *Dynamic Aspects of Speech Production*, Tokyo (University of Tokyo Press) 85–105.

GILES, S.B. and MOLL, K.L. (1975) 'Cinefluorographic study of selected allophones of English /1/', *Phonetica* 31, 206–27.

GRANDGENT, C.H. (1890) 'Vowel measurements', *Pub. Mod. Lang. Assoc.* 5, 148–74.

— (1892) *German and English Sounds*, Boston (Ginn and Company).

GRÜTZNER, P. (1879) 'Physiologie der Stimme und Sprache', in H. Hermann, *Handbuch der Physiologie*, vol. I, part 2, Leipzig (Vogel) 3–238.

HADEN, E.F. (1938) *The Physiology of French Consonant Changes*, Language Monograph no. 26, Linguistic Society of America, Baltimore.

HARDCASTLE, W.J. (1972) 'The use of electropalatography in phonetic research', *Phonetica* 25, 197–215.

HARDCASTLE, W.J. and ROACH, P.J. (1977) 'An instrumental investigation of coarticulation in stop consonant sequences', *Work in Progress*, no. 1, (Phonetics Laboratory, Dept. of Linguistic Science, University of Reading) 27–44.

HERRIES, J. (1773) *The Elements of Speech*, London (Dilly).

JONES, D. (1932) *Outline of English Phonetics*, 3rd ed., Cambridge (Cambridge University Press).

JONES, S. (1929) 'Radiography and Pronunciation', *Brit. J. Radiology* 2, 149–50.

KAISER, L. (1936) 'The shape of the palate and its effect on speech sounds', in D. Jones and D.B. Fry (eds.) *Proc. 2nd Int. Congr. of Phonetic Sciences*, London 1935, Cambridge (Cambridge University Press) p.22.

— (1942) 'Biological and statistical research concerning the speech of 216 Dutch students, IV', *Archives Néerlandaises de Phonétique Expérimentale* 18, 1–58.

KELLER, KATHRYN C. (1971) *Instrumental Articulatory Phonetics: an Introduction to Techniques and Results*, Norman (Summer Institute of Linguistics of the University of Oklahoma) Summer Institute of Linguistics Publications in Linguistics and Related Fields, 31.

KENRICK, W. (1784) *A Rhetorical Grammar of the English Language*, London (Cadell and Longman) facsimile reprint, Scolar Press, London.

KENT, R.D. (1976) 'Models of speech production', in N.J. Lass (ed.) *Contemporary Issues in Experimental Phonetics*, New York (Academic Press) pp.79–104.

KENT, R.D. and MINIFIE, F.D. (1977) 'Coarticulation in recent speech production models', *J. Phonetics* 5, 115–33.

KINGSLEY, N.W. (1879) 'Surgery or mechanism in the treatment of congenital cleft palate', *New York Medical J.* 29, 484–92.

KIRITANI, S. (1977) 'Articulatory studies by the X-ray microbeam system', in M. Sawashima and F.S. Cooper (eds.) *Dynamic Aspects of Speech Production*, Tokyo (University of Tokyo Press) 171–94.

KOZHEVNIKOV, V.A. and CHISTOVICH, L.A. (1965) *Speech: Articulation and Perception*, Moscow (Nauka), (trans. Joint Publications Res. Service U.S. Dept. of Commerce 1967).

KRUISINGA, E. (1935) *An Introduction to the Study of English Sounds*, Groningen (P. Noordhoff N.V.).

LACLOTTE, F. (1899) 'L'Harmonie vocalique', *La Parole* 1, 177–88.

LADEFOGED, P. (1957) 'Use of palatography', *J. Speech Disorders* 22, 764–74.

— (1967) *Three Areas of Experimental Phonetics*, London (Oxford University Press).

LENZ, R. (1888) 'Zur Physiologie und Geschichte der Palatalen', *Zeitschrift für vergleichende Sprachforschung* 29, 1–59.

MacNEILAGE, P.F. (1972) 'Speech physiology', in J.H. Gilbert (ed.) *Speech and Cortical Functioning*, New York (Academic Press) 1–72.

MacNEILAGE, P.F. and DE CLERK, J.L. (1969) 'On the motor control of coarticulation in CVC monosyllables', *J. Acoust. Soc. Am.* 45 (5), 1217–33.

McCLEAN, M. (1973) 'Forward coarticulation of velar movement at marked junctural boundaries', *J. Speech Hearing Res.* 16, 286–96.

MENZERATH, P. and DE LACERDA, A. (1933) *Koartikulation, Steuerung und Lautabgrenzung*, Berlin, Bonn (Ferd. Dümmler).

MENZERATH, P. (1935) 'Lautabrenzung und Wortstruktur', *Proc. 3rd Int. Congr. Ling.*, Rome, 19–26 Sept. 1933, Florence (Felice le Monnier) 59–66, repr. 1972 by Kraus: Nendeln/Liechtenstein.

— (1938) 'Neue Untersuchungen zur Wortartikulation' (mit Vorführung

Studies in Lingual Coarticulation

eines Röntgentonfilms von Janker und Menzerath), in *Proc. 4th Int. Congr. Ling.*, Copenhagen Sept. 1936, Cercle Linguistique de Copenhague, 67–75.

MOLL, K.L. (1960) 'Cinefluorographic techniques in speech research', *J. Speech Hearing Res.* 3, 227–41.

MOSES, E.R. (1940 'A brief history of palatography', *Q. J. Speech* 26, 615–25.

ÖHMAN, S.E.G. (1966) 'Coarticulation in VCV utterances: spectrographic measurements', *J. Acoust. Soc. Am.* 39, 151–68.

PANCONCELLI-CALZIA, G. (1957) 'Earlier history of phonetics', in L. Kaiser (ed.) *Manual of Phonetics*, Amsterdam (North-Holland).

PARMENTER, C.E. and TREVIÑO, S.N. (1932) 'Vowel positions as shown by X-ray', *Q. J. Speech* 18, 351–69.

ROUSSELOT, P.J. (1897–1901) *Principes de Phonétique Expérimentale*, Tome I, Paris (H. Welter).

— (1901–8) *Principes de Phonétique Expérimentale*, Tome II, Paris (H. Welter).

— (1924) *Principes de Phonétique Expérimentale* nouvelle edition, Paris (H. Didier).

RUSSELL, G. OSCAR (1928) *The Vowel*, Columbus, Ohio (Ohio State University Press).

SCRIPTURE, E.W. (1902) *The Elements of Experimental Phonetics*, New York (Charles Scribner's Sons).

— (1906) *Researches in Experimental Phonetics: the Study of Speech Curves*, Washington, D.C. (The Carnegie Foundation).

— (1935) 'Overlapping speech sounds', *Nature* 136, 759.

— (1936) 'The Nature of Speech', in D. Jones and D.B. Fry (eds.) *Proc. 2nd Int. Congr. of Phonetic Sciences*, London 1935, Cambridge (Cambridge University Press) 209–20.

SHOHARA, H. (1939) 'Significance of overlapping movements in speech', *Proc. 2nd Bien. Cent. Zone Conf. Am. Soc. Hard of Hearing*, in E.T. McDonald (1964) *Articulation Testing and Treatment: A sensory-motor approach*, Pittsburg (Stanwix Ho. Inc.) 19–27.

SIEVERS, E. (1876) *Grundzüge der Lautphysiologie zur Einführung in das Studium der Lautlehre der Indogermanischen Sprachen*, Leipzig (Breitkopf und Härtel).

SOAMES, L. (1913) *Introduction to English, French and German Phonetics*, 3rd ed. rev. and partly rewritten by W. Viëtor, London (Macmillan & Co.).

STETSON, R.H. (1951) *Motor Phonetics: A study of Speech Movements in Action*, 2nd ed. Amsterdam, (North-Holland). (First ed. 1928 in *Archives Néerlandaises de Phonétique Expérimentale*, 3).

STETSON, R.H., HUDGINS, C.V. and MOSES, E.R. Jr. (1940) 'Palatograms change with rates of articulation', *Archives Neérlandaises de phonétique expérimentale* 16, 52–61.

SWEET, H. (1877) *A Handbook of Phonetics*, Oxford (Clarendon Press).

VIËTOR, W. (1894) 'Kleine Beiträge zur Experimental – phonetik', *Die Neueren Sprachen* 1, Suppl, 25.

— (1898) *Elemente der Phonetik des Deutschen, Englischen und Französischen*, Leipzig (Reisland).

— (1909) *German Pronunciation: Practice and Theory*, 4th ed., Leipzig, (Reisland).

WICTORIN, L. and AGNELLO, J. (1970) 'Speech pattern changes during edentulous and denture conditions. 1 Palatographic study', *Acta Odontol. Scand.* 28, 729–37.

Consonant Rounding
in British English : The Status of
Phonetic Descriptions as Historical Data

I take as my point of departure an observation of David Abercrombie's: 'Labialisation consists of rounding the lips during the production of a segment just as a rounded vowel ... . The segment represented by the letters *sh* in *shall* is a voiceless palato-alveolar fricative; but as most speakers of English pronounce it (as can easily be confirmed by observation) the corners of the lips are brought forward somewhat, and it is therefore labialised ... . The sound would be different if the labialisation were not there' (Abercrombie 1967, p.62). When I first read this, I remember being surprised at the information. I was of course familiar with the notion of rounded vowels in English but I had not appreciated that 'most speakers' had rounded consonants. I began to pay particular attention to this feature of English pronunciation and was even more surprised to discover that most of the energetic lip-rounding in the stream of speech seems to derive from rounded consonants rather than rounded vowels.

It is the case that there are some speakers who have little, if any, lip-rounding in the stream of speech, but prolonged observation certainly confirms David Abercrombie's statement that most speakers, certainly most R P speakers, do have rounding and this rounding does not appear to derive primarily from vowels. Indeed, it seems to be the case that many of the vowels of English that are classified in descriptions as 'rounded' do not always, or even most of the time, appear as lip-rounded in the stream of speech. Thus /u/ and /ʊ/ and /əʊ/ for example, as in 'two' and 'put' and 'goat', appear to be more often un-lip-rounded than lip-rounded. Of the 'rounded' vowels only /ɔ/ as in 'caught' seems to retain some fairly definite lip-rounding in stressed words in the stream of speech. The chief origin of lip-rounding in natural speech seems, rather, to be rounded consonants. The rounded consonants fall into three classes. The first class produces the most marked lip movement and involves the protrusion and eversion of upper and lower lip. This class includes the /ʃ/, mentioned by Abercrombie, and its congeners /ʒ, tʃ, dʒ/, as well as /r/. The second class involves a slight protrusion and eversion of the lower lip and, with some individuals, compression of the corners of the lips. This class includes /f, v, s, z/. The third class contains only /w/ which is characterised by compression of the corners of the lips, with protrusion but no eversion. These three classes appear to constitute a hierarchy such that a speaker who has any rounding at all will round the members of the first class, whereas only speakers with considerable rounding will round the members of the second class. (/w/ when it precedes a non-round vowel is frequently realised in the stream of speech with no visible rounding.)

My claim that most rounding in natural speech derives from 'rounded' consonants rather than from 'rounded' vowels rests on the fact that the consonants will retain their rounding even in the environment of non-rounded vowels. Thus, in 'shy' and 'cheat' and 'jump', for instance, the consonants will be realised as lip-rounded. I have already suggested that 'rounded vowels' will, typically, (except for /ɔ/), fail to round in the stream of speech. I now suggest that they will fail to round in the environment of a non-rounded consonant (e.g. 'two', 'put', 'goat'). However, when the 'rounded' vowels appear in the environment of a 'rounded' consonant the lip-rounding feature appears on the vowel and is even more prominent on the consonant. Thus in 'ruse', 'push' and 'choke' the lip-rounding feature will be particularly prominent on 'rounded' consonants and vowels and remarkably so in a word like 'George' which contains two 'rounded' consonants as well as the vowel which is most likely to retain some rounding independently of a 'rounded' consonant environment. The same striking effect of interaction between the two 'rounded' categories can of course be seen where /w/ occurs in the context of /u/, producing /wu/ 'woo', perhaps the closest rounding one can attest in English speech (for more detailed discussion cf. Brown 1977). It seems then that 'rounded' consonants have an important part to play in English phonology: they provide an environment in which 'rounded' vowels may be realised as phonetically lip-rounded, and, in many speakers, they contribute importantly to the characteristic 'look' of English speech and, of course, as Abercrombie remarks, 'the sound would be different if the labialisation were not there'.

My intention in this study is to look backwards in time from the present day through some of the best-known descriptions of English in the last hundred years. Within this relatively short span of time we shall find consonant rounding treated in a great variety of ways. The scale of variation has, I believe, important implications for the reliability of such descriptions as indicators of the prevalence of features like consonant rounding, features which are non-phonemic but none-the-less typical of the articulatory setting of a language or accent.

I begin with Gimson's description of mid-twentieth-century RP (1962). Gimson notes lip-rounding as a feature of the first class of rounded consonants that we noted. He says of the affricates /tʃ/ and /dʒ/ (p.170), 'The lip position will be conditioned by that of the adjacent sounds, especially that of a following vowel ... though with some speakers a certain amount of lip-protrusion is always present'; and of /ʃ/ and /ʒ/ he comments: 'Some speakers use slight lip-rounding for /ʃ, ʒ/ in all positions; for others, lip-rounding is an effect of the adjacent vowel' (p.184). I assume that the 'lip-protrusion' of the affricates is not dissimilar from the 'lip-rounding' for /ʃ, ʒ/. He describes /r/ as having its 'lip position ... determined largely by that of the following vowel, e.g. *reach* with neutral to spread lips, *root* with rounded lips' (p.201). (My observation suggests that, in the stream of speech, speakers with a tendency to rounding will round both /r/ and /tʃ/ in 'reach' and this feature of protrusion will carry on through the vowel. I do not suggest that this happens if the word is pronounced slowly, in isolation.) The only intrinsically and generally lip-rounded consonant that Gimson recognises is /w/. He does not mention lip posture as a feature of /f, v, s, z/. It is clear that he regards the 'rounded' vowels as the main origin of lip-rounding in speech.

Ida Ward's description of English pronunciation (1962, first published in 1929) makes no mention of the rounding of consonants except to comment that *k* followed by *w* is likely to be lip-rounded (p.195). This treatment seems to be characteristic of the shorter descriptions of English pronunciation, published with students or teachers of English in mind. It is usual for such descriptions to give only an account of those features necessary for the identification of the consonant – those mentioned in the conventional three-term label. The only exceptions are accounts of variation in the realisation of /l/ and /r/, which seem to exert a mesmeric influence on writers describing English at this level. Rounding on consonants is generally not mentioned at all, or mentioned only as assimilation of rounding on to the consonant from a rounded vowel in the immediate environment.

Daniel Jones (1962, first published 1918) provides the most extensive discussion I have encountered of lip position in consonants that are not primarily classified as labial. His verbal descriptions are frequently accompanied by small inset photographs, which illustrate the type of pronunciation under discussion. These photographs necessarily draw our attention to labial features. It is instructive to compare the verbal descriptions with the photographic illustrations. The photograph illustrating /ʃ/ (p.190) shows the corners of the lips compressed, the lips protruded, and the soft inner surface of the lower lip displayed. Jones comments 'there is protrusion in the lips', although later in the discussion he says that 'Some English people use a variety of ʃ made with spread lips. It has a "clearer" acoustic quality than the normal ʃ'. Again, in describing the deviant habits of Danes producing /ʒ/, Jones recommends that 'the lips should be rounded and protruded'. Note two points here: first, whereas Gimson's description does not imply that lip-rounding or protrusion is the norm for /ʃ, ʒ/, Jones' does; secondly, whereas Gimson appears to use the terms 'lip-rounding' and 'protrusion' as equivalent terms, Jones recognises that lip-rounding can occur without protrusion and that protrusion can be 'added' to lip-rounding.

Jones recognises /r/ as being generally rounded and says of the most common variant of /r/ that 'many English people pronounce **r** with a certain amount of lip-protrusion, especially in stressed position' (p.195); but he does not appear to have followed up this perceptive comment. Nevertheless, it is probably true to say that all types of rounding in the stream of speech, arising from whatever source, are more likely to occur under conditions of stress.

Let us now turn to consideration of our second class of consonants. Jones says very little about the labial articulation of /f/ (and, hence, /v/). He simply states that the stricture is formed 'by pressing the lower lip against the upper teeth' (p.179). However, examination of the photograph accompanying this description clearly shows the lower lip somewhat everted and the corners of the lips compressed. In his discussion of /s/ Jones makes no mention of lip position in the body of the text, but in a footnote he notes that 'subsidiary members with varying lip positions do exist. They are unimportant for ordinary language teaching, but I have been informed that the speech of deaf-mutes can be considerably improved by directing attention to them' (p.185). On /z/, this time in the body of the text, he observes 'Some English people use some lip articulation in addition' (p.189). (The photograph accompanying the description of /s/ (p.185) could be illustrating almost any speech segment. It gives us a clear view of both upper and lower sets of teeth and demonstrates lip-spreading with the corners of the lips well opened. It gives very much more the impression of a man producing a hiss, than of a speaker producing a segment which might form part of a word.)

Like Gimson, Jones regards /w/ as intrinsically rounded, and he correctly notes that 'lip-rounding is closer when long **u:** follows (as in *woo* **wu:**), and may be less close before vowels remote from **u** (as in *wide* **waid**)' (p.206). The photograph illustrating /w/ on page 207 shows the lips squeezed tightly together, the corners maximally compressed, with no apparently possible passage of air.

In general, then, Jones recognises lip position as being relevant to the description of a group of consonants that are not primarily classified as labial consonants. He positively identifies /ʃ/ and /ʒ/ as normally being produced with lip protrusion (and so, we must surely suppose, would describe what he regarded as the sequences /tʃ/ and /dʒ/ as having the same characteristic protrusion). He recognises /r/ and /w/ as rounded. He allows that /s, z/ have 'lip-articulation' in some people's speech and, although he does not recognise this in /f, v/, the photograph of the articulation of /f/ also demonstrates this feature. Even in his earlier very brief description of English consonants, in 1909, usually little more than comments on the three-term labels, he notes of /ʃ, ʒ/ that 'many speakers use lip-rounding' (p.30). It seems clear that whereas Gimson attributes rounding on consonants chiefly to the effect of a rounded vowel environment except in the case of intrinsically rounded /w/, Jones recognises rounding as being an intrinsic feature of at least the class of rounded consonants I have called class one as well as /w/.

I can find no other writer on English who pays the same amount of attention to lip-rounding on consonants as Jones does. Most twentieth-century writers, as I have suggested, ignore the feature completely, even when they pay what may seem to be excessive attention to lip-rounding on vowels.

Thus, J.C. Newland, in his *Voice Production and the Phonetics of Declamation* (1906) proffers the following exercises for the correct degree of rounding in vowels. For the vowel in 'cool', the student is instructed to 'place a thick pencil between the teeth (and) shape the lips lightly round it' (p.67), whereas for the vowel in 'no' he is advised to 'hold a halfpenny or shilling on end between his teeth and he will thereby attain the right measurement' (p.74). Newland does not mention lip-rounding as a feature of consonants.

I had expected to find that the great phoneticians of the nineteenth century would have paid attention to this feature of English consonants. However, in spite of careful accounts of features of lip-rounding in general, particularly by Sweet and Ellis, there is very little comment on consonantal rounding. Sweet, of course, developed the most satisfactory general phonetic account of rounding. In the *Handbook* (1877, pp.13–15) he makes a series of careful observations:

> Rounding is a contraction of the mouth cavity by lateral compression of the cheek passage and narrowing of the lip aperture .... There are three principal degrees of lip-narrowing corresponding to the height of the tongue .... It will be seen that the action of rounding is always concentrated on that part of the mouth where the vowel is formed. In rounding front vowels such as the high-front-round (y), as in the French 'lune', the cheek compression is concentrated chiefly on the corners of the mouth and that part of the cheeks immediately behind them, while in back vowels, such as the high-back-round (u) the chief compression is at the back of the cheeks .... Lip narrowing is therefore something secondary in back-rounded vowels, as it is possible to form them entirely with cheek-narrowing or 'inner rounding' .... The effect of rounding may ... be increased by projecting (pouting) the lips .... If back vowels are pronounced with lip-narrowing alone (without inner rounding as well) we do not obtain the corresponding round vowels but simply muffled varieties of the ordinary sounds.

We may quarrel with the specification of inner rounding, since it always involves sulcalisation of the tongue as well, but, this apart, Sweet does a superb job of sorting out this area. He draws the distinction between 'inner' and 'outer' rounding, a distinction that explains how the 'rounded' vowels of English can be pronounced with no apparent lip-rounding, but still sound like rounded vowels. Besides this, he makes a distinction that other, later writers sometimes use but fail to make explicit: the distinction between simple lip-rounding ('lip-narrowing') of the sort that Newland described as being formed by closing the lips around a pencil, which does not necessarily involve pushing the lips forward but does necessarily restrict the aperture between the lips, and lip-protrusion, which necessarily involves pushing the lips forward but does not necessarily restrict the aperture. (I think even Sweet does not draw the further distinction between protrusion with eversion, where the protruded lips are opened to show the soft inner surfaces, and protrusion without eversion as in /wu/, 'woo'. Sweet's 'protrusion or pouting' appears to include eversion.) The importance of the distinction between simple lip-rounding and lip-protrusion must be clear to anyone who has tried to correct the /ɔ/ vowel (as in 'caught') of a French or Polish speaker who has been taught that /ɔ/ is a 'rounded' vowel. In English this vowel is realised as a 'protruded' vowel, in Sweet's terms, not a 'lip-rounded' vowel.

In spite of his brilliant observations on rounding in vowels, Sweet has little to say on rounding in consonants. He does remark (1908) that 'Rounding on ʃ, ʒ occurs individually in English' (p.44), but here he apparently fails to draw on his own distinction between lip-rounding and protrusion. It is clear that he does not regard lip-rounding as an important feature of English since he classifies these two consonants simply as 'blade-point-open' (p.75). Moreover it is clearly his view that, in general, English speakers do not normally produce 'outer rounding' (lip-rounding or protrusion) in speech. When he discusses the 'organic basis' of English (1877) he remarks 'in many languages such as French and many Scottish dialects, the lips are often protruded in forming rounded sounds, while in others, such as English, the lips are not employed more than is necessary, inner rounding being chiefly relied on' (p.98). (It is not entirely clear to me that this is consistent with his remark in the preceding paragraph where he says of English: 'It has a tendency to labialise back vowels, and even where there is not actual labialisation it gives the vowels generally a muffled sound, so that (ɑ) is not easily distinguished from (ɔ)'.)

The same lack of interest in consonant rounding characterises the work of the two giants whom Sweet hails as the founders of the English School of Phonetics: Alexander J. Ellis and Alexander Melville Bell. Ellis (1875) makes no mention of rounding on any consonant either in his meticulous examination of 'the twenty-six key words of Mr. Melville Bell', or in his 'careful transcripts of the actual pronunciation by Professor S.S. Haldeman, A.J. Ellis, Mr. H. Sweet and Mr. B.H. Smart'. Even his account of 'lip-influence' on /w/ does not clearly identify rounding: 'w, beginning a syllable ... is a consonant having for its basis the most contracted of the vowel-sounds, namely No.27, which sound, being partially obstructed by an inward action of the lips, and then given off by an outward action, is changed from a vowel to a consonant' (p.1204). Again in his later general description of /w/ (1889, p.86*) it is not clear that he is describing a rounded consonant: '(w) a peculiarly English buzzed consonant with nearly closed lips, which are compressed in the middle but inflated on either side by the emitted voice, the back of the tongue raised as for (u)'. It is obviously not the case that Ellis is incapable of describing rounding since in his *Pronunciation for Singers* (1877) he describes the effect of various lip postures in some detail. He urges the aspiring singer to 'try the effect of protruding the lips in a funnel shape, and of bringing the inner parts close and projecting the outer margins ... also try the effect of drawing the lips tightly in, while closing them, bringing the outer margin as near the inside of the mouth as possible' (p.22). I find it difficult to visualise some of the postures Ellis describes, since I do not know whether to interpret the direction of movement as being in a horizontal or a vertical plane. However, in his description of the 'central hisses' in this volume he produces a characterisation of lip posture in /ʃ/ that is remarkably clear: 'Sometimes in England the lips are also considerably protruded for SH, being curved outwards so as to form a trumpet-bell shaped aperture. This is very marked in the command 'hush', and is so well known that the mere assumption of this position of the lips without emitting any breath, is generally understood as an order to be silent' (p.71).

Melville Bell, as far as I can see, does not consider rounding as a feature applicable to consonants. He does make a promising remark in *Visible Speech* (1867): 'the discovery that ... sounds were each susceptible of labial modification ... revealed the principle that the so-called Labial Vowels were all, in reality, compound formations in which a definite lingual quality was involved' (p.16). However, he applies the generalisation only to vowels and glides. Indeed the symbol he provides for lip-rounding also, necessarily, implies 'vowel voicing' (p.35).

There seems little point in plodding on back through time in order to rehearse the names of writers who do not describe or mention rounding on consonants in English. It is perhaps hardly surprising that there should be little interest in this in the works of earlier orthoepists, dictionary makers, and 'forgotten phoneticians' (Abercrombie 1949). They were in most cases struggling to evolve some form of transcription that would distinguish between vowel types. This was clearly a major task, besides which describing rounding on consonants must be seen to be peripheral. Even when they paid attention to consonants, what they were concerned with was a means of distinguishing /s/ from /ʃ/ rather than with detailed description. We must content ourselves with examining the history of consonant rounding as it is described over a period of only one hundred years.

The first mention I can find of consonant rounding is in Ellis (1877), where he writes of the 'trumpet-bell shaped aperture' that characterised some speakers' production of English /ʃ/. Although, for the reasons given above, I would be reluctant to claim that this feature had not existed in English prior to this time, it would be useful to consider the picture of consonant rounding as it is represented in those major works I have mentioned, from Ellis' remark in 1877 up to David Abercrombie's remark in 1967. Do we have a consistent picture of consonant rounding during this period, and, if not, why not?

We have to suppose that rounding on /ʃ/ was not confined simply to a very few speakers, or Ellis would hardly have remarked on it. On the other hand he does not consider that it is the 'norm', since he claims that it only happens 'sometimes'. This seems reasonably consistent with Sweet's 1908 remark that 'rounding on ʃ, ʒ occurs individually in English', again suggesting that rounding is far from being the norm but is not remarkably rare. However, only one year later, in 1909, Jones remarks that 'many speakers use lip-rounding' on these same consonants, and less than ten years later, in 1918, Jones is describing lip-protrusion on /ʃ, ʒ/ as being the norm and is commenting on the deviance of /ʃ/ produced with spread lips. However, Ida Ward, a further ten years later, in 1929 totally ignores this feature. Thirty years after this Gimson (1962) comments that 'with some speakers a certain amount of lip-protrusion is always present'. This suggests to me that Gimson does not view rounding on /ʃ/ as the norm, and that his position is a reversion to that described by Ellis and Sweet. However, less than ten years later Abercrombie (1967) suggests that 'most speakers' of English produce labialisation on /ʃ/.

It would be possible to suggest that rounding of consonants is subject to violent swings of fashion, now popular and 'in', now unpopular and 'out', but this seems implausible. It is more reasonable to suggest that different observers pay particular attention to different phenomena. David Hockney appositely remarks: 'When you walk into a room you don't notice everything at once and, depending on your taste, there is a descending order in which you observe things. I assume alcoholics notice the booze first, or claustrophobics the height of the ceiling, and so on' (Hockney 1976, p.92). So one obvious explanation for different observers commenting on different features is different 'tastes' or interests. We could suggest, for example, in the case of Daniel Jones that an interest in labial characteristics was forced on him from the moment he decided to illustrate his book with photographs showing the lips – although it does seem more reasonable to suppose that he decided to include the photographs because he thought that lip posture was an important and relevant feature.

A second explanation for the variability in the description of the rounding feature may lie in the speech habits of the observer himself. After all, any scholar who sits down to write a major description of an accent that he speaks himself must frequently check the statement he is making against his own pronunciation – he is his own major informant. It may well be that Ellis and Sweet belonged to that section of the received pronunciation speech community that produces little external lip movement and preserves the 'stiff upper lip' suggested by Sweet's description of the 'organic basis' of English. On the other hand, if the photographs in the *Outline of English Phonetics* are typical of Daniel Jones' pronunciation, it looks as if he was a speaker who rounded consonants.

A third explanation for the variability may lie in the sort of access the observer has to the 'speech community' whose habits he purports to describe. The nineteenth-century phoneticians seem, in general, to be anxious to establish the pedigree of their descriptions by insisting that they are describing the speech of men of high standing in the community – professors, judges and clerics. Obviously their best opportunities for detailed observation arose with their close friends and colleagues. Otherwise, we have to suppose, they observed in a fairly *ad hoc* manner the speech of the cleric in the pulpit they happened to be seated in front of, or that of the doctor who was prescribing for them. In these circumstances the visual effect of consonant rounding in the stream of speech may well only have impressed itself upon them 'sometimes' or 'individually'. If they tended to observe, in particular, the speech of older men, members of the establishment, it may well have been the case that few of them did produce much rounding. The phonetician today, with a much more catholic range of received pronunciation speakers offered daily to his observation on television, and with a much more sophisticated battery of data-collecting techniques for serious surveys, will note that women speakers in general appear to produce rounding in speech more than men, and younger speakers more than older speakers, but that in spite of these variations, most speakers do produce some consonant rounding. Despite this prevalence of consonant rounding we would still expect to find that two contemporary phoneticians, asked to comment in general on the speech of a consonant rounding speaker, would select different features of his articulation for attention because of what I shall call the 'Hockney' effect. Only if their attention were specifically drawn to the question of describing articulatory setting would we expect to find both of them paying attention to lip posture and gesture. (We may add that unless terms like 'rounding', 'compression', 'protrusion' and 'eversion' are carefully differentiated, the value of descriptions is in any case rather limited.)

Where does this leave us? We must surely conclude that it is unsafe to rely too much on a particular writer's account of what he judges important, as an indication of a change in characteristic pronunciation features over time. In the limited paradigm example of variable descriptions made within living memory that we have considered here, we find contradictory evidence. This arises from the relative importance that scholars like Jones and Gimson, the writers of the two major descriptions of English pronunciation in this century, ascribe to the feature of consonant rounding in these works. Rather than suppose that consonant rounding has diminished since Jones described it, we must surely suppose that this is simply not a feature that Gimson chooses to focus on, on this occasion. The commonsense of this view is supported by Abercrombie's comment in 1967 that $/\int/$ is labialised by 'most speakers' of English.

The variation we have observed in this study of the descriptive treatment of a feature that is phonologically redundant, but nonetheless plays a part in the characterisation of the articulatory setting of RP (and which may in future have phonological consequences: cf. Laver and Trudgill 1979) clearly shows the danger of basing an argument on what a phonetician does not describe. Such a form of argument is used by some writers to justify a particular line of historical reconstruction. The argument goes thus: A is a fine phonetician, he does not describe the phenomenon P, therefore the phenomenon P did not occur in the language he describes. I give only one example of this form of argument here:

> ... a number of scholars, notably, Dobson (1957), have suggested that when Hart ... wrote *ou* and *ei*, he is to be understood as having meant [ʌw] and [ʏy] as reflexes of ME tense /ū/ and /ī/. There is no evidence in Hart's writings for such pronunciations, *and it would seem unlikely that Hart would fail to record the absence of lip rounding in his reflex of ME /ū/* ... . (Chomsky and Halle 1968, 260; emphasis supplied)

If we can properly assume that lip-rounding is a redundant feature on back vowels in the accent being described, there seems to be no good reason why Hart should record rounding any more than a twentieth-century phonetician necessarily records rounding on consonants. The analysis preferred by Chomsky and Halle may seem attractive to some scholars on historical grounds and on the basis of what Hart does record. What I have suggested in this paper is that little weight can be attached to arguments based on what a phonetician does not describe, discuss or record.

References

ABERCROMBIE, DAVID (1949) 'Forgotten phoneticians', *TPhS 1948*, 1–34. Reprinted in Abercrombie (1965).

— (1965) *Studies in Phonetics and Linguistics*, London (Oxford University Press).

— (1967) *Elements of General Phonetics*, Edinburgh (Edinburgh University Press).

BELL, A.M. (1867) *Visible Speech: the Science of Universal Alphabetics*, London (Simpkin, Marshall & Co.).

BROWN, GILLIAN (1977) *Listening to Spoken English*, London (Longman).

CHOMSKY, N., and HALLE, M. (1968) *The Sound Pattern of English*, New York (Harper & Row).

ELLIS, A.J. (1875) *On Early English Pronunciation*, part IV (Philological Society Extra Volume) London (Asher & Co.).

— (1877) *Pronunciation for Singers*, London (J. Curwen & Sons).

— (1889) *On Early English Pronunciation*, part V (Philological Society Extra Volume), London (Trübner & Co.).

GIMSON, A.C. (1962) *An Introduction to the Pronunciation of English*, London (Edward Arnold).

HOCKNEY, DAVID (1976) *David Hockney by David Hockney*, London (Thames & Hudson).

JONES, DANIEL (1909) *The Pronunciation of English*, Cambridge (Cambridge University Press).

— (1962) *An Outline of English Phonetics*, 8th ed., Cambridge (W. Heffer & Sons).

LAVER, JOHN, and TRUDGILL, PETER (1979) 'Phonetic and linguistic markers in speech', in K.R. Scherer and H. Giles (eds.) *Social Markers in Speech*, Cambridge (Cambridge University Press) 1–32.

NEWLAND, J.C. (1906) *Voice Production and the Phonetics of Declamation*, Edinburgh & London (Oliphant, Anderson & Ferrier).

SWEET, H. (1877) *A Handbook of Phonetics*, Oxford (Clarendon Press).

— (1906) *A Primer of Phonetics*, 3rd ed., Oxford (Clarendon Press).

— (1908) *The Sounds of English*, Oxford (Clarendon Press).

WARD, IDA (1962) *The Phonetics of English*, 3rd ed., Cambridge (W. Heffer & Sons).

PART THREE

HISTORY OF IDEAS IN PHONETICS :
VOICE QUALITY AND VOICE DYNAMICS

The Analysis of Vocal Quality:
from the Classical Period to
the Twentieth Century

In the early literature of phonetics, discussion of speaker-characterising voice quality is often merged with that of paralinguistic tone of voice. This paper is an attempt to trace the history of this interest in these two areas of vocal quality, from the classical period until the beginning of the twentieth century. Indian and Arabic sources have not been included, and comment is confined mostly to Roman, British and American writers.

Classical Writings on the Voice

The explicit classification on a phonetic basis of different voice qualities and tones of voice really began only in the nineteenth century. An interest in the voice goes back, however, to a very much earlier point in time. Hunt (1858) stated that, in ancient Greece:

> The discipline for the formation and improvement of the voice among the Athenians was so comprehensive that, as we are informed by the Roman writers, not less than three different classes of teachers were employed for this purpose, viz. the *vociferarii, phonasci,* and *vocales.* The object of the first class seems to have been to strengthen the voice and extend its compass, the office of the second to improve its quality, so as to render it full, sonorous and agreeable; while the efforts of the third, who, perhaps, were considered as the finishing masters, were directed to the proper intonation and inflection. (quoted by Browne and Behnke 1884, p.8)

Stanford (1967, pp.148–9) says that:

> Besides teachers and performers, two other professional groups in ancient Greece took a special interest in vocal qualities. The physicians ... listened to them in making their diagnoses. Also the writers on 'physiognomics', the art or science of deducing character from physical qualities, had a good deal to say about the supposed relationship between certain kinds of voices and certain kinds of people. Some believed, for example, that people with deep and tense voices were brave, those with high and slack voices cowardly; if disgruntled, one that rises from low to high. If spiteful and morally lax, you are likely to speak with a nasal quality. Greedy and vain people have high, clangy voices like birds; stupid ones bleat like sheep or goats. If you hear a dry quality in someone's voice, look out – he is probably a

wily fellow. And a man's cracked or broken tone should warn you against his gluttony and violence. If he talks with pararhotacism like Alcibiades, he must be haughty, proud and hard-hearted. So, at least, the physiognomists thought.

Part of this earliest interest in voice quality sprang from the classical concern with oratory, and a useful commentary on Greek and Latin writings on oratory, including voice quality and tone of voice, is Austin's *Chironomia* (1806). Like Hunt, he refers to the different sorts of teachers concerned with the voice:

> Phonasci, Vociferarii (and) Vocales, were the common appellations of those who taught the exercise and management of the voice. Tertullian called them Edomatores Vocis. Galen says they recommended to their disciples the frequent use of the warm bath. Cresollius mentions other practices of the Phonasci, some of which are curious, and some he considers useful. (Austin 1806, p.557)

Commenting specifically on the role of the Phonascus, Austin (1806, pp.22–3) writes that:

> It was the custom for the Roman youth to recite weekly, chosen passages from the poets ... . They frequently employed ... Phonasci, whose sole business it was to regulate the modulations of the voice, to manage it by peculiar regimen, and to administer remedies when it happened to be deranged.

In a footnote to this, he quotes a passage from Cresollius' *Vacationes Autumnales*, which can be translated as follows:

> Octavius Augustus ... paid constant attention to the Phonascus, and by these efforts he achieved the object of pronouncing everything with a pleasant and characteristic sort of tone of voice. Galen, who was a very learned and intelligent man, writes of himself 'and I adopted what the Phonasci call voice exercises'. The Emperor Nero, who took great care of his voice, and gave remarkable attention to it, neither said nor attempted virtually anything without the help of a Phonascus.

(Ludovicus) Cresollius was a French Jesuit priest of the seventeenth century called Louis de Cressolles. *Vacationes Autumnales* (1620) was one of the many Jesuit books on rhetoric about that time (Sandford 1938, p.72). Austin supports this last comment by Cresollius on Nero with a quotation (Austin 1806, p.24) from chapter 26 of Suetonius' *Nero*, which is translated in the Loeb edition as:

> So far from neglecting or relaxing his practice of the art after this, he never addressed the soldiers except by letter or in a speech delivered by another, to save his voice, and he never did anything for amusement or in earnest, without a phonascus by his side to warn him to spare his vocal organs and hold a handkerchief to his mouth.

A theme running through much of classical writing on voice delivery in oratory was the avoidance of unpleasant quality. Stanford comments that:

> Another aspect of the speaking voice which the Greeks often men-
> tioned was its quality in terms of timbre and resonance. Modern
> writers variously describe unpleasant voices as 'throaty' or 'nasal' or
> 'guttural' or 'hoarse' or 'thin' or 'harsh' or 'chesty' or 'breathy' and so
> on ... . Pleasant voices are 'rich', 'vibrant', 'warm', ... The Greeks
> deployed a rich vocabulary for qualities of this kind. They especially
> disliked hollowness, coarseness, thickness, roughness, breathiness,
> throatiness, brokenness. (Stanford 1967, p.148)

A final point in Austin's *Chironomia* that is of interest illustrates this 'cosmetic' approach, as it were, to pleasant and unpleasant aspects of vocal quality. As an Appendix to his book (1806, pp.553ff.) he gives a long list of labels for vocal quality from the Greek writer Julius Pollux. Pollux was a 'professor of literature at Athens under the reign of Commodus' (Sweet 1899, p.212), in the second century A.D., the author of a work called *Onomasticon*. Austin quotes from the fourth chapter of Book 2, in the 1706 Amsterdam edition. Austin's English translations of the Greek and Latin labels listed by Pollux are as follows (only the Latin version of the original is given here). Firstly, for the 'good' qualities:

> Altam, high; excelsam, powerful; splendidam, brilliant; mundatam,
> pure; suavem, sweet; illecebrosam, attractive; exquisitam, melodious,
> cultivated; persuasibilem, persuasive; pellacem, tractabilem, engag-
> ing, tractable; flexilem, flexible; volubilem, executive; dulcem, sweet;
> stridulam, sonorous, harmonious; manifestam, distinct; perspicuam,
> perspicuous, articulate.

Secondly, for the 'bad' qualities:

> nigram, obscure; fuscam, dull; injucundam, unpleasing; exilem, pusil-
> lam, small, feeble; angustam, thin; difficilem auditu, molestam, faint;
> subsurdam, obscuram, hollow, indistinct; confusam, confused; ab-
> sonam, discordant; inconcinnam, neglectam, unharmonious, unculti-
> vated; intractabilem, unattractive, unmanageable; impersuasibilem,
> uninteresting; rigidam, rigid; asperam, harsh; distractam, cracked;
> tristem, doleful; infirmam, raucam, unsound, hoarse; aeneam, brassy;
> acutam, shrill, sharp.

Pollux' list is very unsatisfactory, and in the light of the typological labelling principles suggested in Laver (1974) can be seen to be based on no single criterion of description.

Two writers were outstanding in the classical period for analytic comment on voice quality and tone of voice. The first was Cicero, in the first
century B.C., in his two treatises *De oratore* and *Brutus*. The second was
Quintilian, in the first century A.D., in his *Institutiones oratoriae*. Of the two,
Quintilian made the more extensive and systematic comment, but it is as true
of both Quintilian and Cicero as it is of almost all writers on the subject until
the nineteenth century that they mixed, in their descriptive labelling, features

of vocal quality with features of voice dynamics such as pitch, loudness, tempo and continuity (Abercrombie 1967, pp.95–110), and with features of segmental pronunciation. Even when writers in this span of two thousand years successfully managed to isolate a feature that could reasonably be allocated to vocal quality, the labels they chose to use were most often impressionistic imitation labels (such as Cicero's use of a label like 'rough'), or were indexical labels for some physical, psychological or social attribute of the speaker to which the writer imagined the vocal quality was acting as an index (as in Quintilian's use of a label like 'effeminate').

The conflation of impressionistic description and indexical comment can be seen in the following extracts from Cicero's treatises *De oratore* and *Brutus*, (in Watson's translations, 1889):

> Any illiterate Athenian will easily surpass the most learned Asiatics, not in his language, but in sweetness of tone, not so much in speaking well as speaking agreeably. Our citizens pay less attention than the people of Latium, yet among all the people that you know in the city, who have the least tincture of literature, there is not one who would not have a manifest advantage over Quintus Valerius of Sora, the most learned of all Latins, in softness of voice, in conformation of the mouth, and in the general tone of pronunciation. (*De oratore*, Book III, c.XI)

(on Antonius) 'his voice was strong and firm, though naturally hoarse' (*Brutus*, c.XXXVIII); (on Cnaeus Pompeius) 'his voice was sonorous and manly' (*Brutus*, c.LXVIII); (on Catullus) 'his reputed purity of diction was owing chiefly to the sweetness of his voice and the delicacy of his accent' (*Brutus*, c.LXXIV). Cicero also discusses the communication of attitude and emotion in speech, in his commentary on 'tones':

> For every emotion of the mind has from nature its own peculiar look, tone, and gesture; and the whole frame of a man, and his whole countenance, and the variations of his voice, sound like strings in a musical instrument, just as they are moved by the affections of the mind. For the tones of the voice, like musical chords, are so wound up as to be responsive to every touch, sharp, flat, quick, slow, loud, gentle; and yet, among all these, each in its kind has its own middle tone. From these tones, too, are derived many other sorts, as the rough, the smooth, the contracted, the broad, the protracted, and interrupted; the broken and divided, with varieties of modulation; for there is none of these, or those that resemble them, which may not be influenced by art and management; and they are presented to the orator, as colours to the painter, to produce variety. (*De oratore*, Book III, c.LCIII)

Cicero's notion that there are certain features of communication of emotional states that are universal to all human beings, on which are superimposed modulations which are (presumably) culturally relative, recurs repeatedly in writings on the voice up to the present day.

Quintilian, in his very modern-sounding *Institutiones oratoriae*, was the first writer to try to separate features of vocal quality from those of voice dynamics. He had only partial success, but his ideas can be seen to have anticipated major distinctions drawn in the description of vocal quality in current phonetic writing. He also distinguished between a speaker's natural voice (the features arising from the speaker's individual anatomy) and the aspects of voice capable of voluntary control by the speaker (Abercrombie 1967, p.92; Laver 1968).

Quintilian's often quite phonetically-specific ideas can be seen in the following extracts from c.iii of Book xi of his *Institutiones*, (again translated by Watson, 1899):

> The first thing to be considered is *what sort of voice we have*, and the next, *how we use it*. The natural power of the voice is estimated by its *quantity* and its *quality*. Of these, the quantity is the more simple consideration, for it may be said in general that it is either *much* or *little*; but between the extremes of these quantities there are many diversities, and many gradations from the lowest tone to the highest, and from the highest to the lowest. *Quality* is more varied; for the voice is either *clear* or *husky*, *full* or *weak*, *smooth* or *rough*, of *smaller* or *larger compass*, *hard* or *flexible*, *sharp* or *flat* ....

> The general tone of the voice, however, ought to be sweet, not grating.

> In the *management of the voice* there are many particulars to be observed: for besides the three main distinctions of *acute*, *grave*, and *intermediate*, there is need of many other kinds of intonation, as the *forcible* and the *gentle*, the *higher* and the *lower*; and of *slower* or *quicker* time. But between these varieties there are other intermediate varieties: and as the face, though it consists of very few features, is infinitely diversified, so the voice, though it has very few variations that can be named, has yet a peculiar tone in each individual; and the voice of a person is as easily distinguished by the ear as the face by the eye.

It would be tempting to see in this last passage an adumbration of a componential approach to the description of vocal quality, where the 'infinite diversification' Quintilian writes of should come about by the combinations of a small number of basic components, with each component divisible into very many gradations. But it seems more likely that this diversification should properly be thought to mean the variability of the qualities of individual voices due at least in part to the involvement of the variety of anatomically derived features.

Like Pollux, mentioned earlier, Quintilian was interested in the 'cosmetic' aspects of voice production, in oratory at least:

> As to *rules for delivery*, they are precisely the same as those for

language.

For as language ought to be *correct, clear, elegant*, and *to the purpose*, so delivery will be correct, that is, free from fault, if our pronunciation be *easy, clear, agreeable* and *polished*, that is, of such a kind that nothing of the rustic or the foreign be heard in it; for the saying *Barbarum Graecumve*, that a man is 'Barbarian or Greek' is not without good foundation, since we judge of men by their tones as of money by its clink. (*Institutiones*, Book XI, c.III)

This last evocative phrase could hardly put the function of the phonetic, controllable element of vocal quality, as an index of social and psychological characteristics, more concisely. Quintilian continues his comment on 'cosmetic' qualities of the voice, saying that:

If the voice, too, be naturally, so to speak, sound, it will ... not be *dull sounding, gross, bawling, hard, stiff, inefficient, thick*, or on the contrary, *thin, weak, squeaking, small, soft, effeminate* ....

That delivery is *elegant*, which is supported by a voice that is *easy, powerful, fine, flexible, firm, sweet, well-sustained, clear, pure, that cuts the air and penetrates the ear*. (ibid.)

His discussion of cosmetic aspects leads Quintilian on to comment on indexical factors to do with the effect on the voice of various sorts of vocal abuse, and of fatigue:

The voice must not be strained beyond its natural power, for, by that means, it is often choked, and becomes less clear the greater the effort that is used; and sometimes, if urged too far, it breaks out into the sound to which the Greeks have given a name from the crowing of young cocks ....

But the good qualities of the voice, like those of all our other faculties, are improved by attention and deteriorated by neglect. The attention to be paid to the voice by orators, however, is not the same as that which is required from singing-masters; though there are many things equally necessary to both; as strength of body, for instance, that the voice may not dwindle down to the weak tone of eunuchs, women, and sick persons .... It is necessary that the throat be in good condition, that is, soft and flexible, for by any defect in it the voice may be rendered broken, husky, rough or squeaking; ... the throat, when swollen, strangles the voice, when not clear, stifles it, when dry, roughens it, and when affected by spasms, gives forth a sound like that of broken pipes ..... Too much moisture also impedes the voice, and too little weakens it. As to fatigue, it affects the voice as it affects the whole body, not for the present merely, but for sometime afterward. (*Institutiones*, Book XI, c.III)

Like Cicero, Quintilian has something to say about the function of the voice in the communication of emotional states.

The voice is the index of the mind, and has as many variations as the mind itself. Hence, in speaking on cheerful subjects, it flows in a *full* and *clear* tone, and is itself, as it were, *cheerful*; in argument, it arouses itself with its full force, and strains, so to speak, every nerve; in anger, it is fierce, rough, thick .... (ibid.)

Voice Quality and Paralinguistic Description of Tone of Voice

We see thus that phonetic, controllable aspects of speech were of interest to Cicero and Quintilian in their paralinguistic function of acting as 'affective indices' (Abercrombie 1967, p.9) to a speaker's ostensible emotional state as expressed in his tone of voice. This clearly derives directly from their concern with spoken delivery as an art that can be cultivated, and we shall find that comments on voice quality are often found embedded in a discussion of paralinguistic uses of the voice. There are two facets here that are of immediate interest.

The first is that the description of paralinguistic features making up tone of voice is almost always relevant to the description of phonetic voice quality features, because the main difference between vocal paralinguistic features and voice quality's phonetic component is the time scale involved and not so much the identity of the features used (Laver 1980). Paralinguistic features are used on a relatively ephemeral medium-term basis, while the same features, when used as phonetic components in voice quality are quasi-permanent. The way that different writers in the history of phonetics go about the business of constructing a descriptive vocabulary for handling paralinguistic features is thus interesting to a study of voice quality precisely because many of the same phenomena are involved in the two areas.

The second facet is that analytic decisions about which phonic events of vocal quality should be deemed linguistically-relevant in a particular accent, which paralinguistically-relevant to tone of voice, and which relevant to person-characterising voice quality, cannot be taken in isolation. All three strands have to be considered together, and a decision about any one of them has immediate reciprocal implications for the other two. While analytic schemes for describing the phonetic substance of linguistic units are thoroughly well established, the same cannot be said for the substance of paralinguistic units; we have an opportunity here to see the description of voice quality against the background of emerging systems for the description of spoken paralanguage.

There is one further qualification that needs to be made before coming to the work of the early British phoneticians: that is, many writers from the time of Wallis (1653) to the present day comment specifically on the hypothesised long-term articulatory settings (Honikman 1964) of the vocal apparatus that they held to characterise the phonetic aspects of different languages. The concept of an articulatory setting is so central to a phonetic approach to describing voice quality that the account of the historical development of the concept deserves a separate presentation. This can be found in Laver (1978).

Leaving detailed discussion of language-characterising settings aside, this paper will be concerned with two other broad aspects of the history of the analysis of vocal quality. We shall trace the development of the various comprehensive schemes for classifying voice quality on a general, componential basis, which begin to appear in the nineteenth century; and we shall try to follow a number of threads of development in the earlier, less systematic observations on voice quality and paralinguistic features that are scattered through the phonetic literature.

Early British Writings on the Voice

The first systematic commentary on vocal quality in early British works appeared early in the eighteenth century, when Maittaire (1712) wrote about the phonetic, controllable aspects of voice quality and voice dynamics, in a passage which, without acknowledgment, is mostly an extension of some of Quintilian's comments quoted above:

> THE VOICE Two things in it are carefully to be observed; what voice you have, and how to use it.
>
> It may be, as to its Quantity, Great or Small.
>
> As to its Quality, Clear or Thick, Full or Slender, Soft or Harsh, Contracted or Spread, Hard or Easy to be managed, Sharp or Blunt.
>
> The Breath is either Long or Short.
>
> The Good Qualities, as of all other things, so of the Voice are bettered with Care, and impaired through Negligence. Frequent Exercise, Temperance and Frugality conduce much to their improvement.
>
> ... Tis a fault of the voice to be too much stretched or rowling: the mouth is best, when it is Ready, no Precipitate; Moderate, not Slow.
>
> ... Nothing can be worse than a Tone or Cant. A true Pronunciation is ever suited to what we speak. The Affections are either Real and Natural, which need no Art: or else Feigned and Put on; and in these the great Art is to be first moved with them, as if they were Real; then the Voice, as a faithful Interpreter of the Mind, will convey what impressions it has received from our Soul, into those of the Judges or Auditors. It is capable of as many Changes as our Minds; Easy in Chearful Matters; Erect and Firm, when we strive as for the Mastery; Fierce, Harsh and Thick in Anger; Soft, in Begging; Grave, in Persuading; Short, in Fear; Strong, in Exhortation or Narration, Even, between Acute and Grave; in short, it Riseth or Falleth, as the Affections are Raised or Composed. (Maittaire 1712, pp.239–40)

Maittaire also includes an interesting comment on facial expression in speech: 'Small is the motion of the Nostrils and Lips, unless in Scorn and Contempt. We ought always to speak more with the Mouth than the Lips' (ibid., p.241).

An important work in the eighteenth century was Mason's (1748) *Essay on Elocution*. According to R.C. Alston, the *Essay*

> has a particular historical significance because it represents a renewed interest in a neglected art. The interest in pronunciation which is so characteristic of writers on English in the second half of the eighteenth century, and finds expression in numerous treatises on pronunciation and elocution as well as in dictionaries of English, can be traced back to sixteenth century manuals of pulpit oratory, but the movement which was to reach fruition in the works of writers such as Sheridan and Walker has its origins in a complex coincidence of interests: among which are the improvement of dramatic speech (to which Garrick contributed so effectively) and parliamentary debate; the public recitation of poetry; and a concern to 'fix' pronunciation and formulate a universal standard. Mason's *Essay* thus appears at the beginning of an important movement. (Alston, in editorial note to facsimile reprint (1968) of Mason (1748))

Although Mason shared 'a concern to fix pronunciation and formulate a universal standard', and contributed some impetus to the movement Alston describes, he can also be seen as continuing a long-established tradition of an interest in prescriptive cosmetic aspects of voice, started in the classical period and notable in the works of Cicero and Quintilian. Alston acknowledges this, and says that the *Essay*'s

> immediate significance can be seen as related to the re-appraisal of the great classical treatises on oratory by Longinus, Cicero and Quintilian. William Smith's translation of Longinus (1739) was to be reprinted numerous times between 1740 and 1800; William Guthrie's translation of Cicero's *De oratore* appeared in 1742 ... and his translation of Quintilian followed in 1756 ....

> Mason's *Essay* was reprinted in the same year as the first edition, and again in 1751, 1757, 1761 and 1787. (Alston, ibid.)

Mason himself was quite explicit about the value of classical writings:

> Those who desire to be more particularly acquainted with this Subject, and with the several other Branches of Oratory, I would advise not to trust altogether to the Rules of Modern Writers, but to repair to the Fountain Head; and converse with the great Masters and Teachers of this Art among the Antients; particularly, Dionysius of Halicarnassus, Cicero, Quintilian, and Longinus. (Mason 1748, p.39)

It may be necessary to mention here that while Cicero and Quintilian wrote at some length on aspects of spoken delivery relevant to vocal quality, neither Dionysius of Halicarnassus nor Longinus gave it any particular attention. Mason begins with some sensible comments on using a conversational tone of voice in public speaking and reading aloud:

> To avoid all kinds of unnatural and disagreeable Tones, the only Rule

is to endeavour to speak with the same Ease and Freedom as you would do on the same Subject in private Conversation. You hear no body converse in a Tone; unless they have the Brogue of some other Country, or have got into a Habit (as some have) of altering the natural Key of their Voice when they are talking of some serious Subject in Religion. But I can see no Reason in the World, that when in common Conversation we speak in a natural Voice with proper Accent and Emphasis, yet as soon as we begin to read, or talk of Religion, or speak in Publick, we should immediately assume a stiff, awkward, unnatural Tone. If we are indeed deeply affected with the Subject we read or talk of, the Voice will naturally vary according to the Passion excited; but if we vary it unnaturally, only to seem affected, or with a Design to affect others, it then becomes a Tone and is offensive. (Mason 1748, pp.17–18)

The notion of a 'Tone', although rather vague, was widespread in writings on elocution in the eighteenth century. Very often, it seems to be used in the same way that we use the term today in phrases like 'tone of voice'; that is, as a cover term for a wide variety of phonetic phenomena used as paralinguistic cues for conveying emotional information. But there is also a tendency to use 'Tone' to refer to paralinguistic behaviour that the writer condemns as insincere or inappropriate for the particular situation, as in the last sentence of the passage quoted from Mason immediately above. Appropriateness of vocal cues to the speaker's emotional state seems often to be judged on the basis of an imagined iconic resemblance between the vocal behaviour and the mental state to which it is taken to be acting as an index. This may be seen in the following passage from Mason (1748):

The Voice must express, as near as may be, the very Sense or Idea designed to be conveyed by the emphatical word; by a strong, rough and violent, or a soft, smooth, and tender Sound.

Thus the different Passions of the Mind are to be expressed by a different Sound or Tone of Voice. *Love*, by a soft, smooth, languishing Voice; *Anger*, by a strong, vehement, and elevated Voice; *Joy*, by a quick, sweet, and clear Voice; *Fear*, by a dejected, tremulous, hesitating Voice; *Courage*, hath a full, bold, and loud Voice; and *Perplexity*, a grave, steady, and earnest one. Briefly, in *Exordiums* the Voice should be low; in *Narrations*, distinct; in *Reasoning*, slow; in *Perswasions*, strong: it should thunder in *Anger*, soften in *Sorrow*, tremble in *Fear*, and melt in *Love*. (Mason 1748, pp.25–6)

This attribution of indexical characteristics of the speaker to the speaker's voice is easily understandable if we remember the very strong influence on writers such as Mason of Quintilian (see pp. 84–5).

Mason also mentions one specific type of inappropriate use of a 'Tone':

It is false Oratory ... to seek to perswade or affect by mere Vehemence of Voice. A Thing that hath been often attempted by Men of mean

Furniture, low Genius, or bad Taste, among the Antients as well as the Moderns. A Practice which formerly gave the judicious *Quintilian* great Offence: Who calls it not only clamouring, but *furious Bellowing*; not Vehemence, but downright *Violence*.

Besides, an overstrained Voice is very inconvenient to the *Speaker*, as well as disgusting to judicious Hearers. It exhausts his Spirits to no Purpose. And takes from him the proper Management and Modulation of his Voice according to the Sense of his Subject. And, what is worst of all, it naturally leads him into a Tone. (Mason 1748, pp.7–8)

Bayly (1758), in a phonetically sophisticated book, discusses 'tones', and distinguishes clearly between anatomically-derived and phonetic, controllable features of the voice:

The voice itself is indeed a gift of nature; but with respect to the tone it is extremely in the power of affectation, or ill habit to hurt it, and of art to improve it. The most remarkable ill tones are perhaps such as arise from what is called speaking through the nose and in the throat. Of guttural tones there is great variety. Some are like the bleating of a sheep, or noise of a raven; some resemble the croaking of a frog, and quacking of a duck: All which seem to be owing to some trick of compressing the wind pipe in such a manner as to confine the tone in the throat instead of letting it pass freely out. The voice is also often hurt by another trick; that of shutting the teeth, and confining the tone within the mouth instead of opening the teeth and lips properly so as to bring it out with fulness and rotundity. (Bayly 1758, pt.3, pp.180–1)

Thomas Sheridan (1762) follows Cicero in asserting the universality of vocal means for communicating strong emotions, and he distinguishes very clearly between language and 'tones':

Every one will at once acknowledge that the terms anger, fear, love, hatred, pity, grief, will not excite in him the sensations of those passions, and make him angry or afraid, compassionate or grieved; nor, should a man declare himself to be under the influence of any of these passions, in the most explicit and strong words that the language can afford, would he in the least affect us, or gain any credit, if he used no other signs but words. If any one should say in the same tone of voice that he uses in delivering indifferent propositions from a cool understanding, 'Sure never any mortal was so overwhelmed with grief as I am at this present' .... Sure, no one would feel any pity for the distress of the [speaker] .... We should either believe that he jested, or if he would be thought serious, we should be moved to laughter at his absurdity. And why is this? But because he makes use of words only, as the signs of emotion, which it is impossible they can represent; and omits the use of the true signs of the passions, which are the tones,

89

looks and gestures.

This will serve to shew us that the language or sensible marks by which the emotions of the mind are discovered, and communicated from man to man, are entirely different from words, and independent of them ... the language of the animal passions of man ... should be fixed, self-evident, and universally intelligible. (Sheridan 1762, pp.100–2)

In 1781, Sheridan gets closer to a modern conception of the coded, arbitrary nature of paralinguistic features, while still maintaining the universality of affective indices to the most basic emotional states:

Tones may be divided into two kinds; natural, and instituted. The natural, are such as belong to the passions of man in his animal state; which are implanted in his frame, by the hand of nature; and which spontaneously break forth, whenever he is under the influence of any of these passions. These form a universal language, equally used by all the different nations of the world, and equally understood and felt by all. Thus, the tones expressive of sorrow, lamentation, mirth, joy, hatred, anger, love, pity, etc. are the same in all countries, and excite emotions in us analogous to those passions, when accompanying words which we do not understand.

The instituted tones, are those which are settled by compact, to mark the different operations, exertions, and emotions of the intellect and fancy, in producing their ideas; and these in a great measure differ, in different countries, as the languages do.

The former of these, it is evident, neither require study nor pains, when we are ourselves under the influence of any of those passions, as they are necessarily produced by them; ....

With respect to the latter, it will require great pains, and much observation, to become master of them. (Sheridan 1781, pp.120–1)

Nowadays, we would prefer to believe that many of his 'natural tones' are more culturally relative, more 'instituted' than Sheridan suggests, but he puts the distinction between 'natural' and 'instituted' elements in the communication of attitude and emotion very succinctly.

Fenning (1771, pp.180–1), without acknowledgement, copies Mason (1748, pp.25–6) in the passage quoted above ('Love [is expressed] by a soft, smooth, languishing Voice', etc.), for which Fenning has 'Love is expressed by a soft, smooth, languishing tone', and so on.

Herries, in his book *The Elements of Speech* (1773) makes some of the most perceptive and phonetically interesting comments on vocal quality to be found before the nineteenth century. He writes, for example, that

Others, who are not accustomed to expel their breath with the same freedom through the nostrils as through the mouth, pronounce the three nasals m, n, and ng, very imperfectly, which produces that dull disagreeable sound, which we call sneveling or SPEAKING THROUGH

THE NOSE. The latter term is entirely wrong, because it is the defect of NOT speaking thro' the nose which occasions that impropriety in articulation. Sometimes this habit arises from an excess in taking snuff, which ought always to be avoided by a publick speaker or singer. (Herries 1773, pp.55–6)

Herries also has a nice comment on a particular type of voice used in public speaking:

Many of our public speakers have had their powers of utterance enervated and restrained in their younger years. At home and at school they have been put under a false REGIMEN. They perhaps have been told 'that it was not PRETTY, it was not genteel to breathe too strongly, to roar out the words, and bellow like a clown; it was quite vulgar, it grated their ears, it was enough to fright a person'. The young gentleman takes the hint. He begins to speak FINE. He minces out his words, and warbles his modulations like an Italian singer. What is the consequence? His voice as he grows up retains the same unmanly quality. He dare not, he cannot exert it. He speaks upon the most important, the most alarming subjects, with the delicate tone of a waiting-gentlewoman.

Let this effeminate mode of education be banished from our land. (Herries 1773, pp.99–100)

This theme is continued, in a discussion about the function of the voice as an indexical clue to physical features such as a speaker's physique, and the possibility of drawing wrong indexical conclusions:

Do we not often behold men of the most robust habit of body, speaking in public, with such a weak, puerile voice, that if we were to trust to the testimony of our ears alone, we should conclude that their constitution was quite enfeebled and decayed. From hence we may infer, that a strong BODY is not always accompanied with a strong VOICE. (Herries 1773, p.106)

Finally, Herries discusses some details of the inter-relationship of factors of pitch with those of vocal quality:

The true criterion of just speaking is, when each of the articulate sounds is uttered forcibly and distinctly. But we find that whenever we go beyond our natural pitch, we lose the command of articulation. Our tones are weak, shrill, and broken. Every excess of passion has a tendency to straiten the glottis, and render the voice more acute. This we may observe in the sharp, hurrying voice of anger, the plaintive wailings of grief, the clear-gliding warblings of joy. If, therefore, a public speaker is deeply animated with his subject, his voice insensibly ascends, and sometimes is carried to such a pitch that he loses all command of it. Cicero informs us, that when Gracchus, an eminent pleader at Rome, was in the vehement parts of his discourse, his voice became too high and squeaking. To remedy this inconvenience, he placed a servant behind him, with a pitch-pipe in his hand, who, at such a time, sounded a note in unison with the medium of his voice, on which he immediately descended to his usual sweetness. (Herries 1773, p.152)

It may be of interest here to note that James Rush, who was a major figure in the later history of analysis of vocal quality, was very scathing about this anecdote, and about classical writings generally. In his characteristically jaundiced and irascible tone he wrote that:

If one should be disposed to believe in the vocal perfection of the Greeks, through any other than their own testimony, he might well question the authority of their Roman eulogists: since they themselves, the pupils of the Greeks, display no better analysis and system in their institute of elocution. We may fairly estimate their discrimination, when with the same pen that deals out the extravagancies of praise upon the oratorical action of their masters, they gravely give us, as proof of their own nicety in vocal matters, the story of one of their famous orators having occasion for a Pitch-pipe, to enable him to recognize his own voice, and affectedly to govern his melody, through the more acute perceptions of a slave, who now and then blew this little regulating trumpet at his elbow!! (Rush 1859, p.675n (5th edition of *Philosophy of the Human Voice* (1827))

Writings on Vocal Quality
in the Nineteenth Century

In the nineteenth century, attempts at explicit, general componential schemes for describing voice quality begin to appear. Interest in the subject of delivery, and of tone of voice was also still maintained (particularly in America). We have noted Austin's *Chironomia* (1806). Although this had only one British edition, and no American edition, Haberman (1954, pp.117–18) says:

it exerted an enormous influence upon elocutionists. In England, A.M. Hartley called it 'incomparably the ablest treatise on delivery in general that has yet appeared in our language'. In America, a lot of writers, among them Caldwell, Bronson, Bacon, Fulton and Trueblood, and, as late as 1916, Joseph A. Mosher, were indebted to this extraordinary book.

This is to overestimate its value, but it gives us an idea of the general interest during the nineteenth century in the voice.

In Britain during this time, Willis (1829) wrote that 'Thus we say that a man has a clear voice, a nasal voice, a thick voice ...', and by Sweet's time, attempts to set up a voice quality classification on a phonetic basis were becoming frequent (in America, at least), although none of them began to approach any degree of comprehensiveness. Sweet (1877, pp.97–9) distinguished between 'clear', 'dull', 'harsh' and 'nasal' qualities, and expanded this list in his *Primer of Phonetics* (1890b, p.69), to the following set of qualities: 'clear quality', 'dull quality', 'nasality', 'wheeziness' and 'gutturality'. Sweet was probably the first writer to assert quite explicitly that vocal quality is susceptible of systematic componential description, when he wrote that 'besides the various modifications of stress, tones, etc., the quality of the voice may be modified through whole sentences by various glottal, pharyngeal and oral influences' (1877, p.97). This position was re-asserted in *The History of Language* (1900, p.136), when he wrote 'the general quality of the voice is likely to be modified by changes in the shape of the throat and mouth passages, which give rise to the various qualities of voice known as clear, dull, muffled, nasal, wheezing, strangled voice'. He also drew a clear distinction between anatomically derived features of the voice and controllable, phonetic modifications, when he wrote that modifications of voice quality

> must be carefully distinguished from those which are due to peculiarities in the organs of speech themselves. Thus defects in the palate may cause permanent nasality (together with a peculiar hollowness of sound), an abnormally large tongue, gutturality, etc. All of these peculiarities are inseparable from the individual. (1877, p.99)

It is perhaps a little surprising that Sweet stopped short, in considering anatomically derived aspects of the voice, at those that arise from some abnormal anatomical factor, and did not go on to the logical conclusion that nearly *all* speakers can be distinguished on the basis of differences of organic anatomy even within the range of whatever might be considered normal variations of anatomy.

The interests of vocal quality classification in the nineteenth century were probably most advanced by the efforts of the American elocutionists. The first and most influential of these was James Rush. Son of one of the signers of the Declaration of Independence, Dr Benjamin Rush, James Rush was a physician who was educated at Princeton and at the University of Pennsylvania, where he was awarded his M.D. degree. He then spent a year at the University of Edinburgh in 1810, as a student of Moral Philosophy under the Scottish philosopher Dugald Stewart. It was during the year he spent in Edinburgh that he became interested in the writings of Bacon (Gray 1943), and from then on put great emphasis, following Bacon, on the value of objective scientific observations, which had its influence on his approach to the description of speech.

In 1827, he published the first of six editions of *The Philosophy of the Human Voice*. Hale (1954 p.226) comments that 'In publishing a vocal philosophy which gave a physiological foundation and explanation of vocal theory, Rush gave an entirely new and different emphasis to the study and teaching of speech'. (By 'the study and teaching of speech' Hale is referring to the American tradition of interest in rhetoric and elocution.)

Rush gives an extensive commentary on the description of vocal quality. He deserves to be considered in some detail; the quotations given below are taken from the enlarged fifth edition published in 1859. Early in his book he gives a very clear enunciation of one of the most basic characteristics of phonetic analysis:

> A description of the different modes and forms of sound in the human voice, without exemplification by actual utterance, is always insufficient and often unintelligible. With a view to facilitate instruction, it is desirable to discover the mechanical movements of the organs, together with action of the air upon them; that a reference to conformations and changes of the organs, and to the impulses of the air, may enable an observer to exemplify to himself, the description of vocal sounds, by using the known physical means which produce them. (Rush 1859, p.131)

Rush begins with his divisions of 'vocal sound':

> All the constituents of the human voice, may be referred to the five following Modes: Quality, Force, Time, Abruptness, Pitch. The details of these five modes, and of the multiplied combination of their several forms, degrees, and varieties, includes the enumeration of all the Articulation and the Expressive powers of speech. (Rush 1859, p.67)

The first mention of vocal qualities states that

> The thirty-five elements of speech may be heard under four different kinds of voice; the Natural, the Falsette [sic], the Whispering, and that improved quality, to be presently described under the name of the Orotund (Rush 1859, p.138).

He discusses the 'natural' voice in these terms:

> The natural voice is said to be produced by the vibration of the glottis. This has been inferred, from a supposed analogy between the action of the human organ, and that of the dog, in which the vibration has been observed, and on exposing the glottis during the cries of the animal; and from the vibration of the chords, by blowing through the human larynx, when removed from the body. The conclusion is therefore probable, but until it is seen in the living function of the part, or until there is sufficient approximation to this proof by other means, it cannot be admitted as a portion of exact physiological science. (Rush 1859, p.139)

It is a little surprising that Rush, by 1859, had not heard of Manuel Garcia's success with a dental mirror as a laryngoscope in seeing the vocal folds in action, reported in 1854.

'Falsette' is described as follows:

> The Falsette is a peculiar voice, in the higher degrees of pitch, beginning where the natural voice breaks, or outruns its compass. The piercing cry, the scream, and the yell are various forms of the falsette .... The striking difference in quality, between the natural and the falsette voices, has created the idea of a difference in the respective

94

mechanisms, not only of their kind of sound, but likewise of their pitch. It has been supposed, that the falsette is produced at the 'upper orifice of the larynx, formed by the summits of the arytenoid cartilages and the epiglottis' (Dodart): and the difficulty of joining it to the natural voice, which is thought to be made by the inferior ligaments of the glottis, is ascribed to the change of mechanism in the transition. On this point I have only to add that the falsette ... may be brought downward in pitch, nearly to the lowest degree of the natural voice; ... and since the natural voice may by cultivation be carried above the point it instinctively reaches, it suggests the inquiry, whether these voices may have a different agency of mechanism [rather than by] an extension of the powers of the same organization. (Rush 1859, p.142)

Rush starts his discussion of 'Whispering' by saying that 'The Whispering voice is well known', but goes on to declare that

We are not acquainted with the mechanical cause of *whisper*, as distinguished from *vocality*. It has been ascribed to the operation of a current of air on the sides of the glottis, while its cords are at rest; whereas vocality is said to proceed from the agitation of the air by the vibration of those cords. This however is merely an inference from analogy, and has a claim to possibility, but no more. (Rush 1859, p.146)

A longer section is devoted to the description of 'Orotund' voice:

The voice now to be described, is not perhaps in its mechanism, different from the natural; but it is rather to be regarded as an eminent degree of fulness, clearness and smoothness in quality; and this may be either native or acquired.

The limited analysis, the vague history of speech by the ancients, and the further confusion of the subject by commentators upon them, leave us in doubt whether the Latin phrase, 'os rotundum'; used more to our purpose in its ablative, 'ore rotundo', by Horace, in complimenting Grecian eloquence; referred to the construction of periods, the predominance or position of vowels, or to quality of voice. Whatever may have been the original signification of the phrase, the English term 'roundness of tone', specifying as we may suppose the kind of quality, seems to have been derived from it. (Rush 1859, p.151)

Rush goes on to give a specification of what he meant by 'orotund' voice, although he concedes that he knows 'how difficult it is to make such descriptions definite, without audible illustration' (p.152). He writes:

On the basis of the Latin phrase, I have constructed the term Orotund; to designate that assemblage of attributes which constitutes the highest character of the speaking voice.

By the Orotund, or adjectively, the Orotund voice, I mean a natural, or improved manner of uttering the elements with a fulness, clearness, strength, smoothness, and if I may make the word a sub-sonorous quality; rarely heard in ordinary speech, and never found in its highest excellence, except through long and careful cultivation.

By Fulness of voice, I mean a grave and hollow volume, resembling the hoarseness of a common *cold.*

By Clearness, a freedom from aspiration, nasality, and vocal murmur.

By Strength, a satisfactory loudness or audibility.

By Smoothness, a freedom from all reedy or guttural harshness.

By a Sub-sonorous quality, its muffled resemblance to the reson-ance of certain musical instruments. (Rush 1859, p.151)

By 'vocal murmur', Rush meant 'an obscuring accompaniment of sound, as if the whole of the voice had not been *made-up* into articulation. It is not an unfrequent cause of indistinctness in speakers' (Rush, ibid.). He also had this to say about his use of the phrase 'guttural harshness':

There is a harsh quality of voice called Guttural; produced by a vibratory current of the air, between the sides of the pharynx and the base of the tongue, when apparently brought into contact above the glottis. If then the term 'voice from the throat' which has been one of the unmeaning or indefinite designations of vocal science, were ap-plied to this guttural quality, it would precisely assign a locality to the mechanism. (Rush 1859, p.153)

It *is* very difficult to know what he meant, in the absence of an audible demonstration, particularly when many of the aspects of orotund voice that he specifies are only the absence of another quality of the voice (aspiration, nasality, vocal murmur, reedy or guttural harshness). There is also the diffi-culty that two of the factors he prescribes seem to be mutually contradictory – 'a satisfactory loudness' and a 'muffled resemblance to the resonance of certain musical instruments'.

There is, however, one possibility of establishing what it was that Rush meant by labels such as 'Orotund voice'. I have quoted Rush at some length because of the remarkable influence he exercised on the field of elocution. Nearly all the terminologies for the description of voice quality published by American elocutionists for a hundred years after the first appearance of his *Philosophy of the Human Voice* in 1827, up to and including Woolbert (1927), were based on that of Rush. It would be possible, in principle, to elucidate the meaning of some of Rush's terms, if a reasonably detailed continuity of influence could be established from Rush to writers in the twentieth century. It would be too sanguine to hope for more than the most approximate hint of Rush's conceptualisation, but a continuity of teaching and influence *can* be shown. The following discussion is based in part on two interesting review articles about the history of American elocution in the nineteenth century by Gray (1943), and Robb (1954).

William Russell was the first editor of the *American Journal of Education*, from 1826. He was a prolific writer, and of his thirty books sixteen were concerned with elocution. He was a contemporary of Rush, and strongly influenced by him as well as by Austin's *Chironomia* of 1806 (Robb 1954, pp.187–8). With Goldsbury, Russell wrote an American School Reader (1844), in which the following labels were applied to voice qualities: 'harsh', 'smooth', 'aspirated' (whispery or breathy voice), 'pectoral', 'guttural', 'oral', 'orotund', and 'pure tone'. They have no specific label for Rush's 'natural' quality, and do not mention his 'falsette' quality.

Russell founded the School of Practical Rhetoric and Oratory in 1844, with James Murdoch, a well-known actor who had been taught the principles underlying the *Philosophy of the Human Voice* by Rush himself. Robb (1954, p.189) describes Murdoch as 'a leader in the elocutionary movement for fifty years'.

Murdoch and Russell collaborated to produce *Orthophony, or Vocal Culture in Elocution* (1845), which was phenomenally successful, having eighty-four impressions by 1882. They give four basic qualities: 'Whispering', 'Pure Tone', 'Orotund' and 'Aspirated'. In a 'cosmetic' approach, they list various potential faults in quality, such as 'the hollow and false pectoral murmur', 'the aspirate', 'the nasal' and 'the oral' (presumably meaning de-nasal voice). Again, they do not include 'falsette'.

Hamill was a student of Murdoch, and in 1882 published his *Science of Elocution*. In this he lists 'Pure Tone', 'Orotund', 'Aspirate', 'Pectoral', 'Guttural', 'Oral' and 'Nasal'. In the 1886 edition, he added 'Falsetto' [sic].

Fulton and Trueblood (mentioned earlier as having been influenced by Austin's *Chironomia* of 1806), studied under both Murdoch and Hamill, and in 1893 published *Practical Elocution*. They listed 'Normal', 'Orotund', 'Oral', 'Aspirate', 'Guttural', 'Pectoral', 'Nasal', and 'Falsetto' qualities. One of the most interesting aspects of their work is that they chose to call one of their qualities 'Normal', and said that 'the Normal is the natural basis upon which all the other qualities rest, each of which is some modification of or variation from the Normal' (Fulton and Trueblood 1893, p.41).

Finally, Woolbert (1927) is the last writer to be considered here in the continuous succession from Rush, studying under Trueblood. Woolbert is the link with American 'speech science' of the twentieth century, and begins to move towards an acoustic specification, very speculatively and impre-cisely, of the qualities he suggests. 'Orotund' is the 'All-round Resonance', 'Pectoral' the 'Chest Resonance', and 'Guttural' the 'Throat Resonance'. He mentions the term 'Falsetto', but without any acoustic description.

It would be pleasant to be able to demonstrate that the evolution of the descriptive system that had its genetic origin in the work of Rush in 1827 had produced a competent and comprehensive structure by the time Woolbert made his contribution in 1927, a century later. Unfortunately, it has to be said that Woolbert's attribution of particular qualities to principal locations where 'resonance' takes place is not a major improvement on the 'metaphorical' system that Rush himself castigates in his discussion of 'that improved quality of the singing-voice, called by vocalists "Pure Tone"'. Rush wrote that

> there are several terms used to describe the mechanical causes of its different characters and qualities. Among these, the causations implied by the phrases 'voce di testa', and 'voce di petto', or the voice from the head, and from the chest, must be considered as not yet manifest in physiology; and the notions conveyed by them must be hung up beside those metaphorical pictures, which with their characteristic dimness or misrepresentation have been in all ages, substituted for the unattainable delineations of the real processes of nature. (Rush 1859, p.153)

This is perhaps a little harsh as a judgment on Woolbert. The main point to be made here is that enough of Rush's system is visible in Woolbert's work – and more particularly in that of Fulton and Trueblood (1893) – to demonstrate a continuity of teaching and influence spanning the century between Rush and Woolbert. Some hint also emerges from the later writers of what Rush was referring to by his descriptive terms. The chief significance of Rush's work of course extends well beyond the analysis of vocal quality as such: its importance lies, as Hale suggested (1954, p.226) in the insistence he placed on a physiological foundation for the study of speech.

Conclusion

In his article (1949) on 'Forgotten Phoneticians', complementing Firth's (1947) paper on 'The English School of Phonetics', David Abercrombie wrote that 'our antecedents are older and better than we think'. In even this cursory exploration of aspects of vocal quality in the literature on speech, it becomes very clear that modern phonetics has much to gain from the insights offered by our predecessors.

References

ABERCROMBIE, D. (1949) 'Forgotten phoneticians', *TPhS 1948*, 1–34.
— (1967) *Elements of General Phonetics*, Edinburgh (Edinburgh University Press).
ALSTON, R.C. (1968) Editorial 'Note' to facsimile reprint of Mason (1748).
AUSTIN, G. (1806) *Chironomia: or a Treatise on Rhetorical Delivery*, London (T. Cadell and W. Davies).
BAYLY, A. (1758) *An Introduction to Languages, Literary and Philosophical, especially to the English, Latin, Greek and Hebrew*, London (J. and J. Rivington, J. Fletcher, P. Vaillant, R. and J. Dodsley).
BROWNE, L. and E. BEHNKE (1884) *Voice, Song and Speech*, London (Sampson Low, Marston), New York (G.P. Putnam's Sons).
CICERO *Brutus*, trans. J.S. WATSON (1889) London (George Bell and Sons).
— *De oratore*, trans. J.S. WATSON (1889) London (George Bell and Sons).
FENNING, D. (1771) *A New Grammar of the English Language*, London.
FIRTH, J.R. (1947) 'The English School of Phonetics', *TPhS 1946*, 92–132.

FULTON, R. and TRUEBLOOD, T. (1893) *Practical Elements of Elocution*, Boston (Ginn).

GOLDSBURY, J., and RUSSELL, W. (1844) *The American Common-School Reader and Speaker*, Boston (Tappan and Whitmore).

GRAY, G.W. (1943) 'The "voice qualities" in the history of elocution', *Q.J. Speech* 29.

HABERMAN, F.W. (1954) 'English sources of American elocution', in K.R. Wallace (ed.) *History of Speech Education in America*, New York, (Appleton-Century-Crofts) 105–26.

HALE, L.L. (1954) 'Dr. James Rush', in K.R. Wallace (ed.) *History of Speech Education in America*, New York (Appleton-Century-Crofts) 219–37.

HAMILL, S. (1882) *The Science of Elocution*, New York (Phillips and Hunt).

HERRIES, J. (1773) *The Elements of Speech*, London (E. and C. Dilly).

HONIKMAN, B. (1964) 'Articulatory settings', in Abercrombie et al. (eds.) *In Honour of Daniel Jones*, London (Longmans) 73–84.

HUNT, J. (1858) *Philosophy of Voice and Speech*, London (Longman, Browne).

LAVER, J. (1968) 'Voice quality and indexical information', *Br. J. Disorders Comm.* 3, 43–54.

— (1974) 'Labels for voices', *J. Int. Phonetic Ass.* 4, 62–75.

— (1976) 'Language and nonverbal communication', in E.C. Carterette and M.P. Friedman (eds.), *Handbook of Perception*, New York (Academic Press) vol. VII, pp.345–62.

— (1978) 'The concept of articulatory settings: an historical survey', *Historiographia Linguistica* 5, 1–14.

— (1980) *The Phonetic Description of Voice Quality*, Cambridge Studies in Linguistics 31, London (Cambridge University Press).

MAITTAIRE, M. (1712) *The English Grammar*, London (H. Clements).

MASON, J. (1748) *An Essay on Elocution, or Pronunciation*, London (M. Cooper); facsimile reprint, Scolar Press, London 1968.

POLLUX, J. *Onomasticon*, Amsterdam edition 1706.

QUINTILIAN *Institutiones oratoriae*, J.S. Watson (1899) *Quintilian's Institutes of Oratory, or, Education of an Orator*, London (George Bell and Sons).

ROBB, M.M. (1954) 'The elocutionary movement and its chief figures', in K.R. Wallace (ed.) *History of Speech Education in America*, New York (Appleton-Century-Crofts) 178–201.

RUSH, J. (1827) *The Philosophy of the Human Voice*, Philadelphia (Griggs and Elliot); 5th ed. B. Lippincott, Philadelphia 1859.

RUSSELL, W. and MURDOCH, J.E.)1845) *Orthophony or Vocal Culture in Elocution*, Boston (Ticknor).

SANDFORD, W.P. (1938) *English Theories of Public Address, 1530–1828*, Columbus, Ohio (H.L. Hedrick).

SHERIDAN, T. (1762) *A Course of Lectures on Elocution*, London.

— (1781) *A Rhetorical Grammar of the English Language*, Dublin.

STANFORD, W.B. (1967) *The Sound of Greek*, Berkeley and Los Angeles (University of California Press).

SWEET, H. (1877) *Handbook of Phonetics*, Oxford (Clarendon Press).

— (1890) *A Primer of Phonetics*, Oxford (Clarendon Press); 3rd ed., rev., 1906.

— (1899) *The Practical Study of Languages*, London (Dent).

— (1900) *The History Language*, London (Dent).

WALLIS, J. (1653) *Grammatica linguae Anglicanae*, Oxford (Leon Lichfield).

WILLIS, R. (1829) 'Vowel sounds', *Transactions of the Cambridge Philosophical Society*.

WOOLBERT, C.H. (1927) *The Fundamentals of Speech – a Textbook of Delivery*, New York (Harper).

The Keen Prosodic Ear: a comparison of
the notations of rhythm of Joshua Steele,
William Thomson and Morris Croll

Musical prosodists are often dismissed and even held in disdain by the adherents of the traditional approach to prosody. Their merits not being truly recognised, their work has largely been relegated to a minor position and confined to rare-book departments. They have, in fact, made a valuable contribution to quantitative phonetics, for long a neglected branch of study, not only in some aspects of theory, but also in practice by their minute and often amazingly accurate transcriptions of rhythm in the language, while occupying themselves with the study of verse as their prime concern. Their work came as a reaction to the inadequacy and failure of the non-temporal prosody to deal with questions of rhythm, and musical scansion arose in an attempt to remedy the deficiencies of the traditional prosody in this respect. It covers the span of 150 years from Joshua Steele (1775) to Morris Croll (1925), with contributions from John Odell (1806), John Thelwall (1812), James Chapman (1816, 1821), Richard Roe (1823), James Lecky (1887), Sidney Lanier (1880), J.P. Dabney (1901) and William Thomson (1904, 1911, 1923). Later work included major contributions to theory and its application from E.A. Sonnenschein (1925), Thomas Taig (1929) and J.C. Pope (1942).

Unlike the traditional prosodists, they felt that the study of prosody should be preceded by an examination of the most pertinent features of the language and should be related to the actual data. The areas of disagreement with the traditional prosodists stem just from this: the disparity between theory and facts.

The first disagreement concerns the basis of rhythm, the second the unit of rhythm, its nature and use: the third, the range of syllable quantities that these units should contain, the fourth, the method of their assignment. The fifth, related to the first two, concerns the method of scansion. The sixth – and most important – concerns the goal of the analysis, and here two extreme views are represented: the traditional prosodists were interested in the description of metre, the musical prosodists were concerned with the analysis of rhythm.

Regarding the basis of rhythm, the musical prosodists believed in a regular periodicity (Thomson 1904, 1923) or pulsation (Steele 1775; Croll 1925), or a mental beat (Young 1790; Patmore 1857) as constituting the indispensable underlying scheme, permitting measurement and the establishment of a uniform unit of rhythm. In this, they recognise the delimitative function of stress and construct their unit of rhythm accordingly by using stress to signal the incidence of foot boundaries. Here they have partly been influenced by the practice of music, and Steele admits the borrowing, but Thomson uses arguments from the area of psychology, noting that the modality of our perception is such that we tend to perceive from one salient point to another. (This is not altogether an isolated view: the same opinion may be found reasserted later in Fraisse 1964.)

Against this simple and coherent view of a rhythmic base, the attempts of non-temporal prosodists to study only the quantities in isolation from an accentual basis seem condemned to failure and lead only to confusion. Ample evidence of this can be found in the numerous methods of scansion, arbitrarily derived and largely ad hoc, confusing one arbitrary principle of assignment with another, sometimes as often as from one foot to the next. That it is important to have a uniformly established principle of the delimitation of the unit of rhythm is first observed by Steele and then by Roe (1823, p.129) in his criticism of the traditional foot and the method of scansion. Feet not based on the regulative beat are also unthinkable to Thomson (1923, p.173) and in his view the traditional feet are not based on any specific principle. Further support for the accentual base comes from Lecky (1887) who insists that the placement of foot boundary and the ensuing isochrony is dependent on the recognition of stress as the initial element in the foot.

The behaviour of the syllables is seen as the outcome of several factors, but it is always subordinate to the measure in which the syllable occurs. The traditionally accepted two values for the description of syllable quantity are found deficient for a complete description of rhythm in English. They propose nine, which incidentally agrees with the figure quoted by Ellis (1874, p.1131) and Sweet, though the latter finds that three are sufficient for practical purposes (1890, p.43). However, besides accurate transcriptions of syllable quantity, the musical prosodists do not offer any method whatever for the assignment of syllable quantities other than fast tapping.

A number of valid points on rhythm in English have been made by a variety of writers, the pioneering work in this field being done by Joshua Steele in his *Prosodia Rationalis* (1775) where he propounded a scientific approach to the study of rhythm and intonation in English. Before his work a few other minor prosodists had occasionally employed some form of musical notation, but Steele was the first to deal with the subject from a theoretical point of view.

Steele attempts to prove in his book that English has both 'melody' and 'rhythm', and that the rules of music may be applied to the analysis of rhythm and pitch movement in language. The neglect of these aspects of study had left a relatively large area still unknown in his day. It was Steele's hope to fill that gap and to show the way for others to follow. That his start was not easy can be guessed from the preliminary pages of his book. In the preface, Steele finds it necessary to devote a certain amount of space to phonetics, proposing a definition of the vowel and diphthong sounds as well as discussing aspects of the vowel system of English. Further, he traces the sources of disagreement between the grammarians and the prosodists and complains of lack of adequate terminology in the discussion.

Steele conceives speech as consisting of *Melody* (intonation) 'by slides', which may be either 'acute' or 'grave', loud or soft; and of *Measure* or rhythm, distinguished by quantity (long and short) and cadence (heavy and light). With regard to pitch, he finds the chromatico-diatonic scale of music inadequate and proposes to subdivide it into quarter tones to convey the changes in pitch and to adjust the stave accordingly. He admits, however, that it requires an experienced ear to recognise the narrow pitch intervals.

With reference to measure, Steele maintains that 'we must presuppose an exact periodical pulsation, as regular as the swings of a pendulum' (Steele 1779, p.67). The pulsation is marked by the alternation of 'heavy' and 'light' (thesis and arsis) which help to maintain regular periodicity. Each interval between the pulses starts with a 'heavy poize' and comprises the speech material, with any accompanying rests, up to the next heavy poise, but not including it. The advantage of this scheme is that it is related to perception and offers a uniform basis for the assignment of the unit of rhythm. In its internal structure, the interval between the pulses may be regarded as containing either two or three units of time so as to convey the idea of the background of duple or triple time. The cadence itself may be sub-divided into individual syllable quantities, not necessarily corresponding with the individual time of these units, but always being an *integral fraction* of the entire time of the cadence. Here, the term 'quantity' is used by Steele to denote the 'relative value of sounds in duration of time' (Steele 1779, p.116) and it is the function of metre to 'adjust the *quantities* of notes or syllables contained in each *cadence* or *bar*; *rhythmus* is to keep, by its *pulsation*, all the *cadences* of an equal length' (ibid., pp.72–3). The traditionally accepted quantity values were much disliked by Steele as not rendering the actual quantity patterns that exist in the English language. The scheme he adopted for representing syllable quantities is that of music, the notation itself being a modified version of the musical one with its regular sub-divisions. The range of quantities is now greater and comprises eight values. Parts I and II of the Essay consist, in fact, of a systematic presentation of the method of representing the rhythm and intonation of English. All Steele's transcriptions of rhythm, in which the Essay abounds, were made from an auditory impression and followed the rules of the musical grammar. It was Steele's hope that 'when the *cadences* of our language either poetry or prose, are properly marked in our way, every person initiated in the practical knowledge of music will be able to comprehend our meaning, and to read the words according to the *melody* and *rhythmus* we shall mark to them (Steele 1779, p.18).

Even in his age, Steele's work met with little acclaim, apart from occasional signs of interest and enthusiasm, and he was not infrequently referred to as 'the ingenious Mr. Steele'. For the most part, the points he was striving to make were missed by his contemporaries, and were only taken up later by several writers in the nineteenth and twentieth centuries.

The most important contribution to the study of rhythm in English based on Steele's work comes from Dr William Thomson of Glasgow. A London B.A. and, at the time of his first pamphlets on rhythm, Headmaster of Hutcheson's Girls' Grammar School, Thomson showed himself a keen phonetic observer and a discerning critic, well acquainted with the prosodic theories of the day. These he subjected to searching criticism both with regard to theory and notation.

In the early pamphlets *The Basis of English Rhythm* (1904) and *Rhythm and Scansion* (1911), Thomson lays the foundations of his later work, which was to take the form of a voluminous piece of research entitled *The Rhythm of Speech* (1923). This work, for which he was awarded a D.Litt. by the University of Glasgow, embodies the results of many years of investigation into the subject. In it, in addition to the detailed exposition of his views, Thomson furnishes a large amount of transcriptions of rhythm in verse and prose. He puts forward his ideas concerning the principles of speech rhythm and advances several laws. In these he maintains that 'in the rhythm of speech the sounds that count are syllables, more specifically points-of-force (onsets, accents, blows or ictuses)' which he calls syllicts.

'Syllicts vary in strength or loudness, some being specifiable as principal' (1923, p.40) and are then called accents. Accents, in turn, occur at equal intervals, but here Thomson presents a modified view of isochrony, less rigid than Steele's, saying that variety may be added by intervals related as the numbers 2, 3, $4\frac{1}{2}$. Syllicts are also used in determining syllable quantity. Thomson takes care to emphasise that syllable measurement is relative and is reckoned from one syllict to the next. He firmly believes that, within psychological time, each syllable bears to an adjacent syllable a very simple ratio of duration and that it is possible to assign to a syllable a rational number expressing its quantity. The range of quantities that he identifies is considerable and comprises nine values. To cope with such variety, both within measures and in syllables, a certain number of laws had been formulated by Thomson, explaining the factors that govern the principles of rhythm, the structure of the measure and the patterns of quantity. Of particular interest to us may be laws IV and VI – the law of syllict in syllable measurement, and the law of quantity-ratios – and laws VII and VIII dealing with quantity-range in syllables and quantity-range in measures. In addition, laws IX and XV, that is the law of quantity assimilation and the law of tempo in rhythm variation, explain a lot of patterns in the notations that do not conform to the expected scheme, while laws XII and XIII elucidate the more complicated principles of rhythm such as 'unit shifting' and the 'complex measures' as a variation on triple time. Not all of the laws are directly relevant to phonetics; some contain observations of a psychological nature, while others deal explicitly with verse structure. They are a product of many years of observation and attentive listening to the rhythm patterns of language. In the course of these, Thomson had to contend with the popular view that syllables in connected speech are incommensurable, that rhythm is limited to two quantities only, that the same syllable is invariable in quantity, and many others (cf. Thomson 1923, p.235), and his work was meant as a proof to the contrary.

Morris Croll accords a high position to Thomson's work, seeing *The Rhythm of Speech* as a 'new point of departure for students of English verse form' (Croll 1925, ed. 1966, preface). Music is also used as the starting point in discussing the elements of the rhythm of verse in the first chapter of his essay, where he discusses aspects of the theory and outlines the system of notation. Regarding the theory, verse is composed of measures, each indicated by the bar lines, and delimited to the ear by the beats which mark off equal periods of time. Croll maintains that the 'equality of time of these periods is a fundamental fact of rhythm; the rhythm of verse does not arise from equality or similarity in the number of syllables that occupy this time ...' and that 'the interesting quality of the rhythm of English verse is largely due to the fact that equal times are occupied by syllables in different ways' (Croll 1966, p.369). In postulating equal measures, he is conscious that 'there is another element in the form of the measure beside its time. For we could not hear the equality of time between the successive measures, ... unless there were something by which we could mark where one begins and another ends' (ibid., p.370). This delimiting factor is named 'stress'. But it is the measures and not the beats that constitute the line, and they are the unit used to describe the form of verse.

The measures themselves are composed of a number of small sub-units, giving beat in duple or triple time. The character of the measure will also depend on the length of time given to each count within the measure. This information is expressed in the time signature preceding the passage. There are usually five kinds of them (2/8, 2/4, 3/8, 3/4, 3/2), but the most common in English verse is 3/8. It requires, however, a certain amount of training to distinguish them; the ordinary reader is not so skilled in analytical hearing, though he perceives the differences. Two-time and three-time produce different effects and 'some poets are conscious of what causes the difference and take full advantage of the opportunities it offers them' (Croll, 1966, p.374). The beats inside the measure do not necessarily coincide with the syllables contained in the measure. In most cases, they do not do so. The measure can be filled by one, two, three, four or even five syllables either in duple or in triple time. Although the three-syllable arrangement of three-time is possible, a two-syllable arrangement is in fact more common, and Croll shows this with numerous examples from several poets. Much space is given in Croll's essay to exemplifying the various time signatures in verse in both triple and duple time. To bring this distinction closer to an ordinary reader, Croll explains that 'a three-syllable measure in 3/8 time has the effect of being a little faster than ordinary speech, because its unit is similar to that of the short syllables of speech' (p.379), whereas the 3/4 measures have as their unit the long syllable. Croll observes that 'the relation between them is ... ideally, if not actually, a two-to-one relation' (p.379). In turn, 3/2 measures are far less frequent and the thing to be observed about them is that 'the time of the long unit is usually filled by two syllables instead of one ... so that there are always five or six syllables in a measure' (p.384). In exemplifying the distinction between 2/8 and 2/4 time, Croll adds that the poet may require and permit us to hear 2/8 rhythm by 'placing beats at all possible division-points in the measure; whereas if he wants us to hear 2/4 time he must prevent the measures from breaking up so that we could not easily hear a strong secondary beat in the middle of the measure' (p.387). Another point contributed by Croll in the discussion of verse form is the role of the anacrusis. It has often been the source of confusion in noting the form of verse. When appearing in the first line, it is meant to be treated as extrametrical, but it is to be included in the rhythm when it succeeds a measure left incomplete at the end of the preceding line. The remaining space in Croll's essay is devoted to double measure, which is verse written in 4/4 and 6/8 time. It is characteristic of lyric verse and is also found in involuntary rhythmicising. Proceeding methodically, Croll arrives at the last form, the doubly compounded measure consisting of two measures of double time, for which he provides ample illustration.

The value of Croll's work is unquestionable, and together the three prosodists form the core of what may be called the Temporal tradition in the study of verse. Their work may be judged not only from their statements regarding the theory, but also from their practice. Their writings offer a vast body of what might be termed impressionistic 'transcriptions' of rhythm, and useful information concerning linguistic aspects of rhythm at the phonetic, grammatical and syntactic levels may be obtained from a study of their notations. They themselves, on the whole, did not believe that any rules could be adduced for syllable quantity in English, and Croll went even as far as to deny the possibility (1966, p.376). The notations of rhythm can be viewed essentially from two points: the graphic representation and the principles underlying it. The graphic representation is to some extent conditioned by the limitations imposed by printing and, naturally, by considerations of clarity and simplicity. Croll's is the simplest, Thomson's the easiest to print (since it consists only of numerical symbols) and Steele's visually the most attractive and lucid.

As can be seen in figure 1, Steele's symbols are an adaptation of musical notation; the slanted and curved lines attached to the vertical tails represent the pitch movement, the four main symbols ⊢ ⌐ ⌐ | with their dotted versions are used to express eight types of quantity while the symbols at the

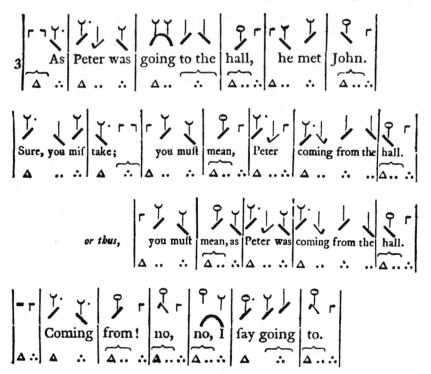

FIGURE 1. Example of Steele's symbols (p.134).

bottom refer to pulsation, or 'heavy' and 'light'. Thomson, in the early stages (1904), employed the musical notation, but abandoned it later in favour of the numerical one (figure 2). In a period of transition, he experimented with the traditional metrical notation involving simple symbols — and ∪ and their combinations, but in the end decided he needed a system independent of music or other associations with traditional metrics.

Croll's simple notation (figure 3) is clearly designed with the difficulties of printing in mind and combines elegance and simplicity.

The form of all the notations has roots in the musical 'grammar of rhythm' and its binary and ternary divisions. Thomson, however, accuses Steele of following it too closely and sometimes using it indiscriminately. Thomson (1923, p.139) explains the relationship between the different types of time by saying that 'by accretion, duple |1 1| becomes |1 1 1|. By dupletic redistribution |1 1 1| becomes |1½ 1½|'. Proceeding in the same manner, he derives the slow triple time by the addition of 1½ to the measure |1½ 1½|. He explains why he is reluctant to use the notation |♪. ♪.| for the last case, because 'it suggests a sub-unit ♪ for which there is no justification; the real sub-unit is the half of 1½, that is $\frac{3}{4}$, not $\frac{1}{16}$' (ibid., p.350).

Quantities are expressed by the three writers in the following way: the

Forest on forest hung a- bout his head

∧| ⅔ 1⅓ 1 | ⅔ 2⅓| 1 1| 1 1 | 3

Like cloud on cloud. No stir of air was there,—

1½ | 2 1| 2 ⌒1½| 1 1|2 1 | 2 ⌒

Not so much life as on a summer's day

∧| 1 ½ 1½ | 2 1| 1 1| ⅔ 1⅓ | 3

Robs not one light seed from the feathered grass,

1½ |1½ 1½| 1½ 1½ | 2 1| 1 2 | 2 ⌒

∧| 1½ 1½|1½ 1½ | 1½ ¾ ¾ |

But where the dead leaf fell, there did it rest.

1 | 2 1 | 1½ 1½ | 3' | 1½ ¾ ¾| 2 ⌒

Keats' 'Hyperion'.

FIGURE 2. Example of Thomson's numerical notation (p.388).

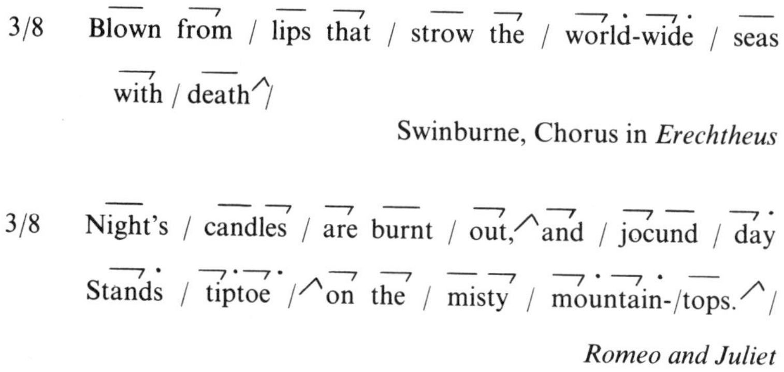

3/8 Blown from / lips that / strow the / world-wide / seas

with / death⌃|

Swinburne, Chorus in *Erechtheus*

3/8 Night's / candles / are burnt / out,⌃and / jocund / day

Stands / tiptoe /⌃on the / misty / mountain-/tops.⌃|

Romeo and Juliet

FIGURE 3. Example of Croll's notation (pp.376, 377).

shorts ½, ⅔, ¾ and 1, and the longs 1⅓, 1½, 2, 2¼ and 3 by Thomson; ⊓, ⌐, Υ, |, for the 'longest, long, short and shortest' by Steele; and ⊔, ─, ⌐, ⌐⌐, ⌐⌐⌐, i.e. 'the half-note, quarter-note, eighth-note, sixteenth-note, thirty-second note' (the last never actually used) by Croll. Their range is the natural consequence of the use of duple and triple time. In the deep structure, however, the essential relationship long: short, short: long, equal: equal is retained.

Some of the principles behind Thomson's notations may be elicited in the following way. Let x represent one syllable quantity and y the next and last syllable quantity in the measure, then the quotient between them may be expressed as $\frac{x}{y} = I$ when $x + y = \Sigma$. From the equations: $Iy = x$; by substitution $Iy + y = \Sigma$, then $y = \Sigma / (I + 1)$. When $\Sigma = 2$ (i.e. the measure consists of two units of time) and when $I = \frac{1}{2}$ is the quotient to be expressed within such a measure, then the quantity values for x, y should be respectively $y = 2/(\frac{1}{2}+1) = 2/1\frac{1}{2} = 4/3 = 1\frac{1}{3}$; $x = Iy = \frac{1}{2} \times 4/3 = \frac{2}{3}$. The quantity values in the foot are therefore $\frac{2}{3}$ and $1\frac{1}{3}$.

This is a useful scheme for translating the quantity ratios into appropriate values in the given time. The ratios $\frac{2}{3} : 1\frac{1}{3}$ thus express the relationship short : long in duple time while preserving the structure of triple time. The fractions permit the conveying of the 'twice as long' relation in the deep structure, when the sum of the units adds up to two. The quantity $1\frac{1}{2}$, in turn, is the result of a sub-division by two of a triple measure, and is itself used as a new unit to form the next measure, the slow triple one, where the quantity $2\frac{1}{4}$ expresses the half-time.

The accuracy with which the three prosodists notated rhythm has enabled us to elicit not only the principles of their system but also those underlying the assignment of syllable quantity. For the purposes of this paper, I have concentrated on examining the di-syllabic measures contained in the writings of the three prosodists. As is known, the rules for the assignment of quantity patterns in di-syllabic feet were formulated by David Abercrombie only in 1964. According to these, two-syllable feet exhibit three different patterns. The first two patterns depend on the phonematic structure of the foot, the third on the presence of a word boundary (Abercrombie 1964, pp.219–20). The quantity patterns and the phonematic patterning correlate as follows:

Pattern A   (C)V^1CV(C) $1+2$ units of time
Pattern B   (C) V C C (C) V (C) *or* (C) V^2 (C) V (C) $1\frac{1}{2} + 1\frac{1}{2}$ units of time
Pattern C   (always involves word-boundary; phonematic structure not relevant) $2+1$ units of time.

Granting the difference of time and accent, I have been interested to see if the three prosodists follow these rules in their notations and to what extent they do so. I have noted, too, how the assignment of patterns differs from Abercrombie's rules and where and when this happens. The results I have tabulated in a simple manner, gaining perhaps in generality and readability, but losing a little on the specificity of detail. In drawing on the examples from the three writers (see Tables on p.109), I have deliberately omitted feet containing rests (they all treat rests as factors of metre), and in the case of William Thomson I have excluded a very small number of feet in musical and modified metrical notation, concentrating exclusively on feet in the last notation, the numerical one, in *The Rhythm of Speech*.

Looking only casually at the notations one notices that:

   i)   The three patterns have validity for the three writers and appear in transcriptions of rhythm of a much earlier period. The figures quoted for the occurrence of such patterns confirm that the 'transcriptions' of rhythm made by the three prosodists need not necessarily be regarded as ad hoc and as being purely and solely impressionistic, but that they reflect the existing linguistic aspects of rhythm.

TABLE 1.   STEELE. 2 syll. Feet: basic patterns

	Pattern A	Pattern B	Pattern C
Triple time	11	26	87
Duple time	—	12	18
Total: 154	11	38	105

TABLE 1a.   STEELE. 2 syll. Feet: Substitution and variation

	Pattern B←C	Pattern C←B	Pattern A←B
Triple time	35	22	10
Duple time	3	—	—
Total: 70	38	22	10

TABLE 2.   THOMSON. 2 syll. Feet: basic patterns

	Pattern A	Pattern B	Pattern C
Triple time	103	353	811
Duple time	70	182	223
Total: 1742	173	535	1034

TABLE 2a.   THOMSON. 2 syll. Feet: Substitution and variation

	Pattern B←C	Pattern C←B	Pattern A←B	Pattern B←A	Pattern A←C
Triple time	296	55	28	5	3
Duple time	367	19	—	83	4
Total: 860	663	74	28	88	7

TABLE 3.   CROLL. 2 syll. Feet: basic patterns

	Pattern A	Pattern B	Pattern C
Triple time	9	60	87
Duple time	—	—	—
Total: 156	9	60	87

TABLE 3a.   CROLL. 2 syll. Feet: Substitution and variation

	Pattern B←C	Pattern C←B	Pattern A←B	Pattern B←A
Triple time	40	14	2	1
Duple time	62	—	—	8
Total 127	102	14	2	9

ii) Within the range of the three patterns an interesting similarity appears between the most prolific transcribers, Thomson and Steele: the incidence of patterns of type A is smallest, next comes pattern B occupying the mid range, and highest is pattern type C. Roughly this relation may be expressed as $1:3:9$.

iii) All three writers have a 'core' of the three basic patterns in agreement with Abercrombie's rules, though in some cases a very large proportion is transferred into duple time. In addition to this, there is an almost equally large area where the assignment of patterns differs from the expected rules. This happens, roughly speaking, along three axes of division: metrical, grammatical and phonetic. I have placed them under the general heading of pattern substitution and variation.

Metrical considerations usually involve a levelling of quantity patterns; here particularly affected are feet type C. Grammatical considerations cover a wider area. I should put here enclitics and cases of 'morpheme isolation' (particularly evident in Steele, Thomson and Croll). Examples of stress suppression, often metrical in origin, may in some cases also belong here. Phonetic considerations involve different assignments of patterns when no other reasons are present, e.g. jocund, swallow (Croll). (Steele also has instances of lengthening under stress.) Here also belong phonetic sub-rules. One of these which is of frequent application concerned pattern A when it contained V^1 in the second vocalic position and both vowels were high. It became then 'equal:equal' $|1 \quad 1|$ in duple time.

In respect of substitutions, the occurrence of pattern A for pattern B is seen as an example of accent variation by Abercrombie, while the substitution of pattern C for B, sometimes met in cases of 'morpheme isolation', to use Abercrombie's terminology, is evident in some adjectives and adverbs used by Thomson, for example 'windy', 'rainy', 'milky', 'fondly', 'faintly'. Here also belongs a quantity variant distinguishing accents of English. As I have already mentioned, the largest group of pattern substitution involves cases that have a 'stressable' part of speech in the unstressed part of the foot, in other words an 'accented' but unstressed word is found in this position (the term 'accented' as used by Abercrombie (1976)). Here pattern B, giving equal quantity value to both parts of the foot, is felt to be more appropriate than pattern C. This substitution is quite common and the examples are varied and numerous in the work of the three prosodists, for example:

That on the green turf suck the honeyed showers
$1 \quad |2 \quad 1| \; 1\frac{1}{2} \quad 1\frac{1}{2}| \; 2 \quad 1|1 \quad 2 \quad | \; 2 \quad \frown$

(Thomson 1923, p.378)

With wild thyme and the gadding vine o' er- grown
$1 \quad | \; 1\frac{1}{2} \quad 1\frac{1}{2} \; \|2 \quad 1|1 \quad 1 \quad |1\frac{1}{2} \quad 1\frac{1}{2}| \; 2^{\frown}$

(ibid., p.373)

When the red fox comes creeping,   dewy-brushed

$\frac{3}{4}$ $\frac{3}{4}$ | 3 |1$\frac{1}{4}$ 1$\frac{1}{2}$ | 1$\frac{1}{2}$ 1$\frac{1}{2}$⌒| 1 1| 2   ⌒

(ibid., p.260)

In addition, a fairly large group of enclitics is to be found here, that is cases where the phonematic structure over-rides the consideration of a word boundary (though not exclusively with this pattern, as the use of pattern A for C is also a possibility). The most common involve pronouns immediately following a verb (as direct or indirect objects) within the same foot. (Some typical instances are mentioned by Abercrombie (1964).) From some of the substitutions it can be seen that despite a large, central core in common, there was also a residue of patterns conveying traces of other accents.

It is evident from the tables presented here that the musical prosodists did not merely follow a whim in their insistence on applying the rules of music for the admeasurement of syllable quantities in their first attempts to render what 'was thought incapable of all rule and measure', and that their transcriptions of rhythm are reliable to a large extent, even if their scansions may appear odd at times. The only serious criticism that can be raised against them is that, with all the wealth of information contained in their notations, they never attempted to relate the results of their auditory findings to the linguistic structure underlying the patterns they so painstakingly sought to transcribe. It now remains for the phoneticians to systematise the data supplied by the musical prosodists and to construct appropriate rules for the diverse patterns contained in their notations.

At this point we may join Steele as spokesman for the three prosodists in saying: 'I think, these small specimens produced, may be our vouchers to prove, that we have discovered the land, and marked out the route which may be followed by others: and therefore, I hope, gallant adventurers will not be wanting, to push these discoveries further, to explore and bring to light those rich curiosities that still lie hid in the interior parts of the country' (Steele 1779, p.46).

References

ABERCROMBIE, D. (1964) 'Syllable quantity and enclitics in English', in Abercrombie et al. (eds.) *In Honour of Daniel Jones*, London (Longman) 216–22. Reprinted in Abercrombie (1965) 26–34.
— (1965) *Studies in Phonetics and Linguistics*, London (Oxford University Press).
— (1976) '"Stress" and some other terms', Department of Linguistics, University of Edinburgh, *Work in Progress*, no. 9, 51–3.
BARKAS, P. (1934) *A Critique of Modern English Prosody (1880–1930)* Halle (Max Niemeyer Verlag).
CHAPMAN, REV. J. (1818) *The Music, or Melody and Rhythmus of Language; in which are explained, and applied to their proper purposes, on principles new in this country, the five accidents of speech, viz. accent, emphasis, pause, and force, or quality of sound, illustrated with symbolic marks, and*

a musical notation: by which are exhibited, and may be perpetuated, the true cadence, metre and rhythmus of the English language; the rational mode of scanning poetry as it ought to be read, and not by the rules of prosody; the tune and time of composition, and the correct manner of reading and speaking. To which are added, outlines of gesture, and a selection of pieces in verse and prose, Edinburgh (Printed by Michael Anderson).

— (1821) *The Original Rhythmical Grammar of the English Language*, Edinburgh (James Robertson).

CROLL, M.W. (1925) 'The rhythm of English verse', Princeton, N.J. (mimeographed). Published in Croll 1966, 365–429.

— (1966) *Style, Rhetoric, and Rhythm*. Essays ... edited by J. Max Patrick et al., Princeton, N.J. (Princeton University Press).

DABNEY, J. P. (1901) *The Musical Basis of Verse*, New York (Longmans, Green & Co.).

ELLIS, A.J. (1874) *On Early English Pronunciation, with especial reference to Shakspere and Chaucer*, Part IV (pp. 997–1432): *Illustrations of the Pronunciation of English in the XVIIth, XVIIIth, and XIXth centuries*, London (Asher & Co.; Trübner & Co.).

FRAISSE, P. (1964) *The Psychology of Time*, London (Dent).

LANIER, S. (1880) *The Science of English Verse*, New York (Charles Scribner's Sons).

LECKY, J. (1887) 'The phonetic theory of English prosody', *TPhS 1885–7*, Monthly Abstracts of Proceedings, Dec. 19, 1884, ii–vi.

ODELL, J. (1806) *An Essay on the Elements, Accents, and Prosody of the English Language*, London (Lackington, Allen and Co.)

OMOND, T.S. (1921) *English Metrists*, Oxford (Clarendon Press).

PATMORE, C. (1857) 'English metrical critics', *The North British Review*, vol. XXVII, 127–61. Reprinted with minor changes under the title 'Essay on English metrical law' as an Appendix to Patmore 1886, vol. II, 217–67.

— (1886) *Poems. Second collective edition*. 2 vols. London (George Bell & Son).

POPE, J. (1942) *The Rhythm of Beowulf*, New Haven (Yale University Press).

ROE, REV. R. (1823) *The Principles of Rhythm*, Dublin (Grainsberry).

SONNENSCHEIN, E.A. (1925) *What is Rhythm? An Essay by E.A.S. ... accompanied by an Appendix on Experimental Syllable-Measurement in which Stephen Jones and Eileen Macleod have co-operated*, Oxford (Basil Blackwell).

STEELE, J. (1775) *An Essay towards establishing the Melody and Measure of Speech, to be expressed and perpetuated by peculiar symbols*, London (Printed by J. Nichols).

— (1779) *Prosodia Rationalis: or, an Essay towards establishing the melody and Measure of Speech, to be expressed and perpetuated by peculiar symbols*, London (Printed by J. Nichols). 2nd amended and enlarged ed. of Steele (1775).

SWEET, H. (1890) *A Primer of Phonetics*, Oxford (Clarendon Press).

TAIG, T. (1929) *Rhythm and Metre*, Cardiff (University of Wales Press Board).

THELWALL, J. (1812) *Illustrations of English Rhythmus*, London (J. MᶜCreery).

THOMSON, W. (1904) *The Basis of English Rhythm*, Glasgow (W. & R. Holmes).

— (1911) *Rhythm and Scansion*, Edinburgh (H. & J. Pillans & Wilson).

— (1923) *The Rhythm of Speech*, Glasgow (Maclehose & Jackson).

YOUNG, W. (1790) 'An essay on rhythmical measures', *Transactions of the Royal Society of Edinburgh*, vol. II, part II, section II, 55–110.

PART FOUR

NATIONAL CONTRIBUTIONS TO
PHONETIC THEORY AND DESCRIPTION

The Greek Contribution to
the History of Phonetics

'Early writers on phonetics and alphabetics have usually had attention paid to them only in so far as they throw light on the pronunciation of their time.' Professor Abercrombie's comment (1949a, p.1), made in the context of English phonetics, is equally true with regard to the ancient Greeks. It is also commonly observed that, as compared with the Sanskrit phoneticians, they were relatively unskilled in the analysis of speech sounds. The rigorous and systematic descriptions of the sounds of Sanskrit by native scholars at a very early period are on a different level of scientific achievement from anything in the ancient history of western phonetics (cf. Allen 1953). Yet it is ultimately the Greek tradition that has, for better or worse, had the greater influence on the terminology and to some extent the categories current in modern phonetics; and an understanding of these is desirable if we are to view our own science in its historical context.

The first contribution of the Greeks, though a major one, tends to be overlooked – that of the 'forgotten phonetician(s)', who developed the Greek alphabetic writing system from a Phoenician original (see e.g. McCarter 1975), a system established in Greece around 800 B.C., although the initial stages of the development may have taken place elsewhere (cf. Cook & Woodhead 1959). This adaptation in itself reveals an awareness, albeit intuitive, of the basic principles of phonemic analysis. From a purely consonantal system the Greeks devised an alphabet with distinct signs for consonants and vowels, the latter being provided by Phoenician consonant symbols not required for Greek. In the case of A, E, and O the choice seems to have been determined by the vowel sound following the initial consonant in the Phoenician names of the letters, namely ʔalep (alpha), he (e ⟨psilon⟩), ʕayin (o ⟨mikron⟩) respectively, the last perhaps on account of a back quality associated with the voiced pharyngal. (It may be noted that, according to the 'classical' version of the Indo-European 'laryngeal theory', the third laryngeal, sometimes identified as [ʕ], has the effect of producing o-vocalism.)

By the time of the creation of the alphabet, the Greek language had lost the semivowel [j], and so the letter yod (iōta) was available to represent the corresponding vowel (I). The semivowel [w] was still to some extent preserved, and the Phoenician waw was adopted with this value in the form F (probably with the Greek name wau, although later, after this sound had been lost, termed digamma from its shape). The more usual form Y was adopted for the corresponding vowel [u], named (h)ū⟨psilon⟩ and placed at the end of the original alphabet after T (tau); later in most dialects the vowel was fronted to [y], and the sign Y was adopted by Latin to render this sound in Greek loan-words, a value it retains in modern phonetic transcription (on the later Greek epithets ⟨bracketed⟩ of certain vowels see further Allen 1974, pp.65, 75f.).

At this stage the prosodic feature of vowel length was not indicated, nor was any such distinction deliberately and generally developed by the Greeks. It came only through the stimulus of historical accident in the case of the mid vowels, where it also disambiguated certain qualitative differences. The digraphs EI and OY became available to indicate long half-close [eː] and [oː] when the diphthongs originally denoted by them merged phonetically with these monophthongs. As a result of 'psilosis' (loss of [h]) in Eastern Ionic, the letter H (from the Phoenician ḥet) became available in a vowel value (ēta) to represent the long half-open [ɛː]; and presumably by analogy with this the Ionians created a differentiated form of O, namely Ω (ō mega) to represent the long half-open [ɔː]. No length distinctions were made in the case of the other vowels, but the Greeks were of course fully aware of the phonological distinction, and referred to the vowels as makron 'long' or brakhu 'short'; those whose length was not indicated in writing (A, I, Y) were termed for this reason dikhrona, literally 'bi-temporal'.

As a result of the general adoption of the Ionic alphabet by other dialects as a replacement for their own local forms (in Athens officially in 403 B.C.), [h] came to be unwritten even where it was pronounced, and was only later re-indicated, together with such features as accentuation, as a 'prosody' in Alexandrian times – a treatment which was strikingly, even if accidentally, prophetic of 'London' phonological theory of the 1950s.

A further process of adaptation was necessary to represent the Greek voiceless aspirated plosives [ph], [th], [kh], for which Phoenician provided no model. In the case of the dental, the symbol for the 'emphatic' (probably pharyngalised) ṭet (thēta) was available and was taken over for this purpose; in the other two series the distinction between aspirate and non-aspirate was achieved (for most dialects) by the device of digraphs (ΠΗ, ΚΗ), although later special symbols were devised for these also – Φ (phei), X (khei) – of which the origins are much disputed. Our own use of digraphs to indicate aspirates derives, however, not from the early Greek usage but from the Latin use of PH, and so on, to indicate the Greek aspirates in loan-words.

The importance of this work of adaptation can hardly be exaggerated. It has been commented that the Indian phonetic acumen was far greater than the Greek; and the Indian writing system indicates those distinctions of vowel length that are missing from the Greek. But the Indian system itself never developed a graphic form that could be readily utilised for general phonetic purposes. Although the underlying analysis is phonemic, it never succeeded in shedding the graphic incubus of a syllabic system ill-suited to the phonological structure of Sanskrit (although it ingeniously avoided ambiguities such as are found in the Mycenaean Linear B). The Devanagari script is in fact a pseudo-syllabic system: each character represents a vowel together with the preceding consonant or consonants, regardless of actual syllabic division. Groups of consonants are written, in variously abbreviated forms, either from left to right or from top to bottom within the character; and the following vowels are indicated by diacritics placed variously above, below, to left or to right of the character (or in the case of short *a* by zero). The fact that such a system survived in a culture of high linguistic sophistication may be due to the characteristic Indian disregard for the written as compared with the spoken word.

The Greeks themselves were well aware of the importance of the alphabet, and its study was sometimes referred to as the 'Old Grammar', or 'Little Grammar' (as opposed to the 'Great Grammar' of more general scope); and the word 'Grammar' itself (*grammatikē* [sc. *tekhnē*]) refers originally of course to the study of writing. Its invention is attributed by Plato to 'some god or god-like man' (*Philebus* 18 B), and later Cicero accords the title of 'Magnus' to the man 'who reduced the sounds of speech, which were infinite in manifestation, to a few written letters' (*Tusculan Disputations* I.xxv.62) – an adequate non-technical recognition of the aims of broad transcription (cf. Abercrombie 1937).

The first explicit classification of sounds by the Greeks is into vowels and consonants, *phōnēenta* and *aphōna*, literally 'possessing voice' and 'voiceless' respectively (the terms are neuter, in agreement with *grammata* 'letters', which was used indifferently in antiquity for both the written and the spoken segments: cf. also Abercrombie 1949b). The first of these terms is translated in Latin as *vocales* (sc. *litterae*), and so is the original source of our category of 'vowels'. The distinction is already found, for example, in a fragment of Euripides, and is a commonplace in Plato and Aristotle. The category of *aphōna*, however, is further subdivided by Plato into *aphōna kai aphthonga* on the one hand, literally 'voiceless-and-soundless' (or alternatively *psophos*, 'noise'), and on the other those sounds which, whilst not 'possessing voice', are not mere 'noise' but have some 'sound' (*Cratylus* 424 C; *Philebus*, loc. cit.). Plato also refers to this second class as *mesa* 'intermediate', and by Aristotle they are termed *hēmiphōna*, literally 'half-voiced' (*Poetics* XX.1456 b), the other consonants being referred to simply as *aphōna*. From the discussions it is clear that *aphōna* (*kai aphthonga*) refers to the plosives and *hēmiphōna* to all other consonants, in Greek *l, r, m, n, s* (to which some Latin writers add the Latin *f*) – in other words the liquids, nasals, and fricative(s), forming the class of continuants. Aristotle further attempts to characterise the three categories of 'voiced', 'voiceless', and 'half-voiced' in terms of their production (*Poetics*, loc. cit; cf. *Historia animalium* IV.ix.535 a), as being articulated by (i) 'voice and larynx without contact', (ii) 'contact of tongue or lip', and (iii) 'contact together with voice'.

117

The distinction between the two types of consonant is translated in Latin by *mutae* and *semivocales*. The first of these terms, 'mutes', is occasionally still found referring to the plosives in old-fashioned modern works; and the modern term 'semivowels' is formally derivable from *semivocales*; but the modern use of the latter term is of course different from that of the ancients (although something of the old sense is retained by Grammont (1946, p.77), who includes under this title 'des spirantes et aussi bien des fricatives et des constrictives'). The exclusion of [h] from the list of *hēmiphōna* by the Greeks is probably due to the absence of segmental indication referred to above; and this model is followed by Latin writers; but it is included in the category by Old Icelandic treatises based on Latin models (which also include the Icelandic *v* and dental fricatives). By contrast the aspirated plosives are mentioned by Sextus Empiricus (fl. *c.* A.D. 200) as being included among the *hēmiphōna* by 'some' scholars; since the Stoic Diogenes Babylonius (reported by Diogenes Laertius) omits the aspirates from his list of plosives, it seems that this doctrine is at least as early as the middle of the second century B.C., and so cannot be accounted for by the change of aspirated plosives to fricatives, for which there is no evidence earlier than the first century A.D. The Greeks in general included among the *hēmiphōna* the combinations *ps*, *ks*, and *zd*, each containing a fricative, simply because they had single symbols for these groups (*psei*, *ksei*, and *zēta*); and it may be that the inclusion of the aspirates was a Stoic aberration based on some kind of analogy with these.

The true 'semivowels' [j] and [w] were not discussed by the Greeks, since by the time the philosophers and grammarians were writing both of these had ceased to exist in their language; and although the semivowels existed in Latin, Latin orthography did not distinguish them from the vowels in writing (both being indicated by I and V), and as consonants they were treated simply as non-syllabic variants of the vowels.

By later Greek commentators the class of *hēmiphōna* was further defined as comprising sounds which whilst not being, like the vowels, independently pronounced in the language, were nevertheless capable of so being, for example 'in hissing and moaning'. This criterion of independent pronounceability had also been used, already by Àristotle (*Poetics*, loc. cit.), in distinguishing the plosives from the vowels and *hēmiphōna*, as 'having themselves no voice, but becoming audible in conjunction with sounds having voice (i.e. the vowels)'; and in the grammarians (e.g. Dionysius Thrax and Dionysius of Halicarnassus) this criterion is usual for the distinction of vowels and consonants in general. As against the vowels (*phōnēenta*) the consonants thus came to be termed *sumphōna*, literally 'voiced in combination (sc. with vowels)', which, through the Latin translation *consonantes*, provides the origin of the modern term for the category.

Basic to this classification is the fact that vowels, but not consonants (in Greek), may form *syllables*, and this term also has its origins in Greek. In a non-technical sense *sullabē* 'group', is applied to speech already by Aeschylus and Euripides; and Dionysius Thrax more specifically explains the term as meaning primarily 'the grouping of a consonant with a vowel'. In the Greek grammarians one finds rules of syllabic division, which specify that a single intervocalic consonant belongs with the following vowel, and that consonant clusters are divided between syllables. There is clear metrical and other evidence in favour of this, but the grammarians also state that the whole cluster belongs with the following vowel if it is a cluster that can occur initially: thus (Herodian) 'in *ktēma* the *kt* is initial in the word; but even when it occurs medially, as in *etikton*, the *k* and *t* are combined'. This doctrine leads to difficulty when the attempt is made, as by Dionysius Thrax, to relate syllabic quantity to syllabic division; for whereas the doctrine correctly prescribes, for example, *er.gon* (resulting in heavy, *qua* closed, first syllable), it wrongly prescribes, for example, *He.ktōr* (which in fact also has a heavy first syllable): so that the quantitative rule then has to be added that a syllable is heavy if the next syllable begins with two consonants. It seems in fact that the syllabification rules were primarily formulated for the practical, graphic purpose of word-division at the ends of lines (rules of which the main principles still persist in typographical practice; cf. Allen 1974, p.99 n.2). In spite of its phonological shortcomings, this formulation does nevertheless indicate a degree of reasoning about the distribution of phonemes, as more recently expressed, for example, by Pulgram (1970, p.46): 'any syllable boundary in any part of the utterance must obey the constraints that prevail in the language under scrutiny at the word boundary'. It remains to mention that the Greeks made no terminological distinction between vocalic length and syllabic quantity, both being referred to as 'long' or 'short' ('heavy' and 'light' are taken over from the Indians), and in the Middle Ages this was to cause a confusion which still persists in some quarters (cf. Allen 1974, p.97ff.).

Within the category of the *hēmiphōna* there is also recognised a special class to which the Greeks gave the strange name of *hugra*, literally 'fluid' (first used in this sense by Dionysius Thrax); this class comprises the Greek *l*, *r*, *m*, *n*, and commentators differ in their interpretation of the term. The most general view is that these sounds are so called in the sense of 'unstable', because in a word like *patros* or *teknon* the medial consonant cluster ('mute + liquid' in old-fashioned English terminology) may be treated for metrical purposes as if it were a single consonant, leaving the preceding syllable light ('short') in quantity if the vowel is short – the so-called 'correptio Attica' of metrics (cf. Allen 1974, p.100ff.). Phonetically this variation may be seen as due to the relatively open articulation of the sounds in question, so that a syllabic 'pulse' may be released by a preceding consonant of greater stricture without being checked by such sounds in its progression to the vocalic peak; in other words, whereas a sequence vccv in Greek and many other languages is generally syllabified vc.cv, a sequence of the type vprv may also be syllabified (as in Attic) v.PRV (for further discussion cf. Allen 1973, p.69ff.). An approach to such a phonetic explanation is perhaps to be seen in the musical writer Aristides Quintilianus (? 3rd cent. A.D.), who states that the first member of the cluster being 'of thicker sound', the second, being 'thinner', is 'elided and suppressed'. This treatment is theoretically possible in any sequence of increasing articulatory apertures; in modern Icelandic it also applies, for example, before a cluster such as [sj] (fricative + semivowel), but in Greek no such other clusters occurred; and in Latin the term (translated as *liquidae*) is further restricted to the consonants *l* and *r*, since clusters of plosive + nasal did not occur in native Latin words. It is in this restricted sense that the term has come down into modern phonetics, where by its very opaqueness it continues to play a useful role; for a single articulatory or acoustic characterisation of just these two sound-types remains a problem, even though various phonological data provide circumstantial evidence for their exclusive membership of a common class.

We have seen that the devisers of the Greek alphabet were well aware of the distinction between the voiceless aspirated and unaspirated plosives; and their early use of the digraphs ΠΗ, ΚΗ suggests an understanding of the nature of the opposition. A terminological distinction is made by the grammarians between *dasea* 'rough', for the aspirated and *psila* 'smooth', for the unaspirated. That these are meant in a 'privative' sense is clear from their use of the same terms to refer to the initial aspirate (glottal fricative) [h] on the one hand and its absence on the other – the so-called rough and smooth 'breathings' (*pneumata*); *psilos* is in fact used privatively in non-technical language (referring to absence of trees, leaves, fur, etc.), and Dionysius Thrax refers to the *dasea* as having the 'addition of breath'. In their application to the 'breathings' the Greek terms are directly translated by the Latin (*spiritus*) *asper* and *lenis*; but in connexion with the plosives they are replaced in Latin by *aspirata* and *tenuis*, the first of which is maintained in modern terminology and the second sometimes found in philological works.

More problematic is the treatment by the Greeks of the distinction between voiceless and voiced plosives. They seem never to have realised the nature of the opposition, and the standard classification, as for example in Dionysius Thrax, treats the voiced plosives as 'intermediate' (*mesa*) between the voiceless aspirates and non-aspirates; the terminology is directly translated into Latin as *mediae*, a name (like *tenues*) still to be found in some relatively modern works. The basis of this terminology has never been satisfactorily explained (for references to some recent discussions see Allen 1974, p.28); and even if it had some phonetic validity for Greek, it would have been inapplicable to Latin, which had no native aspirated plosives. It is in fact only in the last hundred years or so that the laryngal nature of the voice distinction has been generally acknowledged in western phonetics (in India it was already well understood in the earliest phonetic works). Quintilian (*Institutio oratoria* I.iv.16) recommends, as an example of the kind of thing a boy should be taught, the nature of the relationship between *t* and *d* – but does not volunteer any instruction in the matter; the Latin grammarian Marius Victorinus seeks the distinction in different positions of the tongue (in which he is followed by Ben Jonson's *English Grammar*); and the medieval grammarian Hugutio confesses himself unable to discover where the difference lies. In the seventeenth century the English writer William Holder does indeed seem independently to have realised the nature of the distinction, as noted in his *Elements of Speech*; but in the same century John Wallis, who had tried to delay and even suppress Holder's work (cf. Firth 1947, p.115ff.), stated in his *Grammatica linguae Anglicanae* that the distinction lay 'not in the lips or larynx, but in the nostrils'.

Whilst it is clear that the Greeks recognised the distinction of three places of articulation for the plosives – labial, dental, and velar –, they never devised, as did the Indians, a simple terminology for these. Dionysius of Halicarnassus, for example, is aware of the fact that *p*, *b*, and *ph* are 'one set of three mutes, all spoken with a like conformation'; but he has no convenient title for the class, and identifies them by a lengthy description, as those which are produced 'from the edges of the lips, when the mouth is compressed, and the breath, being driven forward from the windpipe, breaks through the obstruction'. Not even in the Latin grammarians do we anywhere encounter such terms as '*dentalis*', '*labialis*', corresponding to the Sanskrit *dantya*, and so on; our own terminology here is of recent creation.

In the earliest forms of the Greek alphabet there was also a consonantal symbol known as *koppa*, derived from the sign for the Phoenician uvular plosive (*qop*); it was employed for Greek only before the back vowels, that is, in contexts where the articulation was retracted, in complementary distribution with the normal velar symbol *kappa*. But the non-phonemic nature of this distinction in Greek was soon recognised, and the use of *koppa* was discontinued (although surviving in the Latin Q and in the lower-case form of this in modern phonetic use).

We have finally to consider the 'prosodic' feature of pitch. Although the melodic accent of ancient Greek is not graphically indicated until Alexandrian times, it was generally well understood at an earlier date, under the title of *prosōidia*, which was firmly established by the time of Aristotle. The term means literally 'tune', 'that to which something is sung', and is exactly translated by the Latin *accentus* (even though the Latin accent was of a dynamic type). The basic pitch distinctions recognised by the Greeks were termed *okseia* 'sharp' (Latin *acutus*), and *bareia* 'heavy' (Latin *gravis*). Another general term used for melodic accentuation in Greek, *tonos*, literally 'stretching', was presumably so applied by analogy with the string tension whereby the pitch of a musical instrument is varied, and does not imply any direct understanding of the action of the vocal cords. Latinised as *tonus*, it provides our own term 'tone'. Apart from the distinction of 'acute' and 'grave' in Greek, a third type of accent could occur on long vowels or diphthongs, comprising a glide from high to low pitch; this was viewed by the Greeks as a combination of acute and grave. Such an analysis is justified in a language where the concept of the 'mora' is applicable (cf. Allen 1973, p.236f.) and was indeed employed by the Greeks under the name of *khronos prōtos* 'primary [measure of] time' (the term '*mora*', lit. 'delay', 'space of time', was not in fact used by Latin writers in any technical sense, but was first so adopted, for metrical purposes, by Gottfried Hermann). The gliding accent was variously termed *ditonos* 'bi-tonal', or *sumplektos* 'compound', later and more generally *perispōmenē*, literally 'bent around', whence the Latin translation *circumflexus*. It is possible that this term refers to the Alexandrian symbol for the accent rather than to its melodic nature; and the names of the other two accents also came to be applied (like the term 'accent' itself) to their written forms as well as to their phonetic realisations.

References

ABERCROMBIE, D. (1937) 'Writing systems', in Abercrombie (1965) 86–91.
— (1949a) 'Forgotten phoneticians', *TPhS 1948*, 1–34 (reprinted in Abercrombie (1965) 45–75).
— (1949b) 'What is a "Letter"?', *Lingua* 2, 54–63 (reprinted in Abercrombie (1965) 76–85).
— (1965) *Studies in Phonetics and Linguistics*, London (Oxford University Press).
ALLEN, W.S. (1953) *Phonetics in Ancient India*, London (Oxford University Press).
— (1973) *Accent and Rhythm*, Cambridge (Cambridge University Press).
— (1974) *Vox Graeca*, 2nd ed., Cambridge (Cambridge University Press).
COOK, R.M. and WOODHEAD, A.G. (1959) 'The Diffusion of the Greek Alphabet', *Am. J. Archaeology* 63, 175–8.
FIRTH, J.R. (1947) 'The English School of Phonetics', *TPhS 1946*, 92–132.
GRAMMONT, M. (1946) *Traité de phonétique*, 3rd ed., Paris (Delagrave).
McCARTER, P.K. (1975) *The Antiquity of the Greek Alphabet and the early Phoenician scripts*, Missoula, Montana (Scholars Press, for Harvard Semitic Museum).
PULGRAM, E. (1970) *Syllable, Word, Nexus, Cursus*, The Hague (Mouton).

The Origin and Early Development
of Chinese Phonological Theory

Most students of classical thought would be likely to reject the view that there was any connection between a particular language and the philosophy or other intellectual modes that developed among its speakers: the idea that, for example, the directions taken by Greek scholarship could in any significant respect be ascribed to the nature of the Greek language. But there is one special exception, in which such a connection is naturally admitted, namely the study of language itself. Linguistics, wherever it has developed autochthonously, has begun as the study of the home language; and it is readily accepted that the nature of this language, whichever it happens to be, has played a significant part in determining the directions linguistic studies would take. In ancient Greece and India, where the languages were rich in word morphology, linguistics first developed as the study of word paradigms; and this, through a search for explanation of the choice of case, eventually led to syntax. The influence of the language on the development of linguistics in China seems no less clear. Classical Chinese had virtually no morphology; morphology is the outward sign of grammar; this, it is assumed, is why there is no study of grammar in Chinese linguistics. Both the general pattern of Chinese linguistics, with its concentration on lexicology and phonology, and the particular methods developed in these two fields, can be reasonably well explained by reference to the nature of the Chinese language and script.

Classical Chinese was largely monosyllabic: most words were (composed of) one morpheme, and most morphemes were (realised as) one syllable. The writing system was, and still is, morphemic: one character represented one morpheme. We may accept Y.R. Chao's observation that 'so far as Classical Chinese and its writing system is concerned, the monosyllabic myth is one of the truest myths in Chinese mythology' (Chao 1968, p.103). The fundamental linguistic unit represented in the consciousness of the speaker is now, and presumably was then, the complex made up of morpheme/syllable/character; this concept is referred to in Modern Chinese as zì.[1] Bimorphemic compounds already existed in the classical language, typically synonym compounds, species compounds and expressive reduplications; but the sense of the unity of morpheme/syllable/character was so strong that every disyllabic expression, even one in which neither element could occur without the other, was and always has been interpreted as consisting of two morphemes, and hence felt as belonging to the class of synonym compounds. Not only native words are thought of in this way, such as xīshuài[2] 'cricket'; the principle is extended to include disyllables that began as loanwords, e.g. bōlí[3] 'glass'.

Like other original traditions in linguistics, that in China sprang from concern about the growing unintelligibility of the ancient texts; in particular, there were many characters in the Book of Odes (songs dating mainly from 900–600 B.C., said to have been compiled by Confucius) that had disappeared from current use by the later classical period. The earliest known work of Chinese linguistic scholarship is a thesaurus of classical and preclassical terms entitled the Ěr Yǎ[4] 'Treasury of Fine Words', traditionally ascribed to a disciple of Confucius, Zǐ Xià.[5] This contains between three and four thousand entries, divided into nineteen sections; the first three sections are devoted to the exposition of important or difficult terms of a general nature, nouns, verbs and figurative expressions, while the remaining sixteen sections are topical groupings entitled Kin, Buildings, Implements, Music, Sky (i.e. calendar and climate), Land, Hills, Mountains, Water, Plants, Trees, Insects (which includes reptiles), Fishes, Birds, Wild Animals and Domestic Animals. Entries in the first three sections are explained by the use of synonymy: they are single items, or lists of related items, glossed by a synonym, or lists of cohyponyms glossed by a superordinate. In subsequent sections the method varies, but includes mainly i) synonymic gloss, as above; ii) reverse definition; iii) descriptive definition. Some entries are citations from the Book of Odes. No indication of pronunciation is given. Examples:

i) dāodāo, tuántuán, …, 'yōu' yě

切切　慱慱　　憂　也

dāodāo, tuántuán, &c. mean 'sad'

wáng, hòu, bì, gōng, hóu, 'jūn' yě

王　后　辟　公　侯　君　也

wáng, hòu, bì, gōng, hóu are 'the royalty'

ii) 'dà qín' wèi zhī lí

大　琴　謂　之　離

'a large lute' is called lí

iii) yàyǔ, lèi 'chū', hǔ zhuǎ, shí rén, xìn zǒu

猰貐　類　貙　虎　爪　食　人　迅　走

yàyǔ is a kind of wild cat, tiger-clawed, man-eating, swift-running

The thesaurus principle established by the Ěr Yǎ continued to be used throughout Chinese history as a method of lexicology; much later its use was extended to Sino-foreign wordbooks and phrasebooks. The work that first gave a systematic representation of how characters are pronounced did not, however, adopt this arrangement; it introduced a very different method of classifying characters, grouping them according to a component of the written symbol. This was the Shuō Wén Jiě Zì[6] 'Explanation of Simple and

Derived Characters'. The Shuō Wén Jiě Zì classification of characters established the lexicographic principle which has been used in dictionaries and encyclopedias right down to the present day. In fact, however, this method, of classifying by 'radical' (to give it its usual English name), is a direct and logical development of the thesaurus system of arrangement as already adopted in the Ěr Yǎ, and results in quite similar semantic groupings.

The Shuō Wén (it is usually known by its abbreviated title) was compiled at the end of the first century A.D. by Xǔ Shèn.[7] It contains 10,516 character entries, of which 1,163 are said to be duplicates. Each character is given in its archaic, 'seal script' form, followed by a gloss which is typically in three parts: semantic – a synonym, or brief definition; palaeographic – an explanation of the origin of the character; and phonetic – an indication of the pronunciation. For example:

háo,   'hǔ   shēng'   yě,   cóng   kǒu   hǔ,   dú   ruò   hào

虖   虎   聲   也   从   口   虎   讀   若   喬

háo means 'noise of a tiger', from kǒu (mouth) and hǔ (tiger), read like hào.

These take up fourteen of the fifteen sections of the work. The fifteenth section is in two parts, a 'postface' and an index of radicals. The postface is a short palaeographic essay containing a classification of characters into six types according to the principle on which they were formed (cf. Chao 1968, pp.103–5; Kratochvíl 1968, pp.148–51). These are, in the order listed in the Shuō Wén, and with Xǔ Shèn's own examples:

	Type	Translation	Examples		Meaning
(1)	zhǐshì[8]	symbolic	上	下	above, below
(2)	xiàngxíng[9]	pictorial	日	月	sun, moon
(3)	xíngshēng[10]	phonetic (compound)	江	河	river, river
(4)	huìyì[11]	semantic (compound)	武	信	arms, loyalty
(5)	zhuǎnzhù[12]	modified	考	老	deceased, old
(6)	jiǎjiè[13]	transferred	令	長	order, grow

Type (1) are non-representational iconic symbols, e.g. 上 (old 二) shàng 'above'; 下 (old 一) xià 'below'. Xǔ Shèn gives very few of these, preferring to interpret in terms of the next wherever possible. Other examples that have been given include 八 bā 'eight', symbol of divisibility, and the numbers 二 èr 'two' and 三 sān 'three'.

Type (2) are pictorial representations, e.g. 日 (old ⊙) rì 'sun'; 月 (old 𝒟) yuè 'moon'. Others: 木 (木) mù 'tree'; 門 (門) mén 'door'; 水 (水) shuǐ 'water'; 女 (女) nǚ 'woman'. Xǔ Shèn includes in this category indirect representations such as 大 dà 'big', picture of man with arms outstretched; 工 gōng 'skill, artisan', picture of carpenter's square.

Type (4) are meaningful combinations, e.g. 武 (modern 武) wǔ 'arms, military', consisting of 戈 'lance' and 止 'foot' – by Shuō Wén time 止 meant 'stop', so this character was later explained as 'fighting to stop fighting'

(Chao says 'cf. idea of "a war to end all wars"'), but the probable explanation is the simpler one of marching under arms; 信 xìn 'loyalty, belief', consisting of a man standing by his word. Other examples are 明 míng 'bright', sun and moon; 反 fú 'submit', kneeling man and hand; 東 dōng 'east', sun seen in tree as at sunrise.

Type (5) are modifications of another character with related meaning, e.g. 考 kǎo 'old, deceased, "the late"', interpreted by Xǔ Shèn as a modification of 老 lǎo 'old' by deflection of one stroke. But according to Karlgren (1940), 考 is a phonetic compound, type (3) below, with radical 老 'old' and phonetic 丂 kào, made to look like a modification of 老 because the 丂 element got fused into it. Chao doubts the reality of this class; another traditional example is 尸 shī 'corpse', said to be a variant of the character 人 rén 'man (human being)', presumably deformed in some way.

In characters of these four types, there is no phonetic principle at work. In the two remaining, there is. Type (6) are 'phonetic loans', characters transferred from their original morpheme referent to another one that is homophonous with it. 令 was originally a pictorial representation of a man and a bell, and was the character for líng 'bell'; it was borrowed to represent the homophone lìng 'to order'. The two were probably cognate; in Xǔ Shèn's other example, 長 cháng 'long' transferred to zhǎng 'to grow', they certainly were. But this category is now thought of primarily as one involving transference to non-cognate homonyms, e.g. 來 lái 'kind of wheat', picture of growing grain, 'borrowed' to represent lái 'come'; 壴 kǎi 'triumphal music', picture of a drum, for qǐ 'how?' (O.C. k'ər, k'jər); 凡 fán 'sail', picture, for fán 'all'.

In type (3), which are the most numerous, the phonetic loan has been backed up by the addition of another character signalling the meaning, resulting in a phonetic-semantic compound, usually referred to simply as 'phonetic compound'; e.g. 江 jiāng 'river', with 工 gōng as phonetic element and (a reduced form of) 水 'water' as semantic element; 河 hé 'river', 可 kě as phonetic element and again 'water' as semantic (both pairs were near-homonyms in Old Chinese). Other examples: 隹 zhuī 'dove' (itself a picture) occurs as phonetic element in 椎 chuí 'hammer', with semantic 木 'tree, wood'; in 誰 shuí 'who?', with semantic 言 'speech'; in 維 wéi 'to tie, guiderope', with semantic 糸 'silk'; in 推 tuī 'to push', with semantic 手 'hand'; and various others, all near-homonyms in Old Chinese (when there were fewer exact homonyms than in the modern language).

Some of Xǔ Shèn's explanations are fanciful: for example, he explains the character 名 míng, meaning 'personal name', which consists of the character for 'mouth' surmounted by that for 'night' (the latter a variant of the 'moon' picture), with the words 'at night it is dark and people cannot see one another, so they use their mouths to call out their names'. Some of his interpretations have been disproved by recent discoveries of early forms of characters in inscriptions and on oracle bones, to which he did not have access; and the meanings he assigns to simple characters that no longer occur alone, but only as elements in others, seem at times to be guesswork based on his interpretation of their origins, without textual evidence. But the vast majority of his analyses are right; and the general theory (which he ascribes to an imperial tutor of former times), with the possible exception of the doubtful type (5), can certainly be accepted as valid.

As a means of ordering the characters, Xŭ Shèn adopted the following principle. Out of the ten thousand or more he was able to identify 540 such that all other characters contained at least one of the 540 as a component part. This set of 540 was then used as 'head characters' for the purpose of classifying the remainder. He arranged them in a reasonably natural order based on what seemed to be the dominant configuration of strokes; this yielded small sets of around 5–10 characters, within which further ordering was achieved roughly by degree of complexity (number of strokes).

Under each head character was entered, first itself, and then all other characters identified by having it as their 'radical' component, in apparently arbitrary order. This system is still in use, though the number of radicals was progressively reduced in two dictionaries of the Ming dynasty, first to 360 and then, in the Zì Huì[14] of around 1580, to the modern inventory of 214; and the number of strokes became the dominant ordering principle, not only of the radicals themselves but also of the characters listed under each.

What determined Xŭ Shèn's choice of radical? In the case of characters of types (1), (2), (4), (5) and (6) the choice was largely arbitrary; but there were relatively few characters belonging to these types that were not themselves among the 540 head characters, where the question of which part was the radical did not arise. The vast majority of characters other than the 540 head characters were of type (3); that is, they consisted of two parts, one semantic and the other phonetic in value. And here Xŭ Shèn's choice of radical was not arbitrary, since he adopted as a principle what had already emerged as a natural pattern in the Ěr Yǎ. Looking at the later sections of the Ěr Yǎ, one finds that, because the characters in a section share a common meaning, they tend to share a common semantic element. So those in Section 14 typically have the 'tree' radical mù,[15] those in Section 17 the 'bird' radical niǎo;[16] those in Section 6 have 'metal', 'bamboo', 'cloth' and so on. Xŭ Shèn turned this into a general principle, always selecting the semantic and not the phonetic element as the radical, under which to list the character. So in paving the way for future lexicographers Xŭ Shèn ensured that there was much less mismatch between dictionary and thesaurus than there is in European languages, because the indexing principle of the dictionary is based on the semantic element in the written symbol.

But the consistent choice of the semantic element as radical also has a consistent side-effect: it clearly identifies the phonetic element wherever there is one, since that is the part left over. Wherever possible Xŭ Shèn made use of this element as an indicator of the pronunciation. Let us look at the most typical form of entry in the Shuō Wén. By far the most frequent is the following:

wèi, 'bào' yě, cóng yán, wèi shēng

謂 報 也 从 言 胃 聲

wèi is 'to announce', from yán (speak), wèi sound.

The character 謂 is made up of the character 言 'speech' functioning as semantic element (pronunciation irrelevant) and the character 胃 wèi functioning as phonetic element (meaning irrelevant). Both halves now serve a lexicological function: 言 as the 'radical', for indexing purposes, and 胃 as the indicator of pronunciation.

By the time the Shuō Wén was written, however, at least a thousand years had passed since the main period of evolution of the script; and many pairs of characters, the one serving as 'phonetic' element in the other, were no longer exact homonyms – if indeed they ever had been. In the case of 胃 and 謂 they are: both are, in Karlgren's reconstruction, Old Chinese gjwəd, Middle Chinese jwei. Xǔ Shèn clearly tolerated some departure from exact homonymy: he used the same formula 'sound ___' not only for instances that did not match for tone but also for others where there was a minor difference in consonant or vowel, for example:

pú, 'shuǐ cǎo' yě, huò yǐ zuò xí, cóng cǎo, pǔ shēng

蒲 水 草 也 或 曰 作 席 从 艸 浦 聲

pú is 'a water plant, sometimes used for making mats'; from cǎo (plant), pǔ sound.

where pú[17] had voiced initial (O.C. b'wo, M.C. b'uo) and pǔ[18] voiceless (O.C. p'wo, M.C. p'uo). In practice Xǔ Shèn was accepting about the same degree of homonymy as had gone into the making of the script in the first place. Where one character was used as phonetic element in another, the morphemes they represented were often not identical in pronunciation but might differ in a variety of features: voicing/aspiration, nasality, palatality, type of stricture, vowel quality, or combinations of these (see Karlgren 1940, passim). For Xǔ Shèn, if one character had another one as its phonetic, that was normally enough reason for him to accept the latter as its 'sound'; in other words, the entry under 'sound' was not yet a true indication of pronunciation, and the concept of the syllable as a phonological unit had not yet fully emerged from the complex notion of 'character'.

But that it was already well on the way can be seen from the other type of pronunciation gloss found in the Shuō Wén. Characters of types (1), (2), (4) and (5) have no phonetic element, and so could not be treated in the same way. Most of those that are themselves head characters, as well as a few others that are very common, mostly of type (4), are left without any phonetic gloss at all. But in a minority of instances, Xǔ Shèn introduces another formula: dú ruò ___[19] 'is read like ___', or dú yǔ ___ tóng[20] 'is read the same as __'. This is used with less common characters, like the 'noise of a tiger' cited above; and it is also occasionally added to the entry for a character which already has a phonetic element where that element is for some reason unsatisfactory as an indication of the sound: because it is very rare, or it has more than one reading – or perhaps because it is felt to be *markedly* different in pronunciation. Here both forms of gloss are combined in a single entry:

dù, 'bì' yě, cóng pǔ, dù/duò shēng, dú ruò dù

啟 閉 也 从 攴 度 聲 讀 若 杜

dù is 'to close off', from pǔ (to strike), dù/duò sound, read like dù.

where the dù reading had final vowel (final voiced stop in Old Chinese, but lost by Shuō Wén time), the duò reading had final consonant (voiceless stop); thus the phonetic element, left by itself, would have been ambiguous as a pronunciation guide. In the following, however, the justification seems to be different:

tiǎo, 'sì jí' yě, cóng xuè, zhào shēng, dú ruò tiǎo

窕 肆 極 也 从 穴 兆 聲 讀 若 挑

tiǎo is 'frivolous', from xuè (cave), zhào sound, read like tiǎo

(the original sense of the character was 'secluded', hence the 'cave' radical). Here the phonetic has only one reading, nor is it at all rare; the reason for the additional gloss appears to be that by this time the difference in pronunciation between it and its 'host' character had become rather striking – probably zhào[21] was voiced initial, palatalised, open vowel, while tiǎo[22] was voiceless initial, unpalatalised, mid vowel.

So while on the face of it there is not much difference between the two forms of the gloss, '__ sound' and 'read like __' (both simply refer one character to another), there is an important difference in principle. The former means 'this part of the character indicates its phonetic value'; it involves no concept of an independent phonetic symbol. The latter means 'this character is pronounced like that one'; the second character is brought in only as a phonetic notation. The latter is therefore the first step towards an abstract phonological analysis. Xǔ Shèn was not, in fact, the first person ever to think of glossing a character in this way, as being pronounced like another one: there are odd instances in the classical texts, sometimes accompanied by a descriptive note. Wáng Lì (1936; I, p.107) quotes the following from the Spring and Autumn Annals:

yán nǎi zhě nèi ér shēn, yán ér zhě wài ér qiǎn

言 乃 者 内 而 深 言 而 者 外 而 淺

nǎi is spoken interior and deep, ér is spoken exterior and shallow

recalling Downer's comment that 'such descriptions mean little to anyone except the originator' (1963, p.128) – although given that nǎi was O.C. nəg (M.C. nɑi), ér was O.C. ɲjəg (M.C. nʒji), it is perhaps not too fanciful to interpret 'interior and deep' as 'open back vowel' and 'exterior and shallow' as 'close front vowel'. But Xǔ Shèn was the first to make systematic use of character homonymy in what was, in fact, a work of linguistic scholarship. In so doing, he set Chinese scholarship along the path of phonological analysis.

As a technique of phonological analysis the use of homonymy has severe limitations, since it is confined within an extremely restricted circularity. In the century or two following the appearance of the Shuō Wén it was superseded by a new technique, which eventually became to be known as 'turning (i.e. inverting) cutting', fǎnqié[23] ('countersegmentation' might be an appropriate English rendering). By this method the pronunciation of a character is stated by reference not just to one other character but to two, which then have to be combined. The formula is exemplified by

dōng, dé hóng qiè
東 德 紅 切
dōng is (represented by) the segmentation of dé hóng

(M.C. tūŋ, tək ɣūŋ). In other words, to find the pronunciation of dōng[24] take the initial sound of dé[25] and the final sound of hóng[26] and combine them. This is still, of course, circular; but the circle is very much wider, as in the pronunciation guide in a modern English dictionary.

This method is known to have been used in a third century phonological commentary on the Ěr Yǎ, the Ěr Yǎ Yīn Yì[27] by Sūn Shúrán,[28] which is now lost. Few fǎnqiè renderings from before A.D. 600 have been preserved in the context of the works in which they originally appeared. But from 600 onwards there is a wealth of such material, and it is known that many of the fǎnqiè renderings contained in the principal works now extant were taken over from earlier sources without change.

The most important single work, which represents the high point of the early phonological tradition, is the Qiè Yùn[29] 'Segmental Rhymer'. This was produced by a government research team directed by Lù Fǎyán[30] and published in 601. For many centuries it was lost, as was an eighth century revision of it the Táng Yùn[31] 'Tang Rhymer' by Sūn Miǎn.[32] It was known, however, through an extant further revision, the Guǎng Yùn[33] 'Enlarged Rhymer' (full title 'Great Sung Revised and Enlarged Rhymer') by Chén Péngnián[34] and Qiū Yǒng,[35] published in 1007–8, which was the version used by all subsequent scholars until the twentieth century. In the first decade of this century portions of early manuscript copies of both Qiè Yùn and Táng Yùn were found in the far northwest of China, by Paul Pelliot and Aurel Stein, in the great Buddhist collection that had been preserved in the Tunhuang caves. These showed that the Guǎng Yùn did in fact carefully conserve the original fǎnqiè renderings given by the authors of the Qiè Yùn. Subsequently further manuscripts were found in other parts of China, making it possible to reconstruct the major portion of the Qiè Yùn or its earlier, Táng Yùn revision. Much of this material was made available in an edition prepared by Luó Chángpéi[36] and Wèi Jiàngōng[37] entitled Shí Yùn Huì Biān.[38]

Just a few years later than the Qiè Yùn is another important work of 'contrasegmental' phonology, the Jīngdiǎn Shì Wén[39] 'Character Analysis of Classical Texts', by Lù Démíng,[40] who died in 630. According to Karlgren (1940, pp.8–11), it was quite independent of the Qiè Yùn, but based on the same dialect, that of Chángān,[41] the capital at that time (modern Sian); and it often serves to confirm the Qiè Yùn interpretations. Lù Démíng quotes extensively the fǎnqiè renderings of earlier writers. This, together with Lù Fǎyán's Preface to the Qiè Yùn which shows that the authors were aware of the phenomenon of diachronic change and had deliberately preserved distinctions recorded by their predecessors, suggests that the fǎnqiè were seen as a method of maintaining traditionally accepted standards of pronunciation.

The fǎnqiè technique presupposes an analysis of every syllable into two parts, an initial and a final. Wáng Lì (1936, I, p.107) suggests that this originated with a small number of etymologies, known since classical times, by which certain morphemes were explained as the fusion of two others, e.g.

ér yǐ wéi ěr, zhī hū wéi zhū

而 己 為 耳 之 乎 為 諸

ér yǐ becomes ěr, zhī hū becomes zhū

(O.C. ɲjəg zjəg becomes ɲjəg; ṭjəg g'o becomes ṭjo), though these 'natural segmentations' were never used as phonetic renderings.

The initial segment consisted of just the initial consonant. The final included everything else: vowel, final consonant if any, prosodic value (palatal, labial or open), and tone. The final thus corresponded exactly to what functioned as the rhyming element in verse, not only in post-classical times but also as far back as the Book of Odes itself (see Karlgren 1940, pp.90–110, for the actual rhymes contained in these songs). By the time of the Qiè Yùn, this two-part structural analysis had become explicit: that is, the elements 'initial' and 'final' had been recognised, and given names, niǔ[42] and yùn.[43] The latter in fact means 'rhyme'. The former means 'a knot', and its use in the sense of 'initial' has not been explained.

The Qiè Yùn was a phonological dictionary which had the specific purpose of establishing standardised rhyme tables for use in poetry, including the poems composed by candidates for the public service examinations. The characters are therefore classified under their finals, a total of 206 distinct finals being recognised. These are distributed over the four tones, so that the actual number of distinct syllabic rhymes is much less: 61 in all, or 95 if those in -p -t and -k are counted separately rather than as tonal variants (see below). The finals are tabulated at the end of the work; but there is no notation for them, nor is there any explicit analysis in phonetic terms. The only explicit phonetic terminology at this stage is found in the analysis of the tones.

131

In the Nán Shĭ[44] 'History of the South (Southern Kingdom)', the biography of Shĕn Yuē[45] (441–513) refers to an essay he wrote called Sì Shēng Pŭ[46] 'Gamut of the Four Tones', and recounts the now well-known story of the answer Shĕn Yuē gave to the Emperor Wŭ Tì who asked him to explain them: 'Tiān Zĭ shèng zhé'.[47] This illustrated the four tones in the order in which he had listed them (M.C. t´iēn tsí ʃjæ̀ŋ tjæt); it also expressed the loyal sentiment 'The Son of Heaven is holy and wise'. Shĕn Yuē called the tones píng, shăng, qù, rù,[48] terms which likewise are appropriate in both sound and meaning: they were in fact instances of their respective tones (M.C. b´jwāŋ, ʒjáŋ, k´jwò, nʒjəp), but they could also be – and subsequently usually were – understood as descriptive labels, since the words meant 'level', 'rising', 'going' and 'entering': the first were, in fact, level in tone, the second rising, the third falling and the fourth 'stopped', that is ending in a plosive consonant. Note that these do not correspond to the four tones of Modern Pekingese.

Shĕn Yuē thus treated the stopped syllable as a *tonal* variant of the others; and this became the established interpretation. It makes very good sense provided the stopped syllables are matched with the corresponding syllables with *nasal* finals; and this is the practice adopted in the Qié Yùn, and followed in the subsequent mainstream tradition. Hence any one rhyme had potentially either three or four tonal variants according to whether it was closed or open, e.g.:

closed type	kām	kám	kàm	kap	(34 rhymes)
open type	kā	ká	kà		(27 rhymes)

Of the 61 rhymes, only 34 were of the closed type; the absence of a fourth, 'entering' tone with the remainder is thus presented as a systematic gap. There are also accidental gaps in the other three tones, since none of the 61 rhymes occurs in all three; there are 57 in level, 55 in rising and 60 in falling tone. This, together with the 34 in stopped tone, makes up the total of 206 yùn (finals) referred to above. The number of characters (morphemes) in each rhyme is of course very variable; the most numerous category is the level tone.

The initials were not tabulated, since they did not form part of the rhyme; but systematic study of the fănqiè renderings by later scholars revealed that 32 initials were kept distinct; and if the interpretation was taken strictly on the basis of the first character used in each rendering, ignoring 'chains' of renderings that arise because the same character may be used to render both an initial and a final, it could be shown that some further distinctions were actually being made, resulting in an inventory of 47 initials in all. The difference arises because 15 out of the 32 initials can occur both with palatalised and with non-palatalised finals; the two are, of course, clearly set apart in the finals themselves, but the distinction is also treated as a feature of the initial consonant, so that in the fănqiè rendering of a palatalised syllable the initial character is also regularly one that stands for a palatalised syllable; and likewise with the non-palatalised.

Similarly with the finals: if one takes the fǎnqiè renderings rather than the tabulation it turns out that the number of finals actually distinguished is 290 (90 if the tonal categories are ignored) instead of the 206 (61) appearing in the tables. In other words the theory that is embodied in the fǎnqiè *practice* makes more distinctions than are recognised in the classification scheme; especially if only the direct renderings are taken into account.

The fǎnqiè technique clearly had the potential for being developed into a systematic notation. Theoretically it would have been possible to select a set of 32 characters to represent the initials and 206 for the finals and use these all the time. But instead of this the scholars preferred to vary the characters used in the fǎnqiè renderings. This was partly no doubt, as suggested by Wáng Lì, to preserve traditional renderings, and also to avoid using any character in the rendering of itself. But the fact is that, in the native tradition, no need was felt for a more systematic notation. This same reluctance to conceive of a character as ever being a purely phonetic symbol is evident throughout Chinese history; in the fourteenth-century Sino-Mongolian script, in which Chinese characters are used to represent Mongolian, over twice as many characters are used as the actual number of syllables recognised as distinct. The same principle holds in the transliteration of foreign names in Chinese today.

So reliable and consistent was the work of the early phonologists that, despite the absence of any concrete phonetic descriptions, the fǎnqiè renderings of the Qiè Yùn and its revisions have been the primary source for the reconstruction of Middle Chinese. Bernhard Karlgren, the Swedish scholar who first systematically reconstructed the sound systems of both Middle Chinese (500–700 A.D.; his term is 'Ancient Chinese') and Old Chinese (800–600 B.C.; his term is 'Archaic Chinese'), wrote (1940, p.3): 'By a lucky chance, rich sources of highly varying kinds (rhyme dictionaries, foreign transcriptions, loanwords in Korean and Japanese and the testimony of strongly diverging daughter dialects) combined to throw light on one definite stage of the evolution of the Chinese language: the language spoken in Ch'ang-an [Chángān], the capital, in Suei and early T'ang time (sixth and early seventh century A.D.). This language [is] most fully represented by the dictionary Ts'ie yün [Qiè Yùn].'

Table 1 shows the reconstructed 32 initials of the Qiè Yùn system, as embodied in the fǎnqiè renderings. If we count as distinct those occurring in palatalised and those occurring in non-palatalised syllables, shown separated by a slash /, the total becomes 47. Karlgren's Ancient Chinese has 37, since he keeps apart ʧ &c. and ʧj &c. as separate sets ('supradental' and 'palatal' affricates and fricatives), and likewise j and ∅, but not the other pairs of palatalised and non-palatalised.

Table 2 shows the reconstructed 61 finals of the Qiè Yùn system. These

133

TABLE 1. Reconstructed Qiè Yùn initials

p/pj   p'/p'j   b'/b'j   m/mj
t   t'   d'   n   l/lj
ʈ   ʈ'   ɖ'   ɲ
ts   ts'   dz'   s   z
ʧ/ʧj   ʧ'/ʧ'j   ʤ'/ʤj   nʒj   ʃ/ʃj ʒj
k/kj   k'/k'j   gj   ŋ/ŋj   χ/χj ɣj
ʔ/ʔj
∅/j

TABLE 2. Reconstructed Qiè Yùn finals

uŋ,-k/juŋ,-k   uoŋ,-k   jwoŋ,-k
oŋ,-k
ie/wie   i/wi   e   ei/wei
jwo   ju   uo
iei/iwei   jæi/jwæi   ɑːi/uɑːi   aːi/waːi   ai/wai   aj/waj   uɑi   ɑi   jwai
jen,-t/jwen,-t   juen,-t   jɛn,-t   juən,-t   jən,-t   uən,-t   ən
jan,-t/jwan,-t   ɑn,-t   uɑn,-t   aːn,-t/waːn,-t   an,-t/wan,-t   ien,-t/iwen,-t   jæn,-t
  /jwæn,-t
ieu   jæu   (iau)   ɑu
ɑ   uɑ/juɑ
a/ja/wa
jaŋ,-k/jwaŋ,-k   ɑŋ,-k/waŋ,-k
aŋ,-k/jaŋ,-k/waŋ,-k/jwaŋ   ɛŋ,-k/wɛŋ,-k   jæŋ,-k/jwæŋ,-k   ieŋ,-k/iweŋ,-k
jəŋ,-k/jwək   əŋ,-k/uəŋ,-k
jəu   əu   iəu
jəm,-p
ɑm,-p   ɑːm,-p   jæm,-p   iem,-p   am,-p   aːm,-p   jam,-p   jwam,-p

represent the ones that are tabulated. Taking account of all finals normally kept apart in the fǎnqiè renderings, shown by a slash, the total becomes 90. It will be noted that these additional distinctions are largely a matter of labialised/non-labialised, except with a back vowel where they are palatalised/non-palatalised; these were later elaborated into a theory of 'grades' (see below). The sixteen major groupings shown in the table are the shè[49] 'classes of final' recognised in the later tradition.

In the tables, I have used a simplified form of representation designed to illustrate the achievements of the early phonologists, and to give some idea of the distinctions that they were aware of, rather than to give an accurate account of reconstructed Middle Chinese. For Karlgren's work on Ancient (Middle) Chinese, see his *Études sur la Phonologie chinoise* (1915–26) and 'The reconstruction of Ancient Chinese' (1922); for his work on Archaic (Old) Chinese, and on the origins of the characters, see *Grammata Serica* (1940). A great deal of further work has been done following up Karlgren's achievements and revising and amplifying his conclusions, but his interpretation remains fundamentally valid (cf. Chao 1940).

It has been pointed out in the discussion of the initials and finals that there were a number of secondary distinctions embodied in the contrasegmental phonology, though less consistently or explicitly; and that these all relate to variation in the y/w prosody of the syllable. This pattern of prosodic systems was a marked feature of North Chinese in Chángān times, and still is today. The intuition of the fǎnqiè scholars was to show y-prosody twice over, as a feature both of initial and of final (cf. Chao 1940, p.207; Downer 1963, p.129); in this they show an awareness of the fact that it colours the whole syllable. On the other hand w-prosody can be treated simply as a feature of the final; there are no pairs of initials that have to be interpreted as (independently) labialised/non-labialised. Exactly the same is true in Modern Pekingese, where a systematic interpretation requires palatality as a term in two distinct systems (cf. Halliday 1959: Appendix A): i) a prosodic system of 'open /y/w/yw (ɥ)' in the syllable as a whole (which can, of course, be represented as a feature of the final), as well as ii) a distinct system of 'y/non-y' in (certain of) the initials – although the actual sets of morphemes falling into these various classes are now quite different.

Such was the phonological theory that evolved, first as an adjunct to lexicology and palaeography and then as an interpretation of poetic form, in the native Chinese scholarly tradition. It had almost no labelled categories, but was beginning to make use of tabulation, at the end of the Qiè Yùn but also already in the Yù Piān[50] 'Jade Tablet' by Gù Yěwáng[51] which appeared in 543. Although it would be foolish to assert that this tradition was totally free of all outside influences, since aspects of Buddhist thought had been known in China for a long time, it was clearly indigenous to China in all its essentials. During the Tang dynasty (7th–10th centuries), however, a major influence came into Chinese phonology from outside China. At this period Indian phonetic theory was introduced, and this led to a considerable shift in orientation.

The Indian tradition was explicit: it involved labels for phonetic categories, and also the idea of notation – derived from the nature of Indian writing, which is of course phonological. But Indian linguistics had, naturally, evolved in the study of Indian languages, and these languages make some phonological distinctions not found in Chinese and ignore others that are found in Chinese. The effect on Chinese phonological theory was therefore somewhat mixed.

It is beyond the scope of this paper to trace the history of subsequent developments. A summary may be found in Downer's 'Traditional Chinese phonology' (1963, especially pp.131–40). On the basis of Indian concepts, during the Tang dynasty the initials and finals of the Chinese syllable were step by step classified and described. The concept of niǔ was superseded by one of zìmǔ;[52] this originally meant simply the character used for writing the niǔ, but then evolved to mean 'category of initial described phonetically and designated by a standard symbol' (Downer's 'initial matrix'). These are said to have been first enumerated by Shǒu Wēn[53] in the Sānshíliù Zìmǔ Tú[54] 'Charts of the Thirty-six Initials' some time in the ninth century. Shǒu Wēn selected certain of the characters used as the initial element in the fǎnqiè renderings and used them as category headings. Since the starting-point was Indian phonetic theory, some of the distinctions made in Chinese were ignored, although the 36 initials also incorporated certain new ones, referred to below. Following the Indian categories, the initials were labelled as follows:

chún yīn[55]	'labials'	p p′ b′ m
shé yīn[56]	'linguals'	t t′ d′ n ṭ ṭ′ ḍ′ ɳ
chǐ yīn[57]	'dentals'	ts ts′ dz′ s z ʧ ʧ′ ʤ′ ʃ ʒ
yá yīn[58]	'molars'	k k′ g ŋ
hóu yīn[59]	'gutturals'	χ ɣ j ʔ

To these were added shéchǐ yīn[60] 'lingual dentals' to account for l and nʒj; and finally a category of chīng chún[61] 'light labials' was separated out from the labials to account for the newly emerging labiodental series which was evolving from pjw- p'jw- b'jw- and mjw- (Modern Mandarin f- f- f- and m/w-). All distinctions of palatalised/non palatalised were ignored, including the by then clearly distinct series of palatal and 'supradental' (modern retroflex) affricates and fricatives. Degrees of voicing were distinguished as follows:

qīng[62]	'clear'	(1)
cì qīng[63]	'semi-clear'	(2)
zhuó[64]	'clouded'	(3)
cì zhuó[65]	'semi-clouded'	(4)

(1) were voiceless unaspirated plosives, affricates and fricatives, and ʔ. (2) were voiceless aspirated plosives and affricates, and χ. (3) were voiced (and aspirated) plosives and affricates, and ɣ. (4) were voiced fricatives, nasals, lateral, and j.

Thus the zìmǔ were a rather unsatisfactory compromise which tended to blur the phonologically clear system of the fǎnqiè renderings, with its implicit system of 32 initials plus 15 prosodic variants. Downer writes (1963, p.134): 'Compared with the earlier *faanchieh* [fǎnqiè] system, the *tzyhmuu* [zìmǔ] in some cases make subphonemic distinctions, in other cases merge phonemically distinct initials'. This was a consequence of importing a set of categories deriving from the description of very different languages, compounded by the difficulties caused by the complex and far-reaching changes that were taking place in the Chinese language itself. In a sense what was blurred was the whole concept of phonology, as it shifted from the purely abstract conception developed in China towards a much more concrete interpretation based on the description of articulatory processes.

The classificatory scheme of initials was now built into the rhyme tables. The earliest extant full treatment is the Yùn Jīng[66] 'Mirror of Rhymes', by an unknown author in the late Tang dynasty. This contains 43 rhyme tables, with all syllables (i.e. all occurring combinations of initial and final) set out in tabular presentation. The labial/non-labial distinction maintained in the Qiè Yùn renderings of finals was now explicitly recognised and labelled, with the terms kāi kǒu[67] 'open mouth' and hé kǒu[68] 'closed mouth', these being known as the two hū[69] (lip postures, from the sense of hū 'to blow', and therefore 'round the lips'). A partial indication of vowel gradation, with the open vowel, had also been incorporated in the Qiè Yùn renderings, suggestive of some regular contrast along the lines of a/ɛ/ja; this was also a feature that was undergoing considerable change. The Yùn Jìng recognises four grades, interpretable as ɑ/ɛ/jɛ/ia (Downer 1963, p.135); they are applicable only to the open vowel series, and even there it is rare to find one final that is said to occur in all four. They are collectively known as děng[70] 'grades'; the grades are not given separate labels, though Downer (1963, p.134 and n.) mentions a later work in which they are referred to as kāi[71] 'open', fā[72] 'released', shōu[73] 'gathered' and bì[74] 'closed' – words which, like the names of the tones, also exemplify the categories they are describing.

By the time of the Sung dynasty (about 950–1250) the impact of Indian linguistics had led to an extremely rich if sometimes rather confusing era of development within Chinese phonology, a development that continued over a thousand years, right up to the introduction of western linguistics at the end of the nineteenth century. Wáng Lì remarks of Láo Nǎixuān,[75] author of the Děngyùn Yī Dé[76] 'Thoughts on the Děngyùn (graded finals)' (1883), that he was probably the last of the Chinese linguists to have been uninfluenced by western scholarship. Throughout this period there were two parallel strands, that of gǔyīnxué[77] 'ancient phonology', concerned with research into the sound system of antiquity, and jīnyīnxué[78] 'modern phonology', concerned with the ongoing study of the contemporary language; and most scholars tended to specialise mainly in either one or the other. A notable representative of the 'ancient' school was Jiāng Yǒng[79] (1681–1762), whose Yīnxué Biànlùn[80] 'Phonological Discussions' not only gave a detailed exposition of Sung phonological theory but also contained sections on the evolution and ontogenesis of speech sounds. As an example of the 'modern' school could be cited Jiāng Yǒng's older contemporary Pān Lěi[81] (1646–1708), a brilliant phonetician who travelled all over China studying and recording the dialects, and then, having used this material for the purpose of establishing an idealised phonological system for the contemporary language, threw all his field notes away.

The phonology remained a phonology of the syllable, always analysed into initial and final, with the initials classified by place and manner of articulation and the finals by rhyme, vowel grade, labialisation and tone. There was a clear distinction between systematic and accidental gaps: between syllables regarded as theoretically impossible, and those regarded as theoretically possible but happening not to occur. The specific features of the theory derive, as we have seen, from the later period, following the introduction of Indian linguistic scholarship. But much of the basic conceptual framework was already present in the Qiè Yùn tradition.

The syllable was conceived of as a structural unit, consisting of the elements 'initial' and 'final'. The way of looking at the syllable was akin to that of Firthian prosodic phonology (cf. Palmer 1970). There was no concept of further segmentation into phoneme-type units, but rather systems of contrasting features which interacted without being rigorously localised. There was a readiness to interpret according to function in the system, without being bound by the particular nature of the exponents: for example, the treatment of the stopped syllable as a tonal variant along with level, rising and falling. Perhaps the most striking feature of the approach – and it is something that forms part of the same overall intellectual stance – was its essentially abstract quality. Being implicit, it remained purely phonological. This is perhaps the only condition under which a purely phonological theory can arise. Be that as it may, the early Chinese tradition seems to be the only instance in history where such a theory has ever actually arisen.

NOTE. Chinese words are given in Pinyin, the official Chinese romanised orthography for modern Standard Chinese (Pekingese). Words cited from Old and Middle Chinese, and the tables of initials and finals in Middle Chinese, are based on Karlgren's *Grammata Serica*, but are given in a simplified form using only standard IPA symbols without diacritics. It should be stressed that this paper is intended solely as a contribution to the history of Chinese linguistics and not to the history of the Chinese language. The main source for the Qiè Yùn system is Wáng Lǐ's *Chinese Phonology*, which is written from the same point of view.

To avoid excessive intrusion of Chinese characters into the English text, wherever possible these have been omitted and put into a list at the end. A raised number following the transcription of a Chinese word refers to its position in the list.

I am most grateful to Professor Gordon Downer for pointing out certain errors in the original draft.

List of Characters
for Chinese words appearing in transcription in the text

1. 字	22. 窾	43. 韻
2. 蟋蟀	23. 反切	44. 南史
3. 琅璃	24. 東	45. 沈約
4. 爾雅	25. 德	46. 四聲譜
5. 子夏	26. 紅	47. 天子聖哲
6. 說文解字	27. 爾雅音義	48. 平上去入
7. 許慎	28. 孫叔然	49. 攝
8. 指事	29. 切韻	50. 玉篇
9. 象形	30. 陸法言	51. 顧野王
10. 形聲	31. 唐韻	52. 字母
11. 會意	32. 孫愐	53. 守溫
12. 轉注	33. 廣韻	54. 三十六字母圖
13. 假借	34. 陳彭年	55. 唇音
14. 字彙	35. 邱雍	56. 舌音
15. 木	36. 羅常培	57. 齒音
16. 鳥	37. 魏建功	58. 牙音
17. 蒲	38. 十韻彙編	59. 喉音
18. 浦	39. 經典釋文	60. 舌齒音
19. 讀若	40. 陸德明	61. 輕唇
20. 讀與　同	41. 長安	62. 清
21. 兆	42. 紐	63. 次清

64. 濁	70. 等	76. 等韻一德
65. 次濁	71. 開	77. 古音學
66. 韻鏡	72. 發	78. 分音學
67. 開口	73. 收	79. 江永
68. 合口	74. 閉	80. 音學辨論
69. 呼	75. 勞乃宣	81. 潘耒

References

CHAO, YUEN REN (1968) *Language and Symbolic Systems*, Cambridge (Cambridge University Press).

— (1940) 'Distinctions within Ancient Chinese', *Harvard J. Asiatic Studies* 5.

DOWNER, G.B. (1963) 'Traditional Chinese phonology', *TPhS*.

HALLIDAY, M.A.K. (1959) *The Language of the Chinese 'Secret History of the Mongols'*, Oxford (Blackwell: Publications of the Philological Society 17) Appendix A 'Phonological (prosodic) analysis of the New Chinese syllable (Modern Pekingese)' reprinted in F.R. Palmer 1970.

KARLGREN, BERNHARD (1915–24) *Études sur la Phonologie chinoise* Stockholm (Archives d'études orientales) 4 volumes.

— (1922) 'The reconstruction of Ancient Chinese', *T'oung Pao* 21.

— (1940) *Grammata Serica: script and phonetics in Chinese and Sino-Japanese*, Stockholm (Museum of Far Eastern Antiquities = *Bulletin of the Museum of Far Eastern Antiquities 12*).

KRATOCHVÍL, PAUL (1968) *The Chinese Language Today: features of an emerging standard*, London (Hutchinson: Hutchinson University Library).

PALMER, F.R. ed. (1970) *Prosodic Analysis*, London (Oxford University Press) Language and Language Learning 25.

WÁNG LÌ 王力 (1936) Zhōngguó Yīnyùnxué 中國音韻學 'Chinese Phonology', (Commercial Press) 2 volumes.

The Devising and Adoption of the Chinese
Phonetic Symbols (zhùyīn fúhào)

In September 1928 the Ministry of Education of the Republic of China
formally recognised two forms of the National Alphabet (guóyīn zìmǔ) as
aids to the pronunciation of the Chinese ideographs (i.e. characters) (Lǐ 1934,
p.174; Fāng 1969, p.58). The first form of the National Alphabet was the
Chinese Phonetic Alphabet (zhùyīn zìmǔ), which had already been proclaimed in November 1918; the second was the National Language
Romanization (Guóyǔ Luómǎzì). As the evolving of the first may be of some
interest to phoneticians in the West, I shall try to tell the story of the devising
and adoption of this system from its beginnings in 1912 to the early 1930s,
when it became widely accepted and was used in schools all over China. In
my account I have drawn heavily on Guóyǔ Yùndòng Shǐgāng ('A History of
the National Language Movement') by Lǐ Jǐnxī, who was active in the
promotion of the Phonetic Alphabet from the start.

Chinese scholars through the ages had always been aware of the variety
and complexity of the Chinese dialects. During the latter half of the nineteenth century many scholars made suggestions for simplifying the writing
of the Chinese characters or for the use of symbols to represent the pronunciation. Scholars such as Lú Zhuàngzhāng, Wáng Bǐngyào, Wáng Zhào
and Láo Nǎixuān were among those who had expended much time and effort
in this field.

In 1911 the monarchy was overthrown and China became a republic. It
being generally felt that the flourishing of a nation and the unification of its
language were closely connected, the Minister of Education, Cài Yuánpéi,
called the first of a series of conferences on language and pronunciation in
Peking (Běijīng) on 10 July 1912. This one, known as the Provisional
Education Conference, passed a resolution on 7 August for the use of a
phonetic alphabet as an aid to pronunciation. In December of the same year
the Ministry further proclaimed a constitution for the Conference on the
Unification of Pronunciation, appointing Wú Jìnghéng chairman of the
Conference (Lǐ 1934, pp.50–3; Fāng 1969, pp.17–18; Ní 1948, pp.66–7; Shào
1937, p.82). The main clauses of the constitution were as follows:

1. Composition of membership;
    a) Members are to be appointed by the Ministry of Education with no
    fixed quota.
    b) Two members from each province are to be nominated by the

provincial governor, one member each from Mongolia and Tibet to be nominated by their respective authorities in Peking, and one Overseas Chinese member to be nominated by the Overseas Chinese Association.

2. Qualifications for membership. The following are eligible for membership:

a) those versed in phonology;

b) those versed in philology;

c) those versed in one or more foreign languages;

d) those with a knowledge of many Chinese dialects.

3. Function of the Conference:

a) The Conference shall standardise the pronunciation of all Chinese characters; the resulting pronunciation shall be called the Authorised Standard National Pronunciation.

b) The Conference shall analyse the sounds of Chinese characters and reduce them to their simplest components, and shall, in addition, fix the total number of such components.

c) The Conference shall adopt a phonetic alphabet, each symbol of which shall represent one of the sound components of Chinese.

All together eighty people were made members of the Conference, among them thirty-odd appointed by the Ministry of Education and about a dozen delegates from the Ministry; the remainder represented the provinces (Lǐ 1934, pp.51–3; Fāng 1969, pp.18–21). As it happened, many of the members were from Jiāngsū and Zhèjiāng provinces – seventeen and nine respectively. Of the others, eight were from Zhílì (i.e. Héběi), four each from Húnán, Fújiàn and Guǎngdōng, three each from Húběi, Sìchuān and Guǎngxī, two each from Shāndōng, Shānxī, Shǎnxī, Hénán, Gānsù, Ānhuī, Jiāngxī, Fèngtiān (i.e. Liáoníng), Jílín and Hēilóngjiāng, one each from Yúnnán, Guìzhōu, Xīnjiāng and Mongolia. There was one member whose place of origin was not known.

On 15 February 1913 the Conference on the Unification of Pronunciation held its first session with forty-four members present (Lǐ 1934, pp.53–4; Fāng 1969, pp.21–2; Ní 1948, p.67; Shào 1937, p.82; Zhōu 1961, pp.33–4, 61). Wú Jìnghéng was elected chairman, and Wáng Zhào, vice-chairman. The first task of the Conference was the standardisation of pronunciation. The most frequently used words, chosen from among homophones classified in Yīnyùn Chǎnwēi (1726) by Lǐ Guāngdì (1642–1718) and others, were duplicated and distributed to each individual member who then noted down the pronunciation of each word in his province, using a set of phonetic symbols previously prepared by the steering committee for this purpose. (As will be seen, these symbols eventually became the Chinese Phonetic Symbols.) On the following day the representative of each province handed in his list of words with their pronunciation indicated by symbols, and the pronunciation recommended by the largest number of members became the standard pronunciation for each particular word. These pronunciations were later adopted for the officially sponsored 'National Pronouncing Dictionary' published by the Commercial Press in 1919. After more than a month, the pronunciation of over 6,500 words had been fixed and, in addition, that of over 600 words of recent origin or in vulgar use, including scientific and technical terms, had also been standardised.

The next task was the analysis of sounds and the devising of a set of phonetic symbols (Lí 1934, pp.54–6; Fāng 1969, pp.22–3; Ní 1948, p.68). This proved just as controversial as the standardisation of pronunciation. Twenty or thirty systems were proposed, representing broadly three schools of thought:

1. Those who advocated symbols similar to kana (i.e. Japanese syllabic writing) and proposed using part of a Chinese character to represent the sound of the whole: Wáng Zhào, Wāng Róngbǎo, Wáng Yí'ān, Cài Zhāng and others.

2. Those who advocated invented symbols: Mǎ Tǐqián, Wú Jìnghéng, Lú Zhuàngzhāng, Hú Yǔrén and others.

3. Those who advocated the Roman alphabet, such as Yáng Zēnggào; those who advocated modification of the Roman alphabet, such as Wú Jìnghéng and Xíng Dǎo; and those who advocated adding symbols to the Roman alphabet, such as Liú Jìshàn.

All these scholars supported their systems with their publications or cyclostyled leaflets. The discussion was heated, for, as Wú Jìnghéng puts it in his 'The Movement for the Use of the Phonetic Symbols in the Last Thirty-five Years' (1931) (Lí 1934, pp.55–6), every one was hoping to be another Cāng Xié, the legendary inventor of Chinese characters.

However, none of the proposed systems could win general acceptance, and it was finally proposed by Mǎ Yùzǎo, Zhū Xīzǔ, Xǔ Shòucháng (all pupils of Zhāng Bǐnglín), Qián Dàosūn and Zhōu Shùrén (i.e. Lǔ Xùn) that the symbols prepared by the steering committee be approved. They maintained that to unify pronunciation it was only necessary to improve upon the traditional method of spelling in Chinese dictionaries, in which two characters were given, the initial sound of one being combined with the final of the other to give the pronunciation. For this purpose it would be best to use simplified Chinese characters representing various initials and finals. Thereupon the Conference decided to adopt the symbols prepared by the committee and named them the Phonetic Alphabet in accordance with the term proposed by the Provisional Education Conference (Lí 1934, p.56; Fāng 1969, p.23; Ní 1948, pp.68–9; Zhōu 1961, p.61; Shào 1937, p.82).

This approved system may be called the 'simplified character' system, and its inventor may be said to be Zhāng Bǐnglín. The symbols were mostly taken from the ancient seal script. For example, the very first symbol ㄅ is the ancient form of the character 包 [pau] and is used to represent the initial [p]; and the symbol 丂 is the ancient form of the character 考 [hai] and is used to represent the final [ai].

After some further discussion, the Conference also approved the symbols for the five tones and voiced consonants. It then went on to recommend the following ways for the promotion of the National Pronunciation (Lí 1934, pp.57–8; Shào 1937, p.82; Fāng 1969, p.27; Ní 1948, pp.69–70):

1. That the Ministry of Education should request all provincial governors to order their educational officers speedily to provide classes for the instruction of the National Phonetic Alphabet, to be attended by representatives from the various counties. Upon completing their course, these representatives would return to their respective counties and conduct classes for others.

2. That the Ministry of Education should proclaim the approved Phonetic Alphabet without delay.

3. That the Ministry of Education should make gramophone records of the National Pronunciation, to be distributed among the provincial educational authorities, thus avoiding the possibility of errors creeping into the teaching in classes.

4. That the Ministry of Education should substitute the vernacular for Classical Chinese in the curriculum of the earliest years of primary school, or, at least, add the vernacular to the existing curriculum.

5. That teachers of Chinese in primary and secondary schools and in training colleges be required to use the National Pronunciation when teaching.

6. That, after the publication of the 'National Pronouncing Dictionary', all textbooks used in primary schools should have the pronunciation in the National Phonetic Alphabet printed beside each Chinese character.

7. That, after the publication of the 'National Pronouncing Dictionary', all public announcements and notices should have the pronunciation in the National Phonetic Alphabet added to each Chinese character.

On 22 May the Conference on the Unification of Pronunciation was formally closed. This was followed, however, by a change of Minister, and the Ministry shelved the matter. After over a year, Wáng Pú and twenty-four other members of the Conference resident in Peking held a second Conference at which both in January and, again, in November 1915 they requested the Ministry of Education to promote the Phonetic Alphabet. The request in November was accompanied by the information that members of the Conference had already set up classes for the instruction of the Phonetic Alphabet in Peking with their own funds. The Ministry duly approved the experiment, and the Minister of Education of the time, Zhāng Yīlín, went so far as to donate two hundred dollars per month out of his own salary to add to the funds. In December, Zhāng formally requested the President, Yuán Shìkǎi, to give the project his official approval. Nothing came of it, for Yuán soon proclaimed himself Emperor and the political situation became the preoccupation of all men in public life. Nevertheless, Wáng Pú, the organiser of the classes, made great efforts to attract students, so that a large number came to learn the Phonetic Alphabet. Wáng Pú also established the Phonetic Alphabet Press, which, apart from reprinting works like the 'Book of Family Names (Bǎi Jiā Xing) and the 'Thousand Characters Primer' (Qiānzi Wén) with phonetic symbols beside the Chinese characters, also published a forty-page magazine in which all Chinese characters were accompanied by phonetic symbols (Lí 1934, pp.62–3; Shào 1937, p.83; Fāng 1969, p.28; Ní 1948, p.71).

After the death of Yuán Shìkǎi in June 1916, China again became a republic. People in the Ministry of Education were more conscious than ever that the basic problem in raising the standard of education was the problem of literacy. Scholars such as Lí Jǐnxī, Wāng Màozǔ, Chén Màozhì and others wrote articles advocating uniformity of language and literature as well as a uniform national language. This resulted in the foundation in Peking of the Society for National Language Research, its members being representatives from each province (Lí 1934, pp.66–7; Fāng 1969, p.31; Ní 1948, p.71). Its aim was 'the study of the language of our country in order to establish a standard for the use of the educational world' (Lí 1934, p.67). At the first formal meeting which took place in 1917 in Peking with Cài Yúanpéi as chairman and Zhāng Yīlín as vice-chairman, a Plan for Research in the National Language was drafted. It is interesting to note that, though firmly believing in the vernacular as the proper medium for literature (i.e. that literature should be written in the vernacular) the scholars all wrote their articles in Classical Chinese. It was not until at the end of 1917 that a postcard written in the vernacular sent from America by Hú Shì started the fashion of writing in the vernacular.

In 1918 Hú Shì wrote his article 'On a Constructive Literary Revolution' (Hú 1953, pp.55–73) in the vernacular in the journal Xīn Qīngnián ('La Jeunesse'). He stressed the importance of a literature written in the vernacular, which could strengthen the standing of the national language. He advocated the use of polysyllabic compounds, since monosyllables used in the old literary style led to ambiguity when read aloud, because of the large number of homophones in the Chinese language. With the publication of this article the two popular trends of thought of the time – the Literary Revolution and the Unification of the National Language – were fused into one. In order to highlight a literature in the national language, the question of the unification of pronunciation, and consequently that of the Phonetic Alphabet, were again brought into prominence (Lí 1934, pp.70–1; Fāng 1969, p.31; Ní 1948, pp.71–2).

The Phonetic Alphabet adopted by the Conference on the Unification of Pronunciation had not been proclaimed by the Ministry of Education. There had been considerable opposition, on these grounds:

1. The Phonetic Alphabet would adversely affect the traditional Chinese

ideographs.

2. If the Phonetic Alphabet were used on its own (i.e. without Chinese characters), then the traditional literary style would have to be changed.

3. In spite of its use for indicating the pronunciation of the Chinese character, it would not necessarily guarantee the unification of the spoken language.

4. It would be an extra burden on schoolchildren (Lí 1934, p.76).

By 1918 the membership of the Society for National Language Research had increased to more than 1,500. During the Third National United Education Conference held in Hángzhōu in 1917 it was resolved that the Ministry of Education be urged to fix a standard for the national language and to promote the Phonetic Alphabet in all provinces as a preparation for the change-over of Classical Chinese to the vernacular in all primary schools (see below p.155). At the same time the Education Conference of Jiāngsū Province resolved that in all schools in the province classes in the vernacular should forthwith begin.

In 1918 the Ministry of Education called a Conference of the Principals of the Higher Teachers' Training Colleges (Peking, Wǔchāng, Shěnyáng, Nánjīng, Guǎngdōng, Chéngdū, and Shǎnxī), at which it was resolved to add a course on 'The Teaching of the National Language' to the curriculum. It was further specified that the course should consist of special instruction in the Phonetic Alphabet and the National Language (i.e. the vernacular). The Ministry also decided to allocate students from twenty-six provinces among the seven Higher Training Colleges so that teachers in all provinces would be able to teach the National Language (Lí 1934, p.76; Shào 1937, p.83; Fāng 1969, pp.31–2; Ní 1948, p.72).

Before we proceed to the Phonetic Symbols themselves, it has to be explained that a Chinese syllable is traditionally divided into parts: the 'initial' (shēngmǔ) and the 'final' (yùnmǔ). The 'initial' refers to the initial consonant of a syllable, for example *l* [l] in lái ['lai] 'to come'. The 'final' refers to what comes after the 'initial'. It may be any one of the following:

1) a simple vowel, i.e. monophthong, e.g. *a* [ɑ] in ná ['na] 'to take';
2) a diphthong, e.g. *ou* [ou] in gǒu ['kou] 'dog';
3) a triphthong, e.g. *iao* [iɑu] in xiǎo ['ɕiɑu] 'small';
4) a simple vowel or a diphthong plus the nasal *n* [n] or *ng* [ŋ], e.g. *ang* [ɑŋ] in láng ['laŋ] 'wolf', *ian* [iæn] in qiān ['tɕʻiæn] 'thousand'.

2, 3 and 4 may be called 'compound finals'. The 'compound finals' are divided into three parts:

1) 'head' yùntóu – the vowel immediately after the initial and before the main vowel; it may also be called the 'medial'. There are three 'medials':

i [i], e.g. *i* in xiǎo,

u [u], e.g. *u* in kuài ['kʻuai] 'quick',

ü or *u* [y], e.g. *u* in quán [ˈtɕʻyan] ‘complete’.

2) ‘body’ yùnfù – the main vowel in the syllable, e.g. ‘a’ in ‘xiǎo’;
3) ‘tail’ yùnwěi – the final vowel or consonant, for example:
   o in xiǎo,
   n in qiān.

In November of the same year the Ministry of Education formally proclaimed the Chinese Phonetic Alphabet of thirty-nine symbols adopted by the Conference on the Unification of Pronunciation (Lí 1934, pp.76–9; Fāng 1969, pp.32–6; Zhōu 1961, pp.62–4; Shào 1937, p.84). The symbols are given in figure 1.

24 initials			
ㄍ [k]	ㄎ [kʻ]	ㄫ [ŋ]	ㄐ [tɕ]
ㄑ [tɕʻ]	ㄬ [ɲ]	ㄉ [t]	ㄊ [tʻ]
ㄋ [n]	ㄅ [p]	ㄆ [pʻ]	ㄇ [m]
ㄈ [f]	ㄪ [v]	ㄗ [ts]	ㄘ [tsʻ]
ㄙ [s]	ㄓ [tʂ]	ㄔ [tʂʻ]	ㄕ [ʂ]
ㄏ [x]	ㄒ [ɕ]	ㄌ [l]	ㄖ [ʐ]
3 medials			
ㄧ [i]	ㄨ [u]	ㄩ [y]	
12 finals			
ㄚ [ɑ]	ㄛ [o]	ㄝ [ɛ]	ㄟ [ei]
ㄞ [ai]	ㄠ [ɑu]	ㄡ [ou]	ㄢ [an]
ㄤ [ɑŋ]	ㄣ [ən]	ㄥ [ʌŋ]	ㄦ [ɜ˞]

FIGURE 1.

The sign for voiced sounds was a ‘,’ on the upper right-hand corner of the symbol.

To indicate the tones, a dot would be put on one of the four corners of the symbol (figure 2). Thus a dot on the left lower corner represented the ‘lower-even’ tone (i.e. high-rising, Tone II); a dot on the upper left corner represented the ‘rising tone’ (i.e. falling-rising, Tone III); a dot on the upper right corner represented the ‘departing tone’ (i.e. high-falling, Tone IV); a dot on the lower right corner represented the ‘entering tone’ (i.e. a clipped sound followed by a glottal stop). When no dot was placed, the tone was the ‘upper-even tone’ (i.e. high level, Tone I).

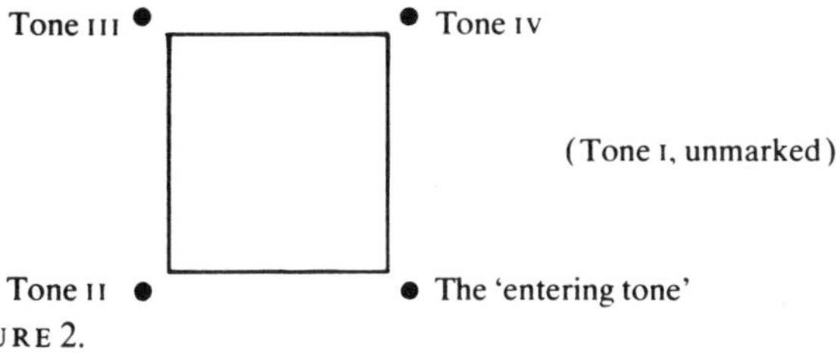

FIGURE 2.

Of the 39 symbols 15

ㄇ ㄈ ㄌ ㄋ ㄏ ㄗ ㄘ ㄙ ㄧ ㄩ ㄛ ㄟ ㄠ ㄥ ㄢ

were devised by Zhāng Bǐnglín.

In April 1919 the Ministry of Education proclaimed the formal sequences of the Phonetic Alphabet (figure 3) (Lí 1934, pp.83–6; Fāng 1969, pp.36–8; Ní 1948, p.73; Zhōu 1961, p.64).

ㄅ [p]	ㄆ [p']	ㄇ [m]	ㄈ [f]	ㄪ [v]
ㄉ [t]	ㄊ [t']	ㄋ [n]	ㄌ [l]	
ㄍ [k]	ㄎ [k']	ㄫ [ŋ]	ㄏ [x]	
ㄐ [tɕ]	ㄑ [tɕ']	ㄬ [ɲ]	ㄒ [ɕ]	
ㄓ [tʂ]	ㄔ [tʂ']	ㄕ [ʂ]	ㄖ [ʐ]	
ㄗ [ts]	ㄘ [ts']	ㄙ [s]		
ㄧ [i]	ㄨ [u]	ㄩ [y]		
ㄚ [ɑ]	ㄛ [o]	ㄝ [ɛ]		
ㄞ [ai]	ㄟ [ei]	ㄠ [ɑu]	ㄡ [ou]	
ㄢ [an]	ㄣ [ən]	ㄤ [ɑŋ]	ㄥ [ʌŋ]	
ㄦ [ɜ˞]				

FIGURE 3.

(In 1931 the three medials ㄧ, ㄨ and ㄩ were moved from their original position and placed after the final, ㄦ – Lí 1934, p.86.)

The compound finals, though not formally proclaimed, generally occurred in the sequence shown in figure 4.

Later, a new symbol ㄜ was added to the Alphabet (Lí 1934, pp.86–8; Fāng 1969, pp.38–40; Ní 1948, p.73; Zhōu 1961, pp.65–6). The symbol ㄛ, which represented the half-close back rounded vowel [o], was pronounced by many as the unrounded vowel [ɤ], but was always pronounced [o] when

ㄧㄚ	ㄧㄛ	ㄧㄝ	ㄧㄞ	ㄧㄠ	ㄧㄡ	ㄧㄢ	ㄧㄣ	ㄧㄤ	ㄧㄥ
[iɑ]	[io]	[iɛ]	[iai]	[iɑu]	[iou]	[iæn]	[in]	[iɑŋ]	[iŋ]
ㄨㄚ	ㄨㄛ	ㄨㄞ	ㄨㄟ	ㄨㄢ	ㄨㄣ	ㄨㄤ	ㄨㄥ		
[uɑ]	[uo]	[uai]	[uei]	[uan]	[uən]	[uɑŋ]	[uʌŋ]		
ㄩㄝ	ㄩㄢ	ㄩㄣ	ㄩㄥ						
[yɛ]	[yan]	[yin]	[yuŋ]						

FIGURE 4.

occurring after [i] or [u] or [y], as in ㄧㄛ, ㄨㄛ and ㄩㄛ. This caused much confusion, so that it was decided to put a dot above ㄛ (i.e. ㄛ̇) to represent the sound [ɤ]. However, since it would be rather inconvenient to add a dot when writing at speed, even apart from the possibility of confusion with tone marks, the dot above the ㄛ was often lengthened to a short vertical stroke

(ㄜ > ㄜ). By 1922 the symbol ㄜ had been included in both the printed form and the regular style of writing in the 'Calligraphic Styles of the Phonetic Alphabet' published by the Ministry of Education, so that there were in all forty symbols in the Phonetic Alphabet.

There was a suggestion in 1920 that the symbol ㄦ be also treated as an initial and grouped with the initials, but this seems not to have been carried out (Lǐ 1934, pp.88–9; Zhōu 1961, p.66; Ní 1948, p.73).

In the meantime three other symbols, ㄪ , ㆬ and ㄫ , were found to be superfluous (Lǐ 1934, pp.89–90; Fāng 1969, pp.40–1; Ní 1948, pp.73–4; Zhōu 1961, p.66).

In 1920, the Committee working on the 'National Pronouncing Diction-ary' decided that ㄪ [v] had the same pronunciation as ㄨ [u] in present-day speech. At the Fourth Preparatory Conference on the Unification of the National Language in 1922, Xú Áng suggested that ㆬ [ɲ] be treated as an allophone of ㄋ [n], while Wáng Pú suggested inclusion of ㄋ- [ni] under ㆬ . However, since ㄋ – (but not ㆬ) was found in the Peking dialect and very few dialects contained both ㄋ – and ㆬ, ㆬ was gradually dropped.

As for ㄫ ([ŋ] in the initial position in a syllable), no formal proposal for its abolition was ever made at any of the five Conferences held between 1919 and 1923, but since in the Peking dialect this sound never occurred in the initial position in a syllable, the symbol ㄫ also gradually disappeared.

On the official 'Chart of the Chinese Phonetic Alphabet' published by the Preparatory Committee on the Unification of the National Language in 1928, it was pointed out that ㄪ, ㆬ and ㄫ were used for indicating the Jiāngsū pronunciation, and not the National Pronunciation. Thus it was made clear that these three sounds did not exist in the National Pronunciation.

The method used to indicate the tones also underwent some changes (Lǐ 1934, pp.91–4; Fāng 1969, pp.41–3; Ní 1948, pp.74–7; Zhōu 1961, pp.66–7). The use of dots placed at the different corners of the symbol, suggested at the Conference on the Unification of Pronunciation in 1912–13, was adopted in the 'Table of the Phonetic Alphabet' (zhùyīn zìmǔ biǎo) published in 1918. This method was similar to that traditionally used for indicating tones, in which a small circle instead of a dot was employed. However, at a meeting of the Preparatory Committee on the Unification of the National Language held in 1920, Wáng Yì suggested that it would only be necessary to indicate the length of the syllable. Tone I and Tone II were to be described as 'long' and left unmarked, while Tone III, Tone IV and the 'entering tone' would be classified as 'short' and indicated with a dot at the lower right corner. At the same time Qián Xuántóng expressed the view that there was no need to mark the tones at all and that the use of hyphenated compound words would be enough to differentiate between tones and between the different meanings of homophones. At the Third Meeting of the Preparatory Committee on the Unification of the National Language held in 1921 Lǐ Jǐnxī proposed that the Ministry of Education proclaim a standard system of tones and suggested that the tones of the Peking dialect be adopted as the standard for the National Language. Lí included in his proposal Chao Yuen Ren's diagram, in which the tones were expressed in musical notation. His proposal was accepted by the Ministry of Education and under the 'cursive' section of the 'Calligraphic Styles of the Phonetic Alphabet' issued in 1922 there was this explanatory note:

> As the 'dot' system of indicating tones may cause confusion when one is writing horizontally, the following marks may be put above the final symbol of the word instead: Tone I: unmarked, unless a word is to be emphasized or lengthened, when a level stroke '——' may be used;
>
> Tone II: ╱ (e.g. | 𝓍́);
>
> Tone III: ⌣ (e.g. | 𝓍̆);
>
> Tone IV: ╲ (e.g. | 𝓍̀);

'entering tone': a dot, as in the other system.

Although this explanatory note dealt specifically with horizontal writing, even in vertical writing the 'diagram' system gradually came to be adopted. In 1931, on the reprinted 'Chart of the Chinese Phonetic Alphabet', the following sentence was added: 'When writing vertically, the tone mark should be placed on the upper right corner of the final sound of the word.' Later, even when writing horizontally, the tone mark was placed on the upper right corner of (instead of above) the final symbol. Thus the method of indicating tones became standardised.

The 'National Pronouncing Dictionary' has been mentioned more than once in the preceding pages, and it would be appropriate to describe the course of its publication. This dictionary recorded the pronunciation of words fixed by the Conference on the Unification of Pronunciation in 1913 in symbols approved by the Conference. After the Conference, a draft of the dictionary was presented to the Ministry of Education, who did not see fit to publish the work (Lí 1934, p.95; Fāng 1969, p.43; Shào 1937, p.83). In 1918, however, Wú Jīnghéng, the chairman of the Conference, rearranged in Shànghǎi the words according to their radicals and named the work the 'National Pronouncing Dictionary'. To the 6,500-odd words whose pronunciation had been fixed by the Conference he added over 6,000 words comprising: 1) essential words which had been left out by the Conference, 2) words the pronunciation of whose subsidiary meanings had not been considered. He further added over 600 words consisting of words in vulgar use and new scientific terms, thus forming a total of over 13,000 words. After completing his draft, Wú travelled to Peking to consult the original members of the Conference, including Chén Màozhì, Wáng Pú, Qián Xuántóng and Lí Jīnxī. After much discussion, the final draft was agreed upon and entrusted to the Commercial Press in Shànghǎi. At the same time the members urged the Ministry of Education to form a Preparatory Committee on the Unification of the National Language to revise the dictionary and eventually the first edition of this dictionary was published in September 1919 (Lí 1934, p.95; Fāng 1969, pp.43–4; Zhōu 1961, p.94n). In the meantime, the Preparatory Committee on the Unification of the National Language had been formed, and the task of revising the 'National Pronouncing Dictionary' had been delegated to three of its members, Qián Xuántóng, Wáng Yí and Lí Jìnxī, who carried out detailed amendments, giving an explanation of their work in 'A Supplementary Note to the "National Pronouncing Dictionary"' (Lí 1934, p.98; Fāng 1969, p.44). In December 1920 the Ministry gave the Dictionary its approval in an official report, quoting the Supplementary Note as follows:

> In this dictionary the pronunciation is based on the 'Universal Pronunciation' (pǔtōngyīn), which was the 'Mandarin Pronunciation' of the old days. This was the pronunciation used for reading aloud in the past several hundred years and is also the one used by 'Mandarin speakers' (pǔtōng huà speakers) in the present. It therefore fulfils the qualification of a universal pronunciation and may be adopted as the national standard. Since the Peking dialect contains the largest number of words which have the same pronunciation as that of Mandarin, nine-tenths of the pronunciation recorded in this dictionary coincide with that of the Peking dialect. However, those pronunciations in the Peking dialect which do not coincide with the universal pronunciation or with the pronunciation used when reading aloud are discarded. (Lí 1934, pp.98–9; Fāng 1969, pp.44–5; Ní 1948, pp.78–9; Zhōu 1961, p.94n; Shào 1937, pp.84–7)

In 1921 the revised edition of the 'National Pronouncing Dictionary' was published by the Commercial Press. It remained in popular use until replaced by the 'National Pronouncing Dictionary of Commonly Used Words' published by the Commercial Press in 1932 (Lí 1934, p.101; Fāng 1969, p.46).

The reference to the Peking dialect leads up to the 'Peking vs. National Pronunciation' controversy (Lí 1934, pp.95–8, 101–2; Fāng 1969, pp.47–50; Ní 1948, pp.78, 79). The question of the National Pronunciation was being widely debated even before the appearance of the 'National Pronouncing Dictionary', and when the first edition of the 'Dictionary' came out in 1919, it became the subject of more argument and debate, especially in Jiángsū Province. By 'National Pronunciation' was meant the pronunciation fixed by the Conference on the Unification of Pronunciation in 1913. This was an artificial pronunciation belonging to no particular province which included the 'entering tone' of the south and the retroflexed sounds peculiar to the north, as well as the voiced initial sounds confined to certain regions. By 'Peking Pronunciation' was meant the pronunciation used by natives of Peking. Advocates of the one and advocates of the other formed rival factions, calling themselves 'teachers of National Pronunciation' and 'teachers of Peking Pronunciation'. Frequent disputes and even occasional fights broke out between them.

Then in 1920 Zhāng Shìyī, head of the English Department of the Nánjīng Higher Teachers' Training College, expressed the opinion that the Chinese Phonetic Alphabet should undergo fundamental revision (Lǐ 1934, pp.95–6; Fāng 1969, pp.48–9; Ní 1948, p.78; Zhōu 1961, p.94n.). He proposed:

1) that the Ministry of Education adopt the spoken language used by those natives of Peking who had completed at least their secondary education as the standard for the National Language;

2) that the Ministry of Education invite phoneticians to analyse and to record scientifically the sounds in the Standard National Language;

3) that the Ministry of Education invite phoneticians, linguists, psychologists and educationalists to devise a phonetic alphabet of the Standard National Language.

These proposals were tantamount to the abolition of the Phonetic Alphabet, upon which so much time and effort had already been expended. Moreover, his idea of using the pronunciation of the natives of Peking as standard aroused widespread opposition. It was, however, supported by the National United Education Conference held in Shànghǎi in the same year, which called upon the Ministry of Education to adopt the Peking pronunciation as the standard and to revise the 'National Pronouncing Dictionary' accordingly. (The idea of adopting the Peking pronunciation as the standard had in fact been proposed in 1911 by the United Provincial General Education Conference; see Lǐ 1934, pp.96–7.) At the same time a similar resolution was passed at the United Conference of the Primary Schools attached to the Teachers' Training Colleges of Jiāngsū held in Chángzhōu. Its members not only refused to recognise the 'National Pronunciation' but also resolved 'not to teach the Phonetic Alphabet before teaching the Chinese characters'.

Then, in November, members of the Preparatory Committee on the Unification of the National Language, Wú Jìnghéng, Lǐ Jǐnxī, Lù Yīyán, Fàn Xiángshàn and others, had an informal conference with leaders of the Peking Pronunciation faction, Zhāng Shìyī, Gù Shí, Zhōu Míngsān and others, in Nánjīng. But the advocates of the Peking Pronunciation were adamant and insisted on fundamental change, so that the meeting broke up without a solution. Though a leader of the National Pronunciation faction, Lǐ Jǐnxī was not, in fact, opposed to a fundamental change of the system. He favoured using the IPA symbols with the Peking pronunciation as the standard if another form of writing was ultimately to replace the Chinese characters, but retaining, for the time being, the Chinese Phonetic Alphabet (Lǐ 1934, pp.97–8).

The 'National Pronouncing Dictionary' appeared at the height of the controversy. It did not help to clarify the issues. For one thing, although the Phonetic Alphabet was used to represent the sounds of the Chinese characters, no tone marks were inserted. Nor was it suggested anywhere of which dialect the tones should be adopted as the standard. In 1920 Liào Yǔchūn proposed adopting as standard the first tone of the Tiānjīn dialect, the second, third and fourth tones of the Peking dialect, and the fifth tone of the dialect of Northern Jiāngsū. But the gramophone records of the National Pronunciation made by Wáng Pú in Shànghǎi used all four tones of the Peking dialect; for the fifth tone they used a shorter version of the Peking Tone IV, described as 'short' but not 'hurried', 'restrained' but not 'concealed'. In 1921 Chao Yuen Ren made his gramophone records of the National Language in America also using the four tones of the Peking dialect and adopting the 'entering tone' of the Nánjīng dialect as the fifth tone, which he described as being 'less precipitate' than that of Northern Jiāngsū. In the same year Lí Jǐnhuī proposed that the four Peking tones be adopted by the Ministry of Education as the standard. Though this proposal was not officially endorsed, the records made by Wáng and Chao were issued with the Ministry's approval. Thus learners of the National Language automatically used the four tones of the Peking dialect. This resulted in a state of 'National Pronunciation with Peking Tones' (Lí 1934, p.102; Fāng 1969, pp.49–50; Zhōu 1961, p.94n).

Then in 1923 a further step was taken when Lí Jǐnxī (1924) issued his 'Table of Words with the "Entering Tones" in the Peking Pronunciation'. In his Preface, Lí says: 'Speakers using the tones of their local dialect created a form of "blue-green Mandarin", which was neither southern nor northern, but a mixture of both. When people felt the want of a uniform tone-system, they looked to one particular dialect for their standard. The natural choice was the tones of the Peking dialect.' Since the 'entering tone' did not exist in the Peking dialect, Lí maintains that all one could do was to look up the tone in Peking Pronunciation of a word with the 'entering tone' in a dictionary or table such as his, and commit it to memory (Lí 1934, pp.102–6; Fāng 1969, p.50). Lí further advocated the adoption of the Peking pronunciation for the very small percentage of words whose National Pronunciation differed from the Peking dialect. Thus both the pronunciation and the tones of the National Language gradually came to be modelled upon the Peking dialect (Lí 1934, p.106).

Also in 1923 twenty-seven members from the Preparatory Committee on the Unification of the National Language were appointed to a Subcommittee for the Revision and Amendment of the 'National Pronouncing Dictionary'. They included Wáng Pú, Qián Xuántóng, Chao Yuen Ren, Lí Jǐnxī and Wú Jìnghéng (Lí 1934, p.107).

In 1924 it was resolved at a meeting of the Preparatory Committee held for the sole purpose of discussing the Dictionary, that the pronunciation of the Peking dialect be adopted as the standard with alternative pronunciations added to many words.

In December 1925 the Subcommittee met, and Wáng Pú, Chao Yuen Ren, Qián Xuántóng, Lí Jǐnxī, Wāng Yí and Bái Zhènyíng were chosen to make a draft of the revised Dictionary. Eventually, after seven months

(March-October 1926) of daily detailed examination and discussion of every word, a twelve-volume draft was compiled in which the prevailing Peking pronunciation was taken as the standard. It differed from the old National Pronunciation in the following main points:

1) ㄪ [v], ㄬ [ɲ] and ㄫ [ŋ] (as an initial), were no longer used;
2) ㄗ [ts], ㄘ [tsʻ], ㄙ [s] became ㄐ [tɕ], ㄑ [tɕʻ], ㄒ [ɕ] respectively when followed by − [i] or ㄩ [y];
3) ㄛ [o] became either ㄜ [ɤ] or ㄨㄛ [uo] except when used as an interjection or when occurring after the bilabials ㄅ [p], ㄆ [pʻ], ㄇ [m] and the labio-dental ㄈ [f]; the diphthong −ㄛ [io] became ㄩㄝ [ye] except when used as an interjection; ㄝ [ɛ] existed only as an interjection and in the diphthongs −ㄝ [iɛ] and ㄩㄝ [yɛ];
4) the 'entering tone' was dropped, characters pronounced according to the fifth tone in the old National Pronunciation being reallocated to one of the four tones of the Peking pronunciation (Lǐ 1934, pp.171–3; Fāng 1969, pp.57–8; Ní 1948, pp.79–80; Zhōu 1961, pp.94–5).

The draft was not immediately printed. Further extensive revision followed, as well as the incorporation of new words, and the material was then rearranged according to the order of the Phonetic Alphabet, so that it eventually became the 'National Pronouncing Dictionary of Commonly Used Words' of 1932 mentioned above. By about 1926, however, learners of the National Language had already adopted the Peking pronunciation and its tones as the standard.

Another event closely related to the promotion of the Phonetic Alphabet was the change-over of Classical Chinese to the vernacular in school syllabuses (Lǐ 1934, pp.107–21; Fāng 1969, pp.51–6; Shào 1937, pp.87–8). It was felt in the early days of the Republic that just as the Phonetic Alphabet could be used to standardise the national pronunciation, so a change in the prevailing literary style would make proclamations and notices intelligible to the masses. A proposal that Classical Chinese be replaced by the vernacular in all primary schools had already been made at the Conference on the Unification of Pronunciation (see above p.144). In 1917 this was again brought up at the Third National United Education Conference by a representative from Húnán, who also recommended the use of the style of 'recorded conversations' and colloquial fiction as a means of bridging the gap between the 'classical' and the 'vernacular', thus creating a universal literary style which would be understood by all. The Conference then proposed that the Ministry of Education standardise the national language and propagate the Phonetic Alphabet in all provinces as a preparation for the change-over from Classical Chinese to the vernacular in all primary schools. At this time the 'Literary Revolution', led by Hú Shì, was at its height, so that many articles written in the vernacular were appearing in newspapers and periodicals. All this made it possible to write books in the vernacular for use in primary schools.

Meanwhile, in Peking, Jiāngsū and Zhèjiāng, some primary schools had already begun to use the Phonetic Alphabet to prepare their own teaching material or even to compile their own textbooks in the vernacular. At the first session of the Preparatory Committee on the Unification of the National Language, Liú Fù, Hú Shì, Zhōu Zuòrén and others proposed the recompilation of all primary school readers in order that only textbooks in the vernacular would be used in the lower forms of all primary schools. This proposal was accepted by the Ministry of Education, which in 1920 ordered that Classical Chinese in the syllabus of the first two years of the primary schools be replaced by the vernacular, though local dialect was to be avoided. Later the Ministry set a definite time limit for phasing out textbooks in Classical Chinese used in primary schools. It also prescribed the teaching of the Phonetic Alphabet as the first step in Chinese lessons, and knowledge of the correct use of the Phonetic Alphabet was laid down as one of the basic requirements for completing the primary stage of education. During this period, in the textbooks for primary schools published by the Commercial Press and the Chung Hwa Book Company (Zhōnghuá Shūjú), lessons on the Phonetic Alphabet preceded lessons with Chinese characters. The problem of replacing Classical Chinese by the vernacular was thus solved, and the importance of the Phonetic Alphabet was again brought to the fore.

The term 'Phonetic Alphabet' itself, however, was soon to be changed to 'Phonetic Symbols' (Lí 1934, pp.231–5, 237–41; Fāng 1969, pp.59–61; Ní 1948, pp.82–4; Zhōu 1961, pp.68–9; Shào 1937, pp.92–4). Many people had disapproved of the term 'Phonetic Alphabet' as suggesting an integral part of the system of writing whereas the purpose of the Phonetic Alphabet was only to indicate the pronunciation of the Chinese characters. When in 1928 the Ministry of Education announced the two forms of the National Alphabet (see above p.141) the first form was still referred to as the Phonetic Alphabet. With the support of others, Wú Jìnghéng proposed at a meeting of the Central Executive Committee of the Chinese Nationalist Party held in April 1930 that the term 'Phonetic Alphabet' be altered to 'Phonetic Symbols'. The proposal was accepted, and instructions were sent to all organisations of the Party that henceforth the term 'Phonetic Symbols' was to be used. The meeting further suggested three ways of promoting the 'Symbols':

1) that members of all branches of the Party be instructed to use the Phonetic Symbols in order to facilitate the dissemination of Party principles;

2) that the National Government order all civil servants to familiarise themselves thoroughly with the Phonetic Symbols so as to be able to assist the illiterate masses;

3) that the Ministry of Education order all teachers and students of the various educational organisations to learn the Phonetic Symbols in order to promote supplementary education for the masses. (Lí 1934, p.234; Fāng 1969, p.61; Shào 1937, p.94)

The government complied with the suggestions. Xíngzhèngyuàn further ordered the Ministry of Education to compile a booklet on 'How to Learn and Teach the Phonetic Symbols' (*Zhùyīn Fúhaò Dúfǎ Chuánxí Xiǎocè*, eventually published by Zhōnghuá Shūjú in 1930 as *Zhùyīn Fúhaò Chuánxí Xiǎocè*). The Ministry thereupon set up a Committee for the Propagation of the Phonetic Symbols. It consisted of eleven members: Wú Jìnghéng, Chao Yuen Ren, Lù Yīyán, Zhāng Shìyī, Liú Lúyǐn, Huáng Zūntáo, Guō Yǒushǒu, Wú Yányīn, Péng Bóchuān, Dài Yìngguān and Wáng Ruìchāng. The Ministry of Education also invited all organisations attached to the Nationalist Party to send representatives to learn the Phonetic Symbols at classes organized by the Committee in order that they could in turn teach their colleagues. At the same time publishers in Shanghai issued many booklets about the Phonetic Symbols.

In May the Ministry of Education ordered all Provincial and City Boards of Education and all state universities to send representatives to attend the Phonetic Symbols Classes. In fact, at the Second National Education Conference in April, Wú Jìnghéng and others had suggested to the Ministry of Education the following aim and methods of propagating the Phonetic Symbols:

1) All Chinese nationals, whether literate or not, should be enabled to use the Phonetic Symbols.

2) The Phonetic Symbols were meant to indicate the National Pronunciation but could, if necessary, be used additionally to indicate dialectal pronunciation.

3) The Phonetic Symbols should be added to all popular reading matter.

4) All educational organizations and popular educational groups should form committees for the study of the Phonetic Symbols and appoint special officers to promote such schemes.

Thus in July the Ministry of Education announced its programme, consisting of twenty-five items, for the propagation of the Phonetic Symbols to be carried out by the education authorities in every province, city and county (Lí 1934, pp.241–6; Shào 1937, pp.96–101; Fāng 1969, p.61; Ní 1948, p.84). The twenty-five items were:

1) All literate persons should learn the Phonetic Symbols in the shortest possible time in order to teach all illiterate persons so that eventually all will be able to read Chinese characters.

2) The promotion of the Phonetic Symbols in all provinces, cities and counties should be preceded by widespread publicity. If necessary, a 'publicity week' might be held for this purpose, as described in the Ministry's 'Outline for a Literacy Campaign'.

3) All provincial and local Boards of Education should set up special Committees for the Promotion of the Phonetic Symbols.

4) A certain number of special instructors should be appointed from among the local Committee for the Promotion of the Phonetic

Symbols or recruited from elsewhere. These instructors should visit various districts, towns and villages in order to give guidance in the promotion of the Phonetic Symbols. At the same time, they should make an investigation of the local dialects and report their findings to the local Board of Education.

5) The aforesaid reports should be submitted to higher education authorities, to be rechecked by the Preparatory Committee on the Unification of the National Language. From the material gathered, booklets on 'The Use of the Phonetic Symbols in Local Dialects' and 'Homophones of Common Occurrence in Local Dialects in Phonetic Symbols' should be compiled with explanations given in the local dialect.

6) The various provinces, cities and counties should send representatives to attend those schools of the national language deemed by the Ministry of Education to have achieved the best results. On returning to their localities, these men should take up the tasks of promoting and teaching the Phonetic Symbols and of investigating the local dialect.

7) Classes on the theory of the Phonetic Symbols should be set up in all provinces and cities, and representatives from all counties and districts sent to attend them. On returning to their localities, these men should promote and teach the Phonetic Symbols and investigate the local dialect.

8) All organizations, schools, factories, shops etc. should set up classes for the study of the Phonetic Symbols for the benefit of their employees and nearby residents.

9) Classes for the study of the Phonetic Symbols should be started in all social and educational organizations such as public reading rooms, public libraries and schools for mass education.

10) The teaching of the Phonetic Symbols should become part of the curriculum of all institutions for mass education and adult supplementary education.

11) All public and private schools should start teaching the Phonetic Symbols as part of regular class work or as an extra-curricular subject; the course should be completed in the shortest possible time. All headmasters, deans, and teachers of Chinese who have not mastered the Phonetic Symbols within a given time limit should be dismissed.

12) All employees in educational or cultural organizations, whether public or private, must learn the Phonetic Symbols in the shortest possible time. Failure to do so would result in dismissal.

13) Publishing houses and printing firms should make a type of Chinese characters with the Phonetic Symbols placed beside them.

14) Whenever possible, all news items in newspapers should be written in the vernacular with the Phonetic Symbols placed beside the Chinese

Characters; alternatively, special columns could be devoted to reading matter fit for the masses, written in the vernacular with the Phonetic Symbols placed beside the Chinese characters.

15) All popular periodicals, journals and literature for the masses should be written in the vernacular with the Phonetic Symbols placed beside the Chinese characters.

16) Name-plates of organizations, street signs and shop signs, signs at railway stations and bus and tram stops, as well as propaganda material, slogans and advertisements written in the vernacular, should have the Phonetic Symbols placed beside the Chinese characters.

17) All announcements in schools and other organizations for the benefit of the public should be written in the vernacular with the Phonetic Symbols placed beside the Chinese characters.

18) Dr Sun Yat Sen's will, readers for the masses compiled by the provinces, cities or counties, and all printed propaganda leaflets about Party principles, should have the Phonetic Symbols placed beside the characters.

19) The Phonetic Symbols indicating the National Pronunciation should be placed on the right-hand side of the Chinese characters; where possible, the Phonetic Symbols indicating the dialectal pronunciation, should be placed on the left-hand side.

20) City and county authorities should encourage the publication of local news written in the vernacular, with the Phonetic Symbols indicating both the national and dialectal pronunciation placed beside the Chinese characters.

21) When reprinting notices issued by the central and provincial governments with the Phonetic Symbols indicating the National Pronunciation on the right-hand side of the characters, city and county authorities should insert the Phonetic Symbols indicating the dialectal pronunciation on the left-hand side of the characters.

22) As from January 1931 all organizations under the control of the Chinese Nationalist Party, all government offices, all schools, factories and shops, when engaging staff, should give preference to those conversant with the Phonetic Symbols.

23) All organizations under the control of the Nationalist Party and all government offices should order their employees to learn the Phonetic Symbols within a definite period of time. On special grounds applications may be made for an extention of this period; if approved, applicants would be given a certificate of extention which must, however, not exceed four months, after which, if the Symbols have still not been learned, action may be taken against them for dereliction of duty.

24) During the Period of Political Tutelage, before the Plan for Adult Supplementary Education has been carried out completely, Phonetic Symbols may be placed beside the Chinese characters in petitions and

suits filed by the people. If necessary, Phonetic Symbols may be used in place of Chinese characters.

25) Detailed regulations regarding methods of propagating the Phonetic Symbols and the teaching and learning of the Symbols by employees of government and other organizations and the people will be drafted by the Ministry of Education and announced officially, subject to the approval of the government.

The Ministry of Education's Programme was supported by the Propaganda Department of the Central Executive Committee of the Chinese Nationalist Party, which published its own programme: 'Essential Points in the Propagation of the Phonetic Symbols' (Tuīxíng Zhùyīn Fúhào Xuānchuán Yàodiǎn). The Ministry of Education further published the 'Regulations for the Committee for the Promotion of the Phonetic Symbols in All Provinces, Cities and Counties' (Gé Shěn Shì Xiàn Zhùyīn Fúhào Tuīxíng Wěiyuánhuì Guīchéng). The Provincial and Local Boards of Education responded to the Ministry's Programme and Regulations with great enthusiasm.

Thus under the auspices of the government, the Chinese Phonetic Symbols flourished, if only for a while, for in less than a year the zeal began to cool (Lí 1934, p.250). The cause of this, according to Lí Jǐnxī, was bureaucratic inertia. Although programmes and regulations were handed down from office to office, they seldom resulted in action, those concerned preferring evasion to performing their duties, so that only a very few were genuinely interested in the promotion of the Symbols. But Wú Jìnghéng (1931), in his 'Movement for the Use of the Phonetic Symbols in the Last Thirty-five Years', thought that the problem was a psychological one: society still looked down upon the Phonetic Symbols (Ní 1948, p.86). Then, after 1933, schools again turned their attention to the study of Classical Chinese and the Phonetic Symbols again fell into neglect. However, in spite of dwindling popular interest, the Phonetic Symbols held their own and continued to receive official support. After the Second World War, interest in them revived. Today, the Phonetic Symbols appear beside the Chinese characters in various dictionaries and books, and in children's readers and periodicals, published in China, Taiwan, and Hong Kong.

Committees, Societies, Sub-committees, Conferences etc.
  with Pinyin forms
Calligraphic Styles of the Phonetic Alphabet: Zhùyīn Zìmǔ Shūfǎ Tǐshì
Chart of the Chinese Phonetic Alphabet: Guóyīn Zìmǔ Dānzhāng
Chinese Phonetic Alphabet: zhùyīn zìmǔ
Chinese Phonetic Symbols: zhùyīn fúhào
Committee for the Propagation of the Phonetic Symbols:
  Zhùyīn Fúhào Tuīxíng Wěiyuánhuì
Conference of Principals of the Higher Teachers' Training Colleges:
  Quánguó Gāoděng Shīfàn Xiàozhǎng Huìyì
Conference on the Unification of Pronunciation: Dúyīn Tǒngyīhuì
Fourth Preparatory Conference on the Unification of the National
  Language: Dì-sì Cì Jiàoyùbù Guóyǔ Tǒngyī Chóubèihuì

Chinese Phonetic Symbols

'Literary Revolution': Wénxué Gémìng
National Alphabet: guóyīn zìmǔ
National Education Conference: Quánguó Jiàoyù Huìyì
National Language Romanization: Guóyǔ Luómǎzì
National Pronouncing Dictionary: Guóyīn Zìdìan
National Pronouncing Dictionary of Commonly Used Words:
　　Guóyīn Chángyòng Zìhuì
National United Education Conference: Quánguó Jiàoyùhuì Liánhéhuì
Plan for Research in the National Language: Guóyǔ Yánjiū Diàochá zhī
　　Jìnxíng Jìhuàshū
Preparatory Committee on the Unification of the National Language:
　　Guóyǔ Tǒngyī Chóubèi Wěiyuánhuì
Provisional Education Conference: Línshí Jiàoyù Huìyì
Society for National Language Research: Guóyǔ Yánjiūhuì
Sub-committee for the Revision and Amendment of the National Pronouncing
　　Pronouncing Dictionary: Guóyīn Zìdiǎn Zēngxiū Wěiyúanhuì
Table of the Phonetic Alphabet: Zhùyīn Zìmǔ biǎo

References

CHAO, YUEN REN (1957) *Mandarin Primer*, Cambridge, Mass. (Harvard
　　University Press) p.85.
FĀNG SHĪDUÓ (1969) *Wǔshi Nián Lái Zhōngguó Guóyǔ Yùndòngshǐ*, 2nd. ed.,
　　Táiběi (Guóyǔ Rìbàoshè).
HÚ SHÌ (1953) *Hú Shì Wéncún*, vol. I, Táiběi (Yuǎndōng Túshū Gōngsī).
LǏ GUĀNGDÌ (1726) *Yīnyùn Chǎnwēi*, Facsimile ed., (1971) Táiběi (Xuéshēng
　　Shūjú).
LÍ JǏNXĪ (1924) 'Jīngyīn Rùshēng Zìpǔ', *The Eastern Miscellany* (Dōngfāng
　　Zázhì), vol. xxi, pp.L62-97.
—— (1934) *Guóyǔ Yùdòng Shǐgāng*, Shànghǎi (Commercial Press).
NÍ HǍISHǓ (1948) *Zhōngguǒ Pīnyīn Wénzì Yùndòngshǐ (Jiǎnbiān)*, Shànghǎi
　　(Shídài Shūbào Chūbǎnshè).
SHÀO MÍNGJIǓ (1937) *Guóyīn Yángé Liù Jiǎng*, Shànghǎi (Commercial Press).
WÚ JÌNGHÉNG (1931) 'Sānshí Wǔ Nián Lái Zhī Yīnfú Yùndòng', *Volume
　　Commemorating the Thirty-fifth Anniversary of the Commercial Press in
　　Shanghai (Shànghǎi Shāngwù Yìnshūguǎn Sānshí Wú Zhōunián Jìniànkān)*
　　part II, pp.25-60, Shànghǎi (Commercial Press).
ZHŌU YǑUGUĀNG (1961) *Hànzì Gǎigé Gàilùn*, Peking (Wénzì Gǎigé
　　Chūbǎnshè).

Three Trends in Phonetics:
the Development of Phonetics as a Discipline
in Germany since the Nineteenth Century

In the third edition of his *Grundzüge der Phonetik zur Einführung in das Studium der Lautlehre der indogermanischen Sprachen* (1885, pp. 1ff.), Eduard Sievers locates phonetics in the border area between physics, physiology, and linguistics and goes on to say that the two science disciplines in this study of human speech have as their main aim the establishing of the general laws concerning the nature and the formation of sounds, whereas the linguist follows up all the ramifications of these basic laws in the different languages and dialects. But Sievers then further subdivides the linguistic orientation of phonetics into the analysis of living languages as the most immediate and most important pursuit, particularly in connection with the practical study of modern languages, and into the historical and comparative branch, which tries to elucidate the different sound processes whose beginning and end points the language-historian has set up through his comparative methods. Whereas the theoretical and scientific phonetician puts his classificatory system with its strict separation of sounds at the centre of his endeavour the historical phonetician is more interested in the systematic survey of the relationships between the categories which the theoretician expends great efforts in keeping distinct.

Sievers sees no way for these three areas of phonetics to be treated equally in one manual because the natural scientist will not have at his disposal the language-specific data that the philologist and the linguist need, and they are hardly able to follow the details of the anatomical, physiological and physical research of the former. The scientist in turn finds little to interest him in a multitude of individual language materials, which do not help him in the investigation into the general principles of speech. Even if a single person were to combine all these different fields of phonetic knowledge and integrate them in one all-round handbook on general phonetics such a book would not meet the needs of the learner, who always approaches the subject from his own one-sided interest and therefore only has the understanding of this or that aspect of it. These considerations led Sievers to give up the idea of a general survey in favour of a monograph on one particular area providing only the necessary generalities and concentrating on the special requirements of one group of phonetic specialists. Sievers' *Grundzüge* was written as the first volume of the *Bibliothek indogermanischer Grammatiken* and thus was to be an introduction to the study of the phonology (in the sense prevalent at the time) of the older periods of Indo-European languages – as the subtitle indicates; therefore its aim is to inform about phonetic problems in connection with an investigation into the Indo-European sound changes. Sievers states quite explicitly that the book neither addresses the phonetic scientist nor does it cater for the requirements of the modern language subjects, in particular foreign language teaching, unless their demands coincide with the language historian's.

In the preface to the third edition, Sievers points out specifically (p.viii) that he has carefully reworded the introductory section in order to give a clearer account of why he is convinced that a general descriptive system of speech sounds meeting all the needs equally is quite impossible, although he is not sure of his success in persuading others since his opinion seems to be more or less unparalleled. Sievers himself had actually changed his mind in this respect and not just provided a more precise wording of his views, for in the second edition of 1881 he did not expound this division of phonetics into three separate areas. On the contrary, he demanded of the linguist that he should first of all become familiar with the indispensable foundations for the further development of the discipline of phonetics ·as laid by the science approach, and that he should build his historical and comparative phonetic studies on these basic research results. Sievers admitted that this goal was still a long way off because of the largely specialised treatment of phonetics: linguistics had learned, or wanted to learn, too little from natural science, and vice versa, and where a mutual exchange of knowledge had taken place it was often accompanied by misunderstandings at the receiving end. This difference between the editions of Sievers' *Grundzüge* constitutes more than a superficial change in exposition; it reveals a break in the theoretical conception of an academic discipline: what used to be regarded as one subject, the unity of which was to be achieved by increased efforts on all sides, is now divided into separate and largely independent specialisations that have no common denominator. Such an attitude in a new scientific subject that is only beginning to establish itself and is making every effort to gain recognition among the *universitas litterarum* is a serious obstacle to its further development and is certainly unique in the history of science. This state of affairs is by no means peculiar to Germany; it has been a characteristic feature of the study of phonetics right down to the present day, as is evidenced by the use of the plural in the name of the International Congress of Phonetic Sciences.

Sievers made a deliberate move away from the medical and physical orientation of the research into speech sounds customary at his time, towards a linguistic outlook that was dominated by the diachronic approach from the 1870s onwards. The five editions of his *Grundzüge* show successive stages of this strengthening of the linguistic point of view. The title of the first edition (1876) was *Grundzüge der Lautphysiologie* and was thus in the tradition of the publications by the Viennese physiologist Ernst Brücke

(*Grundzüge der Physiologie und Systematik der Sprachlaute für Linguisten und Taubstummenlehrer*, 1856; *Die physiologischen Grundlagen der neuhochdeutschen Verskunst*, 1871), and by the general practitioner and lecturer (later professor) of medicine at Leipzig University Carl Ludwig Merkel (*Anatomie und Physiologie des menschlichen Stimm- und Sprach-Organs* (*Anthropophonik*), 1857; *Physiologie der menschlichen Sprache* (*physiologische Laletik*), 1866). In his preface (p.vi), Sievers mentions Merkel as his most important source. In his opinion Merkel had been neglected unduly in favour of Brücke, whose rigid systematisation was beginning to hamper the advance of phonetic research rather than furthering it. Then Sievers goes on to pay tribute to the long co-operation with his friend Jost Winteler, whose book *Die Kerenzer Mundart des Kantons Glarus* (1876) he was able to consult frequently, obviously before its publication. And finally he refers to Helmholtz's *Die Lehre von den Tonempfindungen als physiologische Grundlage für die Theorie der Musik* (1862).

The second edition of Sievers' book appeared in 1881 under the new title of *Grundzüge der Phonetik*, which was to stay through all the subsequent editions. In its preface (pp.v–vii), Sievers stresses the new insight he gained through the study of the English and Scandinavian authors: Ellis's *Early English Pronunciation*, Sweet's *Handbook of Phonetics*, Storm's *Engelsk Filologi* and through them Bell's *Visible Speech*, of which he was unable to get a copy. He admits that the first edition of his book would have turned out differently if he had known these fundamental treatises of modern phonetics when he wrote it. He regards Sweet's *Handbook* as the best comprehensive survey of general phonetics, and he recommends it to the German phoneticians who believe that by setting up general sound systems in the usual schematic way they fulfil the phonetician's task (yet another dig at Brücke!). Sievers praises the practical orientation of the English phoneticians in contrast to the highly theoretical rut into which phonetics in Germany had slipped. The increase in size from 150 pages in the first edition to 224 pages in the second is due to the incorporation of a greater amount and variety of language data over and above the Germanic languages and German dialects, and to a more detailed discussion of the new literature, for example, on the classification of vowels. It now discusses separately the acoustic analysis of vowels (pp.62–4), the system of the German phoneticians (pp.64–73), which according to Sievers leans too heavily on sound similarities established by ear, and finally the English system of Bell and Sweet (pp.73–80), which he regards as the most perfect one of all vowel systems because it excludes the subjective estimation of acoustic vowel resemblances by using the analysis of articulatory positions as in the case of consonants.

Sievers voices one important point of criticism (pp.vii–viii), however, directed against the attempt of the new school to devise general descriptive systems of phonetics, a mistake for which he had already blamed Brücke. It is in this connection that, *before* referring to Merkel and Brücke, he mentions

Winteler's merit of having shown that, although it is possible to investigate the universal conditions of speech production in a general way, the main concern in the grouping of phonetic phenomena must nevertheless lie in the characterisation of individual language and dialect systems (p.viii). Thus he goes much further in his move towards linguistic phonetics than his English colleagues and rings in the age of phonology much more distinctly. There were also the concepts of phonological structures and systems (in the modern sense) in Sievers' arguments right from the beginning, and these separated him from his predecessors. Thus he says (1876, pp.3–4) that the task of phonetics does not simply consist in a statistical observation of single sounds and their changes because it is not the individual sound that is subjected to certain generally applicable laws of change; there is usually a corresponding development of corresponding sound series in corresponding positions (e.g. in the Germanic sound shift). As a rule, reasons can be given which help to explain the changes of such a sound series from the total set-up of the system and from the special position of that series within it. The concept of the phoneme is also foreshadowed in the advice to the phonetician that he should get a good understanding of the structure of every sound system he is dealing with and that he should not forget that this structure is not determined by the number of fortuitously assembled sounds as such but through the relationships of these individual members to one another.

In the third edition, published in 1885, Sievers expanded the paragraph dealing with the necessity of oral teaching in phonetics (pp.4–5). Whereas the scientific principles of speech production can be presented clearly in writing, it is more and more necessary to strengthen the learner's faculties of observation the greater the emphasis on the application of phonetics in language teaching and in linguistic research. Thus a manual of phonetics for philologists, basically, has to be nothing but a guide to observing language data, and the linguist – more so than the language teacher – requires a vast and detailed knowledge of the sound systems of living languages in order to avoid false explanations in the history of sound processes. This was a well-justified and necessary demand from a highly skilled phonetician whose main aim it was to advance the historical study of the Germanic and Indo-European languages by putting the full potentials of practical phonetics at its disposal. Very few, if any, scholars of diachronic linguistics during the following half century achieved Sievers' competence, which meant that the analysis of sound changes in the general linguistics departments and the specific language departments of German universities, and elsewhere, was gradually turned into a sterile discussion of orthographic symbols. These were invested with phonetic categories, but they lost all links with phonetic reality. Linguistics had not taken Sievers' warning at the end of the preface to the third edition (p.xii) seriously: only when the scholar has gained a thorough grasp of the sound structures and processes of living languages should he move on to the problems in the sound history of earlier language periods;

otherwise the premature application of phonetic propositions would cause more damage than benefit to linguistics. Probably without realising it, linguistics returned to Jacob Grimm's 'letters', which he talked about in his discussion of the Germanic consonant-shift in the 1822 edition of his *Deutsche Grammatik*, and thus undid a century of scholarship that had tried to put comparative and historical linguistics on a scientific basis.

Fifty years later, the same development occurred in that branch of phonetics that Sievers called the study of living languages and in which he foreshadowed the field of phonology: generative phonology has now reached a stage where a highly elaborate phonetic framework, partly borrowed from physics and physiology, is used to specify marks on paper, which the linguist can shift about at his desk attributing deep-seated linguistic generalisations, for example about naturalness, without even understanding the phonetic implications; here again the linguist has completely dissociated himself from phonetic substance and is again dealing with 'letters' of a new and much more sophisticated nature. In both these cases, the separation of phonetics from its scientific connections and the association with linguistics has led to a total destruction of the very essence of phonetic research.

In the fourth and fifth editions (1893, 1901), Sievers expresses his views on experimental phonetics (pp.xi–xii, 2, 8), which had begun to assert itself in a number of publications, for example by Rousselot (1891, 1892, 1897–1901). It is too early for him to come to a definite decision about the usefulness of the new trend for the study of speech sounds, because he has not been able to carry out control experiments. But he does not share the enthusiasm with which experimental phonetics has been greeted even by philologists, because he knows from long experience of phonetic teaching that, although the modern graphic recorders reproduce correctly what is spoken into them, hardly anybody is able to speak normally under these experimental conditions. For the time being he is therefore inclined to believe that the deviations from the speech norm caused by the instruments are as frequent and as great as the mistakes a well-trained phonetician without instruments makes in his observation of phonetically naive speakers, quite apart from the equally great dangers of false interpretations or generalisations of instrumental data. Moreover, what lasting results the experimental analyses have yielded seem to belong to the science side of phonetics and consequently do not fall within the domain of his book. Sievers' criticism is quite correct in view of the primitive instrumentation available at the time, depending entirely on mechanical energy transmission, and on account of the poor methodology, which was neither backed up by an adequate test theory and powerful statistics, nor able to solve the problem of linguistic invariance against the background of an enormous variability of recorded signals. But it is unacceptable from to-day's standpoint to exclude instrumental phonetics from descriptive or historical linguistics, although this is in complete agreement with the tripartite division Sievers proposed.

It is worth enquiring into the reasons why Sievers developed this strong bias towards a purely linguistic outlook away from the physical and physiological sides. Sievers' familiarity with Helmholtz, Merkel and Brücke is well documented; they were his primary sources. Merkel's monumental *Anthropophonik* of 1857 provides, in approximately 1000 pages, a minute description of the anatomy of the speech apparatus and, under the heading of physiology, an equally detailed account of tone and speech-sound formation, largely in acoustic terms. The description of actual speech phenomena takes up only about one quarter and the relation of the mass of anatomical, acoustic and physiological data to the phonetic sound classification is not made clear. The book aims at an encyclopaedic collection of facts about the vocal tract as they were known in Merkel's day. The systematisation of speech sounds relies on the traditional categories known from grammarians (*gutturales, linguales, labiales; liquidae, strepentes, explosivae*) and contains a number of inadequacies largely owing to Merkel's limited knowledge of languages other than his own central German; as when he says that *strepentes* are *consonantes continuae* that are not *liquidae* or *nasales*, and are therefore pronounced neither with larynx vibrations nor through the nose (p.834), and that French distinguishes a light *S* (in *rose, besoin*) and a heavy, sharp one (in *sexe, penser, ancêtre*) for which the tongue is pressed harder against the lower teeth and the air is expelled with greater emphasis (p.869). For *B D G* as against *P T K* Merkel assumes a closed glottis (p.853), which may have been true of his own dialect of German, although he arrived at this categorisation not through observation but by extrapolation from his anatomical system, in which he postulated an open glottis for *P T K* and no vocal cord vibrations for any obstruent so that the phonetic oppositions had to be characterised by a closed glottis. Since there is thus a closure in the lower region of the vocal tract the nose need not be completely sealed off by the velum (p.852), which is again a logical deduction rather than an empirical observation. The mechanism of voicing in the different speech sounds was thus simply not properly understood by Merkel.

The scope of Merkel's classificatory framework is limited although he is convinced that with the sound classes he sets up all languages can be covered (p.835). By comparison, Brücke's *Grundzüge*, which appeared one year prior to Merkel's compendium, but which the latter could not possibly have consulted, is a very slim volume that dispenses with all the anatomical and acoustic detail, and concentrates on a comprehensive classificatory system for all linguistic sound elements. As to exhaustiveness, accuracy, systematic clarity, and linguistic relevance this system is far superior to Merkel's, although it still contains a number of false assignments, particularly among the vowels of foreign languages, again owing to a limited familiarity with the linguistic realities. This articulatory classification is also the basis for a new transcription that is outlined at the end of the 1856 edition and elaborated in a separate article, 'Über eine neue Methode der phonetischen Transscription', presented at a meeting of the Imperial Academy of Sciences in Vienna on 7 January 1862 (Brücke 1863). Its principle is to symbolise the positions, one after the other, taken up by the different parts of the vocal tract involved in the course of speech, and the reader always has to move on to the next position by the shortest path (p.231). Since the notation builds up symbols from elements for the different places and manners of articulation as well as a variety of states of the glottis, that is nine phonation types (pp.235–41), a preliminary physiological analysis of the sounds to be transcribed is inevitable, and Brücke therefore only symbolises sounds the production of which he fully understands. He thus leaves clicks aside because, although he has grasped the principles of the oral air-stream mechanism entirely, he is not familiar with the details of the whole system of clicks (pp.227ff.). The notation is thus iconic in David Abercrombie's sense (1967, pp.114–20) and comparable to Bell's Visible Speech, but far less legible because the shapes for the different articulatory components are not distinctive enough. The system has apparently not been used by anybody else.

It is true that Brücke does not go beyond the classification of individual sounds, a fact which Sievers rightly criticises (1881, p.viii), at the same time pointing out that Merkel, on the other hand, offers a wealth of information outside the schematic system of sound positions and deals with the higher levels of phonetics, that is sound clusters, syllables, words, and sentences, rhythm and pitch in musical notation. This criticism is certainly justified, but Brücke's treatise warrants a little more praise for its concise and systematic treatment of speech sounds in general and for the much better basis it provided for linguistic studies than Merkel's *Anthropophonik*. It should not, however, have been republished in 1876 in more or less its old form (with the omission of the chapter on transcription), because the twenty years since its first publication had seen an advance in the subject, particularly by the publication of Merkel's *Physiologische Laletik* in 1866. This was a shorter and more convenient version of the *Anthropophonik*, leaving out a great deal of the anatomical and acoustic details, getting more language-oriented – no doubt through the example of Brücke, whom Merkel quotes and criticises freely – and finally eliminating many of the false statements of the first edition. For instance the voicing in fricatives and plosives is now recognised as a distinct possibility in languages.

Brücke and Merkel were not primarily interested in the language-specific facts of sound, but – to use Merkel's words (1866, p.2) – in the natural laws that come into play whenever man speaks, in the natural elements and conditions of human language in general. Although the different speech sounds do not all occur in all languages, they can nevertheless be produced by all men because their vocal organs are the same; the physiological analysis of these usable and actually used sounds in language is the principal task. This leads to the natural alphabet on a physiological basis, valid for all languages and containing all the sounds that are found all over the world. The corollary of this scientific attitude was the detailed study of anatomical facts and physiological processes of *Homo loquens* just as much as a general schematisation of the sounds produced by these physical conditions. But this conception of phonetics fitted better in the middle of the nineteenth century than into its last quarter.

In 1861–2 August Schleicher published his *Compendium der vergleichenden Grammatik der indo-germanischen Sprachen*, in which, as distinct from the work of Franz Bopp, or even Jacob Grimm, the evolution of sounds played a very prominent part. Here language is regarded as an organism that develops in prehistoric times and decays in historical periods, and linguistics is included among the natural sciences, which alone provide the key to the explanation of sound change through the physiology of the speech organs. This view Merkel (1886, p.v) regards as representing a very significant advance in linguistics since Jacob Grimm's non-scientific subjective study of letters. Schleicher set out to reconstruct the original Indo-European language and capture the relationships among the different languages of the family by a genealogical tree. He even wrote a fable in the Indo-European parent language. In these attempts he was probably influenced by Darwinian ideas, which he documented in his treatise *Die darwinsche Theorie und die Sprachwissenschaft* of 1863. But in spite of his scientific demands, Schleicher, like his predecessors, did not object to unmotivated exceptions in the historical sound laws he proposed. His approach, like Brücke's, was theory- rather than data-oriented.

Another scholar of comparative linguistics who established the general phonetic point of view in his research and even used Brücke's handbook as his basis was Wilhelm Scherer with his *Zur Geschichte der deutschen Sprache* of 1868. He laid stress on the principle of false analogy and thus got very close to the notion of sound laws which admit no exceptions save in accordance with other laws, the principle that was formulated by H. Osthoff and K. Brugmann (1878, 1, pp.iii–xx, the term 'exceptionless sound laws' going back to Leskien 1876). This beginning of the new era of the so-called Neogrammarians meant a much greater concern with language-specific data and with the laws governing them, because this was in effect the only way to come to grips with the individual sound laws and their lawful exceptions. Thus a thorough study of the development of languages was undertaken, which brought modern languages to the fore because scholars did not want to occupy themselves only with the older periods, but wanted also to investigate actually observable processes in order to draw conclusions from them.

Phonetics was now given a prominent place, shown by the inclusion of Sievers' *Grundzüge* in the *Bibliothek Indogermanischer Grammatiken*, but what was required was no longer just the general principles of physiology, although they provided a necessary basis, but the exact phonetic description of individual language facts in a positivist fashion. This provided the impetus for a stronger bias of phonetics towards linguistics. And since historical linguistics was to become an exact science using the methods of the natural sciences, experimental phonetics soon developed as a new branch to help in the study of sound changes by recording minute details of pronunciation. In this vein, l'Abbé Rousselot investigated the phonetic changes of language in the dialect of a family in Cellefrouin and wrote a comprehensive manual of experimental phonetics. So, through its linguistic orientation, phonetics returned to its affiliation with the natural sciences, although the most prominent German phonetician, Sievers, did not take this step. It was, however, no longer the general laws of sound production in man that occupied scholars but the specific patterns of individual languages. As the new movement did not develop a methodology for connecting a variability of instrumental measurements with linguistic invariants determined by descriptive means, it finally led to the most serious break within the subject of phonetics from the 1920s onwards, namely the institution of phonology as a linguistic subject in its own right, an arts discipline, separated from the natural science of phonetics. This dichotomy was proposed most vigorously by Trubetzkoy in his *Grundzüge der Phonologie*. Not only did the development of linguistic phonetics in its descriptive and historical branches result in this ominous schism, but this independent phonology can also be seen as epitomising the preoccupation with language-specific facts, initiated in Sievers' time, at the expense of research into man's general sound producing and receiving mechanisms.

The Neogrammarians' new attitude towards living idioms produced a growing concern with the description of modern languages, the third area in Sievers' division of phonetics, not only as an academic interest to further man's knowledge, but also in pursuit of a practical aim in the reform of language teaching at school level. French and English took up important places beside Latin and required new methods, including a technique for improving pronunciation. In 1882, Wilhelm Viëtor (under the pseudonym of Quousque Tandem) published a fiery attack against Latin-based methods of instruction in modern languages: *Der Sprachunterricht muss umkehren!* In 1884 the first edition of his *Elemente der Phonetik und Orthoepie des Deutschen, Englischen und Französischen*, appeared; the second edition followed three years later, the third – without the subtitle – in 1894, the fourth in 1898. The quick succession of editions and the fact that the seventh edition appeared in 1923, five years after his death, shows how popular a book it was and how well it coped with a practical need: the preparation of German students and teachers for problems of pronunciation in the two most important foreign languages of the time. Viëtor achieved this aim by contrasting the phonetics of French and English with that of the readers' native language: a good and premature example of contrastive phonology without the term and a good deal better than a lot of what followed more than fifty years later! The intention Viëtor had in writing this manual is stressed by the introductory motto taken from Sweet's *Handbook of Phonetics* (1877): '... If our present wretched system of studying modern languages is ever to be reformed, it must be on the basis of a preliminary training in general phonetics, which would at the same time lay the foundation for a thorough practical study of pronunciation and elocution of our own language – subjects which are totally ignored in our present scheme of education.' Moritz Trautmann published a similar handbook at the same time (Trautmann 1884–6). It was far less successful, because its more theoretical approach allowed for less practical application. Trautmann was obsessed with a new German terminology instead of the established international one and thus cut himself off from all the phonetic literature. He was also strongly opposed to the Bell-Sweet system of vowel classification, which Viëtor adopted, and relied on the acoustic resonances of the vocal tract according to Helmholtz, which is, of course, a great handicap in practical problems of pronunciation teaching.

Viëtor, who was professor of English at Marburg University, joined the Phonetic Teachers' Association, the forerunner of the IPA, in July 1886 and thus, once again, documented his all-consuming interest in the teaching of foreign languages and of pronunciation in particular. He was well acquainted with Paul Passy and Henry Sweet and stood firmly in the tradition of practical phonetics as it had developed especially in England. Sweet, Passy and Viëtor all lectured at two summer vacation courses at Edinburgh University from August 1–15 and August 16–30, 1906, their subjects being phonetics of English, French and German, while others lectured on literature and language (see *Die Neueren Sprachen* 14 (1906–7) p.125). In 1888 Viëtor started a phonetic journal, *Phonetische Studien, Zeitschrift für wissenschaftliche und praktische Phonetik*, Marburg, which ran until 1893; from volume VII it was incorporated as a supplement in the more comprehensive journal *Die Neueren Sprachen*, which he founded in 1894. Eventually, the phonetic supplement as such was given up, too, but a great many articles on a variety of phonetic topics appeared in the language journal for many years to come.

Although Viëtor is certainly the most outstanding figure in the field of descriptive and practical phonetics of individual languages in Germany at the turn of the century, there were many more besides him, mostly schoolteachers, who were fervently interested in the subject and contributed to *Die Neueren Sprachen*. One man must be mentioned especially because he tends to be forgotten in spite of his numerous high-quality publications: Hermann Klinghardt, who was a grammar school teacher in Reichenbach and Tarnowitz/Silesia before he was transferred to the 'Realgymnasium' in Rendsburg/Holstein near Kiel where he taught English, French, and German at all grades from 1893 to 1912. Like Viëtor, Klinghardt was very serious about a reform of foreign language teaching and applied the non-grammatical, direct or imitative method, which relied heavily on pronunciation and consequently on phonetics. He wrote two reports on his experience and success with

170

this technique in teaching English over four years (1888 and 1892). In this connection he also sought support abroad for his ideas on reform and in his book *Das höhere Schulwesen Schwedens* (1887) he gave an account of the Swedish school system and its attempt to supplement classical education by modern subjects.

On October 14–15, 1895, the teachers' association of Danish grammar-schools held its annual meeting in Copenhagen, at which Otto Jespersen gave a paper on the value of phonetics in the teaching of the mother tongue and of foreign languages, which Klinghardt translated into German, together with the discussion, and published in annotated form (Klinghardt 1898). The main points of Jespersen's talk were that anybody teaching any language, beginning with instruction in the mother tongue at nursery school level, has to be familiar with the most important points of phonetics in theory and especially in practice; the teacher must know the articulations and acoustic features of sounds (Jespersen means, of course, auditory), he must be able to produce them and to recognise his pupils' mistakes by ear, and finally to relate these to their articulatory causes, for it is only in this way that he can give useful guidance towards their correction. These demands are as necessary and sensible as they are modern, since they have never been fulfilled in German schools: pronunciation in foreign language teaching is still, on the whole, treated in a most unprofessional way, and the modern 'disease' of dyslexia would be dispersed into thin air in many cases if teachers of reading and writing had a better understanding of the relation between sound and letter.

Klinghardt was in full agreement with Jespersen's view and produced his contribution towards its realisation in his *Artikulations- und Hörübungen* (1897; second edition 1914). The first part of this manual, amounting to about one third of the whole, provides a detailed anatomical description of the vocal organs, particularly the larynx, and of their function for non-speech sounds. The second part then treats German speech articulations and sounds according to the different sections of the vocal apparatus in functional series for practice purposes. The general section is far too detailed and technical for the needs of the foreign language teacher, who receives very little help from six illustrations of the larynx and a thorough presentation of all its components, although Pike (1943, p.34) quotes Klinghardt for emphasising the importance of non-speech sounds for phonetic theory. On the other hand, the limitation of speech sounds to those found in German restricts the usefulness of the book still further, because in this respect it does not go far enough in its general phonetic outline. Though Klinghardt stresses his reliance only on visual inspection (mirror), auditory perception and kinesthetic sensation (p.8), he is nevertheless influenced by the physiological literature of Merkel and Brücke, which, according to his article 'Die Lautphysiologie in der Schule' (1885), he knows very well. Whereas pupils are not to be formally instructed in the anatomy and physiology of the speech organs, but to be trained in articulation and hearing, the teachers should be able to relate sounds to the articulatory movements; their detailed description in physical terms is thus a prerequisite of the teacher's successful instruction (p.303). This attitude applies to all the proponents of practical phonetics of the time. They had emancipated themselves from the natural science field and subordinated their phonetic studies to the linguistic point of view, but they nevertheless believed naively that the more objective an articulatory description is the easier the teaching and mastering of speech processes becomes.

The following example illustrates this misplaced striving for physiological accuracy. In volume 14 (1906–7) of *Die Neueren Sprachen*, Klinghardt (1906a–e), Passy (1906a,b) and a schoolteacher from Hamburg, by the name of Jaeger (1906), have a controversial argument about the formation of the plosives in French and German, spread over no less than eight articles and notes. Klinghardt set the ball rolling by stating (pp.86ff.) that in the French tenues the glottis was closed at the moment of the explosion and that the larynx moved upwards, whereas in German there was an opening and no larynx movement. The observations Klinghardt adduced as proofs were visual perception of the jerking larynx, the need to breathe out after a series of French *p*'s, but to breathe in after a series of German ones, and the burning match experiment. Passy objected to this analysis because he was unable to repeat these observations, although he admitted that Klinghardt's French *p*'s sounded quite normal when he heard him produce them in the match test. Whenever Passy pronounced French *pa* a lighted match went out even though he had to hold it closer to the mouth than for the German syllable. To this Klinghardt rightly replied that to be of any proof value the match has to be held at the same distance from the mouth for all these sounds, and that they should not be followed by the vowel *a*. He finally invokes the help of instrumental phonetics (p.445) to settle the argument. Both phoneticians were, of course, unable to determine the state of the glottis with their means of observation, and the experimental techniques available at the time would not have helped them either. Moreover, Klinghardt did not consider the possibility of using different gestures under the stress of a demonstration experiment, although Passy could detect no auditory deviation from the required French norm. The two scholars were thus applying imitation label techniques in spite of their articulatory terminology, and they were convinced of the need for an objective physical analysis, though this could hardly assist language learners in acquiring the correct pronunciation. And this positivist search for exact articulatory details without relevance to the teaching situation still went on after Passy had accepted the auditory result.

Klinghardt, like all the other practical phoneticians and their mouthpiece *Le Maître Phonétique*, attributed great importance to phonetic transcription in language teaching because it was the only aid to memory in view of inadequate orthographies. The introduction of transcription, how-

ever, has always contained the fallacy that language teachers have easily
fallen for, namely the belief that it helps in the acquisition of actual perfor-
mance and listening skills. Right down to the present day pupils have usually
learned transcription as a second orthography without the slightest improvement in their practical abilities in using a language. When the language
laboratory appeared on the scene fifty years later, transcription lost a great
deal of its attraction, since the correct pronunciation was reproduceable
without a teacher so that the memory problem in the pupils' work outside the
class-room was partly solved. But the new oral method committed an equally
serious mistake when, in its behaviouristic outlook, it believed that correct
stimulus presentation for imitation, and reinforcement by correct repetition
lead to the right articulation. Jespersen knew before the turn of the century
that this method achieves nothing (Klinghardt 1898, p.247).

Klinghardt is best known for his books on intonation, which was treated
only very cursorily in the handbooks of general phonetics (e.g. Sievers) and
the pronunciation of particular languages (e.g. Viëtor). At the time the only
large collection of phonetic texts with intonation marks was Daniel Jones's
Intonation Curves (1909). Thus Klinghardt had to explore new territory when
he realised the importance of speech melody for a good pronunciation, and
he deviated in two ways from the model provided by Jones. His practice
manual (Klinghardt and Fourmestraux 1911) was meant to bring out the
typical patterns of French intonation not, like Jones, the individual pitch
curves of particular speakers on particular occasions. The continuous curves,
being a hindrance rather than a help in the initial teaching, are broken up
into a series of dots each marking the relative height of each syllable; heavier
dots represent stressed syllables. A translation and adaptation of this book,
by the lecturer at Edinburgh University, Miss M.L. Barker, who worked with
Klinghardt in Kötzschenbroda near Dresden after his retirement from his
Rendsburg school, was published in 1923. A second edition of the German
version came out in 1925 in cooperation with P. Olbrich, who added a chapter
on 'intonation in class'.

Klinghardt followed the same principles in his *Übungen im englischen
Tonfall* (1920), which he published in collaboration with Gertrude Klemm, a
native speaker of English who was born in Manchester, of German parents.
Educated in England, she had married and been living in Dresden for a
number of years but still retained an English accent in her German. In this
case he was able to draw on a more extensive literature on pitch by Daniel
Jones, who had also followed his example by using the dot notation (cf.
Jones's reference to Klinghardt in *Outline*, 1956, p.277). Finally, in 1927
Klinghardt's *Übungen in deutschem Tonfall* appeared, again on the same
principles as the intonation excercises for the other two languages. He also
published a more theoretical account of the organisation of speech into units
of enunciation characterised by pitch patterns, and a comparative description of the structures in French, English, and German, under the title

'Sprechmelodie und Sprechtakt', (Klinghardt 1923). In this he rejects the unit of the stress-group, introduced by Sweet and taken over by Sievers, and replaces it with a unit that binds a group of words through their content by a melodic pattern instead of the counter-intuitive rhythmic grouping of a stressed syllable with all unstressed followers in a stress group. We know today that these concepts are by no means contradictory, but complementary.

The practical study of language sounds, as it was practised by German phoneticians at the turn of the century, has the closest links with the English school of phonetics. There is, however, an important difference in that the history of English phonetics is characterised by a long tradition of concern with spelling reform, of the relationship between sound and letter, and of shorthand systems, into which the teaching of English pronunciation to foreigners could be incorporated quite naturally. Such a tradition of practical phonetics was lacking in Germany. Its emergence in connection with foreign language teaching had to break new ground, and it declined as the reform movement came to a halt. The description of the phonetics of German was hampered by the concern with the standard stage pronunciation, an artifical creation of the late nineteenth century, which occupied scholars more than actually observable facts of colloquial speech (see Kohler 1970). Viëtor's *Deutsches Aussprachewörterbuch* of 1912 saw its fifth and last edition, prepared by Ernst A. Meyer, in 1931, whereas the 'Siebs' Pronouncing Dictionary is now in its nineteenth edition (Siebs 1969). When the reform of foreign language teaching was revived in the early 1960s under the new auspices of modern linguistics imported from the States together with the language laboratory, phonetic studies of individual languages were carried out on a phonological basis, with little concern for phonetic substance, by unqualified people without a proper phonetic training, in language departments and foreign language centres.

The two old institutes of phonetics, at the Universities of Hamburg and Bonn, stood outside the movement, although the study of languages was one of the reasons for the foundation in both cases. In Hamburg, the African scholar Carl Meinhof saw the need for phonetics in the investigation of African languages and achieved the setting up of a laboratory in the Colonial Institute in 1910, which was incorporated into the newly established university in 1919. In Bonn, the Romance scholar Wilhelm Meyer-Lübke, in true Neogrammarian tradition, was the sponsor of a phonetics department which was founded in 1921 to help in the training of linguists and especially of modern language teachers.

In Hamburg, Giulio Panconcelli-Calzia became head of the phonetics department. A pupil of Rousselot's, he built up experimental phonetics as a natural science (*Phonetik als Naturwissenschaft* 1948), regarding phonetics as a part of physiology, a sub-section of the study of motion like walking, running, jumping (p.8), at the same time ridiculing the *philologus auricularius furibundus* (p.18). Panconcelli-Calzia never came to grips with the linguistic

174

point of view and he had no criteria for separating normal and deviant phenomena. His theoretical outlook and his experimental and instrumental methods caused all phonetic categories (sound, syllable etc.) to disintegrate. He turned them into fictions of investigation without relevance to the communication process (Panconcelli-Calzia 1947). He thus helped to prepare the ground for the division of the discipline into phonetics and phonology.

In Bonn, the psychologist Paul Menzerath took over the phonetics department and built it up on the principles of research into human communication, so the psychological and linguistic views based on a strictly scientific methodology were dominant right from the start. Although there was a growing concern for acoustic analyses – contrasting with the articulatory approach at Hamburg – a concern that was even intensified under his successors Werner Meyer-Eppler and Gerold Ungeheuer, Bonn is also linked with one of the pioneering studies in speech production: *Koartikulation, Steuerung und Lautabgrenzung* (1933), which Menzerath published together with A. de Lacerda and which rectified the old concepts of positional sounds and of glides.

The Bonn Institute has gone a long way towards a return to a unitary interdisciplinary subject of phonetics, which Sievers abandoned in the third edition of his *Grundzüge*. Although phonetic data have always been subjected to the language aspect, research in Bonn has never been dominated by a narrow linguistic point of view; general questions about sound production and perception in man were taken up again more than half a century after Brücke and Merkel, and experimental and instrumental phonetics were fully integrated into the study of language structures, thus bridging the gap between phonetics and phonology. The abandoning of Trubetzkoy's dichotomy has also been a life-long endeavour on the part of another scholar who, through adverse circumstances, had to do his research outside the universities till, very late in life, he became the first professor of phonetics at Cologne in 1963: Eberhard Zwirner. If one considers that all the new phonetics chairs in Germany, at the universities of Munich, Kiel, and Frankfurt, were filled by people who at least at some stage in their training worked in the phonetics department in Bonn (this also applies to Zwirner's successor), it is not surprising that there is a strong drive among the professional phoneticians in Germany to-day to overcome the one-sided linguistic affiliation of phonetics and re-unite its three trends to form a well-established speech science, which seems to me to be a much better name for our discipline than phonetics. In this process, the Kiel institute also brings in the potential of the British school of phonetics, which I was lucky enough to get to know in David Abercrombie's department in Edinburgh, and through which phonetic descriptions of German as well as substance-based analyses of foreign language teaching and learning are beginning to reappear.

The problem of three areas of Phonetics developing away from each other in the history of German phonetics applies to other countries as well, of course. There is the same need everywhere for a unified discipline of speech science that is open to all the subjects it is connected with: physiology, physics, psychology, linguistics. It is my firm conviction that, to be able to cope with its tasks in such areas as speech pathology and therapy, communications engineering and pronunciation teaching, it should stay an independent subject in independent departments and not amalgamate with one of these fields that by sheer historical accident dominated the development of phonetics much to its disadvantage, for a certain period, namely linguistics.

References

ABERCROMBIE, D. (1967) *Elements of General Phonetics*, Edinburgh (Edinburgh University Press).

BELL, A.M. (1867) *Visible Speech: the Science of Universal Alphabetics; or Self-interpreting Physiological Letters, for the Writing of All Languages in One Alphabet*, London (Simpkin, Marshall & Co.), London & New York (Trübner & Co.).

BRÜCKE, E.W. (1856) *Grundzüge der Physiologie und Systematik der Sprachlaute für Linguisten und Taubstummenlehrer*, Vienna (C. Gerold's Sohn).

— (1863) 'Über eine neue Methode der phonetischen Transscription', *Sitzungsberichte der Philosophisch-Historischen Classe der Kaiserlichen Akademie der Wissenschaften Wien*, 41, 223–85.

— (1871) *Die physiologischen Grundlagen der neuhochdeutschen Verskunst*, Vienna (C. Gerold).

ELLIS, A.J. (1869–1889) *On Early English Pronunciation, with especial reference to Shakspere and Chaucer*, London (Asher & Co.; Trübner & Co.), 5 parts [Early English Text Society, Extra Series 2 (1869), 7 (1869), 14 (1871), 23 (1874), 56 (1889)].

GRIMM, J.L.C. (1819–37) *Deutsche Grammatik*, 4 vol., Göttingen (Dieterische Buchhandlung). 2nd ed. of Vol. 1, 1822.

HELMHOLTZ, H.L.F. VON (1862) *Die Lehre von den Tonempfindungen als physiologische Grundlage für die Theorie der Musik*, Braunschweig (F. Vieweg und Sohn), 3rd ed. 1870.

JAEGER, T. (1906) 'Zur Aussprache von Französisch und Deutsch *P T K*'. *Die Neueren Sprachen* 14, 383–4.

JESPERSEN, O. (1898). See KLINGHARDT (1898).

JONES, D. (1909) *Intonation Curves: a collection of phonetic texts, in which intonation is marked throughout by means of curved lines on a musical stave*, Leipzig/Berlin (R.G. Teubner).

— (1956) *An Outline of English Phonetics*, 8th ed., Cambridge (W. Heffer).

KLINGHARDT, H. (1885) 'Die Lautphysiologie in der Schule', *Englische Studien* 8, 287–323.

— (1887) *Das höhere Schulwesen Schwedens und dessen Reform in modernem Sinne*, Leipzig (J. Klinkhardt).

— (1888) *Ein Jahr Erfahrungen mit der neuen Methode. Bericht über den Unterricht mit einer englischen Anfängerklasse im Schuljahr 1887/88*, Marburg (N.G. Elwert).

— (1892) *Drei weitere Jahre Erfahrungen mit der imitativen Methode (Obertertia bis Obersecunda). Ein Bericht aus der Praxis des neusprachlichen Unterrichts*, Marburg (N.G. Elwert).

— (1897) *Artikulations- und Hörübungen. Praktische Hülfsbuch der Phonetik für Studierende und Lehrer*, Cöthen (O. Schulze).

— (1898) 'Der Werth der Phonetik für den Unterricht in der Muttersprache und den Fremdsprachen', *Englische Studien* 24, 239–64; 25. 162–94.

(Translation with introduction and notes of talk given by Otto Jespersen in Copenhagen in 1895, with discussion that followed).

— (1906a) 'Antwort' (to Passy (1906b)), *Die Neueren Sprachen* 14, 439–45.

— (1906b) 'Französisch P, geprüft an und von einem Pariser', *Die Neueren Sprachen* 14, 510–11.

— (1906c) 'Zur Richtigstellung' (Response to Jaeger (1906)), *Die Neueren Sprachen* 14, 512.

— (1906d) 'Die verschiedene Bildung der Tenues im Französischen und Deutschen' 1, *Die Neueren Sprachen* 14, 85–8.

— (1906e) 'Die verschiedene Bildung der Tenues im Französischen und Deutschen' 2 (Response to Passy (1906a)), *Die Neueren Sprachen* 14, 310–15.

— (1923) 'Sprechmelodie und Sprechtakt', *Die Neueren Sprachen* 31, 1–29. Published separately in same year, Marburg (N.G. Elwert).

— (1927) *Übungen in deutschem Tonfall. Für Lehrer und Studierende, auch für Ausländer*, Leipzig (Quelle & Meyer).

KLINGHARDT, H. and FOURMESTRAUX, M. DE (1911) *Französische Intonationsübungen. Für Lehrer und Studierende*, Cöthen (O. Schulze). 2nd ed., with P. Olbrich, Leipzig (Quelle & Meyer) 1925.

— (1923) *French Intonation Exercises*. Trans. M.L. Barker, Cambridge (W. Heffer & Sons).

KLINGHARDT, H. and KLEMM, G. (1920) *Übungen im englischen Tonfall. Für Lehrer und Studierende*, Cöthen (O. Schulze).

KOHLER, K. (1970) 'Deutsche Hochlautung', *Muttersprache* 80, 238–47.

LESKIEN, A. (1876) *Die Declination im Slavisch-Litauischen und Germanischen*, Leipzig (S. Hirzel).

MENZERATH, P. and LACERDA, A. DE (1933) *Koartikulation, Steuerung und Lautabgrenzung*, Berlin u. Bonn (F. Dümmler).

MERKEL, C.L. (1857) *Anatomie und Physiologie des menschlichen Stimm- und Sprach-Organs (Anthropophonik) nach eigenen Beobachtungen und Versuchen wissenschaftlich begründet und für Studirende und ausübende Ärzte, Physiologen, Akustiker, Sänger, Gesanglehrer, Tonsetzer, öffentliche Redner, Pädagogen und Sprachforscher dargestellt*, Leipzig (A. Abel).

— (1866) *Physiologie der menschlichen Sprache (physiologische Laletik)*, Leipzig (O. Wigand).

OSTOFF, H. and BRUGMANN, K. (1878–1910) *Morphologische Untersuchungen auf dem Gebiete der indogermanischen Sprachen*, 6 vols. Leipzig (S. Hirzel).

PANCONCELLI-CALZIA, G. (1947) *Das Als Ob in der Phonetik*, Hamburg (Stromverlag).

— (1948) *Phonetik als Naturwissenschaft*, Berlin (Wissenschaftliche Editionsgesellschaft).

PASSY, P. (1906a) 'La formation des plosives en français et en allemand', *Die Neueren Sprachen* 14, 253–4.

— (1906b) 'Les plosives françaises: lettre ouverte à H. Klinghardt', *Die Neueren Sprachen* 14, 438–9.

PIKE, K.L. (1943) *Phonetics: a Critical Analysis of Phonetic Theory and a Technic for the Practical Description of Sounds*, Ann Arbor (University of Michigan Press).

ROUSSELOT, L'ABBÉ P.J. (1891) 'La méthode graphique appliquée à la recherche des transformations inconscientes du langage', *Compte rendu du Congrès Scientifique International des Catholiques tenu à Paris 1–6 avril 1891*, 109 ff.

— (1892) *Les modifications phonétiques du langage, étudiées dans le patois d'une famille de Cellefrouin (Charente)*, Paris (H. Welter).

The Development of Phonetics in Germany

— (1897–1901) *Principes de phonétique expérimentale*, 2 vols., Paris (H. Welter).

SCHERER, W. (1868) *Zur Geschichte der deutschen Sprache*, Berlin (Weidmann).

SCHLEICHER, A. (1861–2) *Compendium der vergleichenden Grammatik der indo-germanischen Sprachen*, Weimar (Hermann Böhlau).

— (1863) *Die darwinsche Theorie und die Sprachwissenschaft*, Weimar (Hermann Böhlau).

SIEBS, T. (1969) [*Deutsche Bühnenaussprache*.] *Deutsche Aussprache. Reine und gemässigte Hochlautung mit Aussprachewörterbuch*, ed. Helmut de Boor, Hugo Moser und Christian Winkler. 19th rev. ed., Berlin (Walter de Gruyter).

SIEVERS, E. (1881) *Grundzüge der Phonetik zur Einführung in das Studium der Lautlehre der indogermanischen Sprachen*, Leipzig (Breitkopf & Härtel). 2nd ed. of *Grundzüge der Lautphysiologie* 1876. 3rd ed. 1889, 4th ed. 1893, 5th ed. 1901.

STORM, J.F.B. (1879) *Engelsk Filologi. Anvisning til et videnskabeligt Studium af det engelske Sprog*, vol. 1, *Die lavende Sprog*, Kristiana (A. Cammermeyer). German translation *Englische Philologie* …, Heilbronn (Gebr. Henninger) 1881.

SWEET, H. (1877) *A Handbook of Phonetics*, Oxford (Clarendon Press).

TRAUTMANN, M. (1884–86) *Die Sprachlaute im Allgemeinen und die Laute des Englischen, Französischen und Deutschen im Besonderen*, Leipzig (G. Fock).

TRUBETZKOY, N.S. (1939) *Grundzüge der Phonologie*, Prague (Cercle Linguistique de Prague).

VIËTOR, W. (1882) *Der Sprachunterricht muss umkehren!*, Heilbronn (Henninger).

— (1884) *Elemente der Phonetik und Orthoepie des Deutschen, Englischen und Französischen, mit Rücksicht auf die Bedürfnisse der Lehrpraxis*, Heilbronn (O.R. Reisland).

— (1912) *Deutsches Aussprachewörterbuch*, Leipzig (O.R. Reisland).

WINTELER, J. (1876) *Die Kerenzer Mundart des Kantons Glarus*, Leipzig (C.F. Winter).

PART FIVE

INDIVIDUAL CONTRIBUTIONS TO
PHONETIC THEORY AND DESCRIPTION

An Autobiographical Note
on Phonetics

It is a pleasure to acknowledge one's indebtedness to a school of phonetics that has so long a history as the one represented by David Abercrombie. It is extraordinary how deeply indebted one can be to one's predecessors without knowing it – and in my early experience I was as ignorant of my phonetic ancestors as a person can be.

There was a reason for this. Before starting field work in a Mexican Indian language, my total formal training in phonetics consisted of precisely ten days of lectures on the subject, from a person who – so far as my knowledge is concerned – had never had much training. (It never occurred to me to inquire!) Yet those were days of bliss, excitement, and moulding of much of my future energy investment; they first opened a door of science, which I walked through. My prior contact with languages had not prepared me for live languages: in college, four years of New Testament Greek (not for speaking!); in high school a bit of Latin, and a bit of French taught in a country academy of fifty-two students by teachers who never got through to us that reading (never speaking) French was anything other than a cultural exercise comparable to reading Latin. And in our New England home, in the language melting pot at its hottest, it was taboo to utter a single word in Swedish, even though children of recent immigrants joined us in school classes.

Dr E.L. McCreery of the Bible Institute of Los Angeles in the summer of 1935 had come to Arkansas, where the second session of the Summer Institute of Linguistics (founded by Cameron Townsend, who had had no formal training in linguistics) was held.

The explicit aim and incredible dream of the founder of the Institute was to initiate training to lead to the study of some five hundred languages in the world, to publish top scientific work on them, to teach previously alphabet-less people to read in cooperation with the governments involved, and to translate the New Testament into these languages. Mr Townsend gave lectures on the verb structure of Cakchiquel (a Mayan language of Guatemala into which he had translated the New Testament), and started us reading some general books, and descriptions of American Indian languages. Interrupting his sequence was the special lecture series on phonetics.

Dr McCreery discussed vowels and consonants. I had some trouble with the vowel chart he used. Perhaps one reason was that he was from California, but that the chart originated from a different dialect area. (I thought I found it years later in Bell's *Visible Speech*, 1867). He mentioned tone in about a ten minute section – highly valuable to me a few months later when I found to my surprise that I was working on such material in Mexico, but without having heard of morphophonemics of tone – and with consequent difficulty for many months, until I discovered it for myself.

That fall I started working on the Mixtec of Mexico, with tone, vowel length, glottal stop, and nasalisation all significant and exciting. Townsend asked me to come back to Arkansas the next summer to supplement with Latin American materials the work of Dr McCreery, whose field experience had been in Africa. So through a Mexico City bookstore I ordered sight unseen every book on phonetics in the catalogue of books listed as in print in English. Thus I began to get acquainted with Jones, Sweet, Kenyon, Armfield and some others. It was another world. (It was especially exciting in view of the fact that in 1933, when I had a chance to study Chinese for some three weeks, I was told: 'Pike, the trouble with you is that you do not know how to pronounce the aspirates' – the teacher did not know, apparently, that the aspirates were normal for us under stress, and that it was the unaspirates which gave us the pronunciation trouble.)

That summer of 1936 I was supposed to teach a student to pronounce the sounds of Cakchiquel, of Guatemala (a native speaker of the language was with us). I managed in due season to get explosive alveolar, alveopalatal, and front velar sounds; but the bilabial and the back velar stops baffled me. An old letter turned up recently, showing that I learned about the implosives from correspondence with Dr Thomas F. Cummings, who had helped many missionaries study phonetics and principles of language learning in Biblical Seminary, New York. (I had heard of him in 1934, but was unable to study there because of finance – in Arkansas it cost us only six dollars per month, as we five boys did much of the work ourselves.) Later, from his daughter, I was told about the general organic basis of articulation – going back to Sweet at least – which is very useful in mimicry of style and voice quality. Even now I feel sad that so few phonetics teachers take practical advantage of this view for drills in relation to a sound system as a whole.

In the fall of 1936 Townsend asked me to write on phonetics. This seemed a bit silly, with my near-zero background, but a broken leg gave me writing time in the hospital. So I wrote in bed the drills which later made up much of the first part of my book on Phonemics (1947). (I do not normally recommend this kind of stimulus to our students – 'publish or perish' has grim overtones in such an environment.) The manuscript was sent to Sapir by Townsend, and as a result of his encouragement, Townsend sent me to the University of Michigan to a Linguistic Institute to study with Sapir. This was another stimulus of unmeasurable proportions: it was my first contact with the graduate community of scholars, and the first with professional linguists. I never recovered.

From Sapir I got more phonetics, of Navajo, and the clue to the analysis of tone by frames (the tone had been blocking me for two years by then); this, later, I developed in a book on tone languages (1948). That same summer I studied the dialect geography of New England with Bernard Bloch, who in turn had been trained in dialect recording by Guy Loman (Loman, I think, obtained a Ph.D. in phonetics under Daniel Jones).

By 1939 phonetics was taking up much of my attention, and the analogy of explosive to implosive had gripped me, so that I was extending this to various other phases of phonetics. When this was combined with an attempt to show just how the various movements during the sounds were coordinated or segmented, and combined with a dream of separating phonetics from phonemics (which I first heard about in 1936 when Nida, a student at the Institute, introduced me to Bloomfield's 1933 book on language) eventually led to my 1943 book on phonetics.

Reflected in that book, also, is my early interest in the syllable, based upon stimulus from the etic/emic problem of phonetic long vowel as a two-vowel two-syllable sequence in Mixtec, plus interest in the work of Stetson, which seemed to require an etic versus emic view of that material unknown to its author (since a word like *spa* turned out to have two syllable pulses in his experiments, but was treated by him as only one in the poetry of English). Later, about 1952, the whole problem of the syllable forced me to a split between a phonological hierarchy in contrast with a grammatical one, and in contrast to a lexical hierarchy; the then current American scene as emphasised by Trager had no room for a syllable, since he moved direct from (non-linguistic) phone to phoneme, to morpheme, to syntax, and then to ('metalinguistic') meaning. The change forced on that system, caused by leaving room for a syllable that may be other than phoneme or morpheme, was substantial and not accepted in my country for many years – and even then, with great reserve and without adequate reformulation of theory to allow for it. The combination of the demand for allowing multiple hierarchies (with intersection of them) along with the need for etic versus emic distinctions on each level of each hierarchy was too big a step for most of my contemporaries to consider.

Yet the hierarchy of phonology needed to be extended much beyond the syllable – even to identifying some phonetic characteristics related to dialogue interchange as one speaker responded in phonetic kind to another speaker. And the phonetics of segments and lexical tone needed further integration with voice quality and with the intonation of the voice (again, etic versus emic), with a vast range of differences from language to language to be differentiated from characteristics conditioned by the biological state of the individual (nervousness, for example). Further dimensions were needed, where openness of throat, or contrastive height of larynx, had to be included both in the identification of the phonemes (as in West Africa or in Nepal), and in the general quality of the voice.

As these elements continued to gain my attention, they led to a further impression of the importance of their communicative value. And poets, it seemed to me, could well be encouraged to use, as part of their mechanism for recording their meanings, a notation showing some part of those intonations which in fact helped to carry those meanings. But this suggestion (with a few published samples) did not meet with general acceptance; there was fear of loss of freedom (whether of poet or of other reader) to 'interpret' the cold words as he chose from time to time. Moreover, it was felt (often correctly) that sometimes the poet was not a good reader of his own poetry. Here, in our view, the future begs us to move onward, to train new poets in the notation of intonation just as in their youth they learned their A-B-Cs of vowels and consonants. When that is done, poets with artistic control of intonation should, I maintain, start giving us new beauty currently beyond us; a device for expressing double meanings (one by words, another by intonation) would be at hand.

Thus, I have had my pilgrimage from non-phonetician (who first heard with awe, in college, that a few hours of phonetics could better a man's speech who might have studied a foreign language for twenty years) to a commitment to serve the world with sound manipulation of sounds.

And thus also, we record the pilgrimage of a total monolingual, controlling not five sentences in any language other than English, to an interest in the phonetics of the world. But this starting point, apparently so disadvantageous (in relation to the multilinguals of the continent who had developed so much of the world's linguistic theory) had one interesting asset: it was abundantly clear, from my first contact with phonetics, that the first and second /p/ of *paper* were so much the same that only with great effort, and after much time, could they be heard as different. (Now, we teach students to hear the difference in a few moments, by techniques which were not made available to me in those early days.) The contrast between phonetic and phonemic, between phone and phoneme (still far from certain to some scholars) was a behavioural given, from which unshaken convictions could grow, and on which old and new techniques to train other monolinguals – or multilinguals – could be founded. (Persons interested in more detail of this pilgrimage can one of these days consult a biography, currently being written by my sister Eunice Pike.)

But no person can grow in a vacuum. The most 'independent' suddenly finds himself unable to breathe freely except in an atmosphere developed long before he came on the scene. This atmosphere in which I unknowingly grew up was passed on and enlarged by the British tradition to which Abercrombie has been a contributor – someone with whom I have personally enjoyed very much discussing problems in phonetics, such as, for example, the differences between American and British intonation. We give to him, and to his colleagues – and to his many antecedents, as well, whom he has helped us to know better – our appreciation.

References

BELL, A.M. (1867) *Visible Speech: the Science of Universal Alphabetics; or Self-interpreting Physiological Letters, for the Writing of All Languages in one Alphabet*, London (Simpkin, Marshall & Co.), London and New York (Trübner).

BLOOMFIELD, L. (1933) *Language*, New York (Holt Rinehart & Winston).

PIKE, KENNETH L. (1943) *Phonetics: a Critical Analysis of Phonetic Theory and a Technic for the Practical Description of Sounds*, Ann Arbor (University of Michigan Press).

— (1947) *Phonemics: a Technique for Reducing Languages to Writing*, Michigan Univ. Publ. Ling. 3, Ann Arbor (University of Michigan Press).

— (1948) *Tone Languages: a Technique for Determining the Number and Type of Pitch Contrasts in a Language, with Studies in Tonemic Substitution and Fusion*, Michigan Univ. Publ. Ling. 4, Ann Arbor (University of Michigan Press).

The Phonetic Theory of
John Thelwall (1764–1834)

John Thelwall (a colateral relation to whose phonetic views my attention was first drawn by David Abercrombie) was born and brought up in London, where his father Joseph (1731–72) was a silk merchant in Covent Garden. Thelwall suffered from a lisp and weak lungs (C. Thelwall 1837), and the brief encouragement of a clergyman and teacher called Harvey (I can find no further information about him) taught him the value of elocution and made him aspire to a literary and dramatic career. With the collapse of the family's finances after his father's death, a professional career in these fields seemed out of the question. His interest in writing, oratory, and also politics brought Thelwall into close contact with the intellectual and political life of London in the early 1790s. Thelwall's growing political convictions, fanned by events in France, led him to assume a leading role in the London Corresponding Society – founded by Thomas Hardy and dedicated to Parliamentary Reform – which culminated in his arrest and trial for high treason alongside Horne Tooke, Thomas Hardy, and others (Thompson 1963, pp.19–22). Soon after his acquittal he left London to farm in Wales.

In the period between his father's death and the trial he was briefly articled to a barrister, and then supported himself, his mother and elder brother by freelance journalism and writing. The publication of his first book of poems brought him many friendships, notably, for his speech interests, one with Henry Cline (1750–1827), Professor of Anatomy at St Thomas's Hospital and editor of the *Biographical and Imperial Magazine*. Cline was an adherent of Tooke and attended him while Tooke was in prison in 1794 (see the *DNB* for further details of Cline's life). Thelwall thus became interested in medicine, and in 1791 moved to a house near St Thomas's and Guy's Hospitals to attend Cline's lectures on anatomy, and John Haighton's (1755–1823) on physiology. He wrote later:

> The foundations of my system were laid many years ago, when your [Henry Cline's] kindness offered me the opportunity (not usually enjoyed by any but professed students of medicine) of attaining, under your instruction at St Thomas's some knowledge of the Science of Anatomy; I did not indeed, at that time, perceive all the applications that might be made of the facts and principles illustrated; or suspect that I was studying Elocution, while witnessing the demonstrations and experiments of the Medical Theatre. But the objects impressed

upon my mind, and the conversations I occasionally enjoyed ... gave me an early habit of thinking and of reasoning physiologically ... I continued to labour, with increasing application, for the complete development of my system; persevering in the plan, upon which I had first set out, of uniting theoretical study and scientific analysis with practical experience. (Thelwall 1810, pp.1–2)

Another result of Thelwall's activities in London during this period was contact with Coleridge, which grew from correspondence in 1796 to friendship and mutual visits to Wales and Kendal. Through Coleridge he also became acquainted with Wordsworth, Southey, and Blake, and the combination of his interests in physiology, elocution and verse rhythm encouraged by discussion with these poets probably laid the foundations (at this time) of his theory of prosody. (For a more detailed account of these contacts see Rockey 1979.) In 1801 after two fruitless years attempting to farm in Wales, Thelwall set out on a new career as a professional elocutionist:

The idea had been planted by a friend in Manchester who, on hearing of a clergyman delivering elocutionary lectures in the town, thought Thelwall might profitably do likewise. The suggestion burst upon Thelwall 'in a flood of light'. He would use the same title but change the contents and by a series of 'theoretical and practical disquisitions' build 'the solid foundations of a permanent and useful profession'. (Rockey 1979)

For the next four years he embarked on a life of lecture tours that extended to most major towns of the Midlands, the north of England, and Edinburgh. During this period Thelwall brought together all the strands of his knowledge in the elaboration of 'the Nature and Objects of Elocutionary Science'. This included pathological as well as normal elocution, as a result of his contact with a wide variety of speech defects during the course of his lectures. The combination of an analytical interest in both normal and pathological phonetics has been a continuous tradition in England (as noted by Firth 1946), and a detailed account of Thelwall's theory and practice as the 'first British Speech Therapist' is to be found in Rockey (1977, 1978, 1979).

The success of Thelwall's lectures led him in 1805 to establish an Institute in Liverpool, which moved to London in 1806, first to Bedford Place, and then to 87 Lincoln's Inn Fields. His Institute catered for all the above-mentioned aspects of elocution, and his general lectures were attended by many of the foremost intellectuals of the day, including Godwin, Lamb, and Crabb Robinson. For a period between 1818 and 1822 he re-entered active politics, and during this time purchased and edited a radical journal, *The Champion*; but the whole affair was a ruinous failure and he returned to spend the rest of his life on elocution.

Thelwall never published a completely explicit account of his theories in any field. The range of his interests and activities, the pressures of supporting himself and his family, and his undoubted success as a speech therapist in the period after 1801 kept him more than busy. After 1804 he began to make a serious contribution to elocution theory in various published works; but all, with the exception of *A Letter to Henry Cline* (1810), bear signs of a hasty, though never slapdash, compilation of lecture notes, which would have been filled out in delivery. They lack the conclusive detail that would enable an evaluation of his theoretical position on a number of points. A biographical volume by his second wife was published (C. Thelwall 1837) but a second, promised volume, which was to include his theory of elocution in full detail, never appeared. Charles Cestre (1906) mentions possessing the papers of John Thelwall and they are recorded as having been sold at Sotheby's in 1904, but all further trace of them has been lost.

From 1805 until at least 1826, Thelwall published numerous versions of his elocutionary theory and practice, usually as a preface to samples of verse that were either part of his oratorical repertoire or exercises for normal or pathological elocutionary states. Rather than attempt a synthetic presentation of the 'best' of his theory from all the sources, it seemed best to give an extended quotation from the *Introductory Discourse on the Nature and Objects of Elocutionary Science* (1805) and to quote from later publications only where significant clarification results. This extract from Thelwall (1805) forms Appendix 1 to this paper. I have edited out the longer references to speech therapy (for which see Rockey 1979) and repetitious digressions and illustrations that add nothing directly to the exposition of his ideas.

Any evaluation of Thelwall's views must take account of the people he cites, and brief notes on Wilkins, Holder, Kenrick, Herries, Sheridan, Walker, Crombie, Darwin and Itard are given in Appendix 2. They are all mentioned from the earliest of Thelwall's writings. John Wallis (see Kemp 1972) is mentioned much later (1825, p.113) and although Wallis certainly had a very well developed phonetic theory, I shall compare Thelwall's classification of consonants with that of Holder (1669) because Holder's classification represents a significant codification of articulatory classification prior to Thelwall's. From the classifications given below (pp.195–6) we can construct a table (table 1) combining place and manner categories, adding suggested I P A values where the symbols used are ambiguous. Holder's classification is shown in table 2.

Although Thelwall has considerably reduced the numbers of manner categories, his classification cannot be said to be an advance on Holder, and the specific errors in the placing of Y, the muddle over S, Z, Ch and G=J, while not too surprising in view of the difficulty of assessing kinaesthetic sensations does not advance the taxonomy. The denial that NG involves any contact is on the other hand somewhat surprising. Since he gives no clear account of a vowel classification, we cannot make any assessment of this part of his theory.

Thelwall's views on the role of the larynx in speech were original, particularly his appreciation that vibration state was the basis of more than one

TABLE 1. Thelwall (1805, pp.xxxiv–xxxvi)

	Labial	Labiodental		Lingual		Guttural	Other
			3	1	2		
Mute	P			T		K	
Liquid	M,W	V		N,R,L,Y			NG
Semi-Liquid	B		Th[ð]	D,Z		G,GZ	
Sibilant		F	Th[θ]	G=J[dʒ]	S,Ch	X,KS	
					Sh,Zh		

This table presents the main classificatory categories in Thelwall's articulatory taxonomy. Other units such as H, Q; and categories such as aspirate sonosibilant can be deduced from the text (p.196, below). The symbols in square brackets are IPA equivalents.

TABLE 2. Holder (1669, pp.40–52)

Appulse Occluse		Mute	Murmur-mute	Naso-vocal
	Labial	P	B	M
	Gingival	T	D	N
	Palatick	K	G	N̂ĝ

Appulse Pervious		Blase	Murmure Blase	Sibilant	Murmure Sibilant	Semi-vocal Smooth or free	Semi-vocal jarring
	Labio-dental	F	V				
	Lingua-dental	Th	Dh				
	Gingival			S	Z	L	R
	Palatic			Sh	Zh		

Breath	p	t	k	f	th	s	sh
Voice	b	d	g	v	dh	z	zh

parameter at higher levels, including syllabic function and intonation as well as the voiced/voiceless contrast for consonants. It seems clear that he saw the syllabifying function of the vocal cords as occupying a level between the pre-articulatory air-flow and the perception stages (cf. Malmberg 1963).

His awareness of acoustic and perceptual correlates of speech was sharpened by the views of John Gough (1757–1825) of Kendal, who, blinded at an early age, developed a refined awareness of speech acoustics:

In a previous lecture ... which Mr Gough ... did not happen to hear, the secondary vibrations of the human voice through the whole of the cavities and fibres of the head were expressly traced; the respective characteristic tones were specified and demonstrated, in their connection with the respective organs of promulgation and modification (the *roof*, the *nostrils*, the *maxillaries* ...) The suggestion [by Gough–

RT] of the expansion of the sonorous power and the consequent diffusion of sound, through a wider circuit, in proportion to the *number*
(not *loudness*) of the vibrating unisons, and the application of the
powers of volition to the purpose of bringing the respective vibratory
fibres into the satate of unison required ... will also be found most
especial importance. (Thelwall 1810, pp.34–5)

Although it may be stretching the evaluation too far, I think Gough and
Thelwall should be credited with an awareness of formants. Gough published
a paper (1786) 'On the variety of voices', which I have not been able to
consult. Nicholson (1861) gives a brief biographical account of him.

The other major topic that requires evaluation here is Thelwall's view on
'metrical proportions and rhythmus'. On his own claim he had developed his
views without access to the *Prosodia rationalis* (1779) of Steele, although
when he did have the opportunity to peruse this work, he writes:

I was exceedingly interested in perceiving the musical part of my
theory completely demonstrated, and a system of notation, for the
tones, the qualities and proportions of sound, in spoken language,
invented and applied. Mr Steele was obviously unacquainted with
everything that relates to the physiology of speech ... he had accordingly, prosecuted his researches on musical grounds exclusively; and it
appeared not a little extraordinary, that we should have been conducted to the same practical conclusions. (Thelwall 1810, p.23)

He says elsewhere:

Not even those writers indeed Steele, Odell and Roe appear to have
gone to the bottom of the subject. They have sought for their data in
the rules of inventive and imitative art, instead of appealing to physical analysis, the primary principles of nature, the physiological ne-
cessities resulting from the organization of vocal beings ...

I lay it down, therefore, as the first principle and basis of all
rhythmical theory and analysis, and of all instruction for the improvement of human utterance and composition – that a cadence is a
portion of tuneable sound, beginning heavy and ending light; –
Secondly, that – a foot is a syllable, or number of syllables, occupying
the space or duration of such a cadence (for we have single syllables,
in the English Language ... that, under particular circumstances of
arrangement or emphasis, constitute a foot [i.e. fill out a cadence] by
themselves). Thirdly – that the quantity of every perfect foot (for a
foot may be imperfect – as at the beginning of a clause, or after a
caesure, or a protracted emphasis etc.) must be measured from the
commencement of the syllable in thesis or heavy poise. Therefore I
maintain English has a rhythmus as truely metrical as Greece or
Rome. Some Classical measures NOT Congenial to English. Though
I reject those bunglers who treat every heavy syllable as long and
every light syllable as short.

He (the learner) will, also have to ascend, in due gradation, from the more abstract, to the rhetorical rhythmus: – that is to say, from the skeleton rhythmus, which recognizes only the more inherent qualities of the elements and syllables arranged, to that vital and more authentic rhythmus which results from the mingled considerations of sentiment, pause and emphasis, and assigns to each its just proportions of cadential quantity ... Conversational rhythmus, is indeed very different in effect from the rhythmus of genuine oratory, and still more so from the rhythmus of lyrical or epic poetry; but it is rhythmus still; and the rhythmus of dependent upon the metrical proportions of cadences and feet. (Thelwall 1812)

Both Thelwall and Steele were well aware of the concepts of stress timing, the silent stress, and the independence of syllable quantity from stress. With the continuing dominance throughout the nineteenth century of Classics-oriented metrists it is no wonder that these concepts were not properly appreciated until this century. It was left to David Abercrombie to elaborate some of the basic details (1964; see also Croll 1925).

In conclusion, although Thelwall occurs in references by Pike (1945, p.4) and Crystal (1969, pp.25, 47) on the topic of intonation, and in Haberman (1949) on speech therapy, he has been hitherto neglected in phonetics. This is perhaps understandable when we consider that publications on elocution are numerous, and that almost every practitioner jealously guarded his skills as personal secrets not to be transmitted to others, and was reluctant to give any formal recognition to earlier sources of knowledge. The continuous English thread of Phonetic interest (Firth 1947) does not assume the coherence of an academic tradition until the mid-nineteenth century with the Bells and Sweet. The lack of more extended publication of Thelwall's phonetic theory can be attributed to the success of his Institute in London. This, and the unfortunate failure of his widow to publish the projected second volume of his biography, no doubt contributed to his neglect until recently. E.P. Thompson has already done much to establish his role in political history, and the very thorough researches of D. Rockey have thrown much light on the major aspect of his career after 1801, speech therapy. The present modest contribution will, it is hoped, provide further information about this phonetic knowledge.

Appendix 1

Thelwall's Phonetic Theory as stated in his *Introductory Discourse*

THE THEORY OF HUMAN SPEECH is an important branch of Natural Philosophy. Correctness of theory is an essential preliminary to practical improvement. The theory of speech is deducible from the Laws of Organic Structure and Physical Action, and those of harmonic perception.

DEFINITION. The Perfection of Speech consists in *a mode of utterance that combines the utmost contradistinctness of Enunciative Expression with the most uninterrupted flow of Vocal Sound.*

APPARATUS. Two Classes of Organs. 1. VOCAL ORGANS – *those portions of the organic system employed in the production, admeasurement, and variation of voluntary and tuneable sounds.* 2. ENUNCIATIVE ORGANS – *those portions and members of the mouth by means of which we superadd to the tuneable impulses of voice, the specific or characteristic of literal and verbal utterance.*

THEORY OF SOUNDS. The sensation of sound is an effect of specific vibration, originating in some stroke or impulse given to a vibratory substance, and thence communicated, by pulses of the agitated air, to the organs of hearing. Demonstration from philosophical experiments – the Bell in vacuo, etc. The modifications and varieties of sound depend – 1. on the nature, force, and modification of the impulse; 2. on the vibratory power, texture, or construction of the immediate substance to which that impulse is given; 3. upon the sympathetic media, whose secondary vibrations co-operate with, and assist in the diffusion or promulgation of the primary vibrations; and 4. on the sanity and susceptibility of the recipient organ.

VOCAL SOUNDS are the ultimate effects of certain impulses of air driven in a specific direction thro' certain resisting and strongly vibratory organs of the throat, and further impelled or retarded, in their passage to the mouth, by the action and reaction of specific apparatus of the glottis, by which those sounds are rendered admeasurable in distinct proportions, so as to be subservient to the purposes of tune or melody in all vocal animals; and, in the human, to the further superaddition of enunciation, syllabication, or speech. The primary vibrations, thus produced, are also still further modified or complicated by the more minute vibrations of certain other organs, to which, either from necessity or volition, the primary impulses are communicated, and by the responses of certain other vibratory portions of the animal frame, brought into unison (by their tension and position) with such resounding organs.

QUERIES *to be considered.* 1. What are the organs of impulse and contact, transmission, response and modification, which produce the phæno-mena of human voice? 2. How far can man be defective in these and live? 3. What are the laws and principles of physical necessity by which the actions of those organs, respectively, are regulated and restrained? 4. How far are those respective actions subject to the control of volition, and capable of improvement, in the effective exercise of their functions, by elocutionary science and cultivation?

REMOTE OR INCIDENTAL ORGANS OF VOICE. 1. The importance generally assigned to particular structure and vigorous sanity of THE LUNGS in the production of elocutionary energy and facility, is not justified either by physiological induction or experience. The lungs that are sufficient for life are sufficient for elocution. They are the mere recipient, or reservoir, for the portions of atmospheric air, the inhalation and exhalation of which are indispensable to vitality, and the forcible expirations of which, being resisted by the primary specific organs of voice, give occasion to the vibrations that produce the phænomena of vocal sound. Judicious elocutionary exercise is the best remedy for some of the diseases that affect the lungs. 2. THE DIAPHRAGM; and 3. The Intercostal Muscles, have each their necessary functions in the regulation of the passive organ, the lungs, and, consequently in impelling the air that is to be vocalized in the glottis. 4. THE TRACHEA, or *Windpipe*, is principally to be considered as a channel for the inhalation and exhalation of the air, and consequent communication of the impulses from the lungs to the immediate organs of voice. The pitch or tone of the voice is affected, to a certain but limited extent, by peculiarities and varieties in the structure, length and diameter of this organ.

PRIMARY OR IMMEDIATE ORGANS OF VOICE. 1. THE LARYNX, *properly so called*, is the specific organ in which the primary pulses or vibrations of voice originate, and by the contractions or expansions of which, and by the modifications of the vibrations and resistance of the respective parts and fibres of which, and their consequent actions and reactions on the stream of breath impelled from the lungs to the mouth, all the varieties of strength and weakness, loudness and softness, shrillness, clearness, and huskiness, are principally, – and the musical gradations of treble, base, &c. are altogether respectively produced. Structure. Component parts. Extent and limitations of its functions. 2. THE⸱ POMUM ADAMI, *or knot of cartilages that surround the larynx*, contributes essentially to the strength and firmness of the voice. Anatomical description. Offices of the respective parts. The Epiglottis. The Thyroides, or scutiform projection. The alternate action and reaction of the Cricoides Annularis, or cartilaginous ring of the glottis, render that organ the primary syllabicator, or metrometer of vocal impulse; from the necessary alternations of which, originate – those specific phænomena, in which our perceptions of musical proportion originate, whether in song or in speech. It determines by the voluntary force, quantum and momentum of its pulsations, the degree of power or force in the original syllabic impulses of voice, and the degrees of rapidity or slowness, continuous implication, or separative distinctness of those impulses; and, by its inevitable alternations, the marked varieties or alternations of heavy and light, in the successive sounds of all tuneable utterance; whether accompanied or unaccompanied by verbal articulation. Thesis and Arsis of the Greeks (△ .˙.). The Muscular fibres and ligaments connected with the complicated apparatus of the Larynx are also to be considered as part of the vibratory chords of the primary instrument of voice. Combined effects of canular and stringed instruments. Enunciative power of the Larynx. Verbal utterance may be produced almost without assistance of the flexible organs of the mouth.

SECONDARY ORGANS OF VOICE. Besides the complication of Organs that produce the primary impulses of voice, there are other portions of the animal frame that modify those impulses, by the superadditions of other responsive vibrations, and produce the characteristic varieties of tone that belong to different passions and emotions of the individual speaker or singer; and contradistinguish the voice of one individual from another, even when speaking or singing in the same pitch or key. This has been illustrated by the observations of Mr John Gough.

Correspondent phænomena are exhibited in the voices of musical Instruments of the same denomination and apparent structure. The same strings of the same length and tension, tho braced into perfect unison, as far as relates to *note*, will not produce the same characteristic *tones* in different instruments.

Constantaneous vibrations may be complicated to a considerable degree. The succession of notes which constitute what are called simple melodies, do not consist of absolute single tones. Each note communicates to the ear a harmonized combination of vibrations in partial unison; a complication of tones differing perhaps in their physical properties, as assuredly in the physical qualities of the vibrating fibres by which they are propagated. The responsive vibration of fibres in the body of musical instruments may be proved by experiments on the violin, piano-forte, &c. This has been further illustrated by Mr Gough.

Parallel phænomena result from parallel causes, in the complication of the human voice.

The principal organs of modification are, 1. THE ROOF OF THE MOUTH; for the full and swelling tones. The ora rotunda. Formation and action of mouth most favourable to these. 2. THE NOSTRILS – are principally concerned in the modification of certain deep, solemn, trumpet-like tones. Mode of organic action. Sensation. There is a wide distinction between impressive and offensive nasality. 3. THE MAXILLAS, and cellular cavities, &c. and 4. the Integuments and bones of THE SKULL, assist in the production of certain varieties of rich and powerful, but soft and tender intonation. Mode of action that communicates the original impulses to these organs. Sensation by which they are accompanied. Responsive tones or echo of the voice. Experiments that illustrate these phænomena. 5. THE CHEST, and whole superior moiety of the trunk from the Diaphragm upwards, constitute a part of the apparatus of voice. Effect of submersion of the chest upon the voice. Objection from the effect produced upon the sounds of musical instruments when transmitted over an aqueous surface: obviated by further experiments. Appeal to the sense of touch, during the time of elocutionary exertion. Experiments on the effect of bringing certain portions of the body into contact with the back or arms of the chair, while reading or speaking. Characteristic tones may be produced by proper attention to the position and vibrations of the chest. Causes. Excessive pectoralism, or sepulchral hollowness of tone, is not so much a necessary consequence of physical organization, as of inattention and habit. Physiological knowledge is of the highest importance to Elocutionary Science and cultivation. The power and tones of the voice are capable of very extensive improvement. Feebleness, coarseness, dissonance or monotony are seldom necessary consequences of mere physical causes.

ENUNCIATIVE ORGANS, or *Organs of verbal utterance*. The Phænomena of Speech are produced by a complication of constanteous as well as successive actions. The want of proper analysis of this complication has caused much confusion of language upon the subject, both among the ancients and moderns; and serious practical mistakes. This may be illustrated from Dr Itard's account of the Savage of Aveyron. Classification and description of the Organs of enunciation, and their respective functions. Independently of the Lower Jaw (whose motions are highly assistant, tho not indispensable, to distinct utterance) and the Nostrils (which form the sound assigned to *ng*) they are five in number; three of which are duplicated, or in pairs. Three of them are also active, performing their functions by their own proper action – *i.e.* The Tongue, the Uvula, and the Lips; and Two are passive (*i.e.* the front teeth, and the gums, particularly the upper, into which those teeth are inserted) having the elements formed upon them by the action of the other organs. The description of the attributes and functions of these respectively includes the entire anatomy of the elements of verbal utterance. [The element or sound belonging to a letter is unfortunately, sometimes a *very different*, always *a distinct* thing from its name.]

LINGUAL ELEMENTS. *Class 1* – formed by contact of the tongue with the rough part of the upper Gums and Teeth – D.T. G = J.L.N.R. (initial or trilled). Y (initial or consonant). Z (tuneable or sonisibilant). *Class 2* – formed by contact of the end of the tongue with the gums, or root of either the upper, or the under teeth, according to the conformation of the mouth; with different degrees and forms of swell in the middle or the back part of the tongue *towards* the roof of the mouth – S = C. Ch. Sh. Zh. *Class 3* – formed by protrusion of the tongue against, or between the edges of the front teeth – Th (tuneable, or sonisibilant). Th (aspirated or sibilant). GUTTURAL ELEMENTS – formed by action of the Uvula and the root of the Tongue – G.K.Q.X KS, or GZ.R (final). Ch. (Scottish). There are two aspirates represented by the letter H. one of them is simple; the other, capable of combination in immediate succession with a hard consonant, partakes of the nature of a guttural. LABIAL ELEMENTS B. and P.M. and the initial or liquid W. LABIO-DENTALS – F and V. The German V. is a sound intermediate between our V. and our liquid W. and therefore occasionally confounded with both. The cockney vulgar pronounce the German element for both V. and W. and are therefore supposed to transpose them: which, tho it sometimes occurs, is not generally the case.

The position of the lips has something to do with the ultimate neatness and perfection of every enunciated sound; particularly the vowels. THE LOWER JAW facilitates, by its motions modifying the cavity of the mouth, the utterance of the vowels; but they may all be formed, perfectly, with clenched teeth, by proper attention to the aperture of the lips. (Spurious Lock-Jaw).

The lips appear to be the only enunciative organs whose functions cannot be dispensed with, or supplied by any substitution, in the process of distinct and intelligible speech. NG. is a pure nasal, formed by the nostrils alone, without assistance from any of the organs of the mouth. Great inconvenience results from having no simple character to represent this simple sound. No part of the organic action either of N or G, takes place in the formation of the nasal liquid; called by the French a nasal vowel: but the French N. is not exactly the English NG.

DEFINITIONS. The elements are divisible into vowels and consonants. A VOWEL *is an element, or specific modification of voice, formed by modification of the cavity and aperture of the mouth, without contact of organs.* The practical varieties are, therefore, almost infinite; and different numbers and descriptions of these modifications are adopted in different languages. In Scotland they have some that are unknown in England. Precision and Simplicity of the Italian scale. A CONSONANT (a sounding together) *is an element formed by the contact or combined action of two organs.* Consonants are sub-divided into Mutes, Liquids, Semi-Liquids and Sibilants. A MUTE *is a pure stop, – the contact being so complete as to suspend the vocal vibration*: it can, therefore, only be sounded in conjunction with another element. There are only three, T.K.P. A LIQUID *is a tuneable element, formed by gentle contact of two organs in a state of vocal vibration, and capable of unlimited duration and flexure of tone, without change of character.* There are eight – L.M.N.NG.R.V.W.Y: to which some have added Z. but it has a mixture of sibilancy. A SEMI-LIQUID *is a partially tuneable element, formed by the motion of one organ upon another, or by the motion of two organs in contact, and consequently limited in its duration, by the limits of the line of action thro' which it can be formed:* of these we have B.D.G.Q.X GZ.Th.Z. and Zb. The latter four may be called sonisibilants. A SIBILANT *is an element formed by gentle contact of organs and an impulse of breath, without vocal vibration;* as C S.Sh.Ch.F.G J.Th.X KS. The simple ASPIRATE is neither vowel nor consonant; having neither vocalization nor contact. X GZ. and X KS. are compounds; but Ch. is not a compound of TSH. ST (coming together) always form a compound: even when the former terminates, and the latter begins a word: unless there be an intervening grammatical pause. Descriptions of anatomical position are to be taken with great latitude, because different formations of mouth require different positions of the organs. The analysis of the harmonic qualities of the elements, and their classification according to their musical and other inherent properties, is a study of considerable importance, both in elocution and in composition. Researches and classification of Wilkins; of Holder; Kenrick; Herries; Sheridan; Walker; Crombie; Darwin, etc.

[*This part of the subject being minutely critical, does not admit of compres-*

sion by analytical outline.]

It is requisite, also, to consider the necessary, the practicable, and the desirable quantities of elements. All elements are capable of quantity, but the mutes T.K.P. (and it is sometimes graceful to prolong the stop occasioned by these, by holding them a little while between the organs); but none of the consonants, except the tuneable elements (liquids and semi-liquids) should have any more quantity assigned to them, than is necessary for distinct audibility. Much discredit is brought upon our language, especially in singing, by the unnecessary quantity given to sibilants, as well as by the unnecessarily frequent use of them in composition. The vowels having a natural tendency to monotone, are the proper elements to quantity in song; the liquids having a necessary tendency to inflection, are the proper elements of quantity in speech. That composition will be most graceful in which the cadences are most frequently articulated by a liquid; but most energetic in which the articulation is most frequently by semiliquids. Mutes are bad articulators of cadences, but sibilants much worse. [*See hereafter for the definitions, &c. of articulation and cadence*]. Of the liquids some contribute more to energy, and some to melody. Of the semiliquids, those are the best articulators that have least tendency to sibilance.

SYLLABICATION. *A syllable is an intimate articulation of distinct elements in a single impulse of voice.* If the elementary sounds of letters were taught in the first instance, instead of their names, there never could be any difficulty or indistinctness of syllabication. The Physical properties of syllables, as well as their elements and accents, ought to be well considered ...

PULSATION AND REMISSION. The primary action of the organs of voice, in the formation of syllabic impulses, and the laws of physical necessity, by which those actions are dictated and limited, have not been sufficiently considered. The simplicity of the laws of Nature, even in her most complicated operations, may be illustrated in the laws of Gravitation; of Chemical Attraction; of Mechanical Impulse, and of Organic Action. Animal volition is limited by the primary laws of physical necessity .... The application of this principle to the actions of the ENUNCIATIVE ORGANS will explain why certain elements can, and others cannot be pronounced in immediate succession or combination. It is necessary, both in speech and composition, to consider what letters are, of necessity, *absolutely mute*, in such modes of succession; and what elements produce a laboured and ungraceful effect, under such circumstances, when they are not omitted in pronunciation. Writers sometimes present combinations to the eye, which no effort of human organs can present, with distinct and intelligible articulation, to the ear. Several of our elements are in pairs; being formed by similar positions or actions of the enunciative organs – as liquid and sibilant (V. and F.) – or semi-liquid and sibilant (Z. and S.) – or semi-liquid and mute (D. and T.B. and P.G. and K.) of these td, pb, kg, cannot be uttered in implicative succession; and the inverse of these, and the immediate combination of the rest, will have either a feeble, or an elaborate and ungraceful effect, or both. No element, but the initial R. (which is a trill, or element formed by a circle of action) can be duplicated in immediate intimate succession by the organs, tho often duplicated to the eye; but several of them can be prolonged, with or without a circumflex accent. Certain elaborate and pedantic orators appeal, in all these cases, to the awkward expedient of pronouncing a short vowel between. In good composition these combinations are seldom so used as that dropping one of the elements will injure the perspicuity of the sentence, or the impressiveness of the utterance. The element not uttered is, however, to be so far organically formed, as to modify the termination of the previous element. The state of English orthography is eminently obstructive to the progress of English Elocution. But the application of the primary law of pulsation and remission most extensively important – is that which refers to the action of THE PRIMARY ORGAN OF VOCAL SYLLABICATION, already partially explained in the analysis of the organs of voice. The action and the principle are exceedingly simple; yet there is great difficulty in comprehending it without the assistance of patient oral demonstration: – partly because phænomena perpetually recurring are seldom supposed worthy of deliberate analysis; and partly from the complication of constantaneous actions, and simultaneous impressions. A prejudice against this part of the theory may be entertained – from there being no traces of it, even in the minute and elaborate analyses of ancient writers. This may be accounted for from the prejudices of the ancients, which precluded the practical prosecution of anatomical science. It is this law of physical necessity, which produces the natural *Thesis* (△) and *Arsis* (∴) – or *heavy* and *light* of human speech; with the phænomena of which the Greek grammarians were so familiar, tho entirely overlooked by the moderns, till the time of Joshua Steele.

DEMONSTRATIONS. *The indispensable necessity of the alternations of pulsation and remission in the action of the primary organ of syllabic impulse, and the consequent physical alternations of heavy △ and light ∴ syllables, in all fluent or continuous utterance,* may be proved by uttering, even without elementary accompaniment, the simplest impulse (△) upon which a syllable can be engrafted; when it will be found that before such impulse can be repeated, either a pause ( ) must have taken place, or a sound of another character (∴) which might have served, also, as the basis of a syllable. But a long succession of syllabic impulses, alternately heavy and light (△ ∴ △ ∴ △ ∴) may be uttered without interruption ...

13. Either the light or the heavy poise may be interrupted, so as to form two syllables upon each –
absolutely, – spiritedly. The light poise may be farther
△͡△ ∴   ∴   △͡△ ∴.   ∴
subdivided – spiritually – beautifully.
△͡△∴ ∴ ∴   △   ∴∴ ∴

... 14. These alternations have no necessary connection with long and short, in the Latin language –
Nor in the English –
cĭtĭzēns – rĕvĕlrў – bēautĭful – colōn.

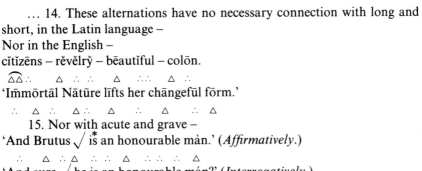

'Ĭmmōrtāl Nātūre lĭfts her chāngefūl fōrm.'

15. Nor with acute and grave –
'And Brutus √ ĭs* an honourable màn.' (*Affirmatively.*)

'And sure √ he is an honourable mán?' (*Interrogatively.*)

... 17. The physical cause of this alternation of heavy and light, and its indispensable necessity, may be demonstrated not only by anatomy, but by the united senses of vision and of touch, on examining the action of the living throat, in the act of energetic speaking.

This principle, and not the mere arrangement of long and short syllables, constitutes the natural basis of rhythmus in language; but the perfection of that rhythmus must depend upon the nice adaptation of quantities, to fill out properly the physical alternation, and preserve a due proportion in the cadences and clauses.

SERIES II – *Principles of Metrical Proportion, and of Rhythmus.*

DEFINITIONS. A cadence is *a portion of tuneable sound (or of organic aspiration) beginning heavy and ending light* | △∴ |. A foot is *a portion of syllabic enunciation occupying the interval of such cadence* |fancy|revelry|beautifully|.

But part of such interval may pass in hiatus or pause: i.e. the action, or the reaction of the primary organ by which the cadence is formed, may be made silently; in which case *the cadence will be occupied by an imperfect foot.* A bar is *a mere technical invention in elocution, as in music, separating cadence from cadence to the eye.* To perform its function faithfully it ought, in general, to be drawn thro' the middle of the letter that articulates the cadences; since the change of cadential action from light to heavy, as well as from heavy to light, in all graceful utterance, generally takes place in the middle of the element – especially of the liquid: for the whole process of speech is by slides and inflections, not by steps and perceptible intervals.

A cadence may be either in common, or in triple time; and in strictness of analysis, either of those cadences may happen to be occupied by feet either of even, or of uneven numbers of syllables ...

Cadences, are sometimes occupied by *feet of four syllables*, and sometimes, tho very rarely, and that only in conversational prose (tho similar

---

*These signs indicate a pause in the speech for the silent stress.

cadences might be admitted in lyric verse) by *feet of five syllables*: which is perhaps the utmost that can ever be delivered in a single cadence, in any clear and intelligible utterance ...

English syllables differ, in quantity, in all the latitude of from eight to one. The integral feet, by which these cadences are occupied, are capable of many technical discriminations: certainly of all that are enumerated in the Classical Gradus. Many of our syllables (like those of every other language) are common; i.e. liable to be long, or short, according to circumstances of emphasis, arrangement, and association ...

As every long syllable is not equally long, and every short syllable is not equally short, some trochaics may be *inherently* as long as some spondees. *Spondees* may, also, be pure (or of exact equality in their syllables,) – as '|Mān's fīrst| diso|-bēdience;'| or impure (both long, but not equally long) – as '|āll our| woe:' and this is a principle inherent in the nature of all languages: for syllables are not meted out by a Winchester measure, according to an arbitrary standard of critical legislation; but derive their quantities from the accidental association of their elements, and other independent circumstances ...

There is great difficulty in analyzing the minute quantities and proportions of syllables, from the extreme shortness of time occupied by each, in due pronunciation. In ordinary discourse, or reading, rather more than three syllables are pronounced in a second; that is to say, the average length of a syllable is about eighteen-thirds; which is at the rate of two hundred syllables in a minute; without allowing anything for pauses ...

LAWS OF CADENTIAL UTTERANCE. The first and most indispensable requisites of intelligible speech, are, of course, the complete formation and clear articulation of the respective elements. The grace and excellence of accomplished elocution, must depend, 1. upon MEASURE, or *the just proportion and clear articulation of cadences or feet.* 2. On MELODY, or *the proper adjustment of the accentual slides, and other musical qualities, to the successive elements and syllables.* 3. on EUPHONY, *or the happy coalescence of those elements and syllables, and the due apportionment of quantities to every element of the respective syllables and words, according to their tuneable qualities, or harmonic capabilities*; and 4. on EXPRESSION, *or the due assignment and distribution of the several kinds of emphases, with the proper intonations of pathos, emotion, sentiment, &c* ... 6. In all smooth and harmonious utterance, the time occupied by each cadence, in a given sentence, or passage, is to be the same, whether the cadence contain one syllable or several; but the momentum, in different passages, should vary, according to the sentiment and subject: as it may also, occasionally, according to the taste or convenience of the speaker or reader. (Thelwall, 1805 xxvii–1v)

Appendix 2
Notes on authorities cited by Thelwall

A full evaluation of Thelwall's knowledge relative to his predecessors and contemporaries can only be made by critical examination of the large body of writings, many of which are now available through the Scolar Press reprints. So far, the only detailed study that gives this kind of perspective is Kemp (1972). Brief biographical and bibliographical notes follow on all those authorities cited by Thelwall.

John Wilkins (1614–72) is briefly discussed by Firth (1947) and Abercrombie (1949). The full-length study by Shapiro (1969) scarcely illuminates our knowledge of his linguistic theory, which is expounded in *An Essay Towards a Real Character* (1668). Suffice it to say that Wilkins presents a sophisticated account of the English vowel system with seven symbols with short and long values. Thelwall does not present any detailed account of the English vowels in his published work as can be seen from the sample given.

William Holder (1616–98) is also very briefly discussed by Firth (1947) and Abercrombie (1949) and more fully in Kemp (1972). He is the subject of a critical study at present in progress by David Abercrombie. His book *The Elements of Speech* (1669) gives a fairly standard account (for that period) of consonant and vowel classification.

William Kenrick (1725?–79) was a dramatist and intimate of the actors Garrick and Coleman. He has an entry in the *DNB* and his *A Rhetorical Grammar of the English Language* (1784) is reprinted in the Scolar Press series. He has sections on vowels and consonants (1784, pp.37–65), but these do not make an advance on Wilkins and Holder.

John Herries (dates unknown) published *The Elements of Speech* (1773) from which the following quotation may be the first reference in English to the term 'chords':

> Larynx. The upper end of the wind pipe forms that curious instrument called the larynx. ... Glottis. The parts which compose the larynx are so disposed as to leave in the midst a small chink or cleft; called the Glottis, which is the sole cause, of voice and modulation. It is of a solid, gristly, and tremulous nature, peculiarly adapted for the production of sound. Its orifice can be widened or contracted, and its sides or chords, either stretched or relaxed, as occasion requires. Hence it is, that it bears a near resemblance to a wind, and a stringed instrument; the one from its form, and the other from its substance. (1773, p.14)

I can find no reference to critical study of Herries nor a mention in the *DNB*.

Thomas Sheridan (1719–88) was the father of the playwright and a teacher of elocution in Bath. He published various books, perhaps the most notable of which was *A General Dictionary of the English Language* (1780), which aimed 'to establish a plain and permanent Standard of Pronunciation'.

But on phonetic classification he is largely implicit. He figures in the *DNB*.

John Walker (1732–1807) was an actor, philologist and lexicographer (see *DNB*). He also published various books connected with elocution, including a pronouncing dictionary based on Sheridan's model (1791). He also based his analysis of intonation (including 'inflexion') on Steele, and Thelwall, as he developed his career as a lecturer on elocution, found Walker's views dominant (Rockey 1979).

Alexander Crombie (1762–1840) was a philologist and schoolmaster in Highgate (see *DNB*). He published *The Etymology and Syntax of the English Language Explained* (1802), which is not in the Alston (1967–72) series, and which I have not been able to consult.

Erasmus Darwin (1731–1802) is well known as a prominent intellectual and scientist (for the most recent biography see King-Hele 1977), but his work on phonetics in connection with his 'speaking machine' has not been evaluated in detail, and he is not mentioned in Firth (1946). Thelwall certainly met Darwin (Rockey 1977) and had read at least the relevant section of *The Temple of Nature* (1803). In a series of articles in *The Panoramic Miscellany* (1826, pp.42–6), and in the *Monthly Magazine* (1825, pp.113–17), he undertakes a critical account of Darwin's articulatory classification. It is also of interest to note that in the latter (1825, p.117) he proposes the use of the symbols ð and θ with their modern I P A values.

Jean-Marc Gaspard Itard (1775–1838) is well known for his work in France with the deaf and dumb, especially with the 'Wild Boy of Aveyron', and not least through Truffaut's superb film. Lane (1976) has recently published a detailed study of Itard's work with this child. According to Rockey (1979), Thelwall visited Itard and the boy in France in 1821 and was critical of some aspects of Itard's work. An obituary by Bousquet (in Schmalz 1848) gives further details of Itard's life.

References

ABERCROMBIE, D. (1949) 'Forgotten phoneticians', *TPhS 1948*, 1–34. Reprinted in Abercrombie (1965) 45–75.
— (1964) 'Syllable quantity and enclitics in English', in Abercrombie et al. (eds.) *In Honour of Daniel Jones*, London (Longman) 216–22. Reprinted in Abercrombie (1965) 26–34.
— (1965) *Studies in Phonetics and Linguistics*, London (Oxford University Press).
ALSTON, R.C. ed. (1967–72) *English Linguistics 1500–1800 (A collection of facsimile reprints)*. London (Scolar Press).
CESTRE, C. (1906) *John Thelwall. A pioneer of democracy and social reform in England during the French Revolution*, London (S. Sonnenschein & Co.).
CROLL, M.W. (1925) 'The rhythm of English verse', Princeton, N.J. (mimeographed). Published in Croll (1966) 365–429.
— (1966) *Style, Rhetoric, and Rhythm*. Essays ... edited by J. Max Patrick et al., Princeton, N.J. (Princeton University Press).
CROMBIE, A. (1802) *The Etymology and Syntax of the English Language Explained*, London.

CRYSTAL, D. (1969) *Prosodic Systems and Intonation in English*, London (Cambridge University Press).

DARWIN, E. (1803) *The Temple of Nature*, London:

FIRTH, J.R. (1947) 'The English School of Phonetics', *TPhS 1946*, 92–132.

GOUGH, J. (1786) 'On the variety of voices', *Manchester Philosophical Society*.

HABERMAN, F.W. (1949) 'Thelwall, his life, his school and his theory of elocution', *Q. J. Speech* 33, 292–8.

HERRIES, J. (1773) *The Elements of Speech*, London; facsimile reprint, Scolar Press, London, 1968.

HOLDER, W. (1669) *The Elements of Speech*, London; facsimile reprint, Scolar Press, London, 1967.

KEMP, J.A. (1972) *John Wallis's Grammar of the English Language*, London (Longmans).

KENRICK, W. (1784) *A Rhetorical Grammar of the English Language*, London (R. Cadell and W. Longman); facsimile reprint,Scolar Press, London, 1968. Originally published as introduction to Kenrick's *New Dictionary of the English Language* 1773.

KING-HELE, D. (1977) *Doctor of Revolution: The Life and Genius of Erasmus Darwin*, London (Faber & Faber).

LANE, H. (1976) *The Wild Boy of Aveyron*, Cambridge (Harvard University Press).

MALMBERG, B. (1963) *Phonetics*, New York (Dover).

NICHOLSON, C. (1861) *The Annals of Kendal*, 2nd ed., London (Whitaker).

PIKE, K. L. (1945) *The Intonation of American English*, Ann Arbor (University of Michigan Press).

ROCKEY, D. (1977) 'The Logopaedic thought of John Thelwall, 1764–1834: First British Speech Therapist', *Br. J. Disorders Comm.* 12.2, 83–95.

— (1978) *Stuttering in Britain in the Nineteenth Century*, Oxford, D.Phil.

— (1979) 'John Thelwall and the Origins of British Speech Therapy', *Medical History*.

SCHMALZ, E. (1848) *Beiträge zu Gehör- und Sprachheilkunde*, III, 137–49, Leipzig (J.C. Hinrichs).

SHAPIRO, B.J. (1969) *John Wilkins, 1614–1672; an intellectual biography*, Berkeley (University of California Press).

SHERIDAN, T. (1780) *A General Dictionary of the English Language*, London; facsimile reprint, Scolar Press, London, 1968.

STEELE, J. (1775) *An Essay towards establishing the Melody and Measure of Speech to be expressed and perpetuated by peculiar symbols*, London (J. Alman).

— (1779) *Prosodia Rationalis …*, London (Printed by J. Nichols). 2nd amended and enlarged ed. of Steele (1775).

THELWALL, C. (1837) *The Life of John Thelwall*, London (J. Macrone).

THELWALL, J. (1805) *An Introductory Discourse on the Nature and Objects of Elocutionary Science*, Pontefract.

— (1810) *A Letter to Henry Cline Esq.*, London.

— (1812) *Illustrations of English Rhythmus*, London.

— (1825) 'Mr. Thelwall's Lecture on the Enunciative Organs and Formation of the Literal Elements', *Monthly Magazine* 60, 113–17.

— (1826) 'Mr. Thelwall's Lecture' *The Panoramic Miscellany*, 1, 41–7, 193, 198, 347–54, 635–42, 796.

THOMPSON, E.P. (1963) *The Making of the English Working Class*, Harmondsworth (Penguin).

WALKER, J. (1791) *A Critical Pronouncing Dictionary and Expositor of the English Language*, London; facsimile reprint, Scolar Press, London, 1968.

WILKINS, J. (1668) *An Essay Towards a Real Character and a Philosophical Language*, London; facsimile reprint, Scolar Press, London, 1968.

PART SIX

WRITING SYSTEMS AND
PHONETIC ANALYSIS

STROFE   III.

Sęs armez il pand ă ſa poſtérité,
Pʋr lęz anʋrtér lʋr témoŋant ſa valʋr,
Dęs ʋmes ętre le konfʋrt.
Lui reçęrçé pʋr ſe bien ſęt
Dęz abitans de Mujęl,
Fonda la męʒon ʋs MEDIÇIS valurʋs.
Là ſont demʋrés lonʒemant :
Apręs FLORANS' an ſon jiron
Pʋr ſęs défanſʋrs lęs rekʋljit.

ANTISTROFE   III.

Depuis du pʋpl' ont mérité la favʋr,
Aians de vʋrtu tʋs lez onʋrs éprʋvés,
Juſk'a tenir le premiʋr liʋ.
Męs travʋrſans mille danjiérs,
Ont ſʋtenu lez aſʋs
Dęs anviʋs fʋs, konſitoiéns anemʋs.
Març' aʋ ſʋlęl ūn' onbre ſuit :
Çęrçant la klęrté dęs valʋrs,
Atręineras pʋrvʋrſe rankʋr.

EPODE   III.

Ki non rekru fęrme tiéndra
Du ſiel bénin ſuporté,
Aʋ ſomęt du pris atéint,
Trionfera de ſęs malins,
Véinkʋr de lʋrs traizons.
Se ſont çukâs é korbʋʋs
Véinemant krians,

FIGURE 1. Part of poem from *Etrénes,* by Jean-Antoine de Baïf, Paris 1574.

Extending the Roman Alphabet:
Some Orthographic Experiments of
the Past Four Centuries

The Roman alphabet did well enough for Latin (though the Emperor Claudius thought it needed supplementing); but it was not so satisfactory for the European vernaculars which later took it over: it did not provide enough sorts for their more complicated phonetic structure. By using digraphs (two letters for one sound), a few new letters (j v w), and assorted accents, they all evolved orthographies of a kind – some more, some less, successful; but for at least the last four centuries these orthographies have been under attack as unsatisfactory makeshifts which fail to do justice to the languages they represent.

They have been held to be deficient for diverse reasons. There have been poets, for example, who considered that verse could only be appreciated if the sound of words was more exactly exhibited than was possible in normal spelling. Such a one was Jean-Antoine de Baïf, whose beautifully produced *Etrénes* (figure 1) was printed in Paris by Denis du Val in 1574; and the same theory was held by Richard Stanyhurst, the eccentric translator of Virgil (1582), and by Robert Bridges (figure 2). Twenty-six letters are inadequate, moreover, for the purposes of scientific and philological discussion, and the construction of a sufficiently exact notation was one of the many early interests of the Royal Society; figure 4c and d, and figure 10, were the work of Fellows. A later attempt is shown in figure 3. A notation having a consistent relation to pronunciation is useful also for more popular needs, such as pronouncing dictionaries, grammars, and foreign language textbooks. Many people have thought that children should be taught to read and write in some modified form of traditional orthography, to which it should act as a transition (cf. figure 7). Others, the commonest critics perhaps, have been thorough-going spelling reformers, advocating a complete break with tradition and the introduction of a simpler and more logical spelling for all purposes.

The most sweeping remedy for the deficiencies of a traditional orthography is to abandon the Roman alphabet altogether, and start again on a fresh basis. Eight such attempts, dating from 1578 to 1962, are shown in figure 4. They all have the same failing: their sorts are too much alike, and however attractive they may look at first sight, the appearance of words as wholes (on which legibility depends) is not sufficiently distinctive. Only three of them, *a, f,* and *h,* ever got as far as being printed from type; *f* and *g* were

Shɛ was in no sɛnse a blɹe-stockiŋ. Shɛ did not wrɹte poɛms bɛcavse shɛ had lɛrn'd the grammar of vɛrse, nor bɛcavse shɛ thavht shɛ had valɹable moral lɛssons for wɛll-intɛntion'd pɛ rple. Hɛr poɛtry is the irrɛprɛssible soŋ of fancy whœse vagaries shɛ wud hav thavht it im- pɛrtinent tu analɹse; and, a'ltho' thɛse rɛcords of her soul wɛr so sacrɛd tu her that shɛ wud hardly show them tu her most intimat frɛnds, shɛ did not appɛ r tu sɛt ɛny grɛit valɹe on thɛm. Thɛy are at wvnce sincɛre and mystɛ rivs, so that Fancy's Following is apt tu giv a rɛ der thɛ imprɛssion that its avthor had sum dɛsperat lɹfe-sɛ crɛt for the spriŋ of her inspiration, and that shɛ wud rɛvɛ l it only in ɛnigma.

> I have forged me in seven-fold heats
> A shield from foes and lovers,
> And no one knows the heart that beats
> Beneath the shield that covers.

If I had mɛt with thatt in Heine's Buch der Lieder, I think I shud hav notɛd it for its ɛxcɛllence, cɛrtɛinly not hav distinguish'd it for diffɛrence; and the same mɹht bɛ sɛd of svm vther lyrics in this bœk; bvt most of those that rɛca'll Heine's manner add svmthiŋ tu it. The followiŋ poɛm is ca'll'd

208

FIGURE 2. From *Collected Essays*, VI, p.208, by Robert Bridges, 1931. Set in Monotype Blado Italic, with special characters cut by Stanley Morison. Edited by Mrs Bridges, with the assistance of David Abercrombie.

designed for purely scientific purposes.

There is no doubt, however, that the Roman alphabet is difficult to beat for legibility and beauty, and a better solution is to take it as a basis, and enlarge its scope by various means. Many experiments on these lines have been made in England. Our orthography is one of the least successful applications of the Roman alphabet (Welsh and Spanish, for example, are much more satisfactory), and every schoolchild learns from painful experience how inconsistently our spelling corresponds to spoken reality. Several of our consonant sounds are represented by digraphs, such as *sh wh ng*. Two distinct, though similar, sounds are both written *th* – compare *than* and *thank*. There is no letter, or even digraph, in English for the sound of the French *j*, though we use it in *measure*. Our many vowel sounds are most confusingly dealt with by the five vowel letters *a e i o u* and their combinations: the words *look* and *pull*, for example, contain the same vowel sound, which however is different from that in either *loop* or *dull*. The unjust treatment of English sounds by our traditional spelling probably accounts for the particular fertility of this country in schemes for the augmenting the Roman alphabet.

One way in which its scope can be enlarged is by use of diacritics (dots, dashes, and other marks placed under or over the letters). Figure 7 is from the title-page of Richard Hodges' *English Primrose* (1644), an ingenious spelling-book, for the use of his pupils, which carried this device to an extreme: it must have been a nightmare for printer and proof-reader. William Johnston published a pronouncing dictionary, in 1764, dedicated to Queen Charlotte in the hope that it might assist her 'in cultivating a right Pronunciation of the English Language'; he made use of italic and black-letter characters, in addition to diacritics (figure 8).

However, mixtures of fount and diacritics are, on the whole, bad expedients. More satisfactory results are obtained by the introduction of new letters, resulting in an *extended* alphabet, and it is the purpose of this article to examine some little-known typographical experiments on these lines, mostly before the nineteenth century, in England and America.

"Where letters are wanting, nothing seems more natural than to borrow them out of that ancient language that is of the nearest affinity', said Edward Lhwyd, F.R.S., in 1707, and the Anglo-Saxon þ and ð have been brought in to do duty for the two *th* sounds by many people, from Sir Thomas Smith, Secretary of State to Queen Elizabeth (figure 9a and b), down to the Oxford English Dictionary. ȝ is another Anglo-Saxon letter which has been frequently borrowed.

Greek letters have also provided extra sorts, especial favourites among the consonants being θ and δ, again for the *th* sounds, and ε and ʏ (ligatured o and ʋ) among the vowels. The latter is well used in figure 1, but most reformers neglected to have their borrowed letters re-cut to accord with whatever roman fount they were using – they simply drew on the nearest Greek fount in size, with poor results aesthetically. John Wilkins, Cromwell's brother-in-law and Bishop of Chester from 1668 to 1672, used peculiar symbols to represent ideas (not sounds) in his *Essay towards a Real Character* (1668), and got James Moxon, the first English writer on typefounding, and author of the *Mechanick Exercises*, to cut them. He took little trouble, however, over the phonetic alphabet in the same book (figure 10). Although the tailed y (representing the vowel in *but*) must have been specially cut, both in upper and lower case forms, no attempt was made to produce suitable forms of α and ɤ, or even to take them from the same fount each time. The carefully designed alphabet of the versatile American Dr William Thornton, however, includes a θ which goes well with roman (figure 11*a*). It also includes (figure 11*d*) a letter for *wh* borrowed from the Gothic alphabet which Bishop Ulfilas invented in the fourth century.

Black-letter founts originally contained numerous abbreviations and contractions used for printing Latin but not employed in English. William Bullokar, an ardent spelling reformer of the second half of the sixteenth century, made black letter, and not roman, the basis of his new system; he was thus able to draw extensively on these disused sorts for new letters (figure 12). Bullokar held the rather extreme view that Sir Thomas Smith and John Hart, his two most notable predecessors, were bound to produce unsatisfactory alphabets for English because they used foreigners to cut their new letters, 'for lack of helpe of skilful men within the realme at that time'. He thanks God that nowadays, however, the printer and workmen are English, and able to help the reformer in fulfilling his aims. Bullokar consulted constantly with Henry Denham, his printer, and abandoned several innovations on his advice. Bullokar's translation of Aesop's Fables, printed by Edmund Bollifant in 1585, provides, I believe, the unique case of an augmented alphabet being used for the signatures.

The possibilities in sheer invention of new letters are more limited than one might suppose: an apparently satisfactory new character will often turn out, in use, to be ill-suited to mixture with the rest of the alphabet, or to be too like letters which already exist. Benjamin Franklin, among his many activities, experimented in spelling reform, and his extended alphabet was produced in 1768, though it was not printed until eleven years later. The total effect is very pleasing (figure 13), but when examined in detail three of the new letters, those for *sh* and the two *th* sounds,

reveal a disturbing similarity both to each other and to h. Franklin was himself a printer, and should have avoided such pitfalls. John Hart, about whom we know little except that he was Chester Herald, had much more success with his new letters, in spite of Bullokar's strictures. His books were beautifully produced: figure 14 is a page from his treatise on the extended alphabet, and figure 15 is taken from his spelling book for children.

The most profitable source of new letters is neither borrowing, nor outright invention, but modification of existing ones. A number of tolerable sorts can immediately be obtained by inversion: ə ɥ ɯ ɔ ʎ ʌ, and frequent use has been made of these, together with the less satisfactory ɐ ʃ ʞ ʍ ɹ ɺ ⱬ. The Anti-Absurd Alphabet (1845) of Major Beniowski, a Polish enthusiast for the reform of English spelling, relied entirely for new letters on inversion (figure 16). Inverted upper-case J, reduced in size to range with the short letters, was used by William Thornton for *sh* (figures 6*f* and 11*c*).

Reversed letters have also occasionally been tried, a successful example being Sir Thomas Smith's reversed z for *sh* (figures 6*a* and 9*f*). A less obviously useful specimen is a reversed h which, together with several inverted letters, was used by an amusing early eighteenth-century writer who signed himself G. W. and who was possibly an Exeter schoolmaster called John White (figure 17).

FIGURE 3. The representation of English dialects in a scientific notation, from Thomas Batchelor's *Orthoëpical Analysis of the English Language*, London 1809.

Provincial Dialect and Pronunciation.	*English Phrases of equiva-lent Signification.*
It s rcɪɣ, s muy pɪnyʉn.	In my opinion, it is wrong.
Hɪy kʉn takl—manɪdy ɪt.	He can perform it.
Wuy dʉ yʉ run ɪt dewn?	Why do you undervalue it?
It s ʉ gud dyob yuw wʉr ewt ʉ hi wey.	It was fortunate that you were absent.
Hɪz muylɪn ʉn tuylɪn kwuyt wiur ɪm ewt.	His labour entirely exhausted him.
Hɪy kumz an—gɪts an—gɪts forʉd—ɪn larnɪn streyn-zyli.	He advances in learning very rapidly.
Uy tuk ʉn went.	I went.
An ewt ʉ hi wey felʉr.	An audacious, mischevous man.
Hey r up tu t—twɪg ɪt.	They understand it.

FIGURE 4. Various attempts to abandon the Roman alphabet and start afresh.

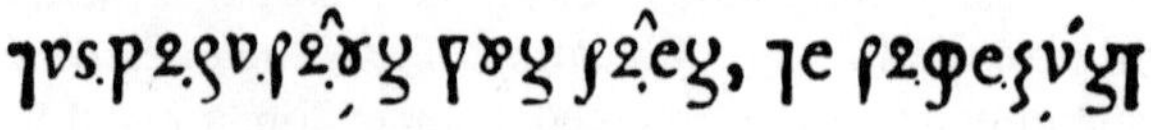

a) Honorat Rambaud (1578).

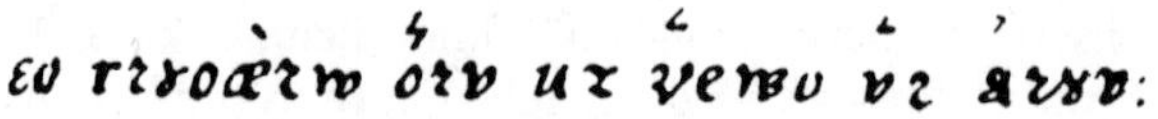

b) Robert Robinson (*c.* 1617).

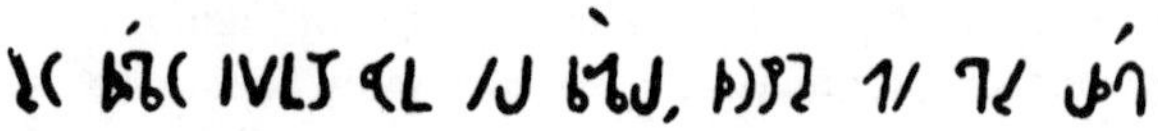

c) John Wilkins (1668).

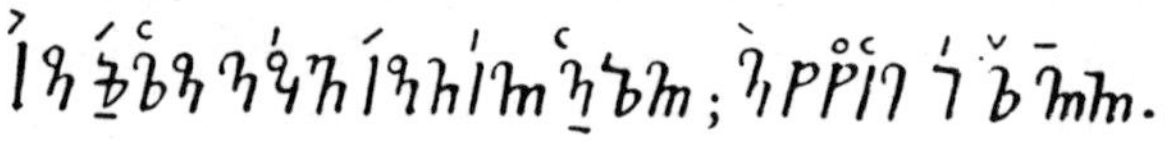

d) Francis Lodwick (1686).

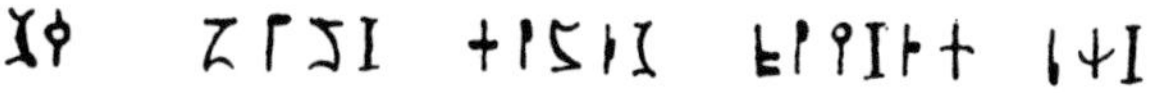

e) Isaac Pitman (1843).

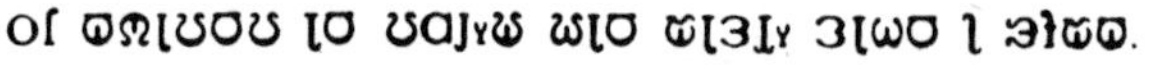

f) A.M. Bell (1867).

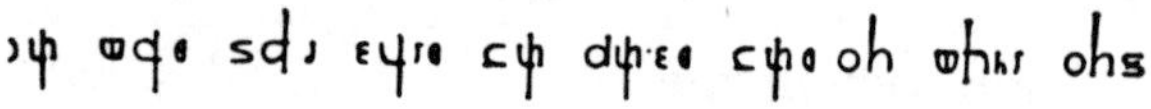

g) Daniel Jones and Paul Passy (1907).

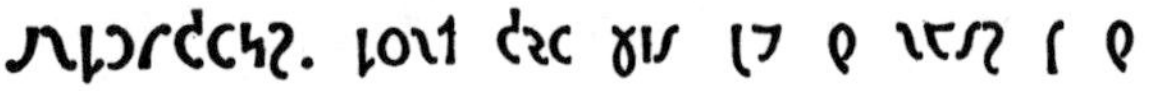

h) The Shaw Alphabet, based on Kingsley Read's entry for the Shaw Competition (1962).

FIGURE 5. Suggested new letters for the *ng* sound in *singing*.

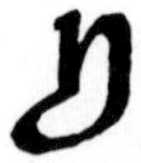

a) Alexander Gill (1619)

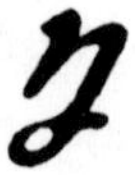

b) Benjamin Franklin (1768)

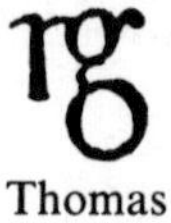

c) Thomas Spence (1775)

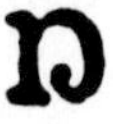

d) William Thornton (1793)

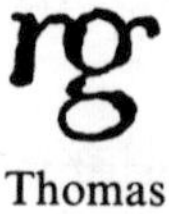

e) Thomas Batchelor (1809)

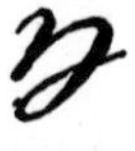

f) Batchelor (script form)

Structural modification is another possibility. Removal of the dot from i produces ı (used, for example, by Batchelor figure 3, Smith figure 9*e*, Wilkins figure 10), but does not make for legibility. Nevertheless, it forms part of the official Turkish alphabet, introduced in 1928. Bars or dashes added to letters were the main standby of Charles Butler, who published in the early seventeenth century an English grammar, and works on bees and the principles of music, in an extended alphabet (figure 18). He also used an inverted t, and a modified long f, with a bar added (figure 6*c*). Sir Thomas Smith produced an extra e letter by adding a stroke (figure 9*g*). William Thornton tried a square o (figure 11*f*).

New sorts can be obtained by ligaturing existing letters. Thomas Spence, who had a stormy political career at the end of the eighteenth century, produced ten by this means for use in his pronouncing dictionary (which was the first to use a scientifically exact notation). It is of particular interest that, although they are not very distinguished, the new letters were cut in Newcastle by Thomas Bewick (figure 19*b*).

An extended alphabet was elaborated by Alexander Gill, teacher of Milton and headmaster of St Paul's from 1608 to 1635 ('a very ingeniose person' wrote Aubrey, 'notwithstanding his whipping-fitts'). Two versions are illustrated in figure 20. The earlier contains numerous new letters, mostly modifications of existing ones, the modifications being added in red ink after the book was printed. The later version, with four new letters only, was less ambitious.

One of Gill's new letters, it will be noticed, was for the consonant *v* in *haven*. This reminds us that in his day u and v were merely alternative forms of the same letter, both being used for the vowel and the consonant ('uvula' was printed 'vuula' in normal practice); the modern differentiation of u for vowel and v for consonant was not established until about 1630. Gill makes u and v into separate letters, but uses them both for vowel sounds. Sir Thomas Smith also produced a new letter for the consonant *v* (figure 9*h*); John Hart, however, as will be seen from figures 14 and 15, anticipates modern usage, and he was apparently the first in England to observe it. The two letters i and j have a similar history. Gill uses j as a vowel symbol, and he, Smith and Hart all use the Anglo-Saxon ȝ for the consonant *j*.

A third letter of the alphabet also originally had two alternative forms – s f. They were never differentiated into separate letters, though Edward Capell, the eighteenth-century editor of Shakespeare, attempted to introduce a distinction between the two forms. He used short s whenever it had the soft sound *z*, but long f when it had the hard sound *ss*; 'ufe' and 'use' were therefore distinguished as noun and verb. The idea, however, never caught on, and f was abandoned at the beginning of the nineteenth century – fortunately, for it is too like f to be a useful member of the alphabet.

The invention of new letters is of considerable importance to phoneticians, spelling reformers, and governments who wish to provide illiterate peoples under their rule with alphabets; and it is still a matter of general interest, as the publicity given to Bernard Shaw's will showed. The early experiments illustrated above are not easily accessible, but they are of more than antiquarian interest. Since the establishment of Phonetics as a science, about a hundred years ago, innumerable extended alphabets have appeared, and there is probably more awareness nowadays of the importance of legibility, appearance, and the needs of the printer; but no fresh principles in the invention of new letters have emerged.

FIGURE 6. Suggested new letters for the *sh* sound in *hush*.

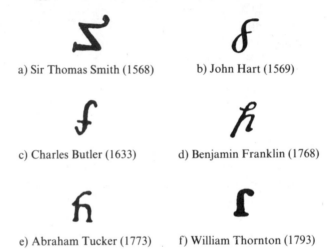

a) Sir Thomas Smith (1568)   b) John Hart (1569)

c) Charles Butler (1633)   d) Benjamin Franklin (1768)

e) Abraham Tucker (1773)   f) William Thornton (1793)

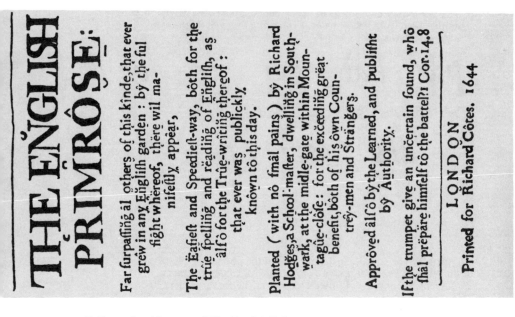

FIGURE 7. From the title-page of *The English Primrose*,
by Richard Hodges, London 1644.

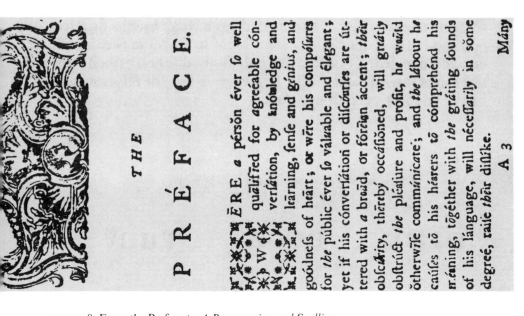

FIGURE 8. From the Preface to *A Pronouncing and Spelling
Dictionary*, by William Johnston, London 1764.

FIGURE 9. Specimen words in the extended alphabet of Sir Thomas
Smith, taken from his *De recta et emendata Linguae Anglicae
Scriptione*, Paris 1568.

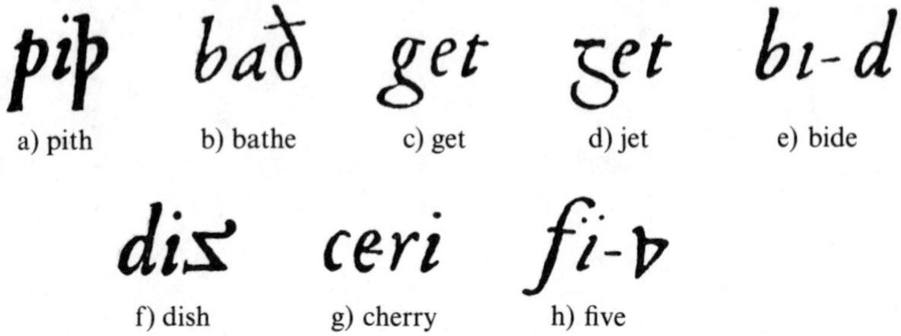

pib   *bað*   *get*   *ʒet*   *bɪ-d*

a) pith   b) bathe   c) get   d) jet   e) bide

diꙅ   *ceri*   *fi-ꝟ*

f) dish   g) cherry   h) five

FIGURE 10. The Creed, illustrating one of the phonetic alphabets of
John Wilkins. From *An Essay Towards a Real Character, and a
Philosophical Language*. Printed by order of the Royal Society, 1668.

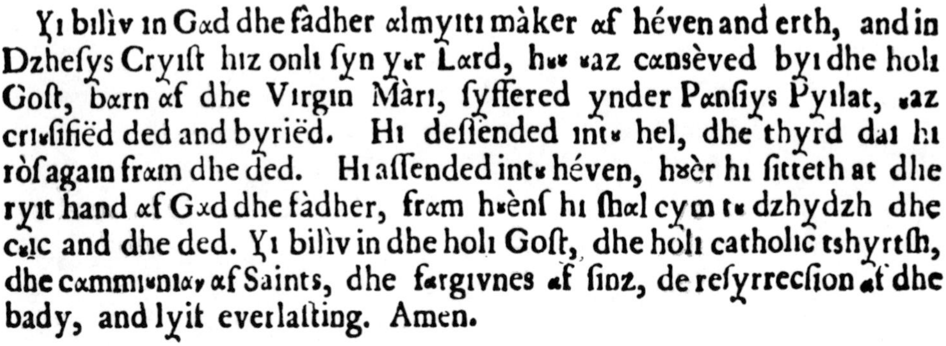

Ɣı bılìv ın Gαd dhe fàdher αlmyıtı màker αf héven and erth, and ın
Dzhefys Cryıſt hız onlı fyn yɪr Lαrd, hʊ ʊaz cαnsèved byı dhe holı
Goſt, bαrn αf dhe Vırgın Màrı, fyffered ynder Pαnfiys Pyılat, ʊaz
crıʊfifiëd ded and byrïëd.   Hı deffended ıntʊ hel, dhe thyrd daı hı
ròfagaın frαm dhe ded.   Hı affended ıntʊ héven, hʊèr hı fitteth at dhe
ryıt hand αf Gαd dhe fàdher, frαm hʊènf hı fhαl cym tʊ dzhydzh dhe
cʊ̈ıc and dhe ded. Ɣı bılìv in dhe holı Goſt, dhe holı catholic tshyrtfh,
dhe cαmmıʊnıαv αf Saints, dhe fɪrgıvnes ɪf fınz, de refyrrecfion ɪf dhe
bady, and lyıt everlaſting. Amen.

FIGURE 11. Specimen words in the extended alphabet of William
Thornton, taken from his *Cadmus, or a Treatise on the Elements of
Written Language*, Philadelphia 1793.

ɵaŋk   **ꝺooz**   **ʃuut**

a) thank   b) those   c) shoot

ʘitʃ   **vɔri**   **pɒɒl**

d) which   e) very   f) pall

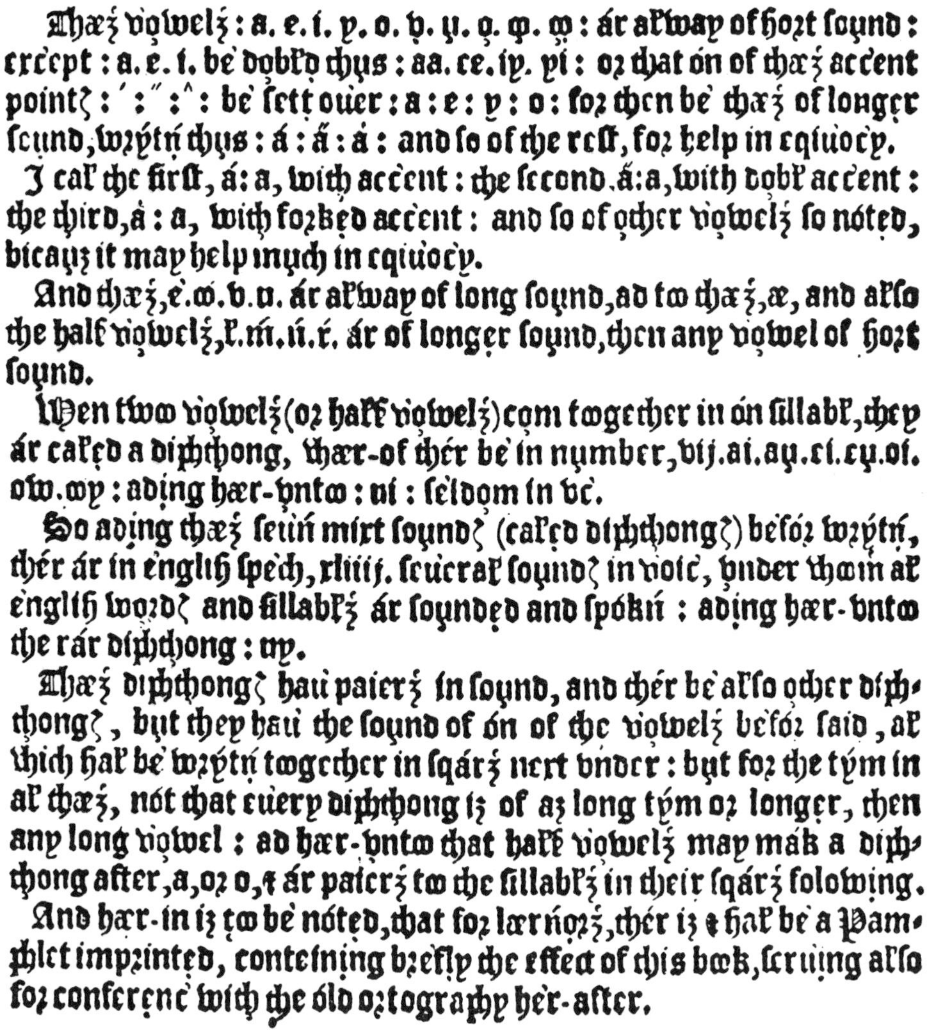

Thæʒ voẃelʒ: a. e. i. y. o. ƀ. u. o̊. ꝏ. ꝏ: ár aƚwaẏ of hoʒt ſoun̄ː
exccept : a. e. i. be dobƚd thus : aa. ee. iy. yi : oʒ that on of thæʒ accent
pointʒ: ´ː ¨ː ^ː be ſett ouer : a : e : y : o : foʒ then be' thæʒ of longer
ſcoun̄,woʒẏtń thus : á : ã : ä : and ſo of the reſt, foʒ help in eqiuocẏ.

J caƚ the firſt, á: a, with accent : the ſeconḋ.ã:a,with dobƚ accent :
the thirḋ,ä : a, with foʒbed accent : and ſo of other voẃelʒ ſo nóted,
bicauʒ it maẏ help inuch in eqiuocẏ.

And thæʒ,e̊.ꝏ.ƀ.u. ár aƚwaẏ of long ſoun̄,ad tꝏ thæʒ,æ, and aƚſo
the half voẃelʒ,ƚ.m̃.ĩ.r̊. ár of longer ſoun̄,then anẏ voẃel of hoʒt
ſoun̄.

Ƚ̃en twꝏ voẃelʒ(oʒ haƚf voẃelʒ)com togetḣer in ón ſillabƚ,theẏ
ár caƚed a diphthong, thær-of thér be' in number,bij.ai.aẏ.ei.eẏ.oi.
ow.ꝏẏ : ading hær-bntꝏ : ni : ſeldom in be̊.

So adin̄g thæʒ ſeuiń mixt ſoun̄ʒ (caƚed diphthongʒ) befóʒ woʒẏtń,
thér ár in engliſh ſpech,xliiij. ſeueraƚ ſoun̄ʒ in voie, bnder thꝏin aƚ
engliſh woʒdʒ and ſillabƚʒ ár ſoun̄ded and ſpókń : adin̄g hær-bntꝏ
the rár diphthong : nẏ.

Thæʒ diphthongʒ haui paierʒ in ſoun̄, and thér be aƚſo other diphthongʒ, but theẏ haui the ſoun̄ of ón of the voẃelʒ befóʒ ſaid, aƚ
Ɨhich haƚ be' woʒẏtń togetḣer in ſqárʒ next bnder : but foʒ the tým in
aƚ thæʒ, nót that euerẏ diphthong iʒ of aʒ long tým oʒ longer, then
anẏ long voẃel : ad hær-bntꝏ that haƚƚ voẃelʒ maẏ mák a diphthong after,a,oʒ o,ꝼ ár paierʒ tꝏ the ſillabƚʒ in their ſqárʒ foloɨing.

And hær-in iʒ tꝏ be' nóted,that foʒ lerńoʒʒ,thér iʒ ꝼ haƚ be a Pamphlet impʒinted, conteining bʒefly the effect of this bꝏk,ſeruing aƚſo
foʒ conferenc' ɨith the óld oʒtographẏ hér-after.

FIGURE 12. The use of Black Letter for an extended alphabet.
From *Bullokars Booke at large for the Amendment of Orthographie
for English speech*, London 1580 (enlarged).

217

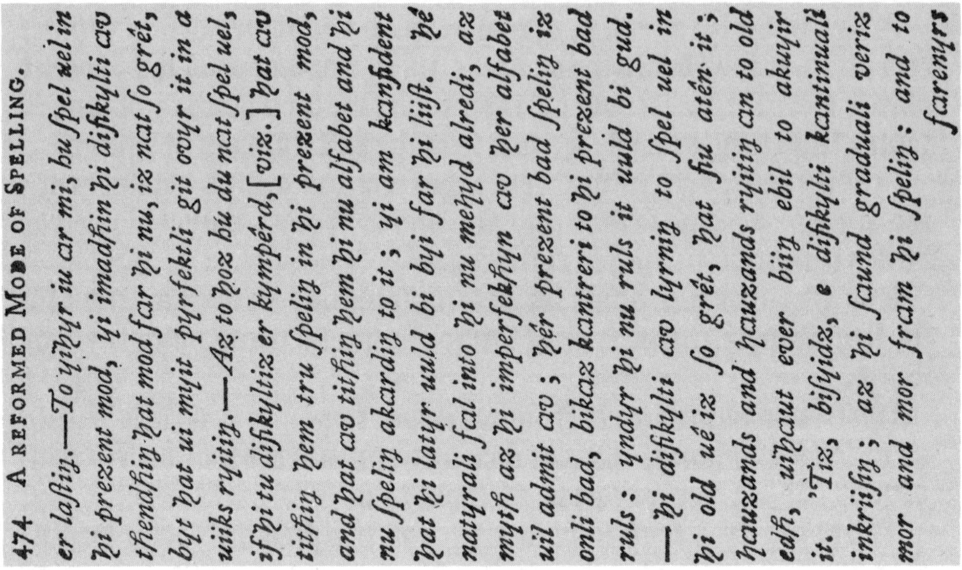

474 A REFORMED MODE OF SPELLING.

FIGURE 13. A page in the extended alphabet of Benjamin Franklin, from *Political, Miscellaneous and Philosophical Pieces*, London 1779.

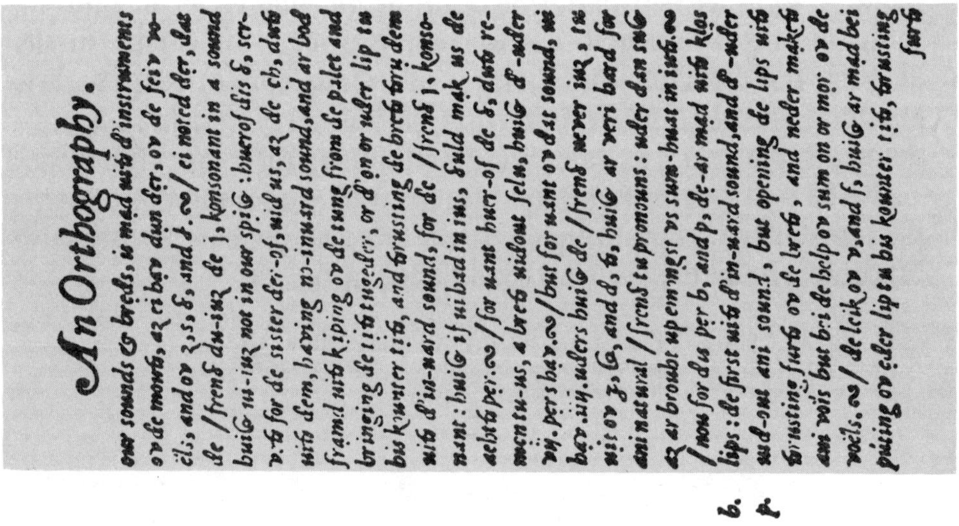

FIGURE 14. A page from *An Orthographie, conteyning the due order and reason, howe to write or paint thimage of mannes voice, most like to the life or nature*, by John Hart, London 1569.

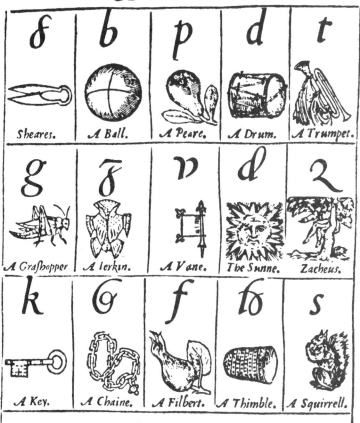

ſ	b	p	d	t
Sheares.	A Ball.	A Peare.	A Drum.	A Trumpet.
g	ᵹ	v	d	2
A Graſhopper	A Ierkin.	A Vane.	The Sunne.	Zacheus.
k	G	f	ƀ	s
A Key.	A Chaine.	A Filbert.	A Thimble.	A Squirrell.

FIGURE 15. a) From *A Methode or confortable beginning for all unlearned, whereby they may bee taught to read English, in a very short time, with pleasure,* by John Hart, London 1570.

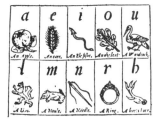

A Methode.

reſort from all townes and Countries, of the
beſt of all profeſſions, aſwel of the own lands-
men, as of aliens and ſtraingers, and therfore
they haue the beſt meanes to take the beſt and
leaue the worſt. And bicauſe I finde no matter in obſeruing the Latine order of their letters, for that no number is vſed by their order as the Greekes haue vſed with theirs : I
haue deuided and parted them, into theyr
ſortes, as ſhall be ſhewed hereafter.

a	e	i	o	u
An Apple.	An eare.	An Eel-ſiſhe.	An oke leaf.	A Woodcock.
l	m	n	r	h
A Lion.	A Mou'e.	A Needle.	A Ring.	A horſe lour.

b) A page from the same book reduced.

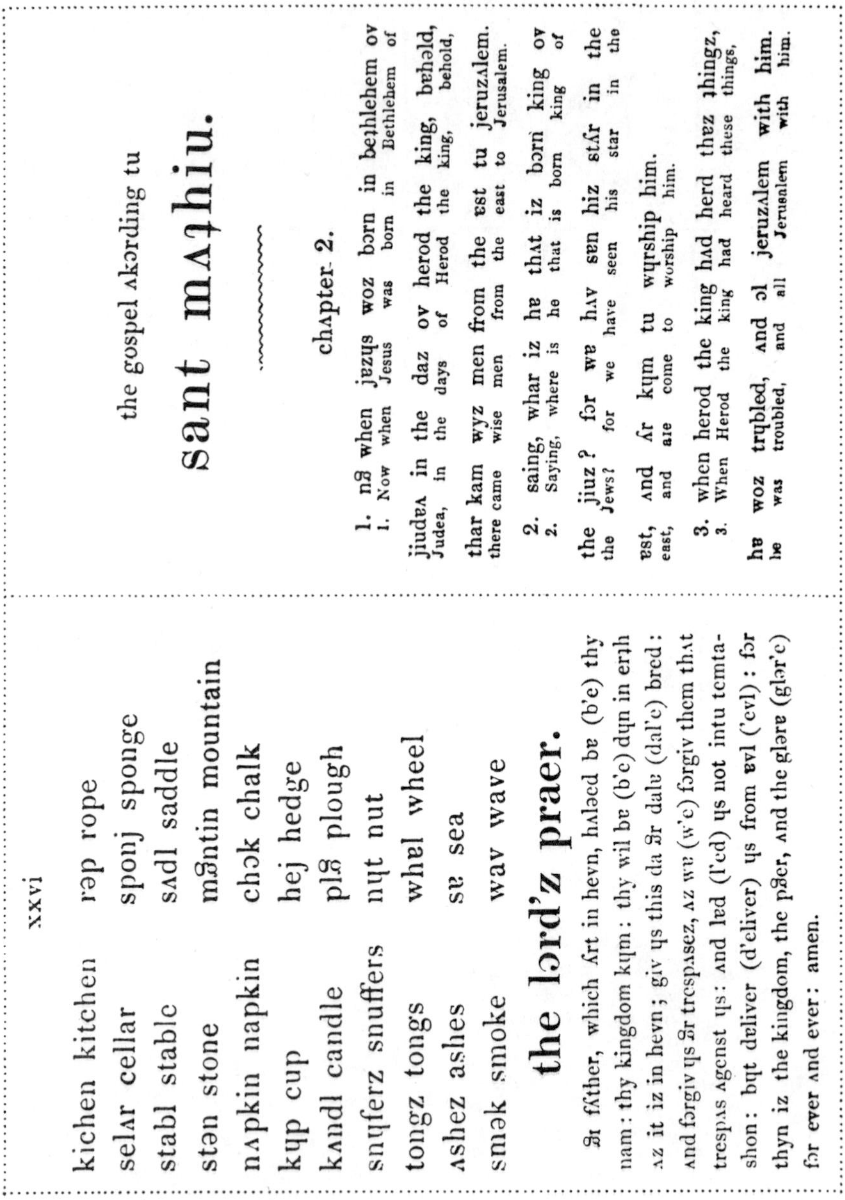

xxvi

kichen kitchen	rɘp rope
selar cellar	sponj sponge
stabl stable	sʌdl saddle
sten stone	mɘntin mountain
nʌpkin napkin	chɔk chalk
kʉp cup	hej hedge
kʌndl candle	plɐ plough
snʉferz snuffers	nʉt nut
tongz tongs	whel wheel
ʌshez ashes	sɐ sea
smɘk smoke	wʌv wave

the lɔrd'z praer.

Ɐr fɐther, which ʌrt in hevn, hʌlɘed bɐ (b'e) thy nam: thy kingdom kʉm: thy wil bɐ (b'e) dʉn in erih ʌz it iz in hevn; giv ʉs this da ɐr dalʉ (dal'e) bred: and fɔrgiv ʉs ɐr trespʌsez, ʌz wɐ (w'e) fɔrgiv them thʌt trespʌs agenst ʉs: and led (l'ed) ʉs not intu temta-shon: bʉt dɐliver (d'eliver) ʉs from ɐvl ('evl) : fɔr thyn iz the kingdom, the pɐer, ʌnd the glɐre (glɐr'e) fɔr ever ʌnd ever: amen.

the gospel ʌkɔrding tu

sant mʌþiu.

chapter. 2.

1. nɐ when jezʉs woz bɔrn in beþlehem ov
   Now when Jesus was born in Bethlehem of
   jiudeʌ in the daz ov herod the king, behɐld,
   Judea, in the days of Herod the king, behold,

   thar kam wyz men from the ɐst tu jeruzʌlem.
   there came wise men from the east to Jerusalem.

2. saing, whar iz hɐ thʌt iz bɔrn king ov
   Saying, where is he that is born king of
   the jiuz? for wɐ hʌv sɐn hiz stʌr in the
   the Jews? for we have seen his star in the
   ɐst, and ɐr kʉm tu wʉrship him.
   east, and are come to worship him.

3. when herod the king hʌd herd thez þhingz,
   When Herod the king had heard these things,
   hɐ woz trʉbled, and ɔl jeruzʌlem with him.
   he was troubled, and all Jerusalem with him.

FIGURE 16. Facing pages from the *Anti-absurd or Phrenotypic Alphabet and Orthography for the English Language,* by Major Beniowski, London 1845.

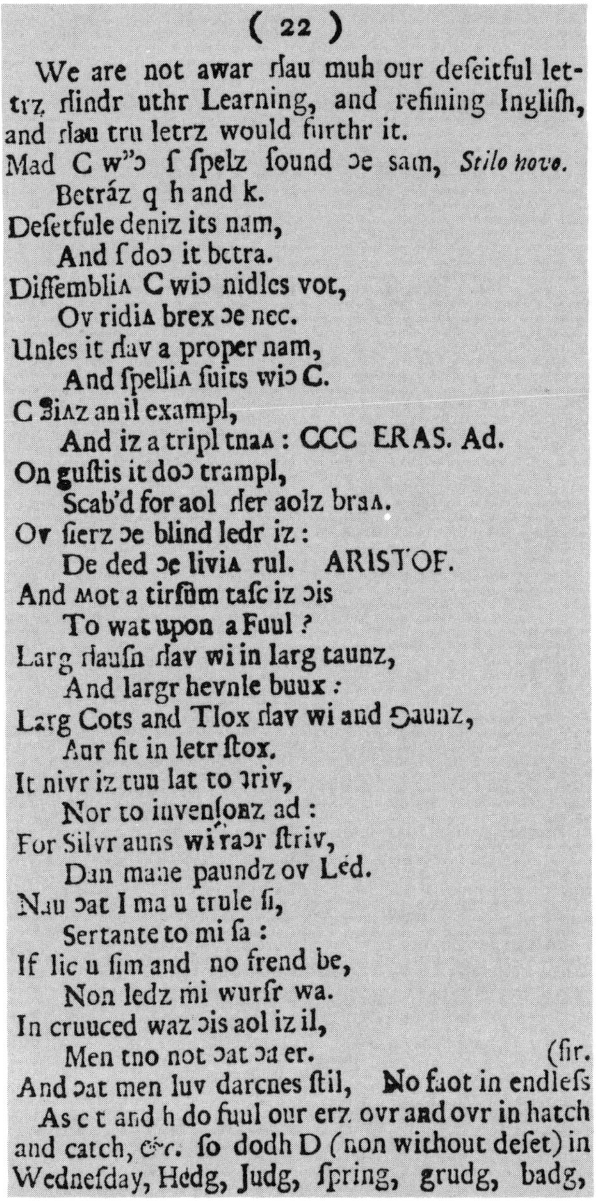

We are not awar ꞁau muh our defeitful let-
trz, ꞁindr uthr Learning, and refining Inglifh,
and ꞁau tru letrz would furthr it.
Mad C w"ɔ f fpelz found ɔe sam, *Stilo novo.*
  Betráz q h and k.
Defetfule deniz its nam,
  And f doɔ it bctra.
Diffembliʌ C wiɔ nidles vot,
  Ov ridiʌ brex ɔe nec.
Unles it ꞁav a proper nam,
  And fpelliʌ fuits wiɔ C.
C Ꞃiʌz an il exampl,
  And iz a tripl tnaʌ : CCC ERAS. Ad.
On guftis it doɔ trampl,
  Scab'd for aol ꞁer aolz braʌ.
Ov fierz ɔe blind ledr iz :
  De ded ɔe liviʌ rul. ARISTOF.
And ᴍot a tirfűm tafc iz ɔis
  To wat upon a Fuul ?
Larg ꞁaufn ꞁav wi in larg taunz,
  And largr hevnle buux :
Larg Cots and Tlox ꞁav wi and Ꝺaunz,
  Aur fit in letr ftox.
It nivr iz tuu lat to ꞇriv,
  Nor to invenfoʀz ad :
For Silvr auns wi raɔr ftriv,
  Ꝺan maꞏne paundz ov Léd.
Nʌu ɔat I ma u trule fi,
  Sertante to mi fa :
If lic u fim and no frend be,
  Non ledz mi wurfr wa.
In cruuced waz ɔis aol iz il,
  Men tno not ɔat ɔꞏd er.   (fir.
And ɔat men luv darcnes ftil, No fʌot in endlefs
  As c t and h do fuul our erz ovr and ovr in hatch
and catch, *&c.* fo dodh D (non without defet) in
Wednefday, Hedg, Judg, fpring, grudg, badg,

FIGURE 17. Verses from *Magazine, or Animadversions on the
English Spelling*, by G.W., London 1703.

Englif orꞇograpi wie dowg

FIGURE 18. Specimen words in the extended alphabet used by
Charles Butler in his *English Grammar*, Oxford 1633.
a) English   b) orthography   c) which   d) though

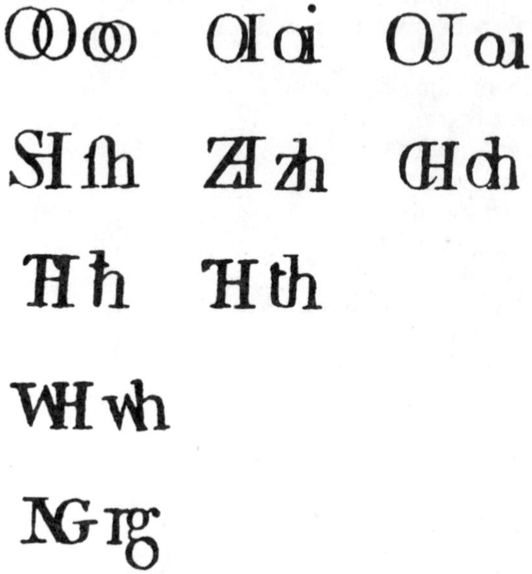

OOoo OIai OJou

SIfh Zzh CHch

Hh Hth

WHwh

NGng

FIGURE 19. a) New letters used by Thomas Spence in his *Grand Repository of the English Language*, a pronouncing dictionary published in Newcastle in 1775; enlarged from the copperplate frontispiece.

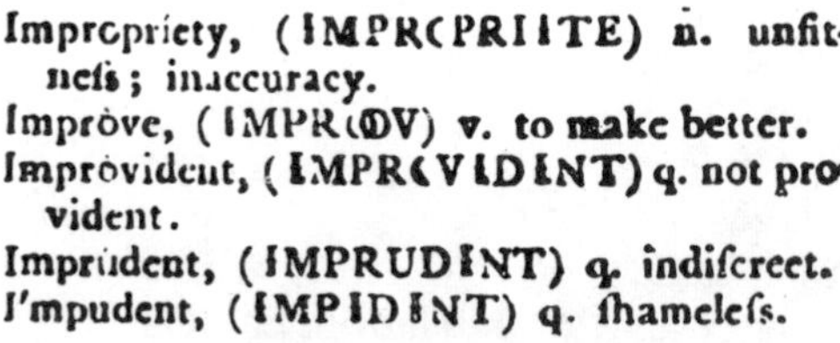

Impropriety, (IMPRCPRIITE) n. unfit-
    nefs; inaccuracy.
Improve, (IMPROV) v. to make better.
Improvident, (IMPRCVIDINT) q. not pro-
    vident.
Imprudent, (IMPRUDINT) q. indifcreet.
I'mpudent, (IMPIDINT) q. fhamelefs.

b) Some entries from Spence's dictionary.

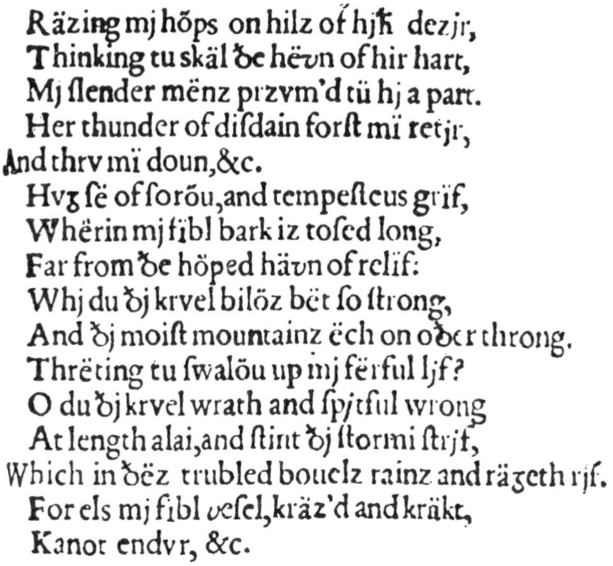

Räzing mj hŏps on hilz of hjⱨ dezjr,
Thinking tu skäl ꝺe hëvn of hir hart,
Mj flender mënz przvm'd tü hj a part.
Her thunder of difdain forſt mï retjr,
And thrv mï doun,&c.

Hvӡ fë of foróu,and tempeſteus grïf,
Whërin mj fïbl bark iz tofed long,
Far from ꝺe höped hävn of relïf:
Whj du ꝺj krvel bilöz bët fo ſtrong,
And ꝺj moiſt mountainz ëch on oꝺer throng.
Thrëting tu fwalöu up mj fërful ljf?
O du ꝺj krvel wrath and fpjtful wrong
At length alai,and ſtint ꝺj ſtormi ſtrjf,
Which in ꝺëz trubled bouelz rainz and räӡeth rjf.
For els mj fïbl vefel,kräz'd and kräkt,
Kanot endvr, &c.

FIGURE 20. Lines from Spenser's *Faerie Queene* in the alphabet used by Alexander Gill in his *Logonomia Anglica*. a) A passage from the 1st edition, London, 1619.

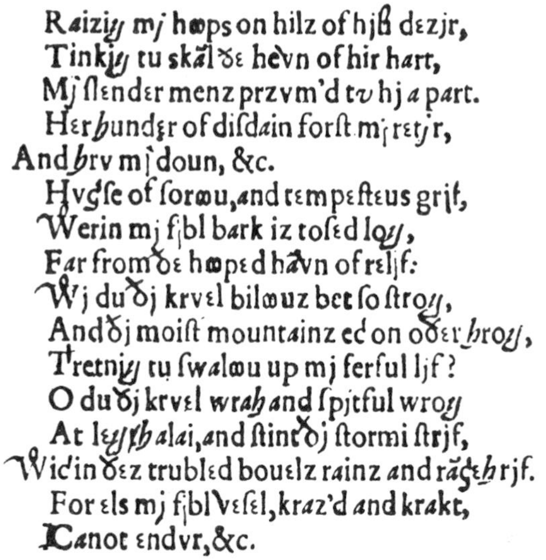

Raizi�📛 mj hꝏps on hilz of hjß dɛzjr,
Tinkjꝏ tu skäl ꝺɛ hèvn of hir hart,
Mj flendɛr menz przvm'd tv hj a part.
Her ɦundɛr of difdain forſt mɩretjr,
And ɦrv mj doun, &c.

Hvɡfe of forꝏu,and tɛmpɛſteus grjɫ,
Werin mj fïbl bark iz tofɛd loꝏ,
Far from ꝺɛ hꝏpɛd hävn of rɛljf:
Wj du ꝺj krvɛl bilꝏuz bet fo ſtroꝏ,
And ꝺj moiſt mountainz ed on oꝺɛr ɦroꝏ,
Tretnjꝏ tu fwalꝏu up mj ferful ljf?
O du ꝺj krvɛl wraɦ and fpjtful wroꝏ
At lɛꝏɦ alai,and ſtint ꝺj ſtormi ſtrjf,
Wicin ꝺɛz trublɛd bouelz rainz and räӡɦ rjf.
For ɛls mj fïbl Vefɛl,kraz'd and krakt,
Kanot ɛndvr,&c.

b) The same passage from the 2nd edition, London 1621.

Extending the Roman Alphabet

References

BAÏF, J.A. DE (1574) *Etrénes ...*, Paris (De l'Imprimerie de Denys du Val).

BATCHELOR, T. (1809) *An Orthoëpical Analysis of the English Language*, London (Didier and Tebbett).

BELL, A.M. (1867) *Visible Speech: the Science of Universal Alphabetics*, London (Simpkin, Marshall & Co).

BENIOWSKI, MAJOR (1845) *The Anti-absurd or Phrenotypic Alphabet*, London (published by the Author).

BRIDGES, R. (1927–35) *Collected Essays* (nine volumes), London (Oxford University Press).

BULLOKAR, W. (1580) *Booke at large, for the Amendment of Orthographie for English speech*, London (Henry Denham).

— (1585) *Aesop's Fables*, London (Edmund Bollifant).

BUTLER, C. (1633) *The English Grammar, or the Institution of Letters, Syllables, and Words, in the English Tongue*, Oxford (William Turner, for the Author).

CAPELL, E. (1760) *Prolusions; or, select Pieces of antient Poetry*, London (J. & R. Tonson).

FRANKLIN, B. (1779) *Political, Miscellaneous, and Philosophical Pieces*, London (J. Johnson).

GILL, A. (1619) *Logonomia Anglica*, London (John Beale); 2nd ed. 1621.

HART, J. (1569) *An Orthographie, conteyning the due order and reason, howe to write or paint thimage of mannes voice, most like to the life or nature*, London (William Seres).

— (1570) *A Methode ...*, London (Henry Denham).

HODGES, R. (1644) *The English Primrose*, London (Richard Cotes).

JOHNSTON, W. (1764) *A Pronouncing and Spelling Dictionary*, London (printed for W. Johnston).

JONES, D. and PASSY, P. (1907) *Alphabet phonétique organique*, supplément au *Maître Phonétique*.

LHWYD, E. (1707) *Archaeologia Britannica*, Oxford (printed at the Theater for the Author).

LODWICK, F. (1686) 'An essay towards an universal alphabet', *Philosophical Transactions* 16, 126–37.

MOXON, J. (1683) *Mechanick Exercises*, London (printed for Joseph Moxon).

PITMAN, I. (1843) 'Phonographic alphabet number 9', *The Phonographic Journal* 2, 107.

RAMBAUD, H. (1578) *La Declaration des Abus que lon commet en escriuant*, Lyon (Jean de Tournes).

ROBINSON, R. (1617) *The Art of Pronuntiation*, London (printed by Nicholas Okes).

SEARCH, E. (*pseud.*, i.e. Abraham Tucker) (1773) *Vocal Sounds*, London (T. Jones, sold by T. Payne).

SHAW, B. (1962) *Androcles and the Lion, an old fable renovated, with a parallel text in Shaw's Alphabet*, Harmondsworth (Penguin Books).

SMITH, T. (1568) *De recta et emendata linguae Anglicae scriptione*, Paris (Robert Stephan).

SPENCE, T. (1775) *The Grand Repository of the English Language*, Newcastle upon Tyne (T. Saint, for the Author).

STANYHURST, R. (1582) *The First Foure Bookes of Virgils Æneis*, London (imprinted by Henry Bynneman).

THORNTON, W. (1793) 'Cadmus, or a treatise on the elements of written language', *Trans. Am. Philosophical Soc.* 3, 262–319.

W., G. (1703) *Magazine, or Animadversions on the English Spelling*, London (printed for the Author).

WILKINS, J. (1668) *An Essay Towards a Real Character, and a Philosophical Language*, London (printed by order of the Royal Society).

Arabic and Roman
Writing Systems for Swahili

Swahili is a Bantu language spoken as a first language by at least a million people living on the coast of East Africa and the off-shore islands. It has a number of dialects; the two most generally described being Kimvita (spoken in the Mombasa area) and Kiunguja (spoken in Zanzibar). The latter form was accepted as standard by 1930 and is normally used in writing. Swahili vocabulary has been much enriched by Arabic, especially in cultural areas relating to Islam, as there is a long tradition of cultural and commercial contact with Arabic-speaking countries. More recently many loan-words have been taken from English.

Swahili is also spoken as a second language by over ten million people and as a lingua franca throughout large areas of East Africa, and into Zaire and other neighbouring countries. It is the national language of Tanzania and the official language of Kenya. Besides East Africa, Swahili is taught at University and similar institutions in West Africa (Ghana and Nigeria), Europe (England, France, Germany, Norway, Sweden, Italy, Poland, Czechoslovakia), Russia, China, India and America.

The earliest known Swahili manuscript dates from 1728. The language was first written in Arabic characters, and many Swahili speakers today – especially Moslems – still use these characters. European missionaries from the mid-nineteenth century wrote the language in Roman characters, however, and almost all published material these days is in Roman.

The inventory of phonemes in Swahili varies somewhat according to which dialect is being described, as does the exact phonetic realisation of the phonemes. However the standard language may be described as having the consonant phonemes shown in table 1. The voiced plosives have an implosive and an explosive allophone; in the case of the palatal phoneme given as plosive, the explosive allophone is also affricate – ([ʤ]).

For some speakers, and historically in the Kimvita dialect (and others), there is a phonemic contrast of aspiration in the voiceless plosives and affricate, that is we have p':p, t':t, ʧ':ʧ, k':k.

Also, and again principally in Kimvita, there is a phonemic contrast between dental and alveolar /t, d/. In most cases the dental forms represent /ʧ/ and /ʝ/ in the standard dialect, but the replacement does not occur in every case, so that the phoneme inventory may be described as wider, although it is difficult to find minimal pairs in every case. The widest inventory

TABLE 1.

	bilabial	labio-dental	dental	alveolar	alveolo-palatal	palatal	velar	glottal
plosive	p b			t d		ɟ	k g	
affricate					tʃ			
fricative		f v	θ ð	s z	ʃ		ɣ	h
lateral				l				
flap				ɾ				
nasal	m			n		ɲ	ŋ	
semivowel				j			w	

TABLE 2.

	bilabial	labio-dental	dental	alveolar	alveolo-palatal	palatal	velar
plosive	p p' b		t̪ t̪' d̪	t t' d		ɟ	k k' g
affricate					tʃ tʃ'		

of plosive/affricate phonemes then would be as in table 2.

In the case of words of Arabic origin there can frequently be heard phones other than those suggested on the chart, e.g. voiceless velar fricative [x], or velarised [ð], but as these are not contrastive they are not described as separate phonemes or even allophones, since their use is not predictable except perhaps in a socio-linguistic sense. In some cases, however, [x] is reflected, even in the Roman spelling, as *kh*.

Vowel phonemes are five in number, symbolised /i e a o u/. Bantu languages normally have either five or seven vowels, rather evenly distributed round the vowel figure. Swahili /e/ and /o/ each have an open and a close allophone in stressed syllables. Other vowels have varying qualities for some speakers, usually related to the stress position.

Swahili nasal phonemes can be syllabic. Otherwise syllables are open and thus all words must end in a vowel, although in some cases this is devoiced (e.g. basi̥ 'O.K.'). Consonant clusters may consist of nasal+C (where C indicates normally a homorganic consonant), or C+semivowel; also N (nasal)+C+semivowel; although by no means all theoretical possibilities occur. A few other consonant clusters exist in loan-words.

Word-stress in Swahili is on the penultimate syllable except in some loan-words. Very few monosyllabic words exist. The question of word-division in writing is, however, not without interest.

The ever-increasing use of Swahili as a lingua franca might seem to suggest the development of a greater variety in the forms of the language; on the other hand a standardised orthography may lead towards the loss of distinctions important in some varieties of the language. For example, neither the Arabic nor the Roman scripts indicate aspiration; and although many scholars have noted it as a phenomenon, invented symbols for it, and marked it themselves in scholarly works, they have not often used it in pedagogical books. (One exception is Meinhof 1910.) It does not seem ever to have been indicated in writing in Swahili for the general public, not even in school texts.

In looking at the different orthographies that have been used for Swahili, there are two variables which have to be taken into account. The first is the kind of Swahili which is being described. Most scholars have described either Kimvita or Kiunguja, though some have looked at other dialects too. The second variable is the native language of the scholar. European writers on Swahili have mainly been German, French or English, though there have also been some Italian and Dutch scholars. Many variations in the orthographic forms used are no doubt due to one or other of these factors. A third variable, one less easily assessed perhaps, is the degree of linguistic sophistication of the scholar. However, since the latter factor is really of little more than anecdotal interest, I have confined this study to the writings of some of the more outstanding scholars.

Comparison is made with the present standard orthography as represented in the Standard Swahili-English Dictionary produced by the Inter-territorial Language Committee (the forerunner of the present Institute for Swahili Research now at the University of Dar es Salaam) in 1939. The committee's work on this dictionary was directed by Frederick Johnson and it was based on A.C. Madan's Swahili-English dictionary (1903). The Inter-territorial Language Committee (later the East African Swahili Committee) was founded in 1930 and its first task was that of standardisation and development of Swahili. Precisely how this standardisation was achieved is a matter for research; but while the work of the committee may be criticised, it has never been seriously challenged.

The Arabic Script for Swahili

Early writings in Swahili in Arabic script show no particular effort on the part of the authors (or copyists) to adapt or extend the range of Arabic symbols. Since most of these early writers were probably bilingual and since they were writing mainly for pleasure or social comment as poets, or for the historical record, and not for pedagogical reasons, and since the readers of these writings might be expected to be familiar with both languages and with the subject-matter, there are no early works that prescribe the relationship between sound and symbol. Later writings by European scholars on the Arabic script as used for Swahili therefore can only describe the current state of affairs. And although there have from time to time been suggestions by both European and Swahili scholars for innovations to make the script fit more closely to the language, on the whole these suggestions have not been taken up. This is no doubt partly because of the weight of tradition, partly because the deficiencies of the script were always more apparent to the

European learner than to the people who were writing and those for whom the writings were intended, and partly because there is now an alternative orthography anyway.

The drawbacks of the Arabic script for writing Swahili are of two types. Firstly, there are no symbols in the traditional script for the phonemes /p/, /g/, /tʃ/, /v/, /ɲ/, /ŋ/; and there are only three vowel symbols, one used for /a/, the other two for /i/ and /e/, /o/ and /u/ respectively. That at least the consonants pose problems even for first-language speakers is implicitly recognised in the fact that beginners are often taught variant symbols for these phonemes; but beyond the learning stage these variants are not often used. Some examples of the variants used are given in table 3 (isolated forms of the letter only being given).

TABLE 3.

Arabic		Variant	
ب	/b/	پ	/p/
غ	/ɣ/	ڠ	/g/
ج	/ʝ/	چ	/tʃ/	(the symbol for /ʃ/ is also sometimes used for /tʃ/)
ف	/f/	ڤ	/v/

The absence of unequivocal symbols for /ɲ/ and /ŋ/ can cause problems for the reader. Frequently nasals are omitted in any case before following consonants, so the most common solution for /ɲ/ and /ŋ/ is to use the symbols for /j/ and /g/ or /ɣ/ respectively. The use of a single symbol for /i/ and /e/ and another for both /u/ and /o/ can also cause confusion, especially when it is considered that nominal stems are overwhelmingly of the pattern CVCV and verb roots of the pattern CVC.

The second drawback of the Arabic script is that there are symbols for phonemes occurring only in Arabic words, symbolising distinctions which are in fact lost in the spoken language as the loan-words become more assimilated. For example the distinction between ق (/q/) and ك (/k/). So there is a choice of two (or more) symbols for some phonemes, and only the writer who knows Arabic well knows which symbol to employ. Many cases of confusion and of hypercorrection occur.

To give an extreme example of the problems of the script, the symbol ی could be used for /j/ /ɲ/ /ˈ/i/ or /e/; while /i/ or /e/ could also be symbolised by Kesra, a stroke below the consonant symbol, for example ٻل *ile* – which word, incidentally, also has to be written as beginning with a consonant (Alif in this case) since vowels in Arabic script can only be associated with consonants. As Swahili often has successions of vowels, the symbols for /w/ and /j/ are often used as vowel signs, with or without an indication that this is so. More detailed accounts of the writing of Swahili in the Arabic script may be found in Allen (1945), Beech (1918) (pp.3–57) et al.

Among European scholars, I would like to consider in detail the work of three: J.L. Krapf, a German missionary who published the first systematic grammar of Swahili in 1850 and from whose dictionary of 1882 I have taken my examples; Bishop Edward Steere whose *Handbook of Swahili* as revised by A.C. Madan (4th ed. 1908) is the source of my second set of examples; and Fr. Charles Sacleux whose studies of Swahili dialects published in 1909 remain unsuperseded, and from whose dictionary (1939) I take my third set of examples. These are all compared with the present standardised form of the language as recognised by the Inter-territorial Language (Swahili) Committee.

But before leaving entirely the subject of the Arabic script, I think it might be worth suggesting that, given the long tradition of literacy in that script and the interrelationship between spelling and pronunciation, it is possible that some at least of the problems encountered by the early European scholars may be related to the fact that their informants seem to have been mainly Muslims of good family and therefore no doubt highly educated and literate in Arabic and Swahili in the Arabic script. Thus Krapf (1882), for example, frequently writes *b* for /p/, though only occasionally *p* for /b/. This could indicate a historical change in pronunciation, it could relate to his German origin – though he is very scornful of Rebmann whom he berates for such confusions and relates it to Rebmann's 'south German origin' (Krapf 1882 p.xiv), or it could perhaps relate to the literary background of his informants. The Rev. J. Rebmann was a German missionary who came to Mombasa in 1837 and who had previously seen some of Krapf's manuscripts which the latter had sent to the Church Missionary Society in London. Rebmann worked on Swahili and gave Krapf some additional vocabulary which Krapf included in his dictionary. Rebmann's main published work, however, is on 'Nika', 'Kiniassa' and 'Nyanja'. The informants would be dictating to Krapf, necessarily slowly; and in fact he quite often gives alternatives without any explanation.

European Systems

The system of Dr Ludwig Krapf. The Preface to Krapf's dictionary (1882) is very entertaining, and he is quite outspoken on the subject of his contemporaries. As to orthography, he regrets (p.x) that 'the standard alphabet of Dr Lepsius' had not been adopted and was sure that all other orthographies of 'other Suahili writers, will and must be absorbed in course of time by that universal alphabet'. In spite of an effort published in 1930 by the International African Institute (see their *Practical Orthography of African Languages*, p.23), and subsequent efforts by various language committees, to bring some such state to pass, so far Krapf's prediction remains unfulfilled. Slightly inconsistently, on p.xiv he writes: 'As to myself, I much regret not having chosen the Amharic Alphabet... . As I was the first European who reduced Suahili to writing, and as there was then no universal alphabet compiled, I might easily have chosen Amharic ... which could evidently suit the Suahili better than the Roman'. He goes on, later, to say: 'However ... I have never regretted having rejected the Arabic mode of writing, which is too imperfect and too ambiguous for writing Suahili in a correct manner'. He also (p.xi) writes an apologia: 'A word may be written with the letter *f*, at another place you may find it written with *v*, or it may be written promiscuously with *z* or *s*, or *j* or *ch*. The author was of opinion, that the book was not only destined for English students, but also for those of other nations who are less accustomed to English pronunciation'! However, if not concerned about consistency, he is at least attracted to economy, for he also writes (p.xiv) 'A perfect alphabet of any language is to contain only such a number of letters which is precisely equal to the number of simple articulate sounds belonging to that language. For this reason we have omitted *x*, which may be rendered by *ks* or *gs*. *Ph* may be given by *f*, as the Italians write – e.g. *Filosofia* for philosophy'. (One may note, however, that in any case the sequences *ks* and *gs* do not occur in Swahili, nor do words of Greek origin.)

Krapf (1882, p.xiii) recognises five vowel phonemes, which he symbolises as *i e a o u*, and in his section on Phonology he gives English words for comparison in pronunciation, namely:

i as *i* in *caprice*, and = *ee* in *feet*; short, like *i* in *pin, pity, little*

e as *e* in *let, met, get, every, hen*; *ê* as in *fête*, or *chair*

a is to be pronounced as *a* in *father, far, papa*

o as *o* in *globe, notice, boy*, and short, like in *not, hot, pot*

u as in *rude, full, bull*, or *oo* as in *tool*.

We may ignore such curiosities as the evident similarity to Krapf's ear (or in his experience) of the vowels in 'fête' 'chair', and in 'notice' 'boy'; also the question as to *which a* in 'papa' (and what pronunciation of that Victorianism) is intended – presumably the same vowel, however, as in 'far'; and the conflation of the qualities for the vowel *u* (always supposing Krapf was not classing the vowels in 'rude' 'full' and 'tool' as the same). Nevertheless it might seem that Krapf was postulating two qualities for at least the vowels *i, e, o* and *u*. More recent scholars (e.g. Tucker and Ashton 1942, p.79) have postulated two qualities for these vowels, and also three for the vowel *a*. Unfortunately, if Krapf *was* intending to postulate more than one quality for the vowel phonemes of Swahili, he gives no indication of the conditions under which the different qualities occur. And indeed, although Tucker and Ashton (1942) suggest a strong correlation between certain allophones and factors such as stress or nasal clusters following the vowel, they also are frequently driven to say that a particular variety occurs 'in less well defined contexts' (p.80).

Whatever its quality, in some words the phoneme nowadays represented as *i*, is by Krapf often represented as *e*, for example -*engia* (-*ingia* 'enter'), *range* (*rangi* 'colour'), *chibene* (*jibini* 'cheese'), *kisema* (*kisima* 'well'), *ela/illa/ila* (*ila* 'except'), -*fea* (-*fia* 'die for') and so on. Tucker and Ashton

(1942) refer to the confusion of spellings of *i* and *e* for what they call the '"weak" sound ɪ' (p.79). However they postulate the use of this 'weak' sound in some unstressed syllables and sometimes before nasal compounds. Stress in Swahili is normally on the penultimate syllable; thus while *-engia, range* and the final vowel in *chibene* can be explained as occurring in unstressed syllables, the other examples cannot. They could perhaps come under 'less well defined contexts' or they could, as I have suggested earlier, be influenced by the lack of distinction in the Arabic script for these vowels. What, however, is one to say of the representation of present-day *i* by *u*? For example *kulla* (*kila* 'each') – I have also heard *u* in this word –, *rusasi* (*risasi* 'bullet'), *-chupuka/-chipuka* 'sprout', *chururika/chiririka* 'trickle'.

/e/ is normally represented by *e* in Krapf, although we do find *i* regularly in the possessive stem *-enyi* (*enye* 'with'). If, then, spelling variation between Krapf and the present standard represented something of a vowel *shift*, it would be in the direction of /e/ to /i/, and not vice versa. Since both vowels have the same symbol in Arabic there is no reason there for the predominance of one over the other. Present /a/ is generally represented by *a* in Krapf, but there are a large number of examples, generally but not exclusively in Arabic loan-words, where *e* is preferred, for example *hei* (*hai* 'alive'), *teary* (*tayari* 'ready'), *biashera* (*biashara* 'business'), *heitimbiki* (*haichimbiki* 'it cannot be dug'), *-seidia* (*-saidia* 'help'), *cheribu* (*jaribu* 'try'), *ketha wa ketha* (*kadha wa kadha* 'several') and so on. There are a few examples with other vowels, for example *kamo* (*kama* 'like'), *luththa* (*ladha* 'taste'), *idili* (*adili* 'right'), *ferasi/farasi* 'horse', *usujai/a* (*ushujaa* 'bravery'), but the overwhelming majority of alternatives to words with *a* have *e*. In unstressed syllables Tucker and Ashton (1942, p.83) point out that something like [ə] 'may occasionally be heard', and in rapid speech 'occasionally the sound is fronted to sound like [e], [ɛ] or even [œ] in unstressed syllables'. (Tucker and Ashton worked partly from recordings made by their informants.) However, Krapf was not recording rapid speech; moreover, many of his examples have *e* in *stressed* syllables, in some cases with the stressed syllable actually marked, for example *magébali* (*majabali* 'rocks') – the stress today is normally on the penultimate syllable in this word. Are we to take it that *some* /e/ phonemes have become lowered while others have become closer? One word suggests movement in both directions within itself: *beredi* 'cool' in Krapf is *baridi* nowadays! However, as John Kelly has pointed out to me, Krapf may have been recording pronunciation (though I myself see no reason why he should not have also looked at Arabic writing) whereas Johnson and the Language Committee may have been recording written forms or spelling pronunciations. Nevertheless the differences between Krapf and later writers do require explanation.

The present vowel /o/ is normally represented by *o* in Krapf, with occasional exceptions, for example *kambu* (*kambo* 'step-parent'), *jogoi* (*jogoo* 'cock'), *-taruka* (*-toroka* 'run away'). Although Tucker and Ashton (1942, p.80) refer to 'confusion between lax [ʊ] and [o] ... in old writings', for Krapf at least the 'confusion' if such it be is all one way.

/u/, then, for Krapf is normally represented *u*, but by far the largest number of exceptions have *o*, e.g. *logha* (*lugha* 'language'), *to* (*tu* 'only'), *omri* (*umri* 'age'), *tómbako* (*tumbaku* 'tobacco'), *shoguli* (*shughuli* 'concerns'), *pango* (*pangu* 'my place') &c. There are a few other reflexes, for example *felani/falani* (*fulani* 'so and so'), *-finika/-funika* 'cover', *sifuria/sufuria* 'cooking pot'. It seems, though, that any vowel movement is rather from /o/ to /u/ than vice versa. If it were a matter of the influence of the Arabic script, one would expect a more equal number of variations each way. *u* and *i* again turn up as alternatives in a few words, as noted under /i/.

Krapf occasionally writes initial vowels, which would not nowadays be written, for example *ilakini* 'but', *estaki* 'reliable', *umbua* (*mbwa* 'dog'). There are some examples which today seem to have undergone metathesis, for example *-ihtaji* (*-hitaji* 'need'), *ihtilafu* (*hitilafu* 'discord'), *-ihtimu* (*-hitimu* 'qualify'). He does not normally write epenthetic vowels; in fact rather the contrary, in many cases where such vowels are written today, he has consonant clusters, for example *pilpili* (*pilipili* 'pepper'), *sermalla* (*seremala* 'carpenter'), *tartibu* (*taratibu* 'carefully'), *orfa/orofa/ghorofa* 'storey'), *-simlia* (*-simulia* 'relate'). These examples, and those of metathesis, might suggest that such words (which are mainly of Arabic origin) are becoming more assimilated into Swahili with its syllable structure of (normally) CV.

When writing words of Arabic origin, there is sometimes for Krapf a very considerable variety of vowel. This must arise partly of course from the varying form of the word in Arabic, but may also reflect the fact that the words in question were not yet fully absorbed into the language. Examples are: *burudi/baradi/baridi/beredi* (*baridi* 'cool'), *ufuthuli/ufathuli/fathili/fathuli* (*-fadhili* 'do a favour').

Krapf is careful to point out (p.xv) that 'there are no diphthongs in Suahili' since even where vowels occur next to each other, each constitutes a syllable. However, when the two vowels are the same, Krapf seems uncertain whether these constitute one or more syllables; at any rate he sometimes writes two vowels (e.g. *bidii* 'zeal'), *bithaa* (*bidhaa* 'merchandise'), and sometimes one with a length mark, e.g. *kondō* (*kondoo* 'sheep'). This leads him into difficulties with stress, and forces him to say that 'the position of the accent ... has great influence on the proper meaning of a word, for example *kóndo* means strife or quarrel, whereas *kŏndō* signifies sheep'. (Modern spellings *kondo: kondoo*; penultimate stress in each case.) Since he occasionally gives a variant, for example *chakā/chakaa*, I do not feel that a distinction is always intended between a double vowel and a long vowel. Nevertheless there are words that he seems to distinguish by vowel length, for example *kānga* 'coconut shoot'; *kanga* 'guinea-fowl' which are both today written *kanga*. Whereas what he gives as *-kaánga/-kānga* 'fry' is written *-kaanga* now.

232

A similar and more serious problem arises from the fact that Krapf normally uses vowel symbols for the semivowels /w/ and /j/. Sometimes he marks such symbols short when they represent semivowels, but by no means regularly, (e.g. 'tŏā or tōáa (*twaa*) means to take, but ku tóa to bring ... out ...; and ku túa to put down ..., and ku tŭa or kuchŭa (*twa, chwa*) ... to set'. (It will be noted that the semivowel /w/ is represented by *either o or u*.) Moreover, he also writes /ɲ/ as *n + i*, and having said that every vowel constitutes a syllable, he then classes as 'words of three or more syllables' examples such as *niúmba* (*nyumba* 'house'), *ónia* (*onya* 'warn'), *fánia* (*fanya* 'do'), *gawánia* (*gawanya* 'divide'), and says that these have the accent on the antepenultimate. Although Krapf very frequently writes *u* for *w* (with or without a short mark), he also uses *w* often initially (though note *ueussi* (*weusi* 'whiteness')), and sometimes medially, for example *kuakwe* (*kwake* 'at his place'). Even where *w* occurs between two vowels he frequently uses *u*, for example *sauasaua* (*sawasawa* 'alike'). Moreover, in passive forms he uses both *u* and *o* (e.g. p.xxix imperative *pendua* (*pendwa* 'be loved'), infinitive *kupendoa* (*kupendwa*). It is really hard to see any justification for the variation here between *u* and *o*. The semivowel /w/ is frequently omitted, especially after /b/ and /m/, for example *bana* (*bwana* 'sir'), *kuba* (*kubwa* 'big'), *utuma* (*utumwa* 'slavery'), *misho* (*mwisho* 'end'); between vowels: *jongoe* (*chongowe* 'a fish'), *hukua* (*hukuwa* 'you were not'); and initially: *api* (*wapi* 'where?'), *-asa* (*-waza* 'think'), *ku inda* (*kuwinda* 'to hunt'), *oga* (*woga* 'fear'). Certainly this semi-vowel is normally pronounced with considerably less lip-rounding than in English; nevertheless several of the examples given would produce homophones without the semivowel (and are often pronounced as homophones today). /j/ is normally written *y* initially and between vowels, but it is regularly written *i* after consonants, for example *-fionia* (*-fyonya* 'chirp'), *niassi* (*nyasi* 'grass'), *jipia* (*jipya* 'new'), *via* (*vya* 'of'), though he sometimes gives alternatives, for example *boniéa/bonyea* 'be dented'. Again, the use of this symbol requires Krapf to mark stress, which he sometimes does, for example *fiónia* (*fyonya*). /y/ occasionally omitted, as in *yee alie penda* (*yeye aliyependa* 'he who loved'); and *i* may function clearly as a syllable as in *babai* (*babaye* 'his father'), *mai* (*mayai* 'eggs'). *y* is also occasionally inserted, as in *chayi/chai* 'tea', *-fayidi/-faidi* 'profit'. It is fair to say that many unsophisticated writers even today are not sure whether to write the semivowel *w* between two vowels one of which is back, or the semivowel *y* between two vowels one of which is front.

With respect to *w*, Krapf writes (p.xiv) '*w* is to be pronounced like ... German *w*. The English *w* is, according to Professor Rothwell's Grammar, p.18, to be considered as a vowel, and not as a vowel and a consonant; therefore the English *w* cannot properly be introduced into the Suahili – e.g. the English *w* in the word *we* is properly = *uih*, or in *went* = *uent*, consequently it is no pure *w* like in German or Arabic'. (Krapf's reference is probably to J.S.S. Rothwell: *Beweise über die Einfachkeit der englischen Sprache, im*

Vergleich mit den andern Sprachen Europas, sowohl lebenden als todten. Ein untrüglichen Wegweiser zum schnellen und leichten Erlernen der englischen Sprache. Munich 1843.) Nevertheless Krapf does also have the letter *v* in his alphabet 'as in *very, view, love, every'*. Possibly then he intends *w* to represent some kind of voiced labial fricative, possibly with historical justification. (See para. 110 in Tucker and Ashton (1942). [β] for orthographic *w* is often heard in Mombasa, as John Kelly has pointed out (personal communication).) Nevertheless, what Krapf writes with *ŭ, u, w* normally is represented by *w* today (though see also the use of *w* for *v* below).

In the case of words which Krapf writes without *w* (e.g. *bana* for *bwana*) he says (p.xv) that 'Elision, or Ejection with the compensation of another letter, takes place in the formation of concrete and abstract substantives – e.g., *mpénzi*, ... from the verb *ku pénda; mapénzi* or *upénzi*. In other words, elision is not attended by the compensation of another letter, but the mode of pronunciation shows that an elision has taken place – e.g. *b'ana* ... for *buána; m'otto* ... for *muotto, m'ezi* for *muezí* [sic] .... The elision ought to be indicated by putting an apostrophe over the place where the letter has been elided'. This somewhat gnomic passage seems to refer to two separate phenomena, since in the derived words (from *-penda* 'move') no elision occurs: whether Krapf detected a variation in pronunciation of the *p* (e.g. aspiration/non-aspiration) or whether he was referring to the *d – z* substitution, the result of historical palatalisation, it is hard to know. In the case of the words (not derived from verbs) involving *w*, one is still at a loss. Perhaps he was referring to a glide from the bilabial consonant which today is symbolised by *w* (and generally pronounced so).

Plosive and affricate consonants are represented for Krapf as *p, b, t, d, ch, j, k, g*. He makes no mention of implosion when describing the pronunciation of the voiced plosives; and the only mention of aspiration is for *p*: '*p* has sometimes an aspirated or explosive sound – e.g. *pepo*, much wind (*p'epo*)' (p.xiii). There is no suggestion as to when aspiration is used, although many writers have considered it to be phonemic. In this respect, however, Krapf may reflect more the modern tendency of the language than perhaps the state it was in when he was writing! He does not mark aspiration in his dictionary.

With respect to the distinction voice/voiceless, Krapf has strictures to observe (p.xiv): 'Mr Rebmann, like most of Southern Germans, has confounded frequently the letters *b* and *p, d* and *t*'. Krapf himself includes under voiced plosives and affricates many items which today are written as voiceless, for example *ku bosa* (*-posa* 'affiance'), *bakuba* (*pakubwa* 'large place'), *buba* (*pupa* 'greed'); *adaka* (*ataka* 'he wants'), *dausi* (*tausi* 'peacock'), *dako* (*tako* 'buttock'); *ujaje* (*uchache* 'scarcity'), *jakula* (*chakula* 'food'), *joo* (*choo* 'lavatory'); *-pigia* (*-pikia* 'cook for'), *ugoga* (*ukoka* 'rice crust'). There are *some* examples of voiceless plosives given where today voiced are used, particularly /ch/ for /j/, for example *chongoo* (*jongoo* 'millipede'), *cheuri* (*jeuri* 'brutality'), *nchema* (*njema* 'good'), but apart from /ch:j/, the majority of cases are of voiceless plosives being written as voiced with as extreme examples *degelea* (*tekelea* 'reach') and *bagada* (*pakata* 'lap'). This may reflect the *lack* of aspiration in Swahili voiceless plosives (except for those which are phonemically aspirated). Other alternatives are *f* for *p/b*: *ku fumbaza* (*-pumbaza* 'amaze'), *ku fomoa* (*-bomoa* 'knock down'); *g*, *y* for *j*: *utagiri* (*utajiri* 'riches'), *uyapokufa* (*ujapokufa* 'although you die'); *t* for *k*: *ku tossa* (*-kosa* 'mistake'); *ch* for *g*: *chego* (*gego* 'molar'), but these are probably dialect forms.

For fricatives the voice / voiceless contrast is only shown by Krapf for *f*: *v* and *s*: *z*. Here it is interesting that although there are some cases of voiced consonants being written where today we write voiceless: *chavu* (*chafu* 'dirty'); *upezi* (*upesi* 'quickly'); the vast majority of deviations are in the opposite direction, namely *ufifu* (*uvivu* 'laziness'), *ófio ófio* (*ovyo ovyo* 'anyhow'), *mafuno* (*mavuno* 'harvest'), *mfufi* (*mvuvi* 'fisherman'); *wasi* (*wazi* 'clear'), *ku sama* (*-zama* 'sink'), *usé* (*uzee* 'old age'), *msaha* (*mzaha* 'joke'), *ku soea* (*-zoea* 'practise'). Tucker and Ashton (1942) do say of /v/ and /z/ that they are not very strongly voiced (pp.92, 93). Are voiced fricatives taking over?

Before leaving the subject of /v/, it is noteworthy that Krapf frequently writes *w*. A nice example of alternation occurs on p.xviii 'w̲itu v̲iangui v̲iote w̲imeiboa laken m̲ui̲vi ame̲virudisha' (*vitu vyangu vyote vimeibwa lakini mwivi amevirudisha* 'all my things were stolen but the thief brought them back'). This *may* be owing to the influence of a proto-Bantu voiced bilabial fricative (see para. 76 in Tucker and Ashton, 1942), but may also have something to do with Krapf's own linguistic background.

Krapf does not distinguish between voiced and voiceless dental fricatives which he writes *th*, though he is obviously unhappy about this, suggesting *th*, *t*, *z*, *s*, *ç*, *dh*, *d* for various Arabic sounds (see p.xiv). He occasionally writes *d* for /ð/: *bidaa* (*bidhaa* 'merchandise'). /ʃ/ is normally *sh*, with occasional dialectal *ch*, for example *chavu* (*shavu* 'cheek'). For /ɣ/ Krapf gives *gh*, occasionally *h*, e.g. *shuhuli* (*shughuli* 'business'), or zero: *orfa* (*ghorofa* 'storey'). For /h/ and /x/ he writes *h* and *kh*, but says '*kh* may be written by *h*, not *k* – e.g. *rokho*, may be written *roho*, not *roko*'. In fact he writes *kh* in many more instances than would attract it today, for example *sakhikhi* (*sahihi* 'correct'). Indeed, today *kh* is very rarely written at all. Occasionally Krapf omits either, for example *itilafu* (*hitilafu* 'discord').

Nasals are written /m/ *m*, /n/ *n*, /ŋ/ *gn*. /ɲ/ is mainly written *ni*, for example *niufa* (*nyufa* 'crack'), *niama* (*nyama* 'meat'), *niota* (*nyota* 'star'); but sometimes *n* as in *nimbo* (*nyimbo* 'songs'), *ku faniza* (*-fanyiza* 'cause to do'), *mnororo* (*mnyororo* 'chain'), *nuelle* (*nywele* 'hair'), *tumekúnŏa* (*tumekunywa* 'we have drunk'). It is also sometimes written *gni* and then seems to represent the combination /ɲj/ which is never written today, for example *muegniewe* (*mwenyewe* 'himself'), *mngiagnagnii* (*mnyang'anyi* /mɲaɲaɲi/ 'snatcher'). In his alphabet, however, Krapf assigns the value /ɲ/ to both *gn* and *ng*, but appears to use *gn* fairly consistently for /ŋ/. He gives no spelling for /ɲ/ in this alphabet (p.xiii). /l/ and /r/ are normally represented by Krapf as standard, with occasional reversal and omission as would be expected given that the distinction between *r* and *l* is basically in foreign words, and that Bantu l/r is frequently lost between vowels. So Krapf writes *bilauli* (*bilauri* 'glass'), *dariri* (*dalili* 'sign'), *fuuliza* (*-fululiza* 'be in sequence') and *chula/chua* (*chura* 'frog'). Also included in his alphabet, Krapf has *dz* which however he does not appear to use for Swahili; and *q* which is used in some Arabic loans.

In spelling these days consonants are almost never written double, though as Tucker and Ashton (1942) note (para.111) 'consonants, especially explosives, may occasionally be lengthened, in order to give special emphasis to a statement'. It is interesting to notice, therefore, that Krapf frequently writes double consonants, and not only (though often) in words with original double consonants in loan words from Arabic. Nor is the phenomenon confined to 'explosives', for example *chappa* 'print', *jeuppe* 'white', *ghubba* 'inlet', *mrabba* 'square', *-letta* 'bring', *-otte* 'all', *hattua* 'step', *matitti* 'breasts', *shadda* 'bunch', *buddi/budi* 'necessity', *akka/wakka* 'burn', *fukka vuka* 'smoke', *kuffa* 'die', *koffi* 'clap', *mkuffu* 'chain', *-passua* 'split', *fenessi* 'jack-fruit', *bussu* 'kiss', *-gussa* 'touch', *usso* 'face' and many others; *luththa* (*ladha* 'taste'), *summu* 'poison', *hammu* 'desire', *janni* 'leaf', *ujanne* 'youth', *-bunni* 'compose', *-salla* 'pray', *mballi* 'far', *milla* 'custom', *telle* 'much', *nuelle* (*nywele* 'hair'), *mwelle* 'bulrush' etc, *marra* 'time', *sirri* 'secret' *burre* 'useless', *hurru* 'free' and so on. It would be difficult to account for these spellings on grounds of stress or vowel quality, but they occasionally appear to be phonemic since Krapf suggests minimal pairs, for example *chapa* 'completely':-*chappa* 'to print'. On the other hand he sometimes gives alternative spellings, for example *batta/bata* 'duck'. On the face of it, it seems hard to account satisfactorily for this phenomenon.

Krapf (p.xv) records stress as occurring on the penultimate syllable in words of two and often three syllables, but on the antepenultimate in 'polysyllables'. As pointed out earlier, many of his examples of trisyllabic words are now pronounced as disyllables (and may have been so then but that Krapf's use of *i* and *u* for /j/ and /w/ as well as for vowels confused the issue). However with regard to the rest, and to 'polysyllables', it is interesting that in fact he was probably referring to words of Arabic origin rather than to polysyllabic Bantu words consisting of a large number of morphemes. In some cases Krapf is referring to word stems or citation forms rather than words in their actual manifestations. And where he marks stress as on syllables earlier than the penultimate, it is in Arabic loans, for example *tháhabu* (*dhahabu* 'gold'), *ku kúbali* 'to agree'. Most of these words nowadays are pronounced with penultimate stress, showing that they are becoming more assimilated into the language.

Another interesting point is that Krapf very frequently writes a noun followed by a possessive as a single word, for example *mtotowangu* 'my child', *watuwakwe* 'his people', *niumbayakwe* 'his house', *nduguzangu* 'my brothers', *mahalipenu* 'your place', *magunimuangu* (*maguuni mwangu* 'in my legs'), and even *juiyetu* (*juu yetu* 'up to us'); and on occasion marks the stress: *babayángu* 'my father'. All subsequent writers have separated these words, but it is interesting that Krapf wrote them together since a) the possessive, where present, almost invariably follows immediately after the noun, whereas the relative positions of other qualifiers are variable – see Maw 1969, p.82 – and b) where a noun is followed by a possessive the accentual place in the noun is not normally realised – see Maw and Kelly 1975, p.5.

At certain points in the language Krapf seems to waver about word division. He regularly separates an infinitive from a verb stem, for example *ku onana* (*kuonana* 'to see each other'), but occasionally puts hyphens between morphemes and sometimes writes the whole form as a single word (which is the present practice). So we get (my slashes at morpheme boundaries) p.xxviii *u/nge dumu* 'you would continue' but *u/nge/kua* 'you would be'; p.xxxiv *yu/wa fanana* 'he resembles'; p.xxxiv *ku ni fania* 'to do for me', under *-fa*: *wa/na ku fa* 'they are dying'.

The system of Bishop Edward Steere. Steere's *A Handbook of the Swahili Language* was completed in 1870 but subsequently revised by Madan. I have used the eighth edition, published in 1908. The Handbook contains an extensive vocabulary. Steere and Krapf worked independently, but each saw the other's work before publication, without, evidently, very much mutual admiration. Krapf's work, however, had been begun much earlier, and Steere's was later revised by Madan, so that it is possible to regard their works as recording the language at different points in time. Steere's vocabulary is of course much shorter than Krapf's great dictionary so that numerical comparisons are impossible; nevertheless comparative trends can be observed.

Steere's alphabet is very similar to Krapf's, but he makes some more accurate remarks. For example he says of /ʝ/ 'Sometimes more like *dy* or *di* in *cordial*'. He separates /ɲ/ and /ŋ/, writing them respectively as *ny* and *ng*'; at other times he is more cavalier in his attitude, for example '*l* and *r* are generally treated as the same letter'. He uses *th* for both /θ/ and /ð/, although recognising that they are distinct sounds, and adds 'In Swahili they may all be replaced by a *z*' (p.9), 'which', says Krapf, 'exact grammarians will scarcely admit' (p.xiv). However, Steere does in his grammar (though not in the vocabulary) write *th* in italics for /θ/. Observation and, perhaps, wishful thinking are displayed in his note (p.12) '*p*, *t*, *k*, and possibly some other letters, have occasionally an ... aspirated sound, such as an Irishman will often give them. This explosive sound makes no change in the letter, but is an addition to it, probably always marking a suppressed *n*' (i.e. Steere does not see aspiration as phonemic. It does indeed at times represent a 'suppressed n', but not only that). He goes on, 'This explosive sound ... is, however, very seldom necessary to the sense of a word, and is noticeably smoothed down or omitted by the more refined and Arabized Swahili'. He adds a nice throw-away comment: 'There are other niceties of pronunciation which a fine ear may distinguish; but as they are by no means essential, and are seldom noticed by the natives themselves, it is not worth while here to examine them particularly' (p.12).

Steere's representations of vowel phonemes show many of the same deviations as Krapf's, but in slightly different proportions. However the most noteworthy difference is that hardly any of Steere's instances occur in stressed position. Steere also, like Krapf, records forms without vowels which today have vowels added as the (mainly Arabic) words become more assimilated, for example *mashuhur* (*mashuhuri* 'famous'), *ilmu* (*elimu* 'education'), *wajib* (*wajibu* 'duty'), *fortha* (*forodha* 'customs house'), *frasi* (*farasi* 'horse'), *cherkhana* (*cherehani* 'sewing machine'). He has, conversely, more frequent examples of initial /i/, for example *illakini* (*lakini* 'but'), *imbu* (*mbu* 'mosquito'), *inchi* (*nchi* 'country'), *iriba* (*riba* 'usury'); and quite often inserts an epenthetic *u* after *m*, for example *-changamusha* (*-changamsha* 'make cheerful'), *-kakamuka* (*-kakamka* 'be firm'). Interestingly, he also on occasions writes double vowels where today we write single ones. (Krapf does this too, but usually gives an alternative form with single vowel, or else he notes that he has taken the item from Steere.) This is normally in a stressed position, preceding a nasal cluster, and applies to the vowels /o/ and /a/, for example *paango* (*pango* 'cave'), *taandu* (*tandu* 'centipede'), *saanda* (*sanda* 'shroud'), *boonde* (*bonde* 'valley'), *koonde* (*konde* 'cultivated plot'). There is no doubt that vowel lengthening occurs in this position, but if that were the reason, all vowels in this position would have been written double. Steere also gives a considerable number of alternatives in some Arabic loans, for example *harufu, harufi, herufi* (*herufi* 'letter'), *marikabu, marikebu, merikebu* (*merikebu* 'warship'), *masakini, maskini, meskini, masikini* (*maskini* 'poor'); and the cluster /ɲw/ gives difficulty: *nuele, nwele, nyele* (*nywele* 'hair'). Words now with metathesis still appear in their earlier forms, though there are less of them in Steere than in Krapf, for example *ihtaji* (*hitaji* 'need').

Considering plosives, with no German background, Steere nevertheless does several times write *b* where today we write *p*, and only once unequivocally *p* for present-day *b*. He also writes *f* occasionally, for example *-fuliza* (*-puliza* 'blow'), *-fingirika* (*-bingirika* 'roll'). He does not write *t* for *d* or vice versa; but writes once *k* for *t*: *-mekameka* (*-metameta* 'glitter'), and several times *l* for *d*, though always with *d* as alternative. He writes once *j* for *ch*: *jongoe* (*chongowe* 'kind of fish'), but never vice versa. His alternants for *j* are all dialectal variants (i.e. *g, d, y*), with one curious spelling *dj*: *Mngazidja* 'Comoro islander'. There is only one example each way of *k*:*g* alternation, namely *garafuu* (*karafuu* 'clove') and *-kutusha* (*-gutusha* 'startle').

Though Steere normally writes *w* for the semivowel, he sometimes gives *u*: *msuaki* (*mswaki* 'toothbrush'), *uayo* (*wayo* 'footprint'), *kua heri* (*kwa heri* 'goodbye'). Sometimes he omits *w*, as in *-loa* (*-lowa* 'be wet'), *mujiza* (*mwujiza* 'miracle'), always in the presence of *o* or *u*. In the same context he occasionally writes *w* where there is none today, for example *mkewo* (*mkeo* 'your wife'), *kiuwaji* (*kiuaji* 'something deadly'). More rarely than *u* for *w*, Steere gives *i* for /j/, as *fiatua* (*fyatua* 'let off'), *fieka* (*fyeka* 'cut down'); and sometimes vice versa, as *mumyani* (*mumiani* 'powdered mummy'). He says (p.288) 'It is in many cases immaterial whether *i* or *y* be written, but where the accent would otherwise fall on it, its consonantal character becomes obvious'. He does not often omit /j/, but frequently inserts it before or after *i*, for example *dayima* (*daima* 'always'), *yayi* (*yai* 'egg'), *rayia* (*raia* 'populace'), *hiyari* (*hiari* 'option').

In fricatives, Steere says (p.271) that *f* and *v* are 'confounded by the Arabs, though in Swahili perfectly distinct' and he never writes *v* for *f* but sometimes vice versa, for example *pofu* (*povu* 'foam'), *jifu* (*jivu* 'ash'); and once *b*: *boruga* (-*vuruga* 'stir'). For /ð/ he only once writes *z*, namely -*fazaa* (-*fadhaa* 'amaze'), in spite of his note on the alphabet, that 'the four Arabic letters *tha*, *thal*, *thod* and *thah* … in Swahili … may all be replaced by a *z*'. (p.9). For /s/ Steere often writes *sh*, and indeed says that (p.377) 'there are … many words in which they are used indifferently …. Many natives seem unconscious of any difference between them'. He occasionally gives *s* for /ʃ/: *msangao* (*mshangao* 'astonishment'). Indeed, considering his view that they are 'used indifferently' it is perhaps surprising how consonant his spelling is with that of today – unless it is that the spelling in the dictionaries has influenced the pronunciation, which is not *very* likely since the dictionaries are all for foreign learners, not Swahili-Swahili. Steere also writes *z* for /s/ and vice versa, for example *nanazi* (*nanasi* 'pineapple'), *zifuri* (*sifuri* 'zero'); *maandasi* (*maandazi* 'cakes'), *majonsi* (*majonzi* 'grief'). /h/ is quite often omitted, for example -*angaika* (-*hangaika* 'be undecided'), *assubui* (*asubuhi* 'morning'). Steere also gives *kh* in words of Arabic origin.

The nasals are usually given as today, with occasional loss of [n] [ŋ] for example *dimu* (*ndimu* 'lime'), *jisi* (*jinsi* 'how'), *kuguni* (*kunguni* 'bug'), *galawa* (*ngalawa* 'outrigger canoe'). /ɲ/ is also occasionally given as *n*: -*danganika* (-*danganyika* 'be cheated').

/l/ and /r/ are only occasionally inverted: -*regea* (-*legea* 'be slack'); *malidadi* (*maridadi* 'showy'). He once gives *u* for /l/: *kifaume* (*kifalme* 'royal') – possibly reflecting the form -*falume*; and once *b* for /r/: -*babuka* (-*raruka* 'be torn').

Steere writes double consonants less frequently than Krapf, and for the same letters (often in the same words – Steere had seen Krapf's dictionary in MS before he published his own, but says (p.ix) 'only 3 weeks before leaving I … was able to examine about half the Swahili-English volume … enough to enrich materially my previous collections', although Madan says (p.xix) 'Dr Krapf's great Dictionary … in its printed form, was in the Bishop's hands too short a time, to allow of his making any use of it for this Edition of the Handbook'. Steere's statement however seems to suggest that he did make use of at least some of Krapf's work.). He does also write *gg* in two words: -*agga* to which he gives the meaning of 'be lost, perish' and separates it from

-aga 'take farewell'. Sacleux gives this word (with single *g*) as dialectal. Steere also gives *daggla* (*dagla* 'short coat'). (I have not found any examples with *gg* in Krapf.) As with Krapf, by far the largest number of occurrences of double consonants in Steere are of *ss*. They seem to follow and precede any vowel, and to precede or follow stress. With Krapf one might have suspected the influence of the German spelling 'sharp' or double *s*, but of course Steere is a different matter.

Steere *sometimes* marks aspiration in his vocabulary where it is distinctive, for example *k'omba* 'galago': *-komba* 'scrape out', but by no means regularly. On stress, Steere refers to 'the universal rule in Swahili, that the main accent of the word is always put upon the last syllable but one' (p.13). In his vocabulary he does, however, occasionally mark stress elsewhere, in some Arabic loan-words. Steere's word division is as it is today.

Comparing Krapf's realisation of Swahili with that of Steere, it is interesting that although Krapf was working mainly in Mombasa and Steere in Zanzibar, their work is not more different. Krapf states (p.x) that 'the form of the book is the Bishop's, while the essence of the [Steere's] Grammar and of the Dictionary are in the main my work' and that Steere 'has utilized my materials'. Krapf says further that, with Rebmann, he once considered the dialect of Zanzibar to be 'low and vulgar' (p.xi) on the grounds that it 'has a very large infusion of Arabic and other foreign words'; and that 'for the best and most original dialect of Kisuahili itself, the people of Patta, Lamu, Malindi, Mombas and Tanga claim precurrence over the inhabitants of Zanzibar and Pemba'. In fact all these have different dialects. However Krapf softens his opinions and writes further (p.xii) 'but latterly it occurred to me that the Zanzibar dialect was not without usefulness, as it is spoken by a very large number of people along the coast, and also affords to the translator the resource of being able to adopt at will an Arabic word when in difficulty for a proper expression in Kisuahili'. Now in fact, if anything, Krapf's dictionary contains a higher proportion of Arabic loans than does Steere's vocabulary. Krapf names a large number of missionaries and others to whom he is indebted in his preface, but does not name any Swahili informants. Steere names five, one of whose language turned out to be 'too learned' for translating the Bible! No doubt this meant, in part, too Arabicised. The differences that show, between the language as described by Krapf and that by Steere, do not then seem to stem very often from a difference of dialect; and indeed so far as possible I have ignored dialectal differences such as /t/, /d/ for /ch/, /ɟ/ in Kimvita (Mombasa): Kiunguja (Zanzibar) dialects.

The system of Fr Charles Sacleux. The work of Sacleux is on a very different plane. I am here dealing with his monumental dictionary (1939), but this was preceded by his work on dialects (1909). The dictionary deals on the one hand with a number of dialects of Swahili and names the citation forms given; and on the other hand Sacleux gives a phonetic rather than a phonological representation. Thus he has an alphabet of 28 'lettres' which he says (p.25) represent 'chacune un son fondamental', but adds diacritics, each of which indicates 'une position déterminée de l'organe vocal'. Some of these diacritics in fact mark phonemic distinctions (as in the case of *ñ* for /ŋ/; others mark allophonic variants (as in the case of some vowel phonemes); others dialectal variants (e.g. dental *d*); others occur only in loan-words (e.g. *ŕ*); and still others signify idiolectal variations (e.g. *g̈:ĝ:r*). Actually his 28 'lettres' include *č* (though not *c*) and *š*, *ž* as well as *s*, *z*, also *æ*, and *ü* as well as *u*. Moreover, he does not always stick to his guns; thus, for *ṇ* he writes *ny*, on the grounds that (p.271) 'Les Swahilis ne paraissant pas fixés entre ṇ et ny', and because *ny* is 'plus pratique et généralement employée par les auteurs'.

Sacleux's list of 'lettres', then, is longer than the alphabets of Krapf or Steere; and when the diacritics are added, is considerably so. For the phoneme /i/ he gives two varieties: *i* oral (moyenne) and *ĩ* nasal (fermée). For /e/ he gives three oral varieties (ouverte, moyenne, fermée) and one nasal (ouverte). For /a/ similarly, three oral and one nasal variety (fermée). For /o/ two oral (moyenne and fermée) and one nasal (moyenne). For /u/ one oral (moyenne) and one nasal (fermée). Nasal vowels he describes as occurring, with certain qualifications, in a 'syllabe fermée avec entrave d'une consonne nasale subséquente' (p.27). While many writers would not admit of closed syllables in Swahili, Sacleux's principle would hold if one spoke of the vowel as being 'followed by' a nasal cluster. Curiously, Tucker and Ashton (1942, p.84) mention nasalisation as occurring in syllables *beginning* with a nasal consonant, and only rarely in those followed by *nz*. Is Sacleux's perception of nasalisation in (generally) more widespread contexts related to his French background? The various degrees of openness of the vowels /i/, /e/, and /o/ Sacleux does not assign to particular places in structure, nor make much attempt to do so; in contrast with Tucker and Ashton (1942, pp.79–82), who have fewer distinctions but attempt to describe distribution.

Sacleux also adds to the inventory of vowels *æ* and *ü*. These vowels he describes as 'inusitées', and gives only *one* citation for the two, namely *kõnsæl/kõnsül* ('du Fr. *Consul*'), which would hardly suffice in itself to have such a sound listed as a phoneme or, as he puts it 'son fondamental'. Without going through the entire dictionary, I have been unable to find other occurrences of these vowels; certainly no words are listed as beginning with either. I fear Gallic patriotism may have overcome prudence here.

Semivowels /w/ (*w*) and /j/ (*y*) he says somewhat tautologously 'En toute rencontre elles font fonction de consonnes' (p.29). Nevertheless, while pointing out (p.25) that there are, properly speaking, no diphthongs in Swahili, he adds that 'Tout au plus peut-on compter comme telles les combinaisons d'une semi-voyelle *w* ou *y* et d'une voyelle, par ex. *ya*, *wa*, yay (pl. mayay)' – the latter written nowadays as *yai* 'egg'. It is curious that Sacleux should have given this last form, since he points out on p.27 that stress is on the penultimate syllable (unless he marks it elsewhere) and that each vowel constitutes a syllable (p.25); nor does he mark stress in the plural form which is certainly *not* on the prefix, as it would be if *yay* constituted a single syllable. In his book on dialects (1909) (p.8) he refers to this as 'contraction de la voyelle finale'.

In the stop consonants, Sacleux notes aspiration and gives voiceless plosives $p:p'$; $k:k'$, also $č:č'$; moreover, he distinguishes dental articulation, so gives $t:t$ (dental, sic): t ('cerebral'). Among voiced stops he distinguishes *d* (alveolar): d (dental), and also writes *dy* as apposed to *dž* for the allophones [ʃ] : [ʤ] of the phoneme now written *j*. He does not give the distribution of these allophones, nor does he list either as a 'son fondamental' in his alphabet, (though he does include *ž* (ʒ) as occurring only in the group [nʤ]. e.g. *ndžia* (*njia* 'road') and in certain loan words (p.30).) He does, however, list *b:* $b̌$ (bilabial fricative), and $g:ġ$ (velar) – evidently *g* is rather forward in position. Obviously Sacleux had an acute ear, and it is therefore curious that he did not note any example of an implosive consonant, although /b/, /d/, /g/ certainly have implosive allophones, and moreover the allophone of /ʝ/ which he writes *dy* is also implosive.

For fricatives he gives $f:v$, $s:z$, $š$ ([ʃ]), also *h* and χ, and $ĝ$ ('ghaïn de l'Ar.'):$r̈$ ('grasseyé' – also for 'ghaïn') and $r̂$ 'ghaïn ... prononciation rigoureuse'. He gives, somewhat strangely, $s̩$, described as 'interdental', which might suggest /θ/, but the words he quotes certainly have present-day *s* (e.g. *s̩ura* 'face'); and $z̩$ 'interdental', which, however, is used for some instances of present /ð/, e.g. *-z̩uru* (*-dhuru* 'harm'). With reference to the distinction /θ/: /ð/, Sacleux is scathing about the use of the spelling *th* which he points out (p.3) is used for four distinct Arabic sounds, and adds sharply 'La décision récente du comité de remplacer le *th* doux par *dh* est un aveu d'erreur en même temps que d'impuissance'. He himself writes $s:z:z̩$ (interdental) which he says is 'conformément à ce que j'ai observé chez les indigènes' – a slight case of having it both ways, I would have thought, since *some* 'indigènes' (unnamed, incidentally) might well write $s:z$, but $z̩$? And even if they did, this must be special pleading, since other distinctions Sacleux makes (e.g. in vowels), they are hardly likely to have written. Again, there seems to me some French influence here.

Nasals are written *m, n, ny* (noted above) and *ñ* (velar). Continuants are noted $l:l^r$ ('intermédiaire entre l et r'):r.

Sacleux does not write double vowels where Steere does, nor does he seem to write them at all except as in the present standard form. He scarcely ever writes double consonants, and where he does, he normally gives an alternative with single consonant, for example *hatta/hata* 'even, until'. In a few cases he gives what seem like phonemic distinctions, for example *ila* 'drawback': *illa* 'except'. One wonders whether these examples might be wishful thinking. In any case, both are written *ila* today, although they came from different Arabic origins. Where he does write double consonants, these are frequently in words which are often emphasised in connected speech, for example *killa* (*kila* 'each').

On stress, apart from word stress, Sacleux (1909) notes (pp.8–9) that 'l'accent oratoire' can move about, and gives interesting examples. He also notes the absence of stress on nouns when followed by 'adjectifs numéraux, possessifs, démonstratifs et indéfinis'. All his remarks on stress seem to be in accord with Maw and Kelly 1975 (p.5), although the little he says on intonation is not easy to interpret.

Table 4 gives the symbols used by each scholar, with alternatives and distinctions. It might be supposed that, since Sacleux uses a larger number of symbols than Krapf or Steere, many of the forms they give that are not the same today would be found in Sacleux to be explainable on the grounds of finer distinctions. For example, words that have *e* in Steere or Krapf and *i* in present-day Swahili might be expected to have *close e* in Sacleux. This however does not seem to be the case. On the whole, where Sacleux's gives a single form, this is normally as today. What does happen occasionally, however, is that (especially in the case of words of Bantu origin) he gives alternative forms as belonging to different dialects. The problem is that these alternatives do not provide a coherent explanation for the variations in the earlier writers' works. Were Krapf and Steere using informants who spoke mixed dialects? This hardly seems likely except in so far as some of their material was taken from other writers (including each other). How reliable is Sacleux's material – some of which he took from other writers (though he is often critical of such material)? He does not name his Swahili informants or give details of his methods of work, although he does name other European informants. Or should we accept that by the time Sacleux was working on his dictionary the language was indeed becoming more standardised? Certainly the Arabic loan-words show less variation in Sacleux than in Krapf or Steere.

TABLE 4.

Phone	Krapf Norm	Substitution	Steere Norm	Substitution	Sacleux
p' p	p	b,f,pp	p	b,f,fy,pp	p' p
ɓ b	b	p,f,bb	b	p,f,bb	b
t' t ʈ	t	d,tt	t	k,tt	t' ṭ ṭ
ɗ d ɖ	d	dd	d	l,dd	}d ḍ

243

TABLE 4. (continued)

Phone	Krapf Norm	Substitution	Steere Norm	Substitution	Sacleux
ʧ̌ ʧ	ch	t,j	ch	t,j	č̆ č
ʃ ʝ	j	d,ch,g,y	j	d,dj,g,y,jj	dy dž
k̓ k	k	g,t,kk	k	g,kk	k̓ k
g̓ g	g	ch	g	k,j,y,gg	g
q	q				
f	f	v,ff	f	ff	f
v	v	f,w	v	f,b	v
θ	th	t	th,*th*		s
ð	th	d,thth	th	z,thth	ẓ
s	s	z,ss	s	z,sh,ss	ṣ s
z	z	s,d	z	s,d,vy,∅	z
ʃ	sh	s,ch	sh	s,ch	š
ʒ					ž
x	kh		kh		χ
ɣ	gh	h,∅	gh		ĝ r̂ ġ ṙ
h	h		h	∅	h
m	m	mm	m	mm	m
n	n	nn	n	m,∅,nn	n
ɲ	gn,ng		ny	n	ny
ŋ		gn	ng'		ṅ

TABLE 4. (continued)

Phone	Krapf Norm	Substitution	Steere Norm	Substitution	Sacleux
l	l	r,ll,∅	l	r,u,ll,∅	l
r	r	l,rr,∅	r	l,b,rr	r
					lʳ
w	u	o,w,∅	w	u,∅	w
j	i	j,∅	y	i,∅	y
i	i	e,u,∅	i	e,a,u,y,∅	i ĩ
e	e	i,a,ee,∅	e	i,a,∅	e è é ẽ
a	a	i,e,u,∅	a	i,e,u,aa,∅	a à á ã
o	o	i,a,u,∅	o	i,a,u,wa,oo,∅	o ó õ
u	u	i,e,a,o,∅	u	i,e,a,o,w,∅	u ũ
Quality unknown	dz				
Quality unknown					œ
Quality unknown					ü

Substitutions are given horizontally; distinctions vertically. No substitutions are given for Sacleux, since he mainly gives alternatives rather than single forms.

The influence of the language background of writers in and on Swahili can often be detected, beginning with the Arabs who saw no real need to add to their orthography for the sake of distinct Swahili phonemes and felt the need to retain distinctions that were necessary for distinguishing sounds in Arabic loans. Krapf's German background shows particularly in his alternation of $w/v/u/o$ for certain sounds. Sacleux's native language, French, leads him to postulate the vowels *æ* and *ü* for loan-words. On the other hand, each noted distinctions often missed by the others, which can also be traced to their own native background. For example, while Sacleux was content to write *s* for both /s/ and /θ/, and *z* for /z/ and /ð/, Steere recognised the distinctions as important although – true to his native writing tradition – he did not always distinguish /θ/ from /ð/, writing both *th*. On the other hand, Sacleux recognised dental /t/ and /d/, and also nasalised vowels. Steere recognised and sometimes symbolised aspiration with reference to the Irish (no doubt he knew many Irish missionaries), and was clear about the distinction between /ɲ/ and /ŋ/. Krapf was of course the pioneer among these three; and each took something from the others. I am not suggesting that any of these scholars had defective perception; what is interesting is what they chose to symbolise.

Of course even allowing for the fact that Krapf's work began considerably earlier than 1850 when he published his grammar, a time-span of some 150 years since he was first recording and the present day is too short to show much in the way of linguistic change, even if the provenance of the speakers and the recordists had been constant. Nevertheless it is plain that there has been a process of standardisation of the writing conventions of the language as well as refinement in the development of recording the actual sounds. There is also clear evidence of progressive stabilisation of forms of foreign words (especially Arabic) and of assimilation of foreign sounds and sequences to fit into the basically Bantu structure of the language. Whether the suggested slight evidence of vowel shifting, principally $e > i$ and $o > u$; and that of devoicing of plosives contrasted with voicing of fricatives, has any real meaning, I think only time can tell.

References

ALI, MOHAMED (1970) *Ulinganifu Wa Maendelezo Ya Kiswahili.* Mimeographed.

ALLEN, J.W.T. (1945) *Arabic Script for Students of Swahili,* (Editorial Committee Tanganyika Notes and Records).

BEECH, MERVYN W.H. (1918) *Aids to the Study of Ki-Swahili,* London (Kegan Paul, Trench, Trübner & Co. Ltd.).

BURT, F. (1917) *Swahili Grammar and Vocabulary,* London (Society for Promoting Christian Knowledge).

HARRIES, LYNDON (undated) *The Swahili-Arabic Script.* Mimeographed.

INTERNATIONAL INSTITUTE OF AFRICAN LANGUAGES AND CULTURES (1930) *Practical Orthography of African Languages,* London (Oxford University Press).

JOHNSON, F. (1939) *A Standard Swahili-English Dictionary,* London (Oxford University Press).

KRAPF, L. (1882) *A Dictionary of the Suahili Language,* London (Trübner and Co.).

MADAN, A.C. (1903) *Swahili-English Dictionary*, Oxford (Clarendon Press).

MAW, JOAN (1969) *Sentences in Swahili*, London (School of Oriental and African Studies, University of London).

MAW, JOAN and KELLY, JOHN (1975) *Intonation in Swahili*, London (School of Oriental and African Studies, University of London).

MEINHOF, CARL (1910) *Die Sprache der Suaheli in Deutsch-Ostafrika*, Berlin (Dietrich Reimer (Ernst Vohsen)).

SACLEUX, LE P.CH. (1909) *Grammaire des dialectes swahilis*, Paris (Procure des PP. du Saint-Esprit).

SACLEUX, CH. (1939) *Dictionnaire swahili-français*, Paris (Institut d'Ethnologie).

STEERE, EDWARD (1908) *A Handbook of the Swahili Language*, London (Society for Promoting Christian Knowledge).

TUCKER, A.N. and ASHTON, E.B. (1942) 'Swahili Phonetics', *African Studies* I, nos. 2 & 3.

VELTEN, C. (1901) *Erlernung der Schrift der Suaheli*, Göttingen (Bandenhoed & Ruprecht).

WHITELEY, WILFRED (1969) *Swahili: the Rise of a National Language*, London (Methuen & Co. Ltd.).

The 1847 Alphabet:
an Episode of Phonotypy

The word *Phonotypy* was coined in the early 1840s by Isaac Pitman. It is not a name for any particular alphabet, but rather for a principle. The principle says that a language should be printed with a set of letters which, in number, and, where practicable, in shape, have a direct relationship with the sound-system of that language. It is a frequent comment that the writing-systems of both English and French are clumsy, and they certainly do not accord with the phonotypic principle. Each language has a system of sounds numbering more than twenty-six, the number of letters provided by the Roman alphabet as now in use. To construct a new alphabet on a phonotypic basis for English, as Pitman wanted to do, extra letters have to be designed and cut.

Pitman himself put forward a number of phonotypic alphabets, and we shall look at some of these. But any alphabet made in accordance with the above principle is phonotypic: the Shaw alphabet, designed by Mr Kingsley Read, and first put before the public in book form in 1962, is a phonotypic alphabet. The book, appropriately, carries a dedication to Isaac Pitman's grandson.

Before looking in some detail at Pitman's work in phonotypy I should like to consider what it was that preceded his decision to attempt a reform of the English writing-system. Pitman's shorthand was first published in 1837. He entitled his booklet *Stenographic Soundhand*, but was soon to adopt the name *Phonography*, by which the system was to be known for many years. The idea of basing a shorthand system on the sounds of the language rather than on the traditional spelling, although not a totally new one, was novel and effective enough to bring about the success of the system. Pitman's originality lay in his combining what he knew of the sound-system of English with what he knew of shorthand. He had used Taylor's shorthand (Taylor 1786) for some years and had made a close study of John Walker's *Critical Pronouncing Dictionary* (Walker 1791). The influence of both can be clearly seen in phonography. Writing in April 1843, Pitman (1843a, p.43) says:

> The basis of this phonetic exposition of universal speech will be found in Walker's 'Principles of English Pronunciation', prefixed to his 'Critical Pronouncing Dictionary', a work which every Phonographer ought to possess; and the foundation of the characters for writing may be traced in Taylor's 'Stenography'.

Some of his characters are in fact identical with Taylor's, and an overall geometric style is common to both systems.

In Walker, the main concern is with the interpretation of the writing-system, and it is the relationship between this and the sound-system that Walker attends to most. His analysis of the sound-system itself is incomplete and, at times, muddled; but most of it finds its way into the earliest versions of Pitman's phonography. Walker deals with the vowels in alphabetical order, and his exposition of the long vowels can be interpreted to give a picture of gradual closing from the vowel of *ball*, through those of *father* and *lane* to the first vowel of *equal*: the vowels of *open* and *coo* are recognised as more rounded and fronter than the vowel of *water*. In Pitman the six key words are *see, say, mar, all, no, do*. Of these the first requires the least opening of the mouth, the second has a 'wider opening': the *no* vowel is made by 'contracting the sides of the mouth a little' and the *do* vowel by 'bringing the organs into a round shape'. The phonographic signs give a dot to the first three vowels, a short stroke to the last three. Pitman seems not to have had a clear appreciation in his 1837 booklet of the back-front and close-open dimensions as separate, and seems, like Walker, to have regarded his six vowels as being arranged along a single conflated continuum with rounding, backness and openness at one end and closeness at the other. This treatment is reminiscent of others in earlier times; Pitman might be said to be here at the end of a long tradition of imprecision in vowel description.

The vowels discussed above are all long. Pitman treats the short vowels as related to the long ones, just as Walker does. It is not always easy to know which short vowel Walker pairs with which long one, and the pairings are sometimes one-to-two rather than one-to-one. Pitman admits to having tried several possibilities before producing his final scheme in which the vowels are paired as: *tea tin*; *pay pet*; *father fat*; *daw dot*; *show shut*; *coo could*. This departs from Walker's scheme notably in that it couples *tea* and *tin*, whereas Walker couples *me* and *met*, *pine* and *pin*. Pitman's consonantal analysis follows Walker.

The system had considerable success and in the ten years following its first publication eight editions appeared (Pitman 1840–7). Each incorporated innovations or modifications of earlier practice, but these details need not concern us here. The importance of phonography for the study of phonotypy lies in the fact that Pitman came to see phonography as merely the first stage of a larger campaign having as its object the replacement of the traditional writing-system by a more rational system, related in its phonetic basis to the phonographic system.

His desire to reform the printed orthography sprang from his experiences as a schoolmaster, and from a deep interest in, and concern for, all matters of social and educational progress. One of the early developments in phonography was the establishment of a country-wide network of persons prepared to work for the propagation of the art: this association was called the Phonographic Corresponding Society. Pitman and his immediate circle

worked energetically with and through these groups, lecturing and address-
ing meetings in numerous towns and villages. When the Phonetic Reform, as
it came to be called, took up the additional task of reforming the traditional
printed medium of English, the existence of these groups provided a ready
channel for publicising this new undertaking. At a meeting held in
Nottingham in June 1843 Isaac Pitman addressed an audience for the first
time on the subject of phonetic printing: and in the following month a
gathering in Birmingham heard him speak again on the same topic. On this
second occasion a practical proposal was put forward for the funding of a
new printing alphabet.

Pitman (1842) had by this time produced a number of experimental
alphabets (figure 1) and printed them in the *Phonographic Journal*, which he
edited and published from his headquarters in Bath. In the earliest stages he
kept closely to the principle that there should be a direct link between the two
branches of the Reform, by designing an alphabet which not only used the
same analysis as the phonographic system but also to a large extent reproduced the phonographic characters, slightly modified for printing. This first
alphabet of August 1842 incorporates *r*- and *l*-hooks, for instance, though it
departs from phonography in the *k*-series. It also uses the ingenious device of
the same character for different consonant clusters, depending on whether
they are syllable initial or final, thus exploiting facts of English consonant
distribution. The second phonotypic alphabet of October of the same year is
Romanic in inspiration; but here too a clear relationship with phonography
can be seen in the shapes for *m* and *n*, and in the use, for the simple vowels, of
dots variously placed with respect to a vertical stroke.

The following month brings four more alphabets, and here again the
vowel letters reflect the influence of phonography throughout, the consonants sporadically. These Romanic alphabets all include characters for *kh*
and *gh*, as Pitman wanted both his phonographic and phonotypic systems to
be available for all languages. During the course of these experiments he
became convinced that it was impracticable to use for phonotypy a system
based on the shapes of the phonographic characters, and also that any non-
Romanic system would be unsuitable; Phonotypic Alphabet no.8, of
September 1843, abandons the earlier type of vowel notation in favour of a
more Romanic one. The alphabets nos.3 to 7 have seven basic vowel letters
instead of six, and no.8 (figure 2) introduces letters for French and German
vowels. No.9 is non-Romanic and based very closely on the phonographic
characters, though this time without using any of the cluster conventions of
that system. No.10, of October 1843, is again Romanic, and is an adaptation
of no.8: it introduces a long series of further experiments leading to a conclusion some three years later. The no.8 alphabet is the subject of a long
commentary in which Pitman discusses some of the problems that arise in
devising a satisfactory alphabet for English. As might be expected, the various
possible ways of grouping and representing the vowels presented the most

VOWELS.				
No	3	4	5	6
e	i i	ſ ٩	ī ī	٩ ٢
a	i i	ɒ ᑯ	ī ī	ᑯ ᑯ
ah	i i	ᑕ ᑐ	ī ī	ᑯ ᒧ
au	ī ī	ſ ١	ī ī	P Γ
o	ɟ ɟ	ʮ ʜ	ī ī	ɒ ʜ
oo	I !	ʟ ᒐ	ī ī	ᕹ ᒪ
uh	ᣔ ᣕ	ᣔ ᣕ	ᣔ ᣕ	ᣔ ᣕ

CONSONANTS.				
No	3	4	5	6
P	P	ᑫ	P	ᑕ
B	ᑲ	P	B	Ð
T	I	Œ	T	ꓶ
D	ᵼ	D	D	Γ
CH	J	ꓨ	C	ꓔ
J	Ŧ	F	J	F
K	Γ	ᒧ	K	ꓘ
G	F	ᒪ	G	K
F	ᑦ	ꓒ	F	ꓛ
V	ᴇ	ʰ	V	ᑐ
TH	T	ꓴ	θ	ꓱ
TH	ꓕ	ᑕ	θ	ꓱ
S	ᑐ	ꓱ	ꓢ	ᑫ
Z	ꓴ	ᶘ	Z	ꓢ
SH	ꓢ	ꓱ	ꓘ	ꓘ
ZH	ꓢ	ᶋ	ꓘ	ꓘ
KH	ꓴ	ꓒ	ᒩ	ꓛ
GH	ᒪ	ᒪ	ꓪ	ᴇ
L	L	J	L	J
R	ᶠ	ᒻ	ꓤ	ᒻ
M	ꓵ	ꓵ	M	ꓵ
N	U	U	ꓠ	U
NG	ꓴ	ꓴ	ꓘ	ꓘ
H	H	H	ꓧ	H

c)

a)

No 7

Vowels ٩٢ ᑯᑯ ᒧᒧ Pſ ɒʜ ᕹᒪ ᣔᣕ

Mutes ᑕ Ð ꓶ Γ ꓱ Ꝺ Ꝺ

Semivocals ᑐ ᑕ ꓱ ꓱ ꓢ ꓢ Z ꓢ ꓠ U

Liquids △ V   Nasals Ω U X   Aspirate H

d)

FIGURE 1. Phonotypic alphabets:
a) no.1,   b) no.2,   c) nos.3–6,   d) no.7.

251

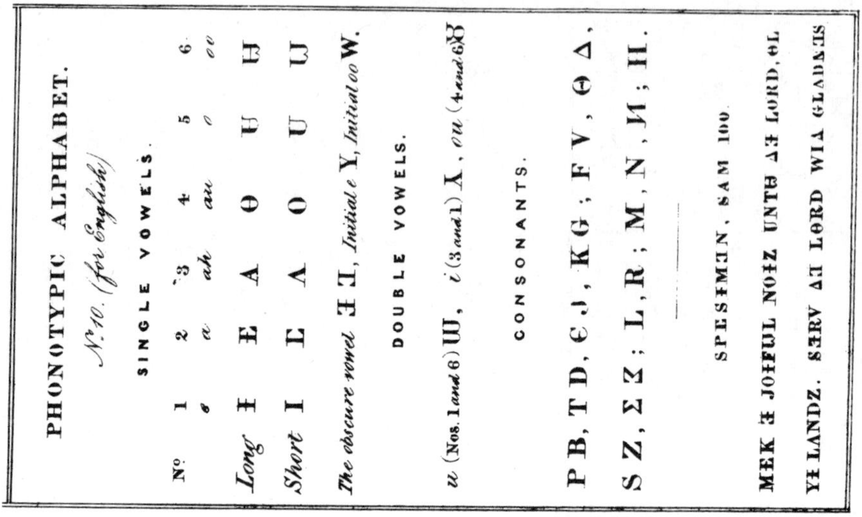

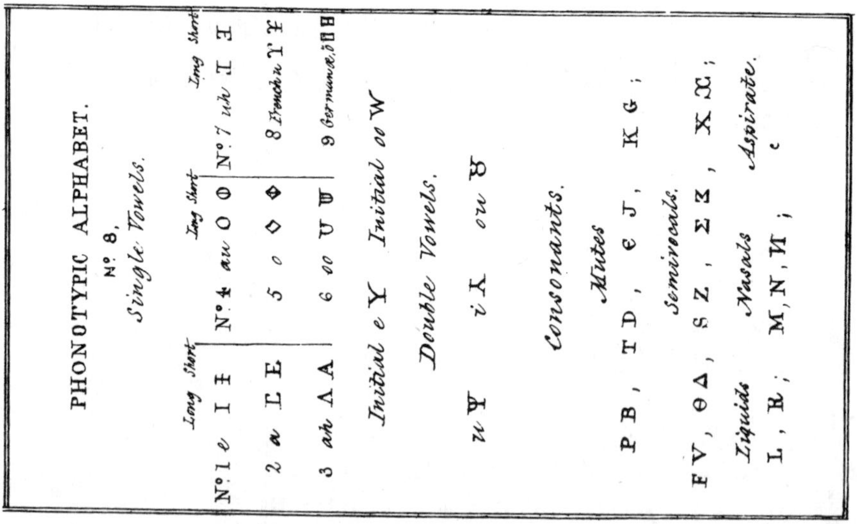

FIGURE 2. Phonotypic alphabets nos.8 and 10.

serious difficulty, and we shall examine these presently. In his commentary Pitman (1843b, p.133) also affirms his belief in an alphabet as close to the Romanic as possible:

> The progress made in Phonetic Printing with the present alphabet, will be so much positive advancement in the cause of truth, equally as though it were accomplished by means of a new alphabet; and the possibility is, that we shall progress far more by using the old letters, than we should by adopting new ones.

At about the time that Pitman wrote this he received a letter from a correspondent enclosing a paper on 'A Phonotypic Alphabet' and telling him of the writer's own work in 'the phonetical analysis of languages'. The writer was Alexander John Ellis.

Ellis, who was eighteen months younger than Pitman, was living at this time in Dorking, where he devoted himself to private researches into a number of subjects. The two men came to their interest in matters of language by different routes. Ellis's university training was in mathematics, but the versatility of his mind, and the leisure that a private fortune bestowed on him, allowed him to develop to the full his polymath sensibility. His interest in the spelling reform question came from two sources, as he himself later explained. One of these was a reading of a tract by R.G. Latham on the subject: this work was almost certainly Latham's *Address to the Authors of England and America on the Necessity and Practicability of Permanently Remodelling their Alphabet and Orthography* of 1834. The second impetus was provided by Ellis's travels in Italy which formed part of a continental tour undertaken after his university studies. Whilst there, he made a number of observations on the dialects of the various parts of Italy that he visited, and thought of devising a notational system which would reflect and unify their range of phonetic variation. Once back in England, he undertook a series of experiments in the design of phonetic systems for general use and for English, although this task was of a dilettante nature and did not at that time belong to the core of his interests. His serious involvement in spelling reform came as a result of the contact with Pitman, a contact brought about through Ellis's reading a notice of the Birmingham meeting mentioned above. He immediately took up the study of phonography, which he mastered in a few weeks, and introduced himself by letter to Pitman. Within the first two months of their correspondence Ellis sent Pitman several alphabets of his own making and a number of papers for inclusion in one or other of the journals that served as organs of the reform, and their acquaintance deepened into a working partnership in the development of phonotypy. The roles taken by the two men in this partnership were rather different. Whereas Pitman was, and had for some time been, involved in the arduous daily business of editing and to a large extent writing his several periodical publications on phonography and phonotypy, in travelling and lecturing, Ellis had leisure to read widely and to devote time to more theoretical aspects of the matter. His wider and more sophisticated training, as well as his knowledge of several European languages, fitted him to take over the role of adviser and consultant, a role he was ready to fill. But he shared the view that Pitman had also come to: that a Romanic base was desirable for the types of alphabet they were working towards. Ellis, in fact, at first preferred alphabets that used the full range of existing founts and sorts together with such devices as turning, rather than those which supplemented the Roman alphabet with new sorts. His own early experiments were of this kind, and he returned in later years to this palaeotypic principle. In matters of principle, then, the two men had already a lot in common, despite their disparate backgrounds and range of experience. During the years from 1843 onwards, Ellis studied tirelessly whatever he could find on the subject of phonetics and writing-systems. He was, of course, self-taught in the subject and, particularly in the early days, tended to look to other authorities for instruction.

The work done jointly by the two started in the late summer of 1843, and culminated in the publication of the so-called '1847 Alphabet' (Pitman 1847). From 1847 onwards their work diverged. On their way towards the 1847 alphabet a great deal of the effort was concentrated on establishing a satisfactory vowel notation. We have seen that Pitman had already carried out the more radical of the experiments before his acquaintanceship with Ellis began. The further development of his Phonotypic alphabet no.10 was the centre of their collaboration. This prototype underwent a bewildering number of changes. The reasons for the changes that were made were of different kinds. Sometimes they were aesthetic reasons. Ellis, for instance, particularly disliked the letters proposed for the seventh vowel in alphabets 3 to 6, and in a letter of 10 August 1843 proposes an uppercase OE digraph to replace them on the grounds that the French vowel he would show in this way is similar in sound. Elsewhere, similarity of letter-shapes led to a modification in the interests of printer and reader. The letter used for the first of the 'double vowels' in Phonotypic alphabet no.8 was suggested by Ellis, to replace a version without the central arm because this original proposal was 'too like Y'. In other cases more theoretical considerations were involved. The differences in the vowel analysis that were most prominent had to do with the labelling of the quantitative vowel classes themselves, the pairing of the vowels, and the status of the so-called neutral vowel. We shall look at each of these.

During the years that led up to the 1847 alphabet both Pitman and Ellis, and particularly Ellis, used a number of names to talk about the 'quantitative' classes of English vowels. The terms *long* and *short* are used by Walker, though he is clear that more than just a difference in duration is involved. Talking about quantity and syllabication he says (Walker 1791, p.71):

> Now the difference between a long and an open vowel is merely the
> greater duration of the former, while the difference between a long

and a short vowel is often an essential difference of sound.

Pitman takes over the terms *long* and *short* in *Stenographic Sound-hand* (Pitman 1837, p.336), and they reappear in the set of phonotypic alphabets that we have looked at. Ellis, even in his earliest communications with Pitman, uses a number of pairs of terms, without always explaining his shift from one to another. His own set of five experimental phonotypic alphabets of September 1843 uses the terms *long* and *short* throughout: but only a few weeks later, in a 'General Phonetical Alphabet' (Ellis 1843) designed for a number of languages, he uses *perfect* and *imperfect* for the same classes. English *feet, mate, father* and *bawl* are *perfect*, as against *fit, met, fat* and *pond*, which are *imperfect*. Even earlier than this Ellis had used the label *long or independent* in a projected phonotypic alphabet that was never printed, and by January 1844 he is taking Pitman to task for using *long* and *short*, and proposes the terms *full* and *stopped* as being more appropriate (Ellis 1844a):

> I now propose full and stopped as accurately indicating the relations of these vowels to each other. I will for the present adopt these names. Long and short should only refer to the time employed in uttering the sounds.

This change is incorporated into Phonotypic alphabet no.12 of April 1844 (Pitman 1844b, p.98).

All of these switches of terminology arise from the attempt to view the English vowel system as made up of a number of pairs of vowels, each pair related in the same way. It is the nature and naming of the relationship that is at issue. All of Ellis's terms and the notions they embody are taken from earlier writers, though Ellis is less than frank in not telling Pitman this. He was at this time immersing himself in the available phonetic literature and getting up a good deal of what Sweet was later to call 'paper phonetics'. Small wonder, perhaps, that his approach to vowel classification underwent such a rapid series of changes. By the time that he came to write his *Essentials of Phonetics* (Ellis 1848a), Ellis had established himself securely as a leader in the field of phonetic research, and felt able to acknowledge his debts in an appendix to the book. One of those to whom he expresses a particular indebtedness is R.G. Latham, whose use of the terms *dependent* and *independent* predates Ellis's. In his *Handbook of the English Language*, the first edition of which appeared in 1841, Latham (1851) has this to say:

> In *fat* the vowel is, according to common parlance, short; in *fate* it is *long*. Here we have the substitution of two fresh terms. For the words *long* and *short*, I substitute, *independent* and *dependent*.

Latham's reason for doing this is illustrated in a further comment on the word *fat*:

> If from this I remove the consonant following, and so leave the *a* at the end of a syllable, instead of in the middle, I must do one of two things. I must sound it either as the *a* of *fate*, or else as the *a* of *father*. Its so-called short sound it cannot retain unless it be supported by a

consonant following. For this reason it is dependent.

It is clear from Latham's remark here that his approach to phonetics is at least in part as a method of interpreting the orthography, since the process of 'removing' the *t* of *fat* is one that can only be envisaged in that way. Also, the 'it' that cannot retain its short sound is the letter *a*, or, perhaps more accurately, some more abstract unit mediated through both the written and the spoken systems. We are concerned here, as in Walker, with the 'powers' of 'letters' (Abercrombie 1949).

The terms *perfect* and *imperfect*, used fleetingly by Ellis, were taken in all probability from Samuel Lee's *Grammar of the Hebrew Language* (Lee 1827, p.14):

> By perfect vowels ... is meant, vowels which, being preceded by a consonant, will constitute a complete syllable in Hebrew orthography. By imperfect vowels is meant, those vowels which are not generally found to constitute syllables without either the addition of another consonant, or of an accent.

Here it is the structure and interpretation of Hebrew orthography which is explicitly under discussion.

In the matter of vowel classification Ellis came down finally in favour of a set of terms which have their origin in early German writing on phonetics and orthography. Ellis, who had a keen admiration for German work in the subject, and who had, like Latham, studied in Germany, chose to see as the 'apologist of phonotypy' not an English writer, but the German poet and essayist Klopstock. Klopstock's works include several pieces on matters of grammar, prosody, orthography and style, and he is credited with the introduction of the terms Umlaut and Ablaut. He devised a modified German orthography and wrote some of his essays on linguistic subjects in it. His *Über die Deutsche Rechtschreibung* contains a brief classification of German long syllables into three types, open, prolonged and truncated (the German terms are *offen*, *gedehnt* and *abgebrochen*). The three types are illustrated, in the *ö*-series, by *Röhre*, *schön* and *gönnte* (Klopstock 1779, p.329). The first type ends the syllable, the second and third types are followed by consonants in the same syllable. Klopstock's analysis aims at replacing with a consistent representation the quantities represented indifferently in the traditional orthography by vowel doubling or post-vocalic -*h*-. The German words *Strahl* and *Saal*, both *gedehnt*, should, in his view, both be written in such a way as to show that they are both the same kind of syllable. The terms Klopstock uses refer to syllable types rather than to classes of vowels, it should be noted.

Ellis's introduction of a threefold vowel classification, similar to that used by Klopstock, has something to do with his views of the nature of the syllable and of syllabication. Like Latham, he held that a syllable-final consonant is a modification of the preceding vowel, and that syllables ending in consonants therefore contain quite different kinds of vowels to those with no final consonant, and this more especially when a vowel can only appear in a closed syllable. Ellis devoted some thought to the way in which syllable division might be shown in phonotypy. One solution was, he suggested, the use of the hyphen, and he put this forward in a paper published early in 1844 (Ellis 1844b). By the time that this had appeared in print, though, the possibility of using the nature of the vowel sounds themselves had occurred to him, derived, as we have seen, from his reading of Klopstock and Latham. This device had the advantage of allowing syllable boundaries and phonetic facts about the vowels themselves to be implied both in the same letter.

Full vowels fall into two sub-classes, long and short, where the duration of the sounds is all that is taken into account: *caught* and *August* both contain full vowels, the first long, the second short. The corresponding stopped vowel is in *cot*. Ellis's full table for these sounds as given in his *Alphabet of Nature* (Ellis 1844c) includes Polish, French, German and Italian examples as well as English ones. The English examples are:

Full		Stopped
Long	Short	Short
neat	*signify* (second vowel)	*knit*
date	*Sunday*	*debt*
psalm		*Sam*
caught	*August*	*cot*
cur	*knocker*	*curry*
bone	*limbo*	
fool		*full*

Each category is differently symbolised in the *Alphabet of Nature* presentation, the symbols for the first row being ī, i and ĭ. Ellis's attempt to extend the distinctions to all languages is an unfortunate one. The stopped vowel, he holds, cannot be separated from its consonant in pronunciation without a simultaneous change in quality. This is a viable observation from the point of view of English, but it is not a genuinely general phonetic observation. He saw that the quality of *cot* was not the same as that of *caught*, and regarded the real stopped equivalent of *caught* to be the vowel of French *bonne*. By attempting to bring together general phonetic categories of duration and quality with statements relevant only to the distributional properties obtaining in syllable patterns in various languages Ellis shows a tendency to conflate what we should now call phonetic and phonological considerations. He does this frequently at this early stage in his phonetic career. In a paper of 1844 (Ellis 1844b), for instance, he gives a table of possible consonant combinations, and in one and the same table combines both the possible combinations of English with those consonant combinations which he found himself able to produce in initial and final positions. Whilst the terms *full* and *stopped* can be appreciated in relation to the facts of English phonetics and phonology (and they are certainly no worse than the traditional *long* and *short*) they make very little sense for Polish, though Ellis, on the basis of a very imperfect acquaintance with the language, gives the Polish words *poddymać*, *pomocy* and *Towarzystwo* as examples of *full long*, *full short*, and *stopped*, *y*.

The inclusion of the distinction in the phonotypic representation of English would have led to what came to be called a tri-typic system. 'A three-type scheme would be perfection of theory but I think it would tend to confuse many' Ellis writes to Pitman on 19 January 1845. Neither was so committed to phonetic accuracy as to make a total sacrifice of practicability at this altar. Pitman had earlier, as we have seen, withdrawn from too idealistic a position in his first phonotypic essays, and in the matter of the tri-typic system both researchers saw that to include letters for all the three classes in their alphabets would be uneconomical and inelegant. Any practical alphabet would work perfectly well with two. This decided, the question arises of which two. Should *full long*, *full short* and *stopped* be grouped as 1 – 2 3 or as 1 2 – 3. The admirable answer, typical of their energetic and open approach, was to try both. The first arrangement was the 1 2 – 3 one, as in Phonotypic alphabet no.12. This arrangement held until January 1846, when it gave way to its alternative. It was therefore the arrangement embodied in the alphabet prevailing in June 1845 when the 'Completion of the phonotypic alphabet' was announced (Pitman 1845). This was a premature announcement, for the version of June 1845 was to be superseded. Indeed it had itself supplanted an alphabet completed in September 1844 which had been presented as definitive. The difference between the two schemes lay not in the actual shapes of the letters used, since these were to a large extent common to both; rather in the use of the letters, and that particularly in unaccented syllables. In the case of a 1 – 2 3 alphabet, the vowels in the second syllable of *signify*, the last two vowels of *asperity*, the second vowel of *cavities*, and of *physical* and the first and third vowels of *phenomena* are all printed identically with the vowel of *feet*, whilst the third vowel of *cavities* and the first of *physical* are printed with the vowel of *fit*, which also appears in words such as *it* and *is*. In the later 1 2 – 3 alphabet, the last two syllables of *complexity* and all but the third of *difficulty* have the same letter as *fit*. The second of the two schemes was, in Ellis's own words, 'the most natural', as well as being nearer to the traditional orthography in that the *fit* letter, which is the traditional Roman one, now appears more often in a page of print. That this should be seen as an advantage is an indication of the way in which the attitudes of the workers changed through the years. They became ever more convinced as time passed of the need to abandon theoretical guidelines and phonetic accuracy in favour of a more empiric approach. The advantages that were to be had from a close resemblance to the existing orthography were progressively given more weight.

Ellis's reinterpretation of the English vowel system in non-quantitative terms was urged by him on Pitman, and the *full* / *stopped* distinction came to make up an important part of the phonotypic alphabets from 1844 onwards. It made its way into phonography also: the seventh edition, of 1845, lists the vowels under these labels, which replace long and short. This innovation was though, on the whole, largely theoretical. Ellis continued to take this three-fold division as the basis of his vowel treatment for some time. In 1848 the names have changed, and the *Teacher's Guide to the Child's Phonetic Primer* of that year treats of *long, brief* and *stopped* vowels. The alphabet in question is the 1847 alphabet, and Ellis (1848, p.5) points out: 'The reader will observe that we have only *two* distinct sets of signs for the vowels, long and stopped.' Ellis later discarded these distinctions.

This innovation of Ellis's is closely linked with a second problem that presented itself to the designers of the early phonetic printing alphabets. We have seen that Walker, and Pitman in his turn, saw the English vowel system as containing a number of pairs of vowels. Once the question of how the relationship between the members of the pairs should be treated has been resolved, the question remains of what the pairs are. Given Pitman's early belief that new letters should show their affiliations in their shape it is of great importance to have the pairs correctly and securely established. Several changes took place as the various editions of the alphabet came out, and Ellis admitted that the pairing of the English vowels was open to some discussion. He changed the pairing of the vowels of *note* and *nut*, which had made its first appearance in the early editions of phonography, replacing it with a relationship between *nut* and *bird*. The phonetic facts were abandoned in favour of the systemic facts of English in the last major change made, in August of 1846. In this the letter for *feet*, which in all variants of the alphabet had been based on Roman *i*, was replaced by a letter based on *e*: at the same time the vowel of *age* was represented by a letter based on *a* rather than, as in earlier stages, on *e*. This had the effect of severing the visual relationship between *feet* and *fit* and establishing it instead between *meet* and *met* and between, to use Pitman's own example, *table* and *tabular*. Ellis pointed out, writing of this change, that 'the etymological relations of the English vowel sounds ... run directly counter to their phonetical relations'. In this final revision the symbolisation which made patent the *long/short* relationship was rejected in favour of one which showed derivational relationships and which accords more closely with the orthography already in use. This is another move away from earlier considerations which had imposed various theoretical requirements on the new script. It is interesting to see Pitman and Ellis rejecting at the eleventh hour a system rather like a modern qualitative phonemic transcription in favour of one that is close to the traditional orthography.

In the matter of the neutral vowel the story is again one of gradual accommodation to the best practical expedient. The central vowel area presented problems from the first. In the earliest of Pitman's alphabets no provision is made at all for these vowels: the six-vowel scheme of Alphabet no.2, for instance, has nothing for schwa or for what is often regarded as its 'long' congener, the vowel of *bird*. These are first introduced in the third alphabet. In his commentary to Alphabet no.8 Pitman remarks that individual preferences might be respected with regard to what vowel is written in words such as *father, tradesman, honour*, and in a later note of November 1843 he suggests that although the sort should be available it should be used sparingly if at all (Pitman 1843c):

> It is considered not only unnecessary, but highly inexpedient, to represent this short obscure vowel in ordinary phonetic printing, as it would change the appearance of words, without sufficient reason, and encourage a slovenly method of pronouncing them. The same may be observed of the long obscure vowel.

By January of 1844 (Pitman 1844a) the Phonographic Corresponding Society had come to the decision that the sorts put forward by Pitman, both based on *E* (only upper case phonetic printing was practised until October 1844) were inappropriate. The new proposal was for the long vowel to be shown by a variant of *U*, thus dissociating it from the short. Ellis at the same time proposed that the names *neutral* and *indistinct* should be given to schwa and the vowel of *bird* respectively, to emphasise their difference which he saw as a difference of function more than of phonetic quality. Much later, in June 1846, an experiment was tried for a brief period in which a letter based on *r* was used as a syllabic: the words *person, manners, character* are written with this letter in the first syllable in the first case, in the final syllable in the last two cases. Pitman records that this experiment 'although based on a true theory, altogether failed in practice', and it was followed by a second experiment with a symbol based on *u*, but so like *u* that it was judged not to be 'of any practical value'. The final decision was to have no special symbol for this vowel but to use the vowels already available, in conjunction with *r* in *r*-final syllables. This is seen in practice in the sample of 1847 phonotypy in figure 3. The adoption of this device accords with the principle that phonotypic representations should be based on careful and deliberate pronunciations such as might be used in the production of words in isolation, a principle that was eventually adopted after various attempts to 'exhibit the common colloquial pronunciation, with all its indistinctness'.

The experiments with the central vowels were amongst the last, and their outcome shows again the willingness of the designers to place considerations of practicality, simplicity and orthodoxy before the more elusive and abstract considerations of phonetic 'truth'. Throughout the long and complex course of their experimentation the two scholars came to a realisation of the real principle that underlies the making of writing systems, a principle that has been well expressed by Abercrombie (1937, p.691): 'When constructing any system of visual symbolisation of speech, convenience must in the long run be the only guide, and practice, not abstract logical principles, the only valid test'. The 1847 alphabet, once established, served as the basis for a further

ĐƐ

FΩNΩTIPIC JURNAL:

PUBLIΣT AT ĐƐ

FΩNETIC INSTITŲΣUN, 5, NELSUN PLAS, BAŦ.

[Nr. 62. FEBRƜERI, 1847. Vol. 6.]

ĐƐ INTRODUCΣUN OV PRINTIŊ, AND ĐƐ SPELIŊ RƐFORM.

Bɛfωr đɛ invenʃun ov đɛ inestimabl art ov Printiŋ, mancɨnd war suŋc in đɛ grωsest ignωrans, and oprest undur đɛ most abject despotizm ov tirani. Đɛ clurji, hɯ bɛfωr đis ɛra held đɛ cɛ ov ɵl đɛ lurniŋ in Ųrup, war đemselvz ignωrant, đo prɤd, prɛzumtųus, arωgant, and artfɯl. Đar dɛvɨsiz war sɯn dɛtected trɯ đɛ invenʃun ov Tɨpografi. Az it ma natųrali bɛ imajind, meni ov đem, az wel az đɛ brɛf men, or rɨturz, hɯ livd bɨ đar manųscripts for đɛ laiti, war veri avurs tɯ đɛ prωgres ov đis invenʃun. Đa went so far az tɯ atribųt it tɯ đɛ instigaʃun ov đɛ devl; and sum ov đem wornd đar hɛrurz agenst ųziŋ suç dɨabolical bɯcs az war ritn wiđ đɛ blud ov đɛ victimz hɯ dɛvoted đemselvz tɯ hel for đɛ profit or fam ov instructiŋ uđurz.

Printiŋ, đarfωr, from its comensment, haz ɵlwaz had sum oponents, actųated bɨ selfiʃ inturests, hɯ in meni casiz pωzest suç influens ωvur đar felω men, az tɯ corupt đar jujments and dɛsiʒunz hwenevur đɛ cwestiun ov its advantejiz or disadvantejiz tɯ mancɨnd cam tɯ bɛ ajitated. Đɛ muŋcs in particųlur war its inveturet opωzurz; đɛ grat majoriti ov đem actiŋ upon đɛ spirit ov an avɤal mad bɨ đɛ Vicur ov Crơdn, in a surmun prɛçt bɨ him at Sant Pɵlz Cros, hwen hɛ dɛclard, "Wɛ must rɯt ɤt printiŋ, or printiŋ wil rɯt ɤt us." Hapili đis supɛriur art wiđstɯd đar hostiliti, and it bɛcam đɛ man enjin bɨ hwiç đar artifisiz, invented tɯ cɛp đɛ pɛpl in supurstiʃun and ignωrans, war dɛtected and puniʃt.

Đɛ prezent projected Rɛform ov ɤr Speliŋ, haz had its fɯl ʃar ov opoziʃun and rɛproç sins đɛ publicaʃun, in 1837, ov đɛ furst ɛdiʃun ov đɛ sistem ov Fonetic Σort-hand hwiç gav rɨz tɯ đɛ Printiŋ Rɛform. Đɛ Pres iz nɤ cumiŋ up tɯ ɤr help, and ? hɯ iz hɛ đat wil dar loŋgur tɯ gansa, and tɯ mutur, az đɛ oracl ov a lɨiŋ spirit, đat a sistem ov Erur hwiç van-glωriusli bosts ov an anticwiti ov but a fų sentųriz, wil prɯv stroŋgur đan Trɯŧ arad in đɛ omnipotens ov an ɛturniti tɯ cum.

THE ENGLISH PHONOTYPIC ALPHABET.

VOWELS.

Ɛ ɛ,	A a,	Ɑ ɑ,	Ɵ ɵ,	Ω ω,	Ɯ ɯ;	I i,	E e,	A a,	O o,	U u,	Ʊ ʊ;
*ee*l,	*a*le,	*a*lms,	*a*ll,	*o*pe,	f*oo*l;	*i*ll,	*e*ll,	*a*m,	*o*n,	*u*p,	f*oo*t;

DIPHTHONGS. COALESCENTS. ASPIRATE.

Ɨ ɨ, Ơ ơ, Ɤ ɤ, Ų ų. Y y, W w. H h.
*i*sle, *oi*l, *ow*l, *yu*le. *y*ea, *w*ay, *h*ay.

CONSONANTS.

P p, B b, T t, D d, Ç ç, J j, C c, G g; F f, V v, Ŧ ŧ, Đ đ,
ro*p*e, ro*b*e, fa*t*e, fa*d*e, e*tch*, e*dg*e, lee*k*, lea*g*ue; sa*f*e, sa*v*e, wrea*th*, wrea*th*e,

S s, Z z, Σ ʃ, Ʒ ʒ; R r, L l; M m, N n, Ŋ ŋ.
hi*ss*, hi*s*, vi*c*ious, vi*s*ion; fo*r*, fa*ll*; see*m*, see*n*, si*ng*.

FIGURE 3. The 1847 alphabet.

series of experiments in the teaching of reading, but these will not occupy us here (Kelly 1979).

The labours of Pitman and Ellis during the ten years that preceded the 1847 alphabet can be said to have established phonetics as a modern science in Great Britain. Prior to 1837 phonetic work had been carried out in the main by isolated individuals as a scholarly pursuit, often one of many. It was often speculative in nature and, whilst sometimes directed to practical ends, it was regarded as limited in what it could achieve. One often senses an almost apologetic note in earlier writings which is missing in the work of Pitman and Ellis. Further, much of the work was imprecise and commonly saw the orthography as a prior object of study. We have seen Pitman and Ellis in their early work taking over from their predecessors some of these attitudes. But they brought much that was new, Pitman a zeal for reform and a degree of energy and application in pursuing this end that is truly impressive, and Ellis a capacity for observation, accurate description and experimentation that set new standards. His training in the natural sciences was all-important here. Perhaps his greatest achievement at this period of his career was to combine these gifts with a close study of the work of others specialising, like Wheatstone, in other but related fields, and to produce for himself a synthesis of all that he found best and most persuasive. (Sir Charles Wheatstone (1802–75) was Professor of Experimental Physics at King's College, University of London, from 1834. He worked and published in numerous fields, including optics, acoustics and electro-magnetism, and was a pioneer in the areas of stereoscopy and submarine telegraphy. He was knighted in 1868.) Ellis did this, though, in no passive spirit. Much of his work of survey and synthesis rejects or modifies the views of his predecessors, and his mastery of the subject was gained through a long process of trial and error. In later years he was to refer to the 'slow and painful' way in which he had come to his competence in phonetics. For example his notation systems during these years are based on the sound-systems of the various languages known to him: none of them is a true general phonetic system. Ellis acknowledges this in a remark made much later in his lifetime that the detailed dialect work that he carried out for his *On Early English Pronunciation* could not have been done during the 1840s because of the lack of an adequate alphabet.

The development of the 1847 alphabet holds much interest for phoneticians, despite the fact that the desired reform never came about, and some of the phonetic theorising behind it was rudimentary and to a certain degree irrelevant. It introduced Ellis to the field in an active way, and provided him with an unequalled opportunity to learn a great deal of both theory and practice in a short time. It also served to introduce the subject of phonetics to people of all classes and ages as something of value.

Pitman and Ellis have the right to be regarded as the founders of modern phonetic studies in Britain, and much that has been seen as an important part of the British tradition is a direct inheritance from their work. One thinks here of the insistence on observation and practical skills, the interest in transcription and its typology, the just balance of theoretical and pragmatic considerations in phonemic analysis and the regard for the practical applications of the subject in all its aspects. The spirit of Pitman and Ellis is to be seen, too, in many of the principles that underlie the International Phonetic Alphabet. But perhaps their greatest contribution to the advancement of phonetics was their intense and serious commitment to the subject. There was no dilettante element in their approach. Pitman often pointed out, when offered advice or criticism by an armchair critic about one aspect or other of the phonotypic alphabets, that at all stages the developments in them were the fruit of practical experimentation with the pen, in the printing office and in the pages of the *Phonographic* and *Phonotypic Journals*. Earlier work in phonetics had often had a distinctly amateur air about it: this era Pitman and Ellis brought firmly to a close.

ACKNOWLEDGEMENTS

My thanks go to Mrs Mary Abercrombie, who put her transcriptions of a part of the Ellis-Pitman correspondence at my disposal; and to the Librarian of the University of Bath, who kindly gave me access to the Pitman Collection housed there.

References

ABERCROMBIE, D. (1937) 'The visual symbolisation of speech', *Pitman's Business Education* 27, August, 689–91.
— (1949) 'What is a "Letter"?', *Lingua* 2, 54–63.
BAKER, A. (1908) *The Life of Sir Isaac Pitman*, London (Pitman).
ELLIS, A.J. (1843) Unpublished. The manuscript is dated September 29th in Pitman's hand.
— (1844a) Unpublished letter of January 21st.
— (1844b) 'On syllabication and the indistinct vowel', *The Phonotypic Journal* 3, no. 26, February, 33–43.
— (1844c) *The Alphabet of Nature*, published in parts as an Appendix to *The Phonotypic Journal*: part 1, June-December, 1844, parts 2 and 3, March-June, 1845. Published as a separate volume by Pitman, Bath, 1845.
— (1848a) *The Essentials of Phonetics*, London (Pitman). Printed in Phonotypy.
— (1848b) *The Teacher's Guide to the Child's Phonetic Primer*, London (Ellis's Phonetic Instruction Books).
KELLY, J. (1979) '"This Great Reform" – Mr Pitman and Mr Ellis at Bath', *Spelling Progress Bulletin* 19, Spring, 10–13.
KLOPSTOCK, F.G. (1779) 'Über die Deutsche Rechtschreibung', in *Sämmtliche Werke*, vol. 9, Leipzig (Göschen) 1844, 325–53.
LATHAM, R.G. (1851) *A Handbook of the English Language*, London. My page reference is to this edition.
LEE, S. (1827) *A Grammar of the Hebrew Language*, London.
PITMAN, I. (1837) *Stenographic Soundhand*, London (Samuel Bagster). Reprinted as Appendix 1 of BAKER (1908): page references here are to that reprint.
— (1840–47) The editions appeared as follows: Second edition, 1840 (January); Third edition, 1840 (September); Fourth edition, 1841; Fifth edition, 1842; Sixth edition, 1844; Seventh edition, 1845; Eighth edition,

1847. The titles of the editions vary. Only the first edition is called *Stenographic Soundhand*. From the fifth edition on, the title *Manual of Phonography* is used.

— (1842) The alphabets appeared as follows: Alphabet no.1, *The Phonographic Journal* 1, no.8, August, 59; Alphabet no.2, *The Phonographic Journal* 1, no.10, October, 74; Alphabets nos.3–6, *The Phonographic Journal* 1, no.11, November, 82; Alphabet no.7, *The Phonographic Journal* 1, no.12, December, 90.

— (1843a) *The Phonotypic Journal* 2, no.16, April.

— (1843b) 'On phonetic printing', Supplement to *The Phonotypic Journal* 2, no.21, September, 133–41.

— (1843c) 'On phonetic printing', *The Phonotypic Journal* 2, no.23, November, 158.

— (1844a) 'On phonetic printing', *The Phonotypic Journal* 3, no.25, January, 1.

— (1844b) 'Phonotypic alphabet no.12', *The Phonotypic Journal* 3, no.28, April.

— (1845) 'Completion of the phonotypic alphabet', *The Phonotypic Journal* 4, no.42, June, 105.

— (1847) 'The English phonotypic alphabet', *The Phonotypic Journal* 6, no.61, January, 2.

TAYLOR, S. (1786) *An Essay Intended to Establish a Standard for an Universal System of Stenography*, London.

WALKER, J. (1791) *A Critical Pronouncing Dictionary*, London.

Henry Sweet's
System of Shorthand

Since the sixteenth century, phoneticians have shown a considerable degree of interest in shorthand, either as devisers, users or interpreters of particular systems (cf. Abercrombie 1937, 1949, 1967, Bell 1869, Firth 1947, Gutzmann 1907, Perrett 1920, Pitman 1837 et seq., Salmon 1972, Sweet 1892, Techmer 1890, Trnka 1937); but the only system devised by a phonetician to achieve widespread and lasting recognition has been Pitman's. Sweet's system, known as Current and published in 1892 as the *Manual of Current Shorthand, Orthographic and Phonetic*, has received limited attention: Butler (1951, pp.170–1) and Read (1972, pp.5–6) devote a few lines to it; Henderson (1971, p.ix) describes it succinctly as 'excellent'; Melin (1927, pp.284–7) discusses some of its main features; Johnen (1917, p.26), Navarre (1909, p.176) and Zeibig (1899, p.153) list it without further comment as one of the many English systems published in the nineteenth century; Faulmann (1895) and Mentz (1910), however, make no reference to it whatsoever. Even Bernard Shaw's sympathetic but sometimes critical interest in it (seen, for example, in the Preface and Act III of *Pygmalion* (Shaw 1941b)) has not resulted in the work becoming better known. In effect, the neglected fate of Current stands in poignant contrast to Sweet's own optimistic assessment of the work's chances of success: 'I consider it the most important piece of work I have yet done .... I think it will make its way in course of time' (Sweet to Storm 1/6/1890; cf. also Sweet to Jespersen 25/3/1893). The purpose of this paper, then, is to describe the background to Sweet's work on shorthand, and to discuss the characteristic features of Current. There are grounds, I believe, for reconsidering the view that Current is an inappropriate system for English; but in any case, from the point of view of Sweet's work on phonetic notation, it does still deserve to be noticed.

There is no doubt that the best known and most generally employed shorthand system in nineteenth-century Britain was Pitman's Stenographic Sound-Hand (1837), subsequently revised and renamed Phonography (see paper by Kelly p.248). Yet Sweet could find little to admire in it: to him it was the 'Pitfall' system (*Manual*, p.xvi)! He was obviously familiar with it (cf. Shaw 1941a), and may even have learned it at King's College School, London, where it was taught to some of the pupils (King's College School, London, 1860). Experience with it, however, led him to conclude that it was one of the poorest systems in existence, on account of its geometric-shaped symbols, its use of the thick/thin distinction and its inherent character of brevity. The latter could lead to serious misinterpretations when transcriptions were being read back such as 'common sand was gone' for 'nature is not so kind' (*Manual*, pp.v–vi, viii). In 1869, therefore, he took up Melville Bell's system of Steno-Phonography (Bell 1869, cf. also Bell 1852), which he continued to use until the early 1880s. In 1877 he had described Steno-Phonography as being 'thoroughly practical in character' (Sweet 1877a, pp.vii–viii; cf. also Sweet 1880, p.13), but by 1883 certain inadequacies in it had become obvious. Consequently, he set to work to produce an improved version. One defect was the principle of attaching a vowel symbol to a consonant symbol after the consonant had been written, even if chronologically the vowel preceded the consonant (*Manual*, pp.xii–xiii). Another was the method of indicating a consonant's place of articulation by the angle of slope of the symbol. Sweet opted instead to use the method of 'projection', that is of descending lines of different lengths set at particular points along a vertical scale. This alteration was to be incorporated into the final version of Current (see the symbols for /p,t,k,ʧ/ in figure 1 by way of example). Further changes included the decision to write vowels smaller than consonants, and to introduce some script forms into the set of symbols Bell had constructed out of purely geometric shapes. The result of the latter change was to make the actual writing of Current more cursive, or to use Bell's expression, more *current*.

Bell's system is capable of notating many non-English sounds, as his examples in Gaelic, Hungarian and Zulu indicate – and there is even a symbol for the notorious epiglottal trill (Bell 1869, Section Second, p.9)! But there still remain certain phonetic features that it cannot notate (although Visible Speech can), such as various diphthongs, tones and voice qualities (see, for example, Bell 1867, p.79). It is possible, then, that a further reason for Sweet's decision to modify Steno-Phonography may have been the wish to have available a general phonetic shorthand to complement Visible Speech (cf. Sweet 1885, p.583, *Manual*, p.xiii), as distinct from a shorthand that was simply faster and easier to write than Steno-Phonography. But as work progressed, he came to accept the impossibility of achieving this goal: 'universality' and 'theoretical symmetry' (*Manual*, p.xiii) became necessarily subordinated to the demands of a system that was 'simpler and easier to read' (Sweet to Storm 3/12/1885), 'less rigorously systematic' (Sweet to Jespersen 26/6/1886), and 'clearer, more practical' (Sweet to Jespersen 8/1/1887). The formal consequences, in addition to those noted above, were the abandoning of the thick/thin distinction (to contrast voiced and voiceless consonants) and the reduction in number of 'awkward down-curves' (*Manual*, p.xiv).

In his work, Sweet was encouraged by the advice and help he received from certain friends and colleagues, especially James Lecky who was responsible for at least two aspects of Current, the low stroke ⟋ for /h/ and the use of two levels for the representation of vowels (*Manual*, p.xiii, xvii). Nevertheless, he also gained considerable inspiration from a detailed study of various continental shorthands, especially Gabelsberger's (1839): 'I have ... had to wade through a mass of German literature on the subject' (Sweet to Storm 2/3/1885; cf. also *Manual*, pp.xiii–xiv). At the same time, he could not have failed to have been conscious of the surge of interest in shorthand amongst the general public in Britain – it became 'as controversial as Home Rule' (Butler 1951, p.126). Not only was dissatisfaction rife with the practical aspects of Pitman's system, but people were avidly discussing and debating the theoretical bases of shorthand. Much of the discussion took place at meetings of the Shorthand Society, founded in 1881, which Sweet joined in 1885 (*Shorthand* 2, 1883–5, p.235), and it is significant that many of what Sweet regarded as the cardinal characteristics of Current (*Manual*, p.xii) were being looked upon in the 1880s as the ideal requirements of any shorthand system. Far from putting forward original points of view, Sweet appears to have developed his system on the basis of opinions which he shared with a number of his contemporaries (see, for example, Anderson 1881–2, idem 1882, pp.126–39, and the various comments in *Shorthand* 2, 1883–5, pp.28–30, 67–8; 3, 1885–9, pp.23–8).

After five years of experimentation and development, Current was ready for publication. Sweet offered it in 1888 to the Clarendon Press who were 'greatly interested', although they had reservations about both the financial factors involved in the production of such a work and the commercial competition (Clarendon Press to Sweet 29/5/1889, 28/1/1890, 5/2/1890). A period of protracted negotiation then followed, during which the Press were compelled to handle Sweet with the utmost tact, assuring him when it became diplomatically necessary to do so, of the work's 'scholarly character', its 'perfection and completeness' and its 'utility for many purposes where the ordinary systems would be wholly useless' (Clarendon Press to Sweet 28/1/1890, 10/2/1890). At one stage, however, they suspended work on the book because of objections from the printers who 'seem to find the book rather a difficult one' since 'the similarity between some of the signs will be too close to avoid error' (Clarendon Press to Sweet 30/6/1891, 6/7/1891, 2/3/1891). Sweet, for his part, refused to allow the work to be published until he was satisfied with the proposed format (Sweet to Storm 26/12/1891). Eventually, however, Current was published in December 1892 in the form of photolithographed manuscript preceded by sections in normal print: no doubt because this was the 'very cheapest form of production' (Satchell, T. to Clarendon Press 8/1/1951). Type had been cut for the shorthand symbols and sorts made from it, but they were never used. Fortunately, the sorts were preserved, and they have been reproduced for the first time in this paper.

As the title of the *Manual* indicates, Current consists of not one, but two styles, a phonetic and an orthographic. The decision to include the latter was taken as late as 1888, and appears to have been owing to the publication that year of a two-style system by the young Cambridge mathematician, Hugh L. Callendar (Callendar 1888); Sweet obviously anticipated Callendar's system providing some strong competition to his own. More interestingly still, he had at one stage intended to include *three* styles, a 'purely phonetic', which would be a shorthand equivalent to the Organic Alphabet, an 'orthographic', which would provide a symbol for each letter of the alphabet and which would cut the normal longhand writing time by a half, and thirdly, an 'elliptical' style, which would be used for verbatim reporting purposes (Sweet to Jespersen 22/6/1888). In the latter, the outline for each word was intended to be distinctive enough for it to be understood even out of context: on reflection, a virtual impossibility (but cf. Sweet 1899, p.27). In the event, the 'purely phonetic' and 'elliptical' styles were amalgamated to form Phonetic Current, a style that was neither a corollary to the Organic Alphabet, nor, superficially at least, a reporter's shorthand. Despite abandoning the 'purely phonetic' style, Sweet nevertheless cherished the idea of a 'rationally constructed system of shorthand' (presumably Current) being used by phoneticians in place of Broad Romic (Sweet 1890, p.viii). Generations of phonetics students are doubtless relieved that he never actively pursued this aim of using Current and the Organic Alphabet for broad and narrow transcriptions respectively! For some years after the publication of Current, he continued to maintain that Phonetic Current could not be written fast enough to be used by a reporter, until a British journalist, Thomas Satchell, demonstrated to him that in fact it could. Sweet, like Satchell, achieved on average a fluently written (and read) 150 w.p.m. – almost as fast as the top speed demanded nowadays of students sitting the advanced shorthand examination of the Royal Society of Arts (Satchell, T., 1952). Sweet's apparent indifference to the needs of the reporter can be explained by the fact that his intention throughout the later stages of the development of Current was to devise a shorthand that would serve the needs primarily of professional persons, not reporters. This is evident in the key-words he uses for several outlines: for example, *adze, Aeolic, censorious, epigraphy, theosophists* – scarcely the type of vocabulary a reporter would be called upon to transcribe in his daily work. Furthermore, an overriding aim of the system was to retain legibility at the expense of brevity.

The pen-strokes for Current are those of cursive longhand, or more accurately, Sweet's English Civil Service style of longhand, and they bear a surprising, and presumably non-accidental, resemblance to the symbols Bell provided for *writing* Visible Speech (cf. Bell 1867, pl. xii). Occasionally, however, a semi-geometric feature such as ` is used; otherwise, the symbols are based on entire letters of the alphabet, parts of letters, or on novel combinations of parts of letters (see figure 1 for examples). All of them are easy to write, both in isolation and sequence, and they avoid any of the 'angularity, jerkiness, sprawliness, and hand-cramping movements' that

Sweet thought so reprehensible in the geometric-based shorthands, especially Pitman's (*Manual*, p.vi). They also accord in general respects with what he considered to be the admirable characteristics of cursive writing as it had developed over the centuries (cf. Sweet 1888, pp.60–3). Shaw, as is well known, was not slow to appreciate this point, but he envisaged the symbols of Current providing a potential basis for primarily a printed alphabet for English (see below in connection with the Proposed British Alphabet).

The phonemic and to some extent the morphophonemic systems and structures of R P provide the linguistic bases of Phonetic Current. Twenty-one vowels (including /ɔə/) and twenty-four consonants are therefore represented, but to permit the writer to notate /x/ and /ʍ/, especially in Scots words, two further symbols are provided. In most cases, there is a one-to-one relationship between symbol and phoneme; in others, a symbol may stand for a sequence of phonemes (for example /-nʃ/), for two or more morphologically related phonemes (for example, the allomorphs of past tense), or even, as in numerous other shorthands, for an entire morpheme (for example, -*ing*). Syllable and morpheme boundaries are sometimes, however, deliberately overlooked, and this results in additional single symbols being used, for example for the /ɪ + ə/ sequence in a word like *carrier*. Conversely, morpheme boundaries may be respected to the extent that homophones such as *find* and *fined* are written differently. This morphophonemic feature is justified on the grounds that a special symbol for some of the allomorphs of past tense acts as a syntactic cue when a passage is being read back.

Figure 1 lists some of the symbols of Phonetic Current. It will be seen that, apart from /l/, consonants are distinguished from vowels by being written with somewhat larger symbols, and that the latter are constructed on the basis of a classificatory analysis of place and manner: places are indicated by projection, and manners by the shape of the symbol. This iconic principle was not by any means an innovation of Sweet's: Pitman and Bell amongst others had used it, although Sweet differs from Bell by relating place to the passive, not the active, articulator. Vowels are written on one of two levels, mid and low (Sweet uses the inappropriate term 'high' for the former), and the symbols for them are constructed from three very simple pen-strokes, a single-hook, a double-hook and a loop (see, for example, the symbols for /ɪ/, /ɷ/ and /ɒ/). By varying their length and the direction in which they face, twenty-four symbols in all can be devised. Eighteen are used for vowels, four for CV sequences, while the remaining two are unused. Ligatures based on some of the eighteen provide symbols for other vowels or vowel sequences (for example, /ɪə,ɔə,ɔɪ,aɪə/). In addition, two 'stroke' symbols serve not only as alternative forms for /ə/, /ɛ/ and /eɪ/, but also as symbols for any vowel when a contracted form is being written (see figure 1). 'Feature-analysis', to use a modern expression, is perhaps not so self-evident with vowels as with consonants, but the pairing of certain 'short' and 'long' vowels should be noted, as well as the principle of using loops for all narrow vowels (in the

Phonemic System

p	ǀ	b	ꞁ	m	ʟ,ſ	f	ℓ	v	∂	θ	o	ð	c
t	ı	d	ꞁ	n	ʟ	s	e	z	∂	ʃ	ꝯ	ʒ	ℓ
k	ǀ	g	ꞁ	ŋ	ʟ	x	0	h	↗,0	ʍ	6	w	ↄ
tʃ	ǀ	ʤ	ꞁ			l	∼	r	ↄ,ↄ	j	ↄ

ɪ	˘	ʊ	∼	iː	⌣	uː	⌣	ɪə	∽	ɛə	⌒	ʊə	ↄ
ɛ	⌢,/	ʌ	◌	ɜː	⌐	ɔː	ↄ	ɔə	○	ʊə	∾	aʊ	◌
a	◌	ɒ	◌	ə	○,/	ɑː	⌣	eɪ	⌒,/	aɪ	⌣	ɔɪ	∾

'Stroke' Symbols for Vowels ⁄, /

Some Sequences

juː	∽	jʊə	⌒	aɪə	◌	aʊə	○	ʊʊə	ↄ	mp	ꞁ	mb	ↄ
nt	ꞁ	nd	ↄ	ns	Ꮟ	nz	Ꮟ	ŋz	Ꮮ	mʃn	J	tn	∖
pt	ſ	ft	ℰ	fts	ℰ	lz	∼	eɪlz	∼	sm	ᑯ	sn	◌
sp	℘	st	℘	sk	℘	sw	ʟ	dw	ↄ	gw	ꞁ	skw	ß
pr	◁	tr	◁	br	◁	gr	◁	θr	ↄ	str	◆	rn	∖
ts	ↄ	fs	ℯ	tθ	◌	sVz	ℯ	ʒVz	ℯ	tʃVr	◁	ŋʃVs	ↄ

Some Contracted Forms

About (bt)	ꞁ	Was (wz)	ℬ	Quite (kw)	ʟ
Seven (sv)	∂	Would (wd)	ℰ	Subject (sb)	ꞁ
Thought (θt)	◍	Yours (jz)	ↄ	Such (sʃ)	∂

FIGURE 1. Some of the symbols of Phonetic Current Shorthand.

sense of the 1890, not the 1877, classification of English vowels) and wide
rounded vowels, and hooks for wide unrounded vowels. Modification of the
basic inventory of symbols either by forming ligatures or by combining
elements from two or more symbols into a new shape whilst still retaining the
basic identities of the symbols, allows sequences of phonemes to be written
more rapidly (see, for example, the symbols for /-nz/, /sk-/, etc.). To avoid
superfluous pen-strokes, some phonemes have 'rising' allographs which can
be joined directly onto the preceding symbol without any intervening stroke
(cf. the two forms of /m/).

The symbols of Orthographic Current are, with the one exception of
that for *ll*, the same as those used in Phonetic Current. In certain cases, their

values are broadly comparable: for example, $p \equiv$ /p/, $b \equiv$ /b/, $i \equiv$ /ɪ/, $e \equiv$ /ɛ/; in others, considerable differences are apparent: for example, $ph \equiv$ /kw/, $c \equiv$ /ʒ/, $a \equiv$ /aɪ/, $u \equiv$ /ɒ/. The systematic use of long up-hook vowels to notate vowel digraphs beginning with e deserves to be noted.

All inventors of shorthands have faced the problem of how to contract a word so that it can be written at speed and yet remain legible. For Sweet, this was the one aspect of Current that he felt he had never solved to his complete satisfaction (*Manual*, p.xv; Sweet to Jespersen 8/6/1893; Sweet to Shaw 26/10/1902). Nevertheless, he sets out in the *Manual* a series of general and particular principles to help the writer determine the best contraction of any word. The primary consideration must be to maintain 'distinctiveness' at all costs (cf. Sweet to Jespersen 22/6/1888), even if this entails retaining segments that in other shorthands would be blithely omitted. On no account has legibility to be sacrificed to brevity. Only if the writer/reader is working with known specialist vocabulary or in a situation with which he is familiar can words be severely pruned, so that they consist of little more than their initial and final segments: for example, *ipecacuanha* can be written as if it were /ɪp ə/, with a space between the last two segments (*Manual*, p.118; *pace* Perrett 1920, p.4). In all other cases, less drastic contraction is appropriate. Thus the accented syllable(s) of a word should be kept, *mutatis mutandis*, together with, where necessary, the initial and final segments of the word. If possible, all vowels should be written with one of the two 'stroke' symbols, or omitted altogether. Consonant sequences may be reduced to a single item. Phonologically inadmissible sequences such as /-ʃz/ and /lm-/ are written with the implication of an omitted /ɪ/, or, as in the case of /sr-/ being used for /θr-/, because the pen-strokes are easier and no ambiguity results from the substitution. (The symbol for /ʒ/ often replaces that for /ʤ/ for the same reason.) 'Position', used in many other shorthands (for example, Pitman, Bell, Rundell) to indicate the character of an adjacent but omitted segment, by means of deliberate raising or lowering of a symbol from its expected position, is employed fairly sparingly. In Current, a high alveolar implies an adjacent high vowel (for example, high /n/ ⊃ /ɪn/), a high vowel a neighbouring labial consonant (for example, high /ɛ/ ⊃ /ɛvə/). An alveolar written lower than expected implies /ʌ/ or /ə/. Occasionally, however, it is useful to know that a segment has not been omitted, and raising is used for this purpose too. By assigning additional phonemic values to certain symbols, the writing process can be further accelerated: for example, the symbol for /ŋ/ also stands for the affixes *con-* and *-ing* as well as for the word *can*. (It will be noticed in passing that Sweet follows the long established convention in shorthand theory of working out the contractions so that the morphological structure of the word is not lost.) 'Arbitraries', that is symbols with no discernible phonemic values, are assigned to frequently occurring words: for example, · stands for *of*, and – for *and*. If no ambiguity is likely to result, whole morphemes can be omitted, thereby reducing a sentence like *She wrote* *most of the book by herself* to *She wrote most of book by self*. Once the rules of phonological contraction have been applied, the final 'phonemic' form of the sentence will be /ʃV roɷt moɷst · bk bV sf/. To help the learner, a list is provided of well over a thousand words and phrases in their contracted forms, many of them having a high frequency of occurrence, as a comparison with the lists in, for example, Thorndike and Lorge (1944, pp.267–70) indicates. It is of historical interest to realise that Sweet's list, although not set out along a rank scale, actually antedates what has usually been considered to be the first *general* frequency count for English (Reed 1895).

Despite having spent five years on the development of Current, Sweet was not altogether satisfied with what he had produced. Six months after the work's publication, he was seriously contemplating changing the symbols for /l/, /ʌ/ and /ə/; in the event, they remained the same (Sweet to Jespersen 8/6/1893). He did, however, begin to use two new symbols, those for /tn/ and /rn/, which had been fortuitously omitted from the *Manual*, but for which sorts had been made (see figure 1). On the other hand, he made no attempt to remove the geometric shapes from the system, being content to regard them as a 'mere excrescence' (Sweet to Jespersen 8/6/1893). He was clearly aware of other shortcomings in the work, for he considered the possibility of re-publishing both styles separately in much more pedagogically oriented forms (Sweet to Jespersen 8/6/1893), and he also told Jespersen of his wish to simplify the system to make it suitable for 'printing' and 'general international phonetic' purposes (Sweet to Jespersen 21/7/1893). Clearly, what he had in mind was not only his earlier plan of a 'purely phonetic' style, but also the precedent of Bell, who had produced several versions of his shorthand, including 'universal' and even 'elliptical universal' ones (Bell 1869). None of these plans came to fruition. He did, however, as a result of discussions with Jespersen and an unnamed English writer of Current, draw up a list of new and modified contractions (Sweet to Jespersen 8/6/1893). Some of the latter were intended to make the words more phonetically transparent: for example, *when*, which in the *Manual* has the phonemic form /wn/ was changed to /wɛ/, and *neither* was altered from /nə/ to /naɪə/. Other changes produced more economically written forms without at the same time any loss of legibility: *afterwards* which had been /ɑːəᵈ/ (where high /d/ implied a neighbouring labial) was altered to /ɑːᵈ/. A third type of change aimed solely at producing more smoothly written forms: thus *easiest* was changed from /zɪst/ to /zst/. On the whole, the effect of these additions and modifications was to leave Current 'modified but slightly' (Sweet to Shaw 20/6/1901).

It was not until 1901 that Sweet embarked on a plan to refashion the entire system, to rid it of its supposedly 'complicated, arbitrary and illogical' characteristics (Sweet to Shaw 26/10/1902), but whatever his intentions, any actual changes seem to have been relatively minor ones. Thus, he introduces a new allograph *ı* for word-final /d/ after a long up-loop vowel, despite the possibility of its being confused with the symbol for /nt/ (see, for

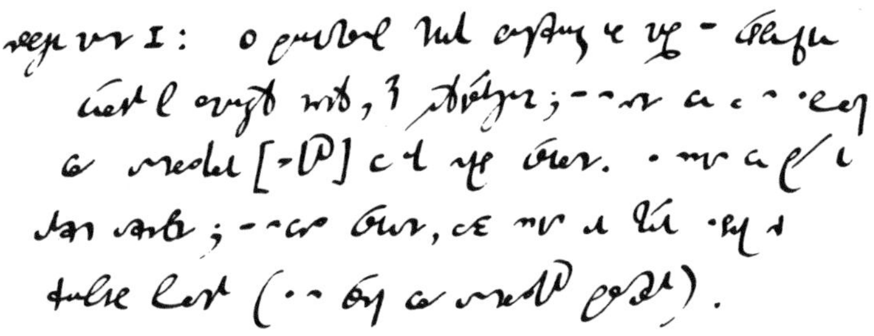

angloꞵsaksn riːdə I: heɾ cynewulf benam sigebryht his rices -(=ond) west seax na wiotan foɾ unryhtum dædum buton ham túnscire; -(=ond) he hæfde þa oþ he ·(=of) slog þone aldor mon [>mn] þe him lengest wunode. ·(=of)* hiene þa c‑ on andred adræfde; -(=ond) he þær wunade, oþþæt hiene an swán ·(=of) stang æt pryfetes flodan (·(=of)* he wræk þone aldormon cumbran).
*An error for -(=ond)

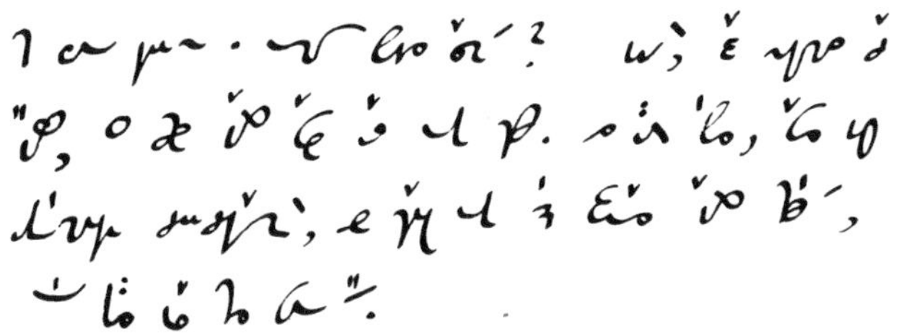

haːbən ziː kyrtsliç ·(=fɔn)iːɾəm fɑtəɾ gəhøːrt? naɪn, zaɪt lɛŋəɾəɾ tsaɪt niçts, ɪç vaɪs nɪçt vas aos iːm gəvɔɾdən ɪst. ɛɾ hatə fɔɾ, viːdəɾ nax ameːɾɪka tsoɾʏk tsøkeːɾən, ɛs gɪŋ iːm dɔɾt tsvaːɾ nɪçt bəzɔndəɾs, miːɾ ɪməɾ nɔx bɛsəɾ viː hiːɾ.

ˈjɑɪ skal ɪnspɑːɾə dem et tʉːsn pʉn', saː en uŋ ɪɾlændəɾ tɪl en gaməl hæɾə. ˈvɔɾlədəs (vls) də', saː dene. ˈdɪ hɑːɾ en datəɾ, vem dɪ teŋkəɾ at jiː tiː tʉːsn pʉn pɔ henəs brølupsdɑː'. ˈdə hɑːɾ jɑɪ'. ˈjɑɪ vɪl tɑː henə me niː tʉːsn'.

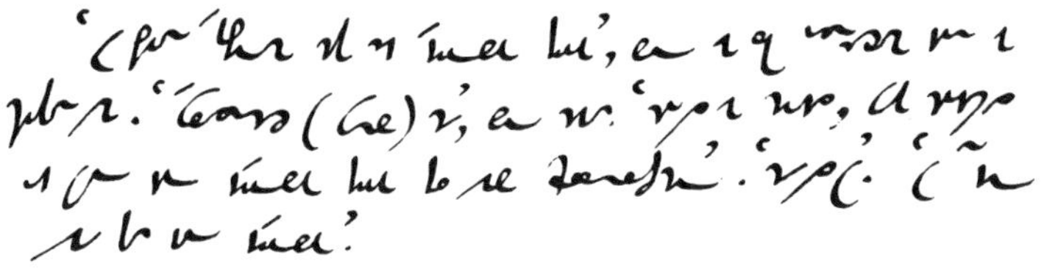

Underlined symbols indicate segments omitted in the shorthand. In the German and Norwegian extracts "=extra-strong stress; '=strong stress; :=medium stress; ˇ=weak stress; ¨=intonation/tone

FIGURE 2. Old English, German and Norwegian in Current Shorthand, transliterated by MKCM. Extracts from Sweet's letter to Jespersen of 8 July 1894.

example, his transcription of *conferred* in his letter to Jespersen of 20/4/1902), and he extends the use of specifically word-final allographs (for example, of /t/) to non-final positions and to those word-final phonemes whose morphological status would not formerly have justified them. A further change, judging by his letters in Current to Jespersen after 1902, appears to have been to use *fewer* contractions than expected. Unfortunately, it is not known for certain what other changes Sweet contemplated making, or indeed introduced into Current (cf. Satchell, T., to Clarendon Press 8/1/1951; Wrenn 1947, p.196). Nevertheless, he felt that his efforts had produced 'encouraging results' (Sweet to Shaw 26/7/1903).

A separate matter was that of adapting Current for the transcription of other languages. Sweet produced, but never published, versions for Old English, German, Norwegian (see the extracts in figure 2) and French. The last has unfortunately not survived (Satchell, T., 1952); a Danish version which Jespersen had been invited to prepare was apparently never devised (cf. Sweet to Jespersen 25/3/1893, 8/7/1894, Sweet to Storm 29/7/1894). The Old English version (1894) is based almost entirely on Orthographic Current, the German and Norwegian (dialect) versions (1887) on Phonetic Current. The latter two necessitated the introduction of some new symbols, for example for German /-xt/ and /-xts/ and for Norwegian [œ] and [ø]. Otherwise, all the symbols can be found in English Phonetic Current, and their phonemic/phonetic values are related as far as possible to those of their English counterparts. Thus, German /ʏ/ and /y:/ are transcribed like English /jɷ/ and /ju:/, and Norwegian [o] like English /oɷ/. In the absence of /w/ in both languages, the symbol for /w/ in English becomes available as an alternative and more quickly written allograph of /v/. By a similar token, the symbol for English /ð/ is used for German /z/. A novel feature of these two adaptations, especially the German, is the introduction of symbols for certain suprasegmentals, stress being marked in virtually the same way as in the Organic Alphabet (cf. Sweet 1890, p.46), and intonation/tone by means of accents.

A possible further adaptation of Current was to be not to a language, but to music. As early as 1875, Sweet had pointed out that a faster method than traditional staff notation could be devised for notating music (Sweet 1877b, p.481), and towards the end of his life he was known to have been experimenting with such a notation (Wrenn 1947, p.196). In view of the sudden resurgence of interest in musical shorthand after 1885 (between 1885 and 1908 no less than twenty-three systems appeared, compared with the eleven between 1776 and 1884 (Navarre 1909, p.830)), it is not improbable that Sweet's 'system of musical notation' (Wrenn) may have involved the use of Current. There is no doubt that cursive symbols can be used effectively for the rapid transcription of music, as, for example, Austin had shown many years previously (Austin [1820]).

Sweet's prophecy of the future success of Current as a shorthand system was not to be fulfilled. A number of interlocking reasons can be put forward in explanation – his own laconic comment that 'most people are too conceited to learn it' (Sweet to Shaw 26/10/1902) may be one very small reason. The indifference and even hostility of the Press and literary journals towards it undoubtedly played a part in discouraging potential learners (see, for example, *The Times* 15/12/1892, p.13, *Daily Chronicle* 13/3/1893, p.3, *Athenaeum* March 1893, p.344. The *Shorthand Herald* politely noted its appearance but failed to review it (*Shorthand Herald* III, iv, February 1893, p.14), and, not surprisingly, Pitman's *Phonetic Journal*, the leading shorthand journal of the day, made no mention of it at all). Another factor is the length of the work (cf. Sweet to Jespersen 8/6/1893), the Phonetic Current section alone of the *Manual* being three times as long as any of the four popular systems of the day: Sloan (1883), Gregg (1888), Kingsford (1888) and Pitman (1889). Furthermore, the presentation of the material in a decidedly more analytical framework than the public would have expected from a book on shorthand was unlikely to have attracted potential learners, as also was Sweet's reticence about the efficacy of Current as a reporter's shorthand (*Manual*, p.xi). More telling still is the fact that the *Manual* was the only means a learner had of acquiring a knowledge of the system: Sweet had at one time intended to teach an earlier version of the system in London (Sweet to Storm 16/12/1886), but nothing came of his plan; he did, however, teach Current to his students at Oxford (Sweet to Jespersen 20/4/1902). Compared with what other shorthand inventors arranged for their students, Sweet's efforts in this respect were minimal. He did not organise any classes, award Certificates of Proficiency, or publish a newsletter or journal to keep users of the system up to date with developments – in effect, he avoided anything approaching such 'vulgar' propaganda (cf. Shaw 1941b), and failed thereby to appreciate the true nature of the contemporary demand for shorthand, as well, of course, as the degree of competition that Current faced. To imagine, as the tenor of his remarks in the *Manual* would suggest (see particularly pp.vii and xii), that in time Current would gradually replace Pitman's Phonography in the estimation of the public was utterly unrealistic. Pitman had truly 'cornered the market': there were innumerable reprints of Phonography, and the system was taught in many parts of the world; it was so pre-eminent in 1888 amongst the shorthand-writers in the House of Commons Press Gallery that almost all of them, out of a total of sixty-four, used it (*Shorthand* 3, 1885–9, p.301); by 1892 the weekly sale of the *Phonetic Journal* had reached 24,000 copies (Johnen 1917, p.27); and by 1895 Phonography had been adapted for the transcription of numerous languages, including Dinka, Malagasy and Chinese (Faulmann 1895, p.157). Shaw certainly understood the world of shorthand publishing, as Sweet did not, when he remarked that if Current were ever to succeed commercially, it would require the 'backing of a syndicate', but even then the result would be only a 'silver-mine' (Shaw to Oxford University Press 16/12/1915). In view of these facts, it is not surprising that the silver-mine, as far as Clarendon Press were concerned, never materialised. For example, between 1896 and 1899 only forty-seven copies of the book were sold, despite extensive publicity in Britain and America (Clarendon Press Record of Sales Figures 1893–1903), and it is little wonder that in the late 1930s the Press were compelled to order the many remaining copies to be wasted.

Amongst a small group of phoneticians and others, attitudes were different, and Current was received favourably – in certain cases, enthusiastically. Passy's review in *Le Maître phonétique* (Passy 1893) prompted Jespersen to step forward as the real champion of Current. He considered it superior on the whole to any other system, even Gabelsberger's of which he had an extensive working knowledge: 'I am much more certain of being able to read my English notes [in Current] of half a year ago than of reading my Danish (Gabelsberger) of two hours ago' (Jespersen 1893, p.168). Furthermore, it was very easy to learn, and 'the pen runs much faster than it [sic] would be possible in any of the angular geometric systems'. He did have reservations, however, about its value as a reporter's shorthand, but for certain types of literary work he considered it ideal, and he used it for some of the preparatory work for his *Modern English Grammar* as well as in his private correspondence with Sweet (Jespersen 1938, pp.215–16). Passy, on the other hand, never took it up, preferring Pitman's system (Findlay 1898, p.152), nor did Storm, despite some periodic admonishing from Sweet (see, for example, Sweet to Storm 8/2/1894; Borchgrevink 1978).

Shaw took a serious interest in it after 1902, although in his literary work he continued to use Pitman. In fact, he preferred Current to Pitman: the difference was between Sweet's 'remarkable and quite legible script', 'the best of the phonetic shorthands' and Pitman's 'much less attractive shorthand', 'possibly the worst system of shorthand ever invented' (Shaw 1941b, p.7, 1941a, Shaw to Oxford University Press 16/12/1915, Shaw 1905). An example of Shaw's ability to write Current is in a marginal note on a prospectus for a new Shorthand and Journalism School in London, where he signs himself in Current as /ʤ brnd ʃɔː/ (Shaw to Sweet 22/10/1902).) On the other hand, he severely criticised Sweet's attempts to make Current into a reporter's shorthand: in his opinion, Sweet had so 'corrupted', 'bedevilled' and 'tortured' it that it had become both 'difficult to learn' and 'useless for ordinary purposes' – worse still, 'the most inscrutable of cryptograms' (Shaw 1947, 1941b, 1941a, 1941b; cf. also Shaw to Belfour 17/10/1947, Shaw to Loewenstein 1948, 1949). Yet inspite of such criticisms – all of which, incidentally, can be firmly refuted – Shaw never tired of drawing people's attention to Current (see the convenient collation of comments in Tauber 1965, *passim*), even if this led him, on occasions, to exaggerate some of its virtues, in particular its 'steady and healthy existence' when the *Manual* lay virtually unsold and was hardly used, and the claim that Gregg took a hint from Sweet and made his system script when Gregg's system (Gregg 1888) was developed quite independently of Sweet's, and appeared four years earlier (Shaw 1941b, p.8).

Quite apart from the question of whether Current could act as a reporter's shorthand or not, at least one person saw a future for it in the teaching of foreign languages. In 1898, J.J. Findlay suggested that it might be taught to school-children to help them acquire a more accurate pronunciation of German (!) (Findlay 1898, p.152), but neither he nor anyone else appears to have tried to put the idea into practice. Some years later, in fact, he changed his preference in favour of Kingsford's so-called 'Oxford' system, whilst still continuing to reiterate the view that shorthand had a part to play in the teaching and learning of languages (Findlay and Bruford 1917).

In connection with alphabets pure and simple, Current received attention in the 1950s when entries were being submitted for the Proposed British Alphabet competition. On Shaw's original suggestion, a number of the entrants modelled their alphabets – initially at least – on the symbols of Current, including the winner of the competition, Kingsley Read (MacCarthy 1969, pp.108–9; Read 1972, pp.7 and 9).

It remains only to chronicle the efforts of two Englishmen to create a more widespread and sensitive understanding of Current amongst the public at large. In 1943, Dr F.J.O. Coddington, a lawyer with a wide knowledge of shorthands who used Current in his professional work, made a tentative offer to Oxford University Press to rewrite the *Manual* with the emphasis on the practical needs of the learner (Coddington, F.J.O., to Oxford University Press 25/2/1943). Unfortunately, nothing came of his offer (Coddington, M., 1978). A few years later, Thomas Satchell, a British journalist and author who spent most of his life in Japan working for an English-language newspaper, suggested the formation of a Current Shorthand Society. In his view, Current was superior to any other system, and it deserved to be better known (Satchell, T., 1952). Regrettably, his suggestion came to nothing, owing to a complete lack of response from the general public (Satchell, G., 1977; Skulstad 1978). Yet he had the satisfaction of knowing that, if only in Japan, he had greatly furthered the cause of Current: 'During the fifty years I have lived in this country [i.e. Japan] I have had many pupils in shorthand and found that the system was easy to learn once it was put into a learnable form. In the form of a series of graduated exercises it was assimilated easily and I had many lady pupils who could read their shorthand notes as easily as they could read longhand. My three daughters all learnt it and used it in business and numerous other clerks in business offices learnt it from me and used it with great success' (Satchell, T., to Clarendon Press 8/1/1951). Satchell could teach a complete beginner with no knowledge of phonetics to use the system fluently in the space of a few weeks (Skulstad 1977).

Should Current be quietly consigned to obscurity as merely one of the many shorthand systems for English that have failed to achieve recognition (and nearly three hundred have appeared since Timothe Bright's *Characterie* of 1588), or is it worthy of further attention? The evidence presented in this paper indicates that it is easy to learn and use, especially for anyone with a knowledge of RP phonology; also, that it can be used as a reporter's shorthand. One might add that, although Sweet based it on RP, it can be adapted with little difficulty to other accents such as Northern and Scottish English, and that it can be written, unlike some other systems, with the writer's normal longhand slope. From the particular point of view of the phonetician, however, it should be regarded, not on a par with Sweet's tangential interests such as Shelley's poetry or Irish politics, but as a further example of one of his central concerns, namely phonetic notation. Current combines the analytical, physiological principles of the Organic Alphabet with the sense of practicality inherent in Broad Romic, and can be said to approximate to Gelb's goal of an 'IPA-stenographic' system for the writing of English (Gelb 1952, p.246).

ACKNOWLEDGEMENTS

I am indebted to the Delegates, Printer and Archivist of the Oxford University Press for their kindness in allowing the shorthand sorts for Current to be reproduced in this paper, and for allowing me to consult papers in the Press's Archives; to the Society of Authors as agent for the Bernard Shaw Estate for permission to quote from certain unpublished letters of George Bernard Shaw, and to Mr Michael Holroyd for drawing my attention to some of these; to Mr Frank Miles of King's College School, London, who made available to me the catalogue of books in use in the School during Sweet's years there; to Miss G. Satchell and Mrs N. Skulstad for invaluable information about Thomas Satchell's work with Current; to Mrs M. Coddington for details of Dr Coddington's plans to rewrite the *Manual*, and for her help in trying to trace other users of Current; and to Fru Louise Storm Borchgrevink for her assistance in clarifying the nature of Storm's attitude towards Current. Shaw Texts © 1981 The Trustees of the British Museum, The Governors and Guardians of the National Gallery of Ireland and Royal Academy of Dramatic Art.

References

ABERCROMBIE, D. (1937) *Isaac Pitman: a Pioneer in the Scientific Study of Language*, London (Sir Isaac Pitman & Sons).
— (1949) 'Forgotten phoneticians', *TPhS 1948*, 1–34.
— (1967) *Elements of General Phonetics*, Edinburgh (Edinburgh University Press).
ANDERSON, T.A. (1881–2) 'The true theory of shorthand', *Shorthand* 1, 115–27.
— (1882) *History of Shorthand With a Review of Its Present Condition and Prospects in Europe and America*, London (W.H. Allen).
AUSTIN, J. [1820] *A System of Stenographic Music*, London (privately printed).
BELL, A.M. (1852) *Steno-Phonography: a Complete System of Shorthand Writing of Unrivalled Simplicity, Brevity, & Perspicuity, Founded On a New Analysis and Notation of Speech*, Edinburgh (W.P. Kennedy).
— (1867) *Visible Speech: the Science of Universal Alphabetics; Or Self-Interpreting Physiological Letters, For the Writing of All Languages in One Alphabet*, London (Simpkin, Marshall & Co.), London & New York (Trübner & Co.).
— (1869) *Universal Line-Writing and Steno-Phonography; On the Basis of 'Visible Speech'*, London (Simpkin, Marshall & Co.).

BORCHGREVINK, L.S. (1978) Personal communication.

BUTLER, E.H. (1951) *The Story of British Shorthand*, London (Sir Isaac Pitman & Sons).

CALLENDAR, H.L. (1888) *A Manual of Cursive Shorthand*, London (C.J. Clay & Sons).

CLARENDON PRESS, OXFORD [*Unpublished*] Letters to Henry Sweet (1889–93) Oxford University Press Archives.

— [*Unpublished*] Record of Sales Figures (1893–1903), Oxford University Press Archives.

CODDINGTON, F.J.O. [*Unpublished*] Letter to the Managing Director of the Oxford University Press, 25/2/1943. Oxford University Press Archives.

CODDINGTON, M. (1978) Personal communications.

FAULMANN, K. (1895) *Geschichte und Literatur der Stenographie*, Vienna (Bermann & Altmann).

FINDLAY, J.J. (1898) 'Some notes on phonetics in relation to the acquirement of modern languages', *Mod. Lang. Q.* 1, ii, 151–3.

FINDLAY, J.J. and BRUFORD, W.H. (1917) *Sound and Symbol: a Scheme of Instruction Introductory to School Courses in Modern Languages and Shorthand*, Manchester (Manchester University Press), London (Longmans, Green).

FIRTH, J.R. (1947) 'The English School of Phonetics' *TPhS 1946*, 92–132.

GABELSBERGER, F.X. (1839) *Anleitung zur Deutschen Rede-Zeichen-Kunst, oder Stenographie*, Munich (F.X. Gabelsberger).

GELB, I.J. (1952) *A Study of Writing: the Foundations of Grammatology*, London (Routledge & Kegan Paul).

GREGG, J.R. (1888) *Light-Line Phonography: the Phonetic Handwriting*, Liverpool (Light-Line Phonography Institute).

GUTZMANN, H. (1907) 'Redner und Stenograph', *Stenogr. Prax.* 1, i, 2–7, ii, 25–9.

HENDERSON, E.J.A. (1971) *The Indispensable Foundation: a Selection from the Writings of Henry Sweet*, London (Oxford University Press).

JESPERSEN, O. (1893) 'Dr. Sweet's kʌrənt ʃɔːthænd', *M Phon*, December, 167–8.

— (1938) *En Sprogmands Levned*, Copenhagen (Gyldendalske Boghandel Nordisk Forlag).

JOHNEN, C. (1917) *Kurzgefasste Geschichte der Stenographie*, Berlin (Ferdinand Schrey).

KING'S COLLEGE SCHOOL, LONDON (1860) [*Unpublished*] Catalogue of *Books In Use*, King's College School, London, Archives.

KINGSFORD, P. (1888) *New Phonography*, Dover (privately printed).

MACCARTHY, P.A.D. (1969) 'The Bernard Shaw alphabet', in W. Haas (ed.) *Alphabets for English*, Mont Follick Series vol.I, Manchester (Manchester University Press) 105–17.

MELIN, O.W. (1927) *Stenografiens Historia*, vol.I, Stockholm (Nordiska Bokhandeln).

MENTZ, A. (1910) *Geschichte der Stenographie*, Leipzig (G.J. Göschen).

NAVARRE, A. (1909) *Histoire générale de la sténographie et de l'écriture à travers les âges*, Paris (Institut sténographique de France).

PASSY, P. (1893) 'Review of Sweet's *Manual of Current Shorthand ...*', *M Phon*, November, 150–1.

PERRETT, W. (1920) *Peetickay: an Essay towards the Abolition of Spelling*, Cambridge (W. Heffer & Sons).

PITMAN, I. (1837) *Stenographic Sound-Hand*, London (Samuel Bagster).

— (1889) *A Manual of Phonography or Writing by Sound*, London (Isaac Pitman & Sons); 22nd ed. of *Stenographic Sound-Hand*.

READ, K. (1972) *Sound-Writing 1892–1972: George Bernard Shaw and a Modern Alphabet*, Reading (University of Reading Typography Unit).

REED, T.A. (1895) 'Tabel ov the frekwensi ov the moast komon w'urdz in the

English langwej', *The Speler*, March, 19–23.

RUNDELL, J.B. (1870) *A Proposal for a Civil Service Shorthand* (Based on Pitman's Phonography), London (Edward Stanford).

SALMON, V. (1972) *The Works of Francis Lodwick: a Study of His Writings in the Intellectual Context of the Seventeenth Century*, London (Longman Group).

SATCHELL, G. (1977) Personal communication.

SATCHELL, T. [*Unpublished*] Letter to the Secretary of the Clarendon Press, Oxford, 8/1/1951, Oxford University Press Archives.

— (1952) 'Dr. Sweet's "Current Shorthand"', *Times Lit. Suppl.* 13/6/1952, 391.

SHAW, G.B. [*Unpublished*] Prospectus for 'The Royal Schools of Shorthand and Journalism' sent to H. Sweet, 22/10/1902, British Library, London, Add.MS.50549.

— [*Unpublished*] Letter to Oxford University Press, 16/12/1915, Oxford University Press Archives.

— [*Unpublished*] Letter to A.O. Belfour, 17/10/1947, George Bernard Shaw Papers (♯3516), Wilson Library, University of North Carolina at Chapel Hill.

— [*Unpublished*] Note to F.E. Loewenstein (1948) for a reply to a letter from Margot Goldrei of 15/4/1948, Shaw Collection, Humanities Research Center, University of Texas at Austin.

— [*Unpublished*] Note to F.E. Loewenstein (1949) for a reply to a letter from Lorain Scott of 5/7/1949, Shaw Collection, Humanities Research Center, University of Texas at Austin.

— (1905) Letter to A. Henderson, 3/1/1905, in D.H. Laurence (ed.) *Bernard Shaw Collected Letters 1898–1910*, London, Sydney and Toronto (Max Reinhardt) 479–506.

— (1941a) Letter to *The Times*, 15/4/1941, 6.

— (1941b) *Pygmalion: a Romance in Five Acts*, Harmondsworth (Penguin Books).

— (1942) 'Preface' to R.A. Wilson (1942).

— (1945) Letter to *The Times*, 27/12/1945, 2.

— (1947) Open Letter, May 1947, in A. Tauber (1965) pp.102–8.

SKULSTAD, N. (1977, 1978) Personal communications.

SLOAN, J.M. (1883) *The Duployan Phonographic Instructor: an Improved Adaptation to the English of the Duployan French Method*, 4th ed., Dublin (W. Leckie).

SWEET, H. [*Unpublished*] Letters to Otto Jespersen (1886–1909), Det Kongelige Bibliotek, København, Ny kgl.Saml. 3975, 4°.

— [*Unpublished*] Letters to George Bernard Shaw (1901–3), British Library, London, Add.MS.50549.

— [*Unpublished*] Letters to Johan Storm (1885–94), Universitetsbiblioteket i Oslo, MS.8° 2402/JIII, JVI.

— (1877a) *A Handbook of Phonetics, Including a Popular Exposition of the Principles of Spelling Reform*, Oxford (Clarendon Press).

— (1877b) 'Words, logic and grammar', *TPhS 1875–6*, 470–503.

— (1880) 'The President's Address for 1877', *TPhS 1877–9*, 1–22.

— (1885) 'The practical study of language', *TPhS 1882–4*, 577–99.

— (1888) *A History of English Sounds from the Earliest Period*, Oxford (Clarendon Press).

— (1890) *A Primer of Phonetics*, Oxford (Clarendon Press).

— (1892) *A Manual of Current Shorthand, Orthographic and Phonetic*, Oxford (Clarendon Press).

— (1899) *The Practical Study of Languages: a Guide for Teachers and Learners*, Oxford (Clarendon Press).

TAUBER, A. ed. (1965) *George Bernard Shaw on Language*, London (Peter Owen).

M.K.C.MACMAHON

TECHMER, F. (1890) 'Beitrag zur Geschichte der französischen und englischen Phonetik und Phonographie', *Int.Zeit.allg.Sprachw.* 5, 145–295.

THORNDIKE, E.L. and LORGE, I. (1944) *The Teacher's Word Book of 30,000 Words*, New York (Teachers' College Press).

TRNKA, B. (1937) *Pokus a vědeckou teorii a praktickou reformu těsnopisu*, Prague (Nákladem Filosofické Fakulty University Karlovy).

WILSON, R.A. (1942) *The Miraculous Birth of Language*, London (J.M. Dent).

WRENN, C.H. (1947) 'Henry Sweet', *TPhS 1946*, 177–201.

ZEIBIG, J.W. VON. (1899) *Nachträge zur Geschichte und Literatur der Geschwindschreibkunst*, Dresden (Gustav Dietze).

Bibliography: the Published Works of
David Abercrombie

1932
'Patois Créole de Martinique', *Le Maître Phonétique*, no.37, p.4.
1933
RECORDING
Langue anglaise (Readings from English literature), Paris, Ultraphone, AP 718–22.
1936
'Icelandic', *Le Maître Phonétique*, no.55, p.51.
1937
Isaac Pitman: a Pioneer in the Scientific Study of Language, with a foreword by A. Lloyd James, London, Pitman; reprinted, with a few omissions, in *Studies in Phonetics and Linguistics*, 1965, pp.92–107.
'The visual symbolization of speech', *Pitman's Business Education*, vol.4, pp.689–90, 698; also in *President's Address and Reprint of Papers of the International Shorthand Congress*, London, 1938, pp.18–20; reprinted, with a few omissions, in *Studies in Phonetics and Linguistics*, 1965, pp.86–91, under the title 'Writing Systems'.
'Two early "transcriptions"', *Le Maître Phonétique*, no.59, pp.34–6.
1945
'A simplification of Icelandic transcription', *Le Maître Phonétique*, no.84, pp.20–1.
1947
'Greek of Cyprus', *Le Maître Phonétique*, no.88, p.29.
1948
'The social basis of language', *English Language Teaching*, vol.3, pp.1–11; reprinted, under the title 'Linguistics and the teacher', in *Problems and Principles*, 1956, pp.1–15; reprinted, under the original title, in Harold B. Allen (ed.) *Teaching English as a Second Language*, New York, McGraw Hill, 1965, pp.15–24.
1949
'Forgotten phoneticians', *Transactions of the Philological Society 1948*, London, 1949, pp.1–34; reprinted in *Studies in Phonetics and Linguistics*, 1965, pp.45–75.
'Teaching pronunciation', *English Language Teaching*, vol.3, pp.113–22; reprinted in *Problems and Principles*, 1956, pp.28–40.
'Some first principles', *English Language Teaching*, vol.3, pp.141–6, 169–71;

reprinted in *Problems and Principles*, 1956, pp.16–27.

'What is a "letter"?', *Lingua*, vol.2, pp.54–63; reprinted in *Studies in Phonetics and Linguistics*, 1965, pp.76–85.

REVIEWS

K.L. Pike, *The Intonation of American English*, 1945 (*Review of English Studies*, vol.25, pp.369–70).

Clive Sansom (ed.) *Speech of our Time*, 1948 (*English Language Teaching*, vol.3, pp.162–3).

1950

'Gaelic', *Le Maître Phonétique*, no.94, pp.30–1.

REVIEWS

Daniel Jones, *The Phoneme: its Nature and Use*, 1950 (*Le Maître Phonétique*, no.94, pp.31–3; reprinted under the title 'On writing and the phoneme', in *Studies in Phonetics and Linguistics*, 1965, pp.134–6).

C.L. Wrenn, *The English Language*, 1949 (*English Language Teaching*, vol.4, pp.137–40).

1951

'Speech recording', *English Language Teaching*, vol.5, pp.208–13.

'Practical uses of speech-recording', *English Language Teaching*, vol.6, pp.26–9; reprinted, together with the preceding, under the title 'The use of recording', in *Problems and Principles*, 1956, pp.84–97.

'The way people speak', *The Listener*, 6 Sept. 1951, pp.385–6; broadcast in the BBC Third Programme on 29 Aug. 1951, under the title 'Local Accent'; reprinted under the title 'R.P. and local accent' in *Studies in Phonetics and Linguistics*, 1965, pp.10–15.

'How Garrick spoke Shakespeare', broadcast in the BBC Third Programme on 9 March 1951; printed in *Studies in Phonetics and Linguistics*, 1965, pp.35–44, under the title 'Steele, Monboddo and Garrick'.

1952

'Rhythm and stress in spoken English', *London Calling Europe*, nos.232, 233.

'Don't judge people by their accents', *News Chronicle*, London, 28 Aug., p.2.

1953

'English accents', *English Language Teaching*, vol.7, pp.113–23; summarised in *Education Today*, vol.3, pp.10–12; reprinted in *The Speech Teacher* (U.S.A.), vol.4, pp.10–18; reprinted in *Problems and Principles*, 1956, pp.41–56.

'Making conversation', *English Language Teaching*, vol.8, pp.3–11; reprinted in *Problems and Principles*, 1956, pp.56–69.

'Phonetic transcriptions', *Le Maître Phonétique*, no.100, pp.32–4.

REVIEWS

P. Henrion, *Petit Mémento de prononciation anglaise*, 1951 (*English Language Teaching*, vol.8, p.33).

K.C. Masterman, *The Power of Speech*, 1952 (*English Language Teaching*, vol.8, pp.28–30).

Bibliography

John Orr, *Words and Sounds in English and French*, 1953 (*University of Edinburgh Journal*, vol.17, pp.60–1).

C. Whitaker-Wilson, *How to Spell*, 1951 (*English Language Teaching*, vol.8, p.33).

1954

'The recording of dialect material', *Orbis*, vol.3, pp.231–5; reprinted in *Studies in Phonetics and Linguistics*, 1965, pp.108–13; reprinted in W.E. Jones and J. Laver (eds.) *Phonetics in Linguistics*, London, Longmans, 1973, pp.1–5.

'Gesture', *English Language Teaching*, vol.9, pp.3–12; reprinted in *Problems and Principles*, 1956, pp.70–83.

'A Scottish vowel', *Le Maître Phonétique*, no.102, pp.23–4; reprinted in *Studies in Phonetics and Linguistics*, 1965, pp.137–8.

REVIEWS

Kenneth Jackson, *Language and History in Early Britain*, 1953 (*University of Edinburgh Journal*, vol.17, pp.136–7).

T.F. Mitchell, *Writing Arabic*, 1953, and H.M. Lambert, *Introduction to the Devanagari Script*, 1953 (*Le Maître Phonétique*, no.102, pp.32–4; reprinted under the title 'On writing and the phoneme' in *Studies in Phonetics and Linguistics*, 1965, pp.131–4).

L. Warnant, *Etudes phonétiques sur le parler wallon d'Oreye*, 1953 (*Modern Language Review*, vol.49, p.513).

1956

Problems and Principles: Studies in the Teaching of English as a Second Language, London, Longmans, 97 pp.; second edition, 1963, under the title *Problems and Principles in Language Study*, London, Longmans, 83 pp. ('The use of recording' omitted). Japanese translation, 1969, Tokyo, Shohakusha, iii + 150 pp.

REVIEWS

W.S. Allen, *Phonetics in Ancient India*, 1953 (*Bulletin of the School of Oriental and African Studies*, vol.18, pp.187–8).

Aasta Stene, *Hiatus in English*, 1954 (*Review of English Studies*, vol.7, pp.63–4).

1957

'Direct palatography', *Zeitschrift für Phonetik*, vol.10, pp.21–5; reprinted in *Studies in Phonetics and Linguistics*, 1965, pp.125–30.

'A Scottish text', *Le Maître Phonétique*, no.107, pp.7–8.

1958

G.W.: Magazine, or Animadversions on the English Spelling 1703, Los Angeles, Augustan Reprint Society (editing and introduction), 32 pp.

'The Department of Phonetics', *University of Edinburgh Gazette*, no.20, May 1958, pp.24–7.

Foreword to D. Ward, *Russian Pronunciation*, Edinburgh, Oliver & Boyd.

REVIEW

R.W. Albright, *The International Phonetic Alphabet: its Backgrounds and Development*, 1958 (*Le Maître Phonétique*, no.110, pp.32–4).

1959

REVIEW

L. Kaiser (ed.) *Manual of Phonetics*, 1957 (*Nature*, vol.183, p.269).

1960

REVIEWS

E.J. Dobson (ed.) *The Phonetic Writings of Robert Robinson*, 1957 (*Review of English Studies*, vol.11, pp.328–9).

W. Nelson Francis, *The Structure of American English*, 1958 (*Le Maître Phonétique*, no.114, pp.32–3).

1963

'Augmenting the Roman alphabet', *The Monotype Recorder*, vol.42, pp.2–17.

'Conversation and spoken prose', *English Language Teaching*, vol.18, pp.10–16; reprinted in *Studies in Phonetics and Linguistics*, 1965, pp.1–9. Japanese translation in *Journal of English Teaching*, vol.2, 1968, pp.45–54.

'Pseudo-procedures in linguistics', *Zeitschrift für Phonetik*, vol.16, pp.9–12; reprinted in *Studies in Phonetics and Linguistics*, 1965, pp.114–19.

REVIEW

Lord Brain, *Speech Disorders: Aphasia, Apraxia and Agnosia*, 1961 (*Developmental Medicine and Child Neurology*, vol.5, pp.77–81 (with Elisabeth Ingram and T.T.S. Ingram)).

1964

English Phonetic Texts, London, Faber & Faber, 125 pp.

'The contribution of phonetics', in Catherine Renfrew and Kevin Murphy (eds.) *The Child Who Does Not Talk*, London, Heinemann (Medical), pp.39–42; reprinted under the title 'Parameters and phonemes' in *Studies in Phonetics and Linguistics*, 1965, pp.120–4; reprinted in W.E. Jones and J. Laver (eds.) *Phonetics in Linguistics*, London, Longmans, 1973, pp.14–18.

'Language and medium', in Catherine Renfrew and Kevin Murphy (eds.) *The Child Who Does Not Talk*, London, Heinemann (Medical), pp.22–8. This paper forms part of chapter 1 of the then forthcoming book *Elements of General Phonetics*, Edinburgh University Press, 1967.

'A phonetician's view of verse structure', *Linguistics*, vol.6, pp.5–13; reprinted in *Studies in Phonetics and Linguistics*, 1965, pp.16–25; reprinted in W.E. Jones and J. Laver (eds.) *Phonetics in Linguistics*, London, Longmans, 1973, pp.6–13.

'Syllable quantity and enclitics in English', in David Abercrombie et al. (eds.) *In Honour of Daniel Jones*, London, Longmans, pp.216–22; reprinted in *Studies in Phonetics and Linguistics*, 1965, pp.26–34.

1965

Studies in Phonetics and Linguistics, London, Oxford University Press, i + 151 pp.

REVIEWS

W.A. Smalley et al., *Orthography Studies*, 1964 (*Archivum Linguisticum*, vol.17, pp.50–3).

Bibliography

A. Sovijärvi and P. Aalto (eds.) *Proceedings of the Fourth International Congress of Phonetic Sciences*, 1962 (*Journal of Linguistics*, vol.1, pp.206–7).

1966
REVIEW

E.R. Moses, Jr, *Phonetics*, 1964 (*Phonetica*, vol.15, pp.42–3).

1967
Elements of General Phonetics, Edinburgh, Edinburgh University Press, 203 pp.
REVIEW

P. Ladefoged, *A Phonetic Study of West African Languages*, 1964 (*Le Maître Phonétique*, no.127, pp.9–11).

1968
'Paralanguage', *British Journal of Disorders of Communication*, vol.3, pp.55–9; reprinted under the title 'Paralinguistic communication' in J.P.B. Allen and S. Pit Corder (eds.) *Readings for Applied Linguistics*, London, Oxford University Press, 1973, pp.31–6.

'Some functions of silent stress', *Work in Progress*, no.2, Department of Linguistics, University of Edinburgh, pp.1–10; reprinted in A.J. Aitken et al. (eds.) *Edinburgh Studies in English and Scots*, London, Longmans, 1971, pp.147–56.

1969
'Voice qualities', in N.N. Markel (ed.) *Psycholinguistics*, Homewood, Illinois, The Dorsey Press, pp.109–34; a reprint of chapter 6 of *Elements of General Phonetics*.

1972
REVIEW

L.F. Brosnahan and B. Malmberg, *Introduction to Phonetics*, 1970 (*Journal of the International Phonetic Association*, vol.2, pp.85–9).

1975
REVIEWS

H. Sweet, *A Handbook of Phonetics*, reprint, 1970, and E.J.A. Henderson (ed.) *The Indispensable Foundation: a Selection from the Writings of Henry Sweet*, 1971 (*Linguistics*, no.147, pp.40–6).

1976
'Using the voice in lecturing', *Work in Progress*, no.9, Department of Linguistics, University of Edinburgh, pp.49–50.

'"Stress" and some other terms', *Work in Progress*, no.9, Department of Linguistics, University of Edinburgh, pp.51–3.

1977
'The accents of Standard English in Scotland', *Work in Progress*, no.10, Department of Linguistics, University of Edinburgh, pp.21–32; reprinted in A.J. Aitken and T. McArthur (eds.) *The Languages of Scotland*, Edinburgh, Chambers, 1979, pp.68–84.

Bibliography

1978

'The indication of pronunciation in reference books', in P. Strevens (ed.). *In Honour of A.S. Hornby*, London, Oxford University Press, pp.119–26.

1979

'Phonetics and phonology', *Work in Progress*, no.12, Department of Linguistics, University of Edinburgh, pp.75–81.

1980

'Fifty years of Phonetics', *Work in Progress*, no.13, Department of Linguistics, University of Edinburgh, pp.1–9.

List of Subscribers

R. H. Barnes, Director, Studio Schools, Cambridge
William A. Bennett, Reader, University of London
Ronald Beresford, Lecturer in Phonetics, University of Newcastle-upon-Tyñe
Thomas Bloor, Lecturer, University of Aston, Birmingham
Keith Brown, Department of Linguistics, University of Edinburgh
Edward Carney, University of Manchester
Jack Carnochan, Professor, s.o.a.s., London
E. Clavering, University of Aston, Birmingham
Anna Morpurgo Davies, Professor, University of Oxford
Jeffrey Ellis, Reader in General Linguistics, University of Aston, Birmingham
Anthony Fox, University of Leeds
Nigel Gotteri, Lecturer, University of Sheffield
Pamela Grunwell, Principal Lecturer, School of Speech Pathology, Leicester Polytechnic
Martin B. Harris, Professor of Romance Linguistics, University of Salford
Gillian R. Hart, Durham University
Leofranc Holford-Strevens, Oxford
Beatrice Honikman, Lecturer, University of London, then Leeds (retd.)
Tony Howatt, University of Edinburgh
Sandy Hutcheson, Lecturer, University of Edinburgh
L. A. Iles, Edinburgh
Siew-yue Killingley, Visiting Lecturer, University of Newcastle-upon-Tyne
John M. Kirk, Junior Research Fellow in English Language, University of Sheffield
Giulio Lepschy, Professor, University of Reading
Maurice Lynch
John Lyons, Professor, University of Sussex
J. Derrick McClure, Department of English, University of Aberdeen
John Mountford, Southampton
Denys Player, Thames Polytechnic
Graham Pointon, Pronunciation Advisor, b.b.c.
Rodney Sampson, University of Bristol
Marion Shirt, Lecturer, University of Leeds
Mórag Fox Simpson, Glasgow
John Spencer, Director, Institute of Modern English Language Studies, University of Leeds
Sam Spicer, Professor, University of Essex

289

Robert B. Stewart, Lecturer, Department of Audiology, University of
  Manchester
Peter Strevens, Fellow of Wolfson College, Cambridge
Ceinwen H. Thomas, 4 Cae Delyn Road, Whitchurch, Cardiff
James Thorne, Professor, University of Edinburgh
Ormond Uren, Lecturer, Birkbeck College, London
J. C. Wells, Lecturer, University College, London
J. L. Woodhead, University of Leeds

The Bell School of Languages, Cambridge
Centre for Information on Language Teaching and Research, London
W. & R. Chambers, Publishers, Edinburgh
Edinburgh University Library
Hatfield Polytechnic Linguistics Group
Mont Follick Library, Department of General Linguistics, University of
  Manchester
Summer Institute of Linguistics (G.B.)
University of Bath Library
University of Birmingham Library
University College London, Department of Phonetics
University of Essex Library
University of Leeds, Department of Linguistics and Phonetics
University of Leeds Library
University of Stirling Library
School of Oriental & African Studies Library, London
West London Institute of Higher Education

Australia
Corinne Adams, Sydney
Chitra Fernando, Macquarie University
John S. Ryan, Associate Professor, University of New England, Armidale
Roger Wales, University of Melbourne

Belgium
L. K. Engels, Section of Applied Linguistics, K. U. Leuven
D. L. Goyvaerts, Professor, University of Brussels (VUB)
Raymond R. Renard, Department of Phonetics, State University of Mons
Max Wajskop, Professor, Director of the Institut de Phonétique, University
  of Brussels
Université de L'Etat, Bibliothèque de Linguistique, Mons

Canada
R. J. Handscombe, Professor, York University, Toronto
L. G. Kelly, Professor, University of Ottawa

Denmark
Eli Fischer-Jørgensen, Copenhagen

Finland
University of Helsinki, Department of Phonetics

France
J. L. Duchet, Faculté des Lettres et des Langues, Université de Poitiers
Peter Stap, Lyon
Brian J. Wenk, Université de Strasbourg
Laboratoire de Phonétique, Université de Besançon

German Federal Republic
Martin K. Ashoff, Universität Trier
W. D. Bald, Professor, University of Aachen
Eugenio Coseriu, Professor, University of Tübingen
Monika K. Delfosse, Universität Trier
Otto Jastrow, Professor, Universität Erlangen-Nürnberg
Dieter Kastovsky, Professor, University of Wuppertal
Muriel Keutsch, Dip. Phon.
Jens-P. Köster, Professor, Universität Trier
Herbert R. Masthoff, Universität Trier
R. C. L. Matthews, Albert-Ludwigs-Universität Freiburg
Joachim Neppert, Universität Hamburg
John Nuttall, Lecturer, University of Paderborn
Elmar Ternes, Professor, Universität Hamburg
Horst Weinstock, Aachen
Institut für Angewandte Linguistik, Universität Erlangen
Institut für Anglistik der Rheinisch-Westfälischen Technischen Hochschule
  Aachen
Institut für Phonetik, Christian-Albrechts-Universität Kiel
Phonetisches Institut der Universität Hamburg
Universitätsbibliothek Bamberg
Universitätsbibliothek Trier

Ghana
Florence Abena Dolphyne, Senior Lecturer, University of Ghana.

Iceland
Heimir Áskelsson, Reader in English, University of Iceland
Hreinn Benediktsson, Professor, University of Iceland

India
Paroo Nihalani, Reader, Central Institute of English & Foreign Languages,
  Hyderabad

Iraq
Kusay A. Ahmad, Department of English, College of Education, University
  of Basrah

Ireland
Anders Ahlqvist, Galway and Helsingfors
Séamas Ó Murchú, University College, Dublin
R. B. Walsh, University College, Dublin

Israel
Shlomo Hofman, Consultant, Speech Disorders, Ichilov Hospital, Tel-Aviv

Japan

Yoshiko Horie, College of Foreign Studies, Yokohama
Sadahiko Ikeura, Professor, Fukuoka University of Education
Yoshihiro Masuya, Professor, Konan University
Hideo Okada, Professor, Waseda University
Graduate School of Languages & Linguistics, Sophia University, Tokyo

Mexico

Kathryn Keller, Summer Institute of Linguistics

Netherlands

Jan Posthumus, Lecturer, University of Groningen
Vrije Universiteit, Amsterdam

Nigeria

Emmanuel Kwofie, Associate Professor, University of Lagos

Norway

Elisabeth Ingram, Professor, University of Trondheim
British Institute, University of Oslo
Telemark Regional College
University of Bergen, English Department

Poland

Leszek Biedrzycki, University of Warsaw

Saudi Arabia

M. H. Bakalla, Associate Professor, University of Riyadh
Hassan Mustapha, Head, Earth Sciences, English Language Centre,
 University of Jeddah

Singapore

Anthea Fraser Gupta, Lecturer, National University
Mun-Kwong Phoon, Specialist Inspector, Ministry of Education
Mary W.-J. Tay, Senior Lecturer, National University

South Africa

A. C. Nkabinde, Professor, University of Zululand

Switzerland

Phonetisches Laboratorium der Universität Zürich

U.S.A.

Archibald A. Hill, Professor Emeritus, University of Texas
Frances Ingemann, Professor, University of Kansas
John J. Ohala, Professor of Linguistics, University of California, Berkeley
John Regan, Professor, Claremont Graduate School
Mo-Shuet Tam, ESL Coordinator, City College of San Francisco
R. S. Weitzman, Professor, California State University, Fresno

Yemen

T. Balasubramanian, Professor, College of Education, Aden

Zimbabwe

Brian Annan, Professor, University of Zimbabwe

Indexes

a) Personal names

Abercrombie, D., 3, 4, 5–6, 9, 12, 56, 57, 64, 67, 68, 73, 74, 76, 82, 83, 85, 98, 108, 110, 111, 115, 117, 122, 167, 175, 176, 181, 184, 186, 191, 201, 202, 208, 256, 260, 263, 265, 278
Abercrombie, Mary, xi
Aeschylus, 119
Agnello, J., 58, 66
Alcibiades, 80
Ali, Mohamed, 246
Allen, J. W. T., 228, 246
Allen, W. S., 35, 36, 37, 45, 48, 115, 116, 119, 120, 122
Alston, R. C., 87, 98, 202
Amman, J. C., 39, 44–5, 47, 48
Anderson, T. A., 267, 278
Antonius, 82
Aristides Quintilianus, 120
Aristotle, 3, 36, 38, 48, 117, 118, 121
pseudo-Aristotle, 38, 44, 48
Armfield, G. Noël, 182
Ashton, E. B., 230–1, 234, 235, 236, 241, 247
Atkinson, H. W., 56, 64
Aubrey, J., 213
Austin, G., 90–1, 92, 97, 98
Austin, J., 274, 279

Bacon, A. M., 92
Bacon, Francis, 93
Bái Zhènyíng, 153
Baïf, J.-A. de, 206, 207, 224
Baker, A., 263
Barkas, P., 111
Barker, Marie L., 173
Batchelor, T., 211, 212, 213, 224
Baudouin de Courtenay, J., 9–10, 11, 13–14, 15–16, 17
Bayly, A., 89, 98
Beech, M. W. H., 228, 246
Behnke, E., 79, 98
Bell, A. M., 7, 8, 19, 20, 22, 23, 25, 30, 31, 51, 72, 73, 76, 163, 167, 170, 176, 182, 185, 212, 224, 265, 266, 268, 269, 271, 272, 278
Beniowski, Major, 211, 220, 224

Benni, Tytus, 12
Bewick, T., 213
Bladon, R. A. W., 61, 64
Blake, W., 187
Bloch, B., 183
Bloomfield, L., 183, 185
Bollifant, E., 210
Bonet, J. P., 44, 48
Bopp, F., 168
Borchgrevink, I. S., 276, 279
Bousquet, J.-L.-E., 202
Bridges, R., 207, 208, 224
Bright, T., 227–8
Bronson, C. P., 92
Brown, Gillian, 68, 76
Browne, L., 79, 98
Brücke, E. W., 162–3, 166–7, 168, 171, 175, 176
Bruford, W. H., 277, 279
Brugmann, K., 168, 177
Bullokar, W., 60, 210, 217, 224
Bulwer, J., 4
Burt, F., 246
Butler, C., 213, 214, 221, 224
Butler, E. H., 265, 267, 279

Cagliari, L. C., 35, 45, 47, 48
Cài Yuánpéi, 141, 145
Cài Zhāng, 143
Caldwell, M., 92
Callendar, H. L., 268, 279
Cāng Xié, 143
Capell, E., 213, 224
Casserius, 38
Catford, J. C., 20, 23, 31
Catullus, 82
Cestre, C., 188, 202
Chao, Y. R., 123, 125, 126, 135, 140, 150, 153, 160
Chapman, J., 100, 111
Chén Màozhì, 145, 150
Chén Péngnián, 130
Chistovich, L. A., 54–5, 65
Chomsky, N., 5, 6, 7, 8, 76
Cicero, 3, 81–3, 84, 85, 87, 89, 91, 98, 117

293

b) SUBJECTS

consonant classification
  Amman's, 41
  by articulatory position, 163, 188, 189
  by organic formation, 21
  by tactile information, 31
  Greek, 117–18
  Holder's, 188
  Lodwick's, 5–6
  manner categories, 188, 189
  place categories, 188, 189
  Thelwall's, 188, 195, 196
  voiced/voiceless contrast in, 189
  Wallis's, 41
consonant clusters, 119–20, 226, 232
consonant distribution, in English, 250
consonant rounding, 67–76
consonant-shift, 165
consonantes continuae, 166
consonants
  and vowels, 4, 21, 23, 31
  as *sumphōna*, 118
  assimilation of first to second, 56
  Chinese, 144, 146
  closed, 41
  coarticulation of combinations of, 62–3
  continuant, 47
  defined, 196
  differences between, 5
  double, 35, 36
  doubling of, 236, 239–40, 242
  final, 56, 131, 132
  formation of, 21
  half-voiced, 117
  hēmiphōna, 117, 118
  homorganic, 226
  initial, 131, 132
  intermediate, 117, 120–1
  joined, 4
  nasalised, 44, 47
  non-stop, 44
  open, 42
  origin of term, 118
  palatographical studies on, 57
  palatalisation of, 59
  place of articulation, 21, 23, 31, 57
  sounded alone, 4
  specification of, 5–6
  Swahili, 225–6, 228, 232, 234–43, 246
  syllabic, 3
  symbol for, 115, 117, 121
  voiced, 6, 41, 56, 189
  voiceless, 6, 41, 117, 189
constriction, 20
constrictives, 118
continuants, 36, 47, 117
continuity, 82
cosmetic aspects of voice, 81, 83–4, 87–8, 97

contrasegmentation, 130–5
conversational tone, 87–8
correptio Attica, 119
CVF (cardinal vowel + formant)
  diagram, 25–7, 29–31
Czech, 13

Dagestan, 28
Danish
  grammar schools, 171
  pronunciation of, 69
  shorthand, 274
deaf, the
  classical references to, 44–5
  education of, 3, 70
  phonetic observation and teaching of,
    37, 42, 44, 202
deaf-mutes, 70
dental(s), 6, 136, 225, 226, 235, 246
Devanagari script, 117
devoicing
  of plosives, 234–5, 246
  of vowels, 226
diachronic, 12–13, 131, 162, 164
diacritics, 121–2, 207, 209, 215, 241
dialect(s)
  Chinese, 131, 141, 142, 149, 150, 153
  effect of, on coarticulation, 61
  geography, 183
  German, 163
  linguists' concern with, 161
  systems, characteristics of, 164
dialogue interchange, 183
diaphone, 11
diaphragm, 193
dichotomies, 40
dictionary
  Chinese pronouncing, 143, 144, 149,
    150–1, 152, 154
  phonological, 131
  pronouncing, 201, 207, 209, 213, 215
  rhyme, 133
  thesaurus and, 127
digraphs, 116, 120, 207, 209, 271
Dinka, shorthand, 275
diphthong(s)
  absence of, in Swahili, 232, 241
  accent on, 121–2
  Chinese, 146
  Greek, 116, 122
  in American English, 30
  in Lodwick's scheme, 6
  in shorthand, 266
  sounds, 102
diphthongal
  gesture, 55
  glide, 30
distinctive features, 3–8

311